SADRACH'S COMMUNITY AND ITS CONTEXTUAL ROOTS

Front cover designed by Bambang Priyono Sudiyono GKJ NEHEMIA, Pondok Indah – Jakarta (Indonesia)

VRIJE UNIVERSITEIT TE AMSTERDAM

SADRACH'S COMMUNITY AND ITS CONTEXTUAL ROOTS:
A Nineteenth Century Javanese Expression of Christianity

ACADEMISCH PROEFSCHRIFT

ter verkrijging van de graad van doctor aan
de Vrije Universiteit te Amsterdam,
op gezag van de rector magnificus
dr. C. Datema,
hoogleraar aan de faculteit der letteren,
in het openbaar te verdedigen
ten overstaan van de promotiecommissie
van de faculteit der godgeleerdheid
op woensdag 16 november 1988 te 15.30 uur
in het hoofdgebouw van de universiteit, De Boelelaan 1105

door

SUTARMAN SOEDIMAN PARTONADI

geboren te Wates (Indonesia)

AMSTERDAM 1988

Promotor   : prof. dr. A. Wessels
Copromotoren   : prof. dr. J. van den Berg
                 dr. Ph. Quarles van Ufford
Referent   : prof. dr. J. Veenhof

DEDICATION

To my father, Soediman Partonadi and my late mother, who raised their children "syncretistically" with love and tolerance, teaching them to seek the truth and to find their own way, with the sole admonition, "You may choose your own religion, but once you have chosen, you must not change. You do not change your religion like you change your shirt."

CONTENTS

ABREVIATIONS

CWME — Commission on World Missions and Evangelism of the World Council of Churches

DZV — *Doopsgezinde Zendings Vereniging* (Dutch Mennonite Mission Society)

GKN — *Gereformeerde Kerken in Nederland* (The Reformed Churches in the Netherlands)

GIUZ — *Genootschap voor In en Uitwendige Zending* (Organization for Home and Foreign Missions)

Haagsche Commissie – Commissie voor de Zaken der Protestantsche Kerk in Nederlandsch Oost en West Indië (Commission for the Affairs of the Protestant Church in the Dutch East and West Indies)

HAZEA — *Hersteld Apostolische Zendinggemeente in de Eenheid der Apostelen* (The Restored Apostolic Mission Church in the Unity of the Apostles)

Indische Kerk – De Protestansche Kerk in Nederlandsch-Indië (The Protestant Church of the Dutch Indies)

IRB — *International Reformed Bulletin*

IRM — *International Review of Mission*

LMS — London Missionary Society

MNZG — *Mededelingen van wege het Nederlandsch Zendeling genootschap*

NGK — *Nederduitsche Gereformeerde Kerken* (The Netherlands Reformed Churches)

NGZV — *De Nederlandsche Gereformeerde Zendings Vereniging* (The Dutch Reformed Mission Organization)

NHK — *Nederlandsche Hervormde Kerk* (The Dutch Reformed Church)

NZG — *Het Nederlansch Zendeling Genootschap* (The Dutch Missionary Society)

NZV — *Nederlandsche Zendings Vereniging* (The Dutch Mission Organization)

RR — *Regeringsreglement* (Regulation 123); the Dutch colonial government's restrictions on missionary activities

RSV — Revised Standard Version

TNI — *Tijdschrift voor Nederlandsch-Indië*

VOC — *Vereenigde Oost Indische Compagnie* (Dutch East India Company)

ZGKN — *Zending van de Gereformeerde Kerken in Nederland* (Mission of the Reformed Churches in the Netherlands)

ACKNOWLEDGEMENTS

At last the tiring though interesting study ends. It is, however, only through the contribution, support, and encouragement of so many that this project was made possible. I owe and express my heartfelt thanks to the following:

Prof. Dr. A. Wessels of the Free University in Amsterdam as promotor. As my professor and promotor he was, of course, my "intellectual father" giving me guidance, critique, and suggestions throughout the writing of this dissertation. However, beyond academic matters, he and his wife were supportive and encouraging, treating me with friendliness, patience, and great understanding, so that I did not feel myself a foreigner in their presence.

Prof. Dr. J. Van Den Berg of the University of Leiden as co-promotor. With great patience he made many valuable suggestions. His eye for detail prevented me from unnecessary error.

Dr. P. Quarles Van Ufford of the Free University in Amsterdam as co-promotor. With his experience working among the Javanese people in Salatiga, Central Java, and his knowledge of Javanese culture, his contributions to the final product of this book were significant.

Prof. Dr. J. Veenhof of the Free University in Amsterdam as referent. He received me hospitably as a fellow minister and made invaluable suggestions for my dissertation.

Drs. J.D. Gort of the Free University in Amsterdam. Even before I arrived in the Netherlands, he and his wife made the necessary contacts enabling me to find a way to continue my study. For their friendship I greatly appreciate and deeply thank them.

Moderamen van de Sektie Java-Sumatra voor Zending en Werelddiakonaat in Leusden and the staff: Mr. M. De Vries (retired secretary), Mrs. Elizabeth Boekestijn (present secretary), Mrs. A. Grasman, and Rev. W.B. Van Halsema.

The following libraries and their staff:

— The Library of the *Zending der Gereformeerde Kerken in Nederland* in Leusden, especially Mr. Peter Van Beek of the Archives section.

— The Library of the *Koninklijk Instituut voor Taal-, Land- en Volkenkunde* in Leiden.

— The Library of the *Hendrik Kraemer Instituut*, especially Mrs. A. Werner.

— The National Archives Office in Jakarta, especially Drs. Amy Darmiyati.

— The *Interuniversitair Instituut voor Missiologie en Oecumenica*, especially Drs. L. Lagerwerf.

The immediate descendants of Kyai Sadrach: Bapak Soepono and Soerprapto Martoseputro in Karangjasa, who allowed me to copy manuscripts and documents as well as explained aspects necessary for my study.

Majelis Gereja Kristen Jawa NEHEMIA in Jakarta for giving me sabbatical leave to undertake this study.

John and Susan Medendorp for improving the English text as well as the bibliography and glossary, and Drs. F. Kirihio for writing the Dutch summary.

My wife Sri Umiyatni for her great patience and understanding as well as her willingness to take on the task of father as well as mother in nurturing our son during my absence.

My son Eko Nugroho Widhi, who with understanding never made any unreasonable demands or requests.

It is not possible to name each and every person who made a contribution to this study. Each one I thank.

DEI GLORIAE ET HOMINUM SALUTI
voor de eer van God en der menschen heil
for the glory of God and the salvation of men

INTRODUCTION

A. Subject of study

1. Sadrach's community

Karangjasa is a small remote village in the southern part of Bagelen, a former residency of Central Java. Since the second half of the nineteenth century it has been well-known to officials of the Dutch colonial government, the Mission of the Dutch Reformed Churches (*Zending van de Gereformeerde Kerken in Nederland*, hereafter ZGKN),[1] and Javanese Christians. This small village was the residence of the great man, Sadrach Surapranata, a pioneer Javanese evangelist who became the charismatic leader of Javanese Christians throughout Central Java. He had great influence on his followers, and was highly respected as their spiritual father. As a result, Karangjasa gradually became the center of Javanese Christianity, a sort of Mecca, as L.W.C. Van Den Berg described it.[2]

The local Dutch colonial government, however, considered Sadrach a rebellious leader who threatened the delicately maintained peace and public order, while the Dutch missionaries generally perceived Sadrach's authority and leadership as going beyond the limits of true Christianity and against the principles of Calvinism.[3] They accused him of leading Javanese Christians astray and regarded his teachings as a mixture of Christian and non-Christian ideas. His community was perceived as pseudo-Christian[4] and a Moslem community dressed in Christian garments.[5] F. Lion Cachet, therefore, gave Karang*jasa*, which means 'the established rock,' the nickname Karang*dosa*, which means 'the rock of sin.'[6]

---

1. See Appendix I.
2. L.W.C. Van Den Berg, "Javaansch Christendom," *De Gids* 25 (1907), p. 257.
3. Petrus Heyting, *Verslag van den toestand de verspreiding enz. der Inlandsche Christenen in de residentie Bagelen en aangrenzende gewesten* (National Archives Office, Jakarta), pp. 2-7.
4. F. Lion Cachet, *Een jaar op reis in dienst der Zending* (Amsterdam, 1896), p. 282.
5. D. Bakker, "Ons Zendingsterrein op Midden Java," *De Macedoniër* 15 (1911), p. 364.
6. Cachet, *Een Jaar*, p. 372. All translations of Dutch and Indonesian or Javanese texts are those of the author.

2

2. The uniqueness of Sadrach's community

The community which emerged around Sadrach originated and grew apart from the established colonial church, *De Protestantsche Kerk in Neder-landsch-Indië*, hereafter *Indische Kerk*) and the missionary community of the Dutch Reformed Church. The members of the community were called *Sadrach's Kring* (Sadrach's Circle)[7] by some, and Javanese Christians[8] by others. They, however, chose to refer to themselves as *Golongane Wong Kristen Kang Mardika* (the Group of Free Christians).[9]

Sadrach's community was a unique religious phenomenon since it was the product of neither the *Indische Kerk* mission nor of any of the other missionary enterprises working in Central Java in the second half of the nineteenth century. Rather, it was the fruit of the missionary activities of lay Euro-Indonesian Christians who felt called to evangelize the Javanese people. Because the community was born from the womb of Javanese culture and was nurtured, developed, and shaped within this cultural framework by those who valued the Javanese cultural background, the result was, not surprisingly, an indigenous community with a Javanese cultural outlook. For this reason, the Dutch missionaries viewed it with suspicion.

3. Sadrach's community as a case study of contextualization

It was the implicit assumption of the missionaries working in Java in the nineteenth century, that Javanese converts had to abandon their culture in order to become truly Christian. Sadrach, however, did not conform to this mold. Although he received the Gospel through personal contact with missionaries, he did not become a typical product of the Dutch missionary endeavor. The community he developed was strongly allied with Javanese culture. Sadrach became an example of independent Christian leadership, and his community became a model of many similar communities throughout the world.

Sadrach's community is, therefore, a case study in contextualization and holds a threefold interest for us. First, being from Central Java, we are interested in the way in which Sadrach, also the son of Javanese soil, was able to integrate his Christian faith and Javanese culture. Second, we are interested in the nature of the Christianity brought by Western mis-

---

7. L. Adriaanse, *Sadrach's Kring* (Leiden, 1899).
8. Van Den Berg, "Javaansch Christendom," pp. 235-269.
9. J. Wilhelm, *Dagboek*, 1883 (Archives of the Dutch Reformed Missionary Society, Leusden), p. 20.

sionaries to Central Java. Finally, our interest lies in the conflict which ensued between Sadrach and the Dutch missionaries.

B. Area and Purpose of Study

1. Area of study

We have defined as our area of study Sadrach's "contextual theology." We have chosen this area in order to come to a better understanding of this Javanese expression of Christianity, in the hope that it will contribute to the contextualizing efforts of the church throughout the world. We begin, therefore, with the term "contextualization."

New forms and patterns of church life and mission relevant to a multifaceted and constantly changing world have been urgently needed. Today greater attempts are being made to "translate" the Gospel from one culture to another. For, doing missions basically means communicating the Gospel in such a way that people of different cultures can understand it in their own "language." Trying to understand God's truth from a cross-cultural perspective and to communicate that truth cross-culturally is a necessity. There has been a growing interest in developing this area of cross-cultural ministry in missions.[10] In short, the church needs contextual theology. Theology which is not contextual, that is, an expression of faith in terms of contemporary society, history, and culture, is considered false.[11]

Contextualization, like the terms incarnation, indigenization, inculturation, and accomodation, means searching for a *local, situational,* or *relevant* theology. Relevant theology relates to the situation and needs of an audience, and therefore, is situational (different from time to time) and local (different from place to place). The Commission on World Missions and Evangelism (CWME) of the World Council of Churches which gathered in Bangkok (1973) under the theme "Salvation-Today" underscored that

> proper theology is reflection on the experience of Christian community in a particular place at a particular time. Thus it will be necessarily be a contextual theology; it will be a relevant and living theology which refuses to be easily universalized because it speaks to and out of a particular situation.[12]

10. Cf. Charles H. Kraft, *Christianity in Culture: A Study in Dynamic Biblical Theologizing in Cross-Cultural Perspective* (New York, 1981).

11. Stephen Bevans, "Models of Contextual Theology," *Missiology: An International Review* 13 (April, 1985), p. 185.

12. "Culture and Identity," Report of Section I of the Bangkok Conference, *IRM*, Vol. 52, No. 246 (April, 1973), p. 190.

While indigenization emphasizes taking the local, traditional religious and cultural elements into account, contextualization, while not ignoring these elements, pays more attention to the socio-political situation. The World Council of Churches defines it as that which "takes into account the process of secularity, technology, and the struggle for human justice."[13] The aspect stressed here is the need for liberation, the predominant feature of the Third World's context. The need for contextualization within the Third World churches thus arises not from a theoretical imperative but from a practical one,[14] and it is therefore *theologia praxeos* (theology of action). Such theology emphasizes God's liberating act from economic, political, and social supression and injustice.

Stephen Bevans concludes that a theology will be contextual if it takes four things into consideration; namely, the spiritual message of the Gospel, the tradition of Christian people, the culture of a particular nation and region, and the social change in that culture due both to technological advances on the one hand, and the struggle for justice and liberation on the other.[15] Therefore, we may say that contextualization as a theological approach is comprehensive in character.[16]

Finally, we should beware of false contextualization which uncritically accomodates to culture — a form of "culture-faith." Unlike "culture-faith," authentic faith is always prophetic, "arising always out of a genuine encounter between God's Word and His world, and moves toward the purpose of challenging and changing the situation through rootedness in and commitment to a given historical moment."[17]

13. Theological Education Fund, *Ministry in Context: The Third Mandate Program of the Theological Education Fund (1970-1977)*, (Bromiley, 1978), p. 20.

14. Robert J. Schreiter, *Constructing Local Theologies* (New York, 1985), p. 27; cf. Bevans, p. 185.

15. Bevans, p. 186.

16. For a discussion on contextualization see: Bruce C.E. Fleming, *Contextualization of Theology: An Evangelical Assessment* (Pasadena, 1980); Krikor Heleblian, "The Problem of Contextualization," *Missiology*, XI: 1, pp. 95-111; B.J.F. Lonergan, "Theology in New Context," *Theology of Renewal*, L.K. Shook, ed. (New York, 1968), pp. 34-46; Lonergan, *Method in Theology* (New York, 1972); Bong Rin Ro, "Contextualization: Asian Theology," *What Asian Christians are Thinking*, Douglas J. Elwood, ed. (Queen City, 1976), pp. 49-58; Schreiter; Boston Theological Institute, *One Faith, Many Cultures,* Ray O. Costa, ed. (New York, 1988); H.M. Kuitert, "Contextueel of academisch? Op zoek naar relevante theologie," *Gereformeerd Theologisch Tijdschrift* 83 (August, 1983), pp. 188-203.

17. Theological Education Fund, *Ministry in Context*, p. 20.

2. Purpose of study

Both Sadrach as leader and the community he founded were extraordinary phenomena which raised many missiological issues in *De Nederlandsche Gereformeerde Zendings Vereeniging* (the Dutch Reformed Mission Organization, hereafter NGZV) and the ZGKN, which took responsibility for the mission fields in Central Java after 1894. In 1891, Cachet executed an investigative tour in Central Java on behalf of the Board of the NGZV and the Synod of the *Nederduitsche Gereformeerde Kerken* (hereafter NGK) and made the following recommendation: "For the glory of the Lord and out of love for the souls, even the soul of Sadrach, the Mission should break from the lying Sadrach who has poisoned the life of the established 'Javanese Christianity' in which Christ no longer has a place."[18] In our study, we will raise the following issues in connection with this view of Sadrach's authority, leadership, and community. With respect to the Dutch missionaries, we ask whether this evaluation was merely the personal judgment of Cachet, or whether it reveals the mission theology of the two organizations he represented. If so, what kind of Christianity and mission theology was brought to Central Java? How did the missionaries perceive the Javanese context in which they worked? Was such a perception justified?

With respect to Sadrach and his community, on the other hand, we ask whether Sadrach's authority and leadership were contrary to Christian or Calvinistic principles. Did Sadrach really betray the truth of the Gospel, or did he understand and interpret the Gospel in an authentically Javanese manner? Could the uniqueness of his leadership and the life of his community be seen as a Javanese expression of a fundamental universal faith which recognized Jesus as Christ and Lord?[19] How far were Sadrach's leadership and the life of his community relevant to the Javanese context of the nineteenth century? These are intriguing questions which reflect the problem of contextualization in the early history of Javanese missions. They reflect, as T. Müller Krüger pointed out, the problem between Christianity "in Western and in Javanese form."[20]

Thus, the purpose of our study is to answer these questions in order to

18. "Om de eere des Heeren, en uit liefde tot de zielen, ook tot de ziel van Sadrach, moest de Zending zich losmaken van leugen Sadrach, die geheel ons zendingsveld vergiftigde, en een 'Javaansch-Christendom' in het leven had geroepen, waarin voor den Christus geen plaats is." Cachet, *Een Jaar*, p. 842.

19. Cf. Rom. 10:9; I Cor. 12:3; Phil. 2:11.

20. T. Müller Krüger, *Sejarah Gereja di Indonesia* [Church History of Indonesia] (Jakarta, 1966), p. 159.

6

get a true picture of Sadrach's "contextual theology" as reflected in his community, and to focus on the problems involved in the issue of contextualization. Accordingly, our study can be properly entitled: *Sadrach's Community and its Contextual Roots: A Nineteenth Century Javanese Expression of Christianity.*

The title and subtitle clearly imply a *local* and *situational* character, i.e., the *Javanese* context of the *nineteenth century.* They also denote the scope and limits of our study, distinguishing it from the previous study by C. Guillot, *L'Affair Sadrach, un Essai de Christianisation à Java au XIXe siècle.*[21] His study focuses on the social aspects of Sadrach's movement. As he has clearly stated in his introduction, his purpose was "to investigate and understand the motives behind the conversion to Christianity of the Javanese people who followed Sadrach in the second half of the nineteenth century."[22] According to Guillot, Sadrach's movement was a struggle against a discriminative colonial society for social equality; equality, therefore, became the dominant motive for conversion. Sadrach was viewed by his followers as the bridge or mediator between the colonized Javanese and the colonizing Dutch.

C. Composition of the Book

In order to describe the life of Sadrach and his community and the theological issues which arose, it is first necessary to give the socio-cultural, political, and religious background of Central Java in the nineteenth century and to examine the way in which the Christian faith was brought by the existing "official" church (the *Indische Kerk*), the Dutch missionary organizations, and lay evangelists. This will be done in Chapter I. In Chapter II, we will describe Sadrach's life from his early youth to his conversion to the Christian faith, and the historical development of his community. In Chapter III the uniqueness of Sadrach's community will become apparent through the description of some aspects of its life.

After Sadrach came in direct contact with the NGZV a conflict with the Dutch missionaries become unavoidable. The theological and missiological issues reflected in this conflict will be discussed in Chapter IV. Chapter V, the final chapter, contains a reflection on Sadrach and his community, which highlights several of the aspects elaborated in the preceding chapters. Through this reflection we hope to arrive at a more

21. C. Guillot, *L'Affair Sadrach: Essai de Christianisation à Java au XIXe siècle* (Paris, 1981); Indonesian edition *Kiai Sadrach, Riwayat Kristenisasi di Jawa* (Jakarta, 1985).
22. Guillot, *L'Affaire Sadrach*, p. 6; *Kiai Sadrach*, p. 2.

comprehensive understanding of Sadrach's "contextual theology" and the life of his community as rooted in the Javanese context.

D. Sources and literature

This study is based primarily on research into the literature available in the forms of reports, minutes, correspondence, articles appearing in various missionary periodicals, as well as diaries and books written by the Dutch missionaries, particularly those who came in direct contact with Sadrach and/or his community.

The National Archives Office (*Kantor Arsip Nasional*) in Jakarta, Indonesia, provided valuable sources regarding the development, life, and problems of Sadrach's community in its first fifteen years. P. Heyting's handwritten report to the Board of the *Indische Kerk* in Batavia (now Jakarta) was an important source. Included in his report are nine appendices, the first five of which contain statistical data on the membership of Sadrach's community and the Javanese community led by the Dutch missionaries. Appendix F is a report made by a Controller in Karangkobar regarding Sadrach's community in that area. Appendices G and H contain letters written by J. Wilhelm, P. Heyting, and P. Bieger. Appendix I contains information about A. Vermeer, a missionary whom Heyting suggested as as associate minister. As the minister of the *Indische Kerk* in Purwareja, Heyting represented not only the interests of his church, but also, indirectly, those of the local Dutch colonial government. His report is basically an argument for the installation of a Dutch associate minister to be in charge of the Javanese Christian community. In addition to Heyting's work, numerous other valuable documents are available including decisions and missives of the Dutch colonial government. Most of them represent the perspective of the Dutch colonial government, and, accordingly, served political purposes.

The Archives Department of the Central Office of the ZGKN in Leusden, The Netherlands, also provided valuable sources. Of great significance is the diary of J. Wilhelm, missionary of the NGZV to Central Java, which covers the period from January 1, 1881 to August 30, 1890. Wilhelm had a personal relationship with Sadrach and was fully involved in the work of his community. As an "insider" who was significantly involved in the development of the community, he viewed Sadrach and his community from a positive, yet critical, perspective. Wilhelm's knowledge of the Javanese people, his personal contact with Sadrach, and his direct involvement with the community lend credence to his personal witness.

Another importance source found in these archives is the Almanac of 1891 which gives some helpful insights into the life of the community.

Minutes of various NGZV gatherings and the personal correspondence of NGZV missionaries represent the views and interests of the NGZV and its missionaries.

Not to be overlooked are the Karangjasa Documents preserved in Karangjasa, Central Java, Indonesia. Although Sadrach left no book by his own hand, there are, nevertheless, authentic documents preserved by and available from his immediate family and associates. Among these documents can be found a short history of the establishment of the Christian community in Karangjasa and Sadrach's biography. Both of these manuscripts were written in Javanese by Yotham Martareja, Sadrach's adopted son. Because they were written while Sadrach was still alive, they reveal Sadrach's personal experience of his newly found Christian faith. Together with the other documents which have been preserved in Karangjasa, we are able to gain some insights into Sadrach's community from a Javanese perspective.

Several articles written for various missionary periodicals during the lifetime of Sadrach (mid-nineteenth century to the early twentieth century) deal with Javanese customs and life. Some deal more directly with the work of individual missionaries, including their opinions regarding Sadrach and the Christian community in Java. These sources provide insight into the personal perceptions of the missionaries, as well as the perceptions of the missionary organizations or denominations which they represented.

Finally, it is necessary to mention two books written about Sadrach's community which were very helpful for our study. The first is Cachet's book, *Een jaar op reis in dienst der Zending*, in which he described the Javanese Christian community he encountered on his inspection tour. His perceptions reflect the view of a man of great authority coming from a highly civilized country. The yardstick by which he measured the situation in Central Java was Western and ethnocentric, and his superior attitude is reflected throughout his book. His judgments on the Javanese in general were harsh —he viewed them as primitive and uncivilized. His judgments on the Javanese Christians were even harsher — he viewed Sadrach as a liar and his community as unchristian.

The second book, *Sadrach's Kring* by L. Adriaanse, also reflects the view of a Dutch missionary, but from a more moderate position. Adriaanse, who lived and worked in Central Java, attempted to understand Sadrach's community from "within." He not only knew Sadrach personally, but he was also familiar with Javanese life and culture. His goal, unlike that of Cachet, was to work with Sadrach and his community with the hopes of building a bridge between the community and the Dutch mission. His book, therefore, is more sympathetic in its approach toward Sadrach's community. Despite his attempts, however, Adriaanse was cautious in his approach to Sadrach. He viewed him as a Javanese evangelist whose knowledge of Christianity was insufficient and misguided in certain areas. He felt that Sadrach has misinterpreted certain points of Christian doctrine and, as a result, the community was weak in areas of Christian truth. Like the other Dutch missionaries, Adriaanse failed to understand Sadrach's community as an expression of the Christian faith rooted in the Javanese context of the nineteenth century.

The sources which originated with the Dutch missionaries and the mission organizations generally record the failure of the Javanese Christian community to be truly Christian. It is our objective in this study to use these sources carefully and critically to contrast the view of the Dutch missionaries with the view of Sadrach and his community.

CHAPTER I

CENTRAL JAVA IN THE NINETEENTH CENTURY

In order to get an accurate picture of Central Java in the nineteenth century, we will first describe the socio-cultural and religious life of the Javanese people. Secondly, we will describe the Christian mission to Central Java, focusing attention on the activities of the NGZV, which played a significant role in the history of Sadrach and his community.

Prior to the second half of the nineteenth century, before the various missionary organizations began their work in Indonesia, christianization of the indigenous people had been carried out by the Protestant Church of the Dutch Indies (*Indische Kerk*) as an continuation of the mission of the Dutch East India Company (*Vereenigde Oost Indische Compagnie*, VOC). Although the mission fell under the official jurisdiction of the colonial government, it never became a priority and was often yielded to other interests. Unlike the eastern parts of Indonesia (e.g., in the Moluccan Islands where the *Indische Kerk* was fairly successful in converting the indigenous people), the role of the *Indische Kerk* in Java became primarily one of maintenance, partly for internal ecclesiastical reasons and partly because the socio-political situation was not conducive to missions. Nevertheless, several lay people together with their Javanese helpers took the initiative and played a significant role in missions during that time. These lay evangelists will be the focus of the third section. The final section will look at some of the obstacles to missions in nineteenth century Java.

A. Javanese Life in the Nineteenth Century

1. *Javanese socio-cultural life and the Dutch colonial government's policy*

a. Social stratification in nineteenth century Java

Socio-culturally, the Javanese people were sharply divided into two groups. The first group, the *wong gede* (great people), consisted of *priyayi* (aristocrats), the ruling class, many of whom were government officials. The second group, the *wong cilik* (little people), consisted of the common people.[1] The *priyayi* were educated and enjoyed many special rights and privileges, the most important of which was access to education for their children. The *wong cilik* were denied such rights by the Dutch colonial government, however, and were thus deprived of the means of social advancement.

The colonial government administration used the *priyayi* as an extension of itself in order to rule the people. The *priyayi*, therefore, represented colonial interests rather than the interests of the common people. The policy was indirect rule with the slogan, "governing people through indigenous rulers." This policy only served to reinforce the existing social structure. The *priyayi*, who usually lived in the cities, developed their own lifestyle and culture. Following the great/court tradition, they utilized symbols and titles to emphasize their greatness.[2] The king's court became the center of Javanese culture and life.

In contrast to the *priyayi*, the majority of the *wong cilik* lived as peasants in rural areas. A small number lived in the cities, working as traders and unskilled laborers. They also developed their own lifestyle and tradition (little tradition) which was regarded as lower and unrefined in contrast to the court.

The *wong cilik* were socio-economically divided into the following strata based on land ownership:[3]

1) The **pondok** were the landless immigrants, newcomers, and other landless people who generally owned no house. This group comprised the largest social category.

---

1. C. Poensen, "Een en ander over de godsdienstigen toestand van den Javaan," *MNZG* 8 (1864), pp. 214-263; *MNZG* 9 (1865), pp. 161-202; C. Poensen, "De Javanen en het Evangelie," *MNZG* 14 (1870), pp. 123-216; C. Poensen, "Het Evangelie op Java," *MNZG* 34 (1890), pp. 391-415.

2. Regarding Javanese titles, see L.W.C. Van Den Berg, *Nota over de Inlandsche rangen en titels op Java en Madura* (n.p., n.d.), especially pp. 12-18 on Central Java. Among other Javanese symbols of greatness was the golden umbrella, not only used by Javanese nobility, but also by the Dutch residents, showing a high social status that they were agents of the great Dutch power. Cf. Heather Sutherland, *The Making of a Bureaucratic Elite, the Colonial Transformation of Javanese Priyayi* (Singapore, 1979), p. 8; Indonesian edition: *Terbentuknya sebuah Elite birokrasi*, trans. Sunarto (Jakarta, 1983), p. 35.

3. M.H.J. Kollmann, "Bagelen onder het bestuur van Soerakarta en Djokjakarta," *Bataviaasch Genootschap van Kunst en Wetenschappen*, Vol. 14 (n.p., 1864), pp. 352-368; C. Poensen, "Iets over de Javaansche Desa," *MNZG* 38 (1894) p. 32; Soemarsaid Moertono, *Negara dan Usaha Bina Negara di Jawa masa lampau* [State and Statecraft in Old Java] (Jakarta, 1985), p. 144; Koentjaraningrat, *Javanese Culture*, (Oxford, 1985), pp. 188-190; *Indonesian edition: Kebudayaan Jawa* (Jakarta, 1984), pp. 200-202.

2) The **lindung** were landless villagers who owned a house and garden but were dependent on the landowners for their livelihood.

3) The **kuli** were the landowners, mostly descendants of the original legendary settlers of the village. They were called *tiyang baku*, or main settlers. Their relationship to the venerated village ancestors was often indicated by their possession of an ancient house or heirlooms, or by their devotion to the sacred graves of the founding ancestors.

Often in traditional village communities a myth or legend existed which told the history of the founding fathers of the village. It was believed that they were members of the ancient royalty who were considered divine and had left the court to wander around as knights or hermits, finally settling down in the village. These myths concerning their sacred origin explains why they and their descendents, the *kuli*, enjoyed prestige in the village community. Even if the *kuli* became poor, they were still treated with respect. In this case, ancestral lines were a higher criterion for prestige than property and material wealth.[4]

The *prabot dusun* was the village administration, consisting of families belonging to the rural elite. The village leader (*lurah*), appointed for life by the *priyayi patuh*, was usually a member of the royal family who held control of the rural areas. His staff, included the *kaum* or *modin*, Islamic officials who performed the religious rituals and ceremonies. This administration met regularly every thirty-five days (*selapan*). They were not paid but maintained the right to cultivate part of the village's communal land in lieu of a salary, which was called *bengkok* or *palungguh*. Other sources of income were taxes and services paid for by the villagers according to the regulations based on village tradition.[5] Next to the *lurah* and his staff was a council of elders (*kasepuhan*), which acted as advisor. These men were highly respected in the village as the creators and sustainers of the village traditions.[6]

The relationship between the *priyayi* and the *wong cilik* was patterned after the *kawula-gusti* (servant-master) model.[7] The gap between the two classes was greater in the nineteenth century than at present. As D. Bakker stated, the common people blindly obeyed and slavishly honored the

4. "De Toestand van Bagelen in 1830," *TNI* (1858) pp. 45-84; J.F.G. Brumund, "Het Landbezit op Java," *TNI* (1859), pp. 48-49.

5. Brumund, "Het Landbezit," pp. 50-51.

6. C. Poensen, "Iets over den Javaan als mensch," *MNZG* 29 (1885), p. 61; Koentjaraningrat, *Javanese Culture*, p. 193; *Kebudayaan Jawa*, p. 205.

7. Poensen, "De Javanen," pp. 141-157; cf. Sartono Kartodirdjo, *Ratu Adil* (Jakarta, 1984), p. 47.

priyayi, and since a person's status was likely to be based solely on birth, it was a form of caste system.[8] The common people were merely *kawula* (servants) and had no right to take part in state affairs. Their role was primarily to serve their *gusti* (master). The relationship was characterized by authoritarianism and paternalism. The *priyayi* were expected to nurture the peasants as their own children, leading and governing them with an iron rod.[9] The greatest merit for the common person was to serve his master faithfully for life. The royal family and the *priyayi* were considered demigods and their commands were thought to be divine.[10] Economically the common people were faithful taxpayers. Socially they were dedicated citizens who obeyed the regulations issued in the name of the king and the colonial government.[11]

b.   The socio-economic situation and governmental policy

The socio-economic condition of the people, particularly those in rural areas, was not improving. The colonial government's policy of forced cultivation, the well-known *Cultuurstelsel* (1833-1867),[12] which was intended to improve economic conditions in the Netherlands following the Javanese war of 1825-1830 (led by the Javanese prince, Dipanegara, against the Dutch colonial government), inflicted great economic harm upon the common people.[13]

As a result of sharp criticism on the part of some conscientious members of the Dutch Parliament after 1855, this policy was gradually abandoned in favor of a more liberal economic policy. Although privatization in the economic sector produced a more favorable climate for business enterprise only those with capital could benefit. In contrast, those without capital, which included the common people in general, were unaffected by the policy and continued to live in the same depressed economic conditions.[14]

8. D. Bakker, "Christelijke Hollandsch-Javaansche Scholen," *De Macedoniër* 15 (1911), p. 268.

9. Sutherland, *Bureaucratic Elite*, p. 30; *Terbentuknya*, p. 74.

10. D. Bakker, "Het Schuldbesef van de Javanen," *De Macedoniër* 15 (1911), p. 241.

11. Poensen, "Javaansche Desa," pp. 30-61. Regarding taxation, see "De Toestand," pp. 77-78.

12. One-fifth of the peasants' land had to be used to plant crops for commodity exports or they were obligated to work on government plantations for sixty-six days per year; Koentjarangingrat, *Javanese Culture*, p. 61; *Kebudayaan Jawa*, p. 67.

13. P. van Akkeren, *Sri and Christ* (London, 1970), p. 38; Koentjaraningrat, *Javanese Culture*, p. 61; *Kebudayaan Jawa*, p. 67.

14. C. Geertz, *The Social Context of Economic Change: An Indonesian Case Study* (Massachusetts, ©1956), as quoted by Koentjaraningrat, *Javanese Culture*, p. 62; *Kebudayaan Jawa*, p. 70.

Moreover, the public schools, an avenue for improving these conditions, were mainly accessible only to the middle and upper classes and did not affect the vast majority of the Javanese people. Initially, only a small number of the Javanese elite sent their children to these schools, while the rest regarded them as the Western agent for christianizing Javanese children and alienating them from their native culture.[15]

Due to these poor socio-economic conditions, Java was flooded by religious movements in the nineteenth century. Occasionally, what began as a religious movement would turn into a protest, or even a radical revolutionary movement. The socio-economic situation, however, was not the sole cause. The presence of the Dutch regime and its stifling influence was widely regarded as a foreign threat to traditional Javanese values. The introduction of Western institutions, administration, and moral values intensively threatened the traditional bureaucracy. The *priyayi* soon overcame their initial suspicion, and because of their special privileges and education, adjusted to the new situation by becoming somewhat westernized and secularized. The traditional religious teachers (*kyai* and *guru*), however, held fast to their traditions. According to Sartono, the religious movements led by these conservative leaders appeared to be the strongest forces against Western penetration. The disagreement between the *priyayi* and the traditional religious leaders originated from basic differences in ideology and social status.[16] The *priyayi* preferred to maintain the "status quo" rather than concern themselves with the interests of the people. They could not be expected, therefore, to be defenders and protectors of the people in such a feudalistic, colonial system. To a certain extent, the *kyais* and gurus, who often stood against the suppressing system, became the heroic defenders and protectors of the common people.

The traditional religious teachers, in fact, played a very decisive role in the community. They stood outside the formal bureaucratic structure of the colonial administration and could, therefore, act independently. Although they were informal leaders, they were very influential, and their authority was acknowledged by the common people. They often challenged the colonial authorities, even though such conflicts between formal and informal leaders usually ended with the purging of the latter and a dissolution of the movements. Nevertheless, these movements remained a latent danger, always threatening to explode. In its attempts to suppress

15. Sutherland, *Bureaucratic Elite*, p. 46; *Terbentuknya*, p. 99.

16. Sartono, *Ratu Adil*, p. 51. For Western penetration of Javanese life since the nineteenth century, through modern transportation, trade or money, new traditions and morality, see also Poensen, "Javaan als mensch," pp. 125-126; Koentjaraningrat, *Javanese Culture*, pp. 60-63; *Kebudayaan Jawa*, p. 66-68.

such movements, the colonial government took pains to file legitimate charges against them. A study of the various colonial archives shows some of the reasons used by the colonial government to justify its frequent seizures of Javanese leaders:

1) Leaders were accused of distorting the true teachings of the religion concerned.
2) Because of the large number of followers, the leaders were regarded as politically dangerous.
3) Leaders were accused of exploiting the religious sensitivities of their followers, inciting them to oppose the colonial government and rulers in favor of a just society ruled by *ratu adil* (the "just king," a messianic figure).
4) Some leaders were accused of deceiving the people for personal material gain.[17]

Many of these reports were tendentious. According to Sartono, several reports were doubtful and misleading, colored by ethnic prejudice and islamophobia, with the result that they tended to view all religious movements as anti-foreign and revolutionary. Such a generalization was, however, erroneous.[18]

Although the traditional religious leaders were blamed by the Dutch colonial government for the social unrest of the nineteenth century, missionary activities were also affected. The ultimate concern of the government was to maintain peace and public order. Java was generally regarded by the colonial authorities as solidly Moslem. Islamic resistance was, therefore, greatly feared, and the authorities were alert to anything that might lead to a disturbance. Peace and public order became the key words for understanding the general policy of the colonial government during this period. Repressive measures were applied to religious movements and their leaders at the first sign of trouble. This policy was combined with restrictive measures taken against the Christian mission through the issuance of Regulation 123 in 1854 (known as *Regeringsreglement*, or R.R., and later as the *Indische Staatsregeling 177*). The Regulation stipulated that every missionary have government permission to work, and that missionary activities be restricted to a given area. It also

17. K.A. Steenbrink, *Beberapa aspek tentang Islam di Indonesia abad ke19* [Some Aspects of Islam in Indonesia in the Nineteenth Century] (Jakarta, 1984), pp. 188-189. Studies on rural movements have been made by scholars such as Sartono, *The Peasants' Revolt of Banten in 1888* ('s-Gravenhage, 1966); *Protest Movements in Rural Java: A Study of Agrarian Unrests in the Nineteenth and Early Twentieth Centuries* (Singapore, 1973), and G.W.J. Drewes, *Drie Javaansche Goeroe's,* (Leiden, 1925).

18. Sartono, *Ratu Adil*, p. 10.

gave the government the right to revoke permission if missionary activities were judged to be disruptive.[19]

One can only conclude that the Javanese feudal system was strengthened in the nineteenth century by colonialism in order to serve the interests of the colonial government. The introduction of a new administration, public schools and institutions, and the improvements made in transportation and agriculture were primarily intended to serve the needs of the Dutch colonial government. Such a feudalistic, colonial system, coupled with repressive policies, brought no improvements in the living conditions of the Javanese people in general.

Although the impact of colonial society began to be felt more intensely in the second half of the nineteenth century, it brought little change to rural life. The Javanese peasants continued to live under simple conditions. The changes introduced by the colonial government did not correspond to the basic needs of housing, clothing, farm equipment, and medical care. The traditional healers (*dhukuns*) continued to play an important role in health care and childbirth. Most of the indigenous schools were *pesantren* and *langgar*, Islamic schools which emphasized religious matters. According to governmental statistics, in 1871, Java had 2,112 *pesantrens* with 45,883 pupils, 8,123 *langgars* with 140,303 pupils, and 756 private religious schools with 6,059 pupils. In the same year there were 76 public schools run by the colonial government serving 7,611 pupils, and 108 non-religious private schools serving 4,890 pupils.[20] With a population at the time of twelve million, it is clear from these statistics that the educational system was inadequate. Not surprisingly, Van Der Chijs reported that in Tegal, Central Java, only three or four out of eight hundred fifty village leaders were able to write their own names in Latin letters.[21] It must be noted, however, that while most of them did not know the Dutch language, they did possess adequate skills in Javanese and Arabic letters.

Because of the simplicity of Javanese rural life, the peasants were

19. Regarding this regulation, see K. Van Dijk, "Article 177 van de wet op Staatsinrichting van Nederlandsch-Indië," *De Macedoniër* 38 (1934), pp. 55ff.; D. Pol, "Article 177," *De Macedoniër* 38 (1934), pp. 344-345; L.W.C. Van Den Berg, "Article 123 RR Nederlandsch-Indië," *De Opwekker* 69 (1924), pp. 213-214; H. Dijkstra, "Article 123 van het Indisch Regeerings-Reglement," *De Macedoniër* 19 (1915), p. 203.

20. J.C. Neurdenburg, "De Eischen van het Inlandsch Onderwijs in Nederlandsch-Indië, Bijlage: Eenige denkbeelden over het Inlandsch Onderwijs bepaaldelijk voor de Javaan," *MNZG* 23 (1879), pp. 124-125.

21. J.A. Van Der Chijs, "Bijdragen tot de Geschiedenis van het Inlandsch Onderwijs in Nederlandsch-Indië," *Tijdschrift voor Indische Taal-, Land- en Volkenkunde* 14 (1864), p. 216.

described by some Dutch missionaries as "children of nature."[22] By this term they did not mean that the Javanese people were uncivilized, but that their lives were closely tied to nature. The Javanese were already permanent land dwellers and were well organized in the agricultural sphere, as their wet rice farms testify. Their lives, however, remained unsophisticated in most areas. In using the term "children of nature," the missionaries meant that the Javanese people lived mainly according to the laws of nature. They did little planning and tended to spend much time on what the missionaries considered to be unnecessary work. In addition, the missionaries viewed the Javanese as sluggish and lazy, characteristics which kept them in severe poverty and prevented them from seeking knowledge of spiritual things and eternal life.

The "slavishness" which has been ascribed to the Javanese must, however, be seen as the result of a series of suppressive regimes, both indigenous and foreign, which prevented the Javanese people from preserving and developing their own identity. Even Western critics, whose evaluations were often less than sympathic, recognized that this extended duress had a negative effect, making the Javanese, in their words, dependent, fatalistic, submissive, and childlike.[23] Jacob Wilhelm, a missionary of the NGZV, was of the opinion that the long process of suppression under the influence of Hinduism, Buddhism, Islam, and Western colonialism distorted the Javanese character and prevented its natural formation. He described the Javanese nature and spirituality as entirely worldly and sensual.[24]

2. Javanese socio-religious life

a. The historical development of religion in Java

Javanese religion is usually considered to be a syncretistic belief system[25]

---

22. D.J. Ten Zeldam Ganswijk, "Iets over de Javanen in betrekking tot Evangelie-predikking in Oostelijk Java," *MNZG* 1 (1857), p. 89. Ten Zeldam Ganswijk used the term "kinderen der natuur," while J.H. Bavinck used "*natuurvolken*" for the same concept. These terms indicate a people whose life is bound closely to nature and community, a homogeneous group. Cf. J.H. Bavinck, "Zending en Cultuur," *Indische Dag* (Heemstede, n.d.), p. 51.

23. Ten Zeldam Ganswijk, p. 94; D. Bakker, *Verhoudingen in Zendingsarbeid contra ds. Fernhout*, (Amsterdam, n.d.), p. 51; S.E. Harthoorn, "Iets over Javaanschen Mohammedaan en Javaanschen Christen," MNZG 1 (1857), p. 190; Poensen, "Javaan als mensch," pp. 51-52.

24. J. Wilhelm, *Dagboek* 1882 (Archives of the Dutch Reformed Missionary Society, Leusden), 1882, p. 17.

25. D.C. Mulder distinguishes between "syncretistic" and "syncretism proper."

resembling a cake with layer upon layer of differing elements, each of which maintains its own character. Such syncretism has, according to Howard P. Jones, made the Javanese people more open-minded and tolerant toward others.[26] The first layer of this "cake" is the early Javanese religion which was based on local ancestor worship. This religion was characterized by a belief in spirits, the worship of objects, and the practice of magic.[27] This is the indigenous religion of Java.

This indigenous faith was subject to several subsequent foreign religious influences. As early as the fourth century AD, Hinduism and Buddhism were imported from India through trade routes. The position of these religions in Java was strengthened through the visits of *brahmans* (upper cast Hindus) and *bhiksus* (Hindu or Buddist monks), who were periodically invited to Java by the Javanese rulers. Although the two religions are different, they peacefully coexisted in Java. Their influence climaxed in Central Java during the eight century with the establishment of a Hindu-Buddhist dynasty which lasted until the tenth century. The Hindu-Buddhist dynasty in East Java was in power from the eleventh through the fifteenth centuries.[28]

Between the fourteenth and seventeenth centuries, the third layer, Islam, was introduced to Java, also as a result of trade. In the northern coastal regions Islam gradually took hold and Moslem sultanates were established. After these areas were firmly islamized, a campaign was launched to reach the interior regions, first by converting the Javanese rulers with the assumption that their people would follow.[29] A mass

"Syncretistic" refers to the addition of alien elements which remain foreign within the original pattern of the religion concerned. Such elements are neither integrated into the religion nor filled with new content. "Syncretism proper," on the other hand, refers to the blending of all elements into one religious system. The color of each element becomes mixed, and the basic orientation is blurred, resulting in a new religion composed of these elements. D.C. Mulder, "The Christian Message to a Changing World," *IRB* 35 (October, 1968), p. 40. About syncretism, see H. Kraemer, *De Wortelen van het Syncretisme* ('s-Gravenhage, 1937); L. Adriaanse, "Syncretisme in Britsch-Indië en op Java," *De Macedoniër* 39 (1935), pp. 293ff.

26. Cf. Howard P. Jones, *Indonesia, Possible Dream* (California, 1971), p. 414.

27. Koentjaraningrat, "Javanese Religion," in *The Encyclopedia of Religion*, ed. Mircea Eliade, ed. (New York, 1987), p. 559; Hendrik A. Van Hien, "De Javaansche Geestenwereld en de betrekking, die toeschijnen den Geesten en de zinnelijke wereld bestaat," *Verduidelijkt door Petangan's of Tellingen bijde Javanen in gebruik* (Semarang, 1896).

28. Koentjaraningrat, "Javanese Religion," p. 560.

29. Moslem penetration of the interior of Java became very intense after the fall of the Majapahit Kingdom in 1518, but islamization of Java was not completed until the reign of Sultan Agung of Mataram in the seventeenth century. See Harun Hadiwijono,

conversion resulted, which explains why Java is now considered a Moslem country. The arrival of Western Christianity in the nineteenth century is not generally regarded as another layer since it failed to take hold, largely as a result of the uncompromising attitude of the missionaries toward the local culture and religion.

b.   The Moslem religious structure of Java

The American sociologist, Clifford Geertz, in his book *Religion of Java*, has recently distinguished three groups within the religious structure of Javanese Islam, i.e., *abangan*, which means red, *santri*, which stands for the Moslem students of the *pesantren*, and *priyayi*, the aristocracy.[30] However, a hundred years prior, the Dutch missionary, S.E. Harthoorn, categorized the religious structure into two groups, *bangsa putihan* (white people) and *abangan*.[31] Another Dutch missionary, C. Poensen, confirmed these divisions, labeling them *de kleine* (the little) and *de groote* (the great).[32] In another article, Poensen used the categories of *abangan* and *putihan* as well.[33] From this we see that nineteenth century Islam in Java was usually divided into two groups, although it is not known why they were called *abangan* and *putihan*.[34] These categories were based on the strength of one's commitment to Islam, which manifested itself in religious practices and rites. In Java a distinction was made between *rukun iman* (Islamic belief), namely, belief in God, angels, sacred books, prophets, the last days (*kiyamat*), and predestination (*takdir*), and *rukun Islam* (Islamic obliga-

Man in the Present Javanese Mysticism, (Baarn, 1967), pp. 5-6; cf. T.W. Arnold, *The Preaching of Islam* (London, 1913), p. 348; H. Kraemer, *Een Javaansche Primbon uit de zestiende eeuw* (Leiden, 1921), p. 56.

30. C. Geertz, *Religion of Java* (Illinois, 1960) and *Abangan, Santri, Priyayi dalam Masyarakat Jawa* Bur Rasuanto, ed. (Jakarta, 1981). *Abangan* refers to the Javanese Moslems who emphasize indigenous religious elements, *santri* refers to those who emphasize Islamic elements, and *priyayi* to those who emphasize Hindu-Buddhist elements. Bachtiar does not agree with the use of *priyayi* as a religious classification. Rather, it refers to a social status — the traditional elite — in contrast to the little people (*wong cilik*), or peasants. See Harsja W. Bachtiar, "The Religion of Java; Sebuah Komentar," *Abangan, Santri, dan Priyayi dalam Masyarakat Jawa*, ed. Geertz (Jakarta, 1981).

31. Harthoorn, pp. 183-212.

32. Poensen, "Een en ander," and "De Javanen."

33. C. Poensen, "Iets over Javaansche Naamgeving en Eigennamen," *MNZG* 14 (1870), pp. 304-317.

34. Koentjaraningrat states that the Indonesian philologist, Soebardi, points out a similar pronounciation between the Arabic word *aba'a* (those who ignore) and the Javanese word *abangan*, and the Arabic *muthi'ah* (those who obey) and the Javanese *putihan*. See Koentjaragingrat, *Javanese Culture*, n. 1, p. 197; *Kebudayaan Jawa*, n. 1, p. 209.

tions), namely, confession (*syahadat*), prayer (*sholat*), fasting (*puasa*) alms giving (*zakat-fitrah*), and pilgrimage to Mecca (*naik haji*).

It is from this perspective that the differences between these two types of Islam should be viewed. Javanese *Islam abangan* holds to the *rukun iman* as does *Islam putihan*, but it also holds to such non-Islamic elements as magic and animism. *Islam Putihan* on the other hand, is more orthodox-puritanical, in the sense that it tries to distance itself from Javanese culture and religions. Scholars refer to Javanese *Islam abangan* as *agami Jawi*, or Javanese religion, and to *Islam putihan* as *agami Islam santri*, or Islam as observed by *santri*.[35] The name *agami Jawi* implies that Javanese elements are dominant in this form of Islam, whereas *agami Islam santri* implies a more orthodox form of Islam. Unlike the adherents of *Islam putihan* who dilligently fulfill their Moslem obligations, those of Javanese *Islam abangan* are not fully committed to the *rukun Islam*. In addition, *Islam abangan* is considered to be syncretistic and more tolerant, whereas *Islam putihan* is regarded as fanatical because of its orthodox puritanism. In the nineteenth century, adherents of *Islam abangan* were sometimes called *tiyang pasek* (Arabic: *fāsiq*, meaning godless) and "pork eaters," while *Islam putihan* were called the holy people (*hellig volk*).[36]

The majority of the Javanese Moslem laity were *Islam abangan*, i.e., outwardly Moslem and Moslem by birth.[37] They were often Moslem in name only, paying lip-service to Islam while remaining "pagan" in their hearts.[38] In the past, the two religious groups lived separately. The *putihan* lived predominantly in the coastal areas of north Central Java and in certain section of the cities, which were called *kauman* (Moslem priestly communities) and *perkampungan Arab* (Arab villages). The mosque at the center usually characterized these areas. The interior parts of Central Java were predominantly populated by *Islam abangan*, i.e., the kingdoms of Yogyakarta and Surakarta, and the residencies of Bagelen and Banyumas.

Of course, the differences between the two Islamic groups are, in reality, not absolute. There is a continuum of beliefs, and what are considered non-Islamic and "paganistic" practices can be found in both the *abangan* and the *santri* circles. Looking at the introduction of Islam to Indonesia, particularly Java, we see that it was heavily influenced by its interaction

35. Regarding *agami Jawi* and *agami Islam santri*, see Koentjaraningrat, *Javanese Culture*, pp. 316-426; *Kebudayaan Jawa*, pp. 310-427; cf. also Geertz, *Religion*.
36. Regarding *tiyang pasek* see Poensen, "Een en ander"; Harthoorn, pp. 183-212.
37. In the 1870's the population of Java was approximately twelve million, nearly all of them Moslem. Only about sixty thousand were puritan — "Islamic soldiers"; cf. Poensen, "Een en ander," p. 216. The total number of hajjis in Java and Madura were: 2,508 in 1879, 2,226 in 1880, 5,224 in 1881. See *MNZG* 27 (1883), p. 138.
38. "De Islam op Java," *De Macedoniër* 2 (1884), pp. 5-15.

with the native religion as well as by Hinduism and Buddhism. In fact, the first Arab missionaries themselves often indulged in selling *zam-zam* (holy Arab water from the sacred well of Mecca, the well of Ishmael) and various amulets for profit. These amulets were considered by some as "pagan."[39] In addition, many of the Arabic books used in the *pesantrens* were known to contain superstitions. It must be remembered that modernist-reformist Islam did not arrive in Java until as late as the early twentieth century via the direct contact of Javanese pilgrims with Arabian Moslems. The Islam that had previously arrived in Java via the trade routes had already been colored by Persian and Indian influences, especially noticeable in the form of mysticism.[40] Such Islamic mysticism fell upon fertile ground in Java since mystical elements were already prevalent in Javanese Hinduism and Buddhism (Shivaism and Mahayana Buddhism). According to Hadiwijono, this brand of Islam easily penetrated Java because the Moslem missionaries focused on the similarities between Islam and Javanese Hinduism. Therefore, Islam has not been entirely successful in changing Javanese beliefs.[41]

c. Mysticism and magic in Javanese *Islam abangan*

Javanese mysticism, which in the past was called *high ngelmu* (religious knowledge), was developed in various mystical schools called Javanese *paguron* (discipleship systems),[42] usually under the leadership of a guru or *kyai*. Emphasis was placed on the questions regarding *sangkan paraning urip* (the origin and destiny of life). The mystery of life was to be grasped through the human experience of unity with the highest reality (*kasunyatan*), known as God, the Absolute, or *Gusti* (Master), among other names. The life of the mystics was one of harsh discipline which included fasting (*puasa*), refraining from pleasure, deliberately seeking hardship (*tirakat*), asceticism (*tapa*), and meditation (*semedi*). They usually became moralists who emphasized good conduct.

J.H. Bavinck pointed out a very important distinction between mysticism and magic. According to him, the highest goal of mysticism is unity with the transcendent, whereas magic is the manipulation of supernatural

---

39. Steenbrink, p. 129.
40. Hadiwijono, p. 6; cf. Niels Mulder, *Mysticism and Everyday Life in Contemporary Java* (Singapore, 1978); *Kebatinan dan hidup sehari-hart orang Jawa* (Jakarta, 1983).
41. Hadiwijono, pp. 251, 254.
42. Regarding *ngelmu* see also chapter IV, section C2b.

powers for various reasons.[43] Magic is also concerned with *ngelmu* (knowledge) of supernatural things, but is considered "lower" than mysticism. It is thought that one can gain extraordinary powers or become invulnerable through the exercise of magic. Through magic, one supposedly can control and direct a supernatural power. According to the animistic, dynamistic elements of Javanese belief, the magical power can be present in a specific part of the human body, e.g., hair, eyes, genitals, fingernails, saliva; in animals which have an unusual appearance, e.g., white elephants, white turtles, white monkeys; or in talismans (*jimat*), e.g., daggers (*keris*), Javanese musical instruments (*gamelan*), the golden carts of Javanese sultans (*kereta kencana*), etc.[44]

We may conclude from our discussion that Javanese *Islam abangan* (*agami Jawa*) is the amalgamation of a variety of beliefs, incorporating several indigenous Javanese beliefs, the most obvious of which are those concerned with the spirit world, including ancestral spirits. Hinduism and Buddhism contributed a number of deities to Javanese *Islam abangan,* although the roles and functions of such deities are often different from those of the original ones, e.g., Dewi Sri, wife of Visnu, who in Javanese belief functions as the goddess of fertility and rice. The concept of incarnation was also incorporated from Hinduism and Buddhism. Orthodox Islam introduced belief in prophets and saints, the sacredness of their graves, and the concept of the oneness of God, God as person, and heaven.[45]

Most of these independent religious movements were based on mystical ideas. They can be distinguished as:

1) movements which focused on mysticism,
2) movements which focused on morality and ethics,
3) movements which focused on the coming of *ratu adil*,
4) movements which focused on the return to original Javanese culture, i.e., nativism,
5) movements which focused on magic and the occult.[46]

What these various movements share, however, is the rich ritual life of

43. J.H. Bavinck, *Christus en de Mystiek van het Oosten* (Kampen, 1934), pp. 56-57; see Hadiwijono, p. 2, n. 5, for the difference between *kebatinan* (mysticism) and *klenik* (magic) in contemporary times.

44. Koentjaraningrat, *Javanese Culture*, pp. 344-345; *Kebudayaan Jawa*, pp. 341-342; Regarding *djimat* see J. Kreemer, "Iets over djimat," *MNZG* 32 (1888), pp. 349-354; C. Poensen, "Djimat," *MNZG* 23 (1879), pp. 229ff.

45. Koentjaraningrat, "Javanese Religion," pp. 560-561.

46. Ibid., p. 562.

Javanese *Islam abangan*, of which the several communal meals (*slametan*) are the most important.[47]

B. Christians Missions in the Nineteenth Century

1. Christianization of the indigenous people by the "official church"

a. The mission of the Roman Catholic Church

The discovery of the "new world" outside of Europe introduced a new era of exploration and trade during the sixteenth and seventeenth centuries which had a great impact upon the Eastern world including Indonesia. The explorations of this period were initiated by Portugese and Spanish sailors out of curiosity and a desire for adventure, commerce, and trade. To this spirit was soon added the desire to bring the Gospel to the heathen. In order to understand the mission activity of the nineteenth century, therefore, we must begin with the important initial work done by the Roman Catholic Church. The Christianity that was introduced at this early stage later went hand in hand with imperialism, as we shall see.[48]

Competition among the two Catholic nations of Spain and Portugal became unavoidable and soon intensified into open hostility. Such hostility was a real hindrance to their sacred mission. Realizing this danger, the two nations appealed to Pope Alexander VI, to act as mediator. Peace talks were held in Tordesillas in 1493, and both parties finally reached agreement by dividing the newly discovered regions into two parts. The regions west of Cape Verde were given to Spain, and the rest to Portugal.[49] So, the Moluccan Islands were given to Portugal and the Philippines to Spain. By 1534, Roman Catholicism, under the auspices of Portugal, had established a foothold in the eastern parts of Indonesia, including the Moluccan, North Sulawese, and Lesser Sundanese Islands. Missionary St. Francis Xavier reached Ambon in 1546. Roman Catholicism continued as the predominate faith among the Christian minority in these areas until the arrival of the Dutch in 1605.[50]

Numerically, Roman Catholic efforts were successful. During the

---

47. For more about Javanese ceremonies and rituals, see Chapter III.

48. H.T. Fischer, *De Verhouding tusschen het Binnenlandsch Bestuur en Zending* in Nederlandsch-Indië ('s-Gravenhage, 1931), p. 4.

49. J. Mooij, *Geschiedenis der Protestantsche Kerk in Nederlandsch-Indië* (Weltevreden, 1923), p. 11. Müller Krüger, *Sejarah Gereja* p. 18.

50. Mooij, *Geschiedenis,* pp. 11-16.

sixteenth century about forty thousand people converted to Christianity, although their motives were political. As Christians they benefitted from the political protection offered by the Portugese authorities, which was an improvement over living under the threatening Moslem sultans. This led, inevitably, to a superficial faith. Therefore, later Western Catholic missionaries could not view them as Christians.

The Catholic missionaries were unable to convince the native Indonesians to chance their lifestyle, however, which remained closely tied to the ancient traditions (*adat*).[51] Inwardly their lives were still empowered by pagan traditions. Since paganism was not successfully defeated, the Gospel did not penetrate their lives. Christianity was like a coat of varnish painted over the indigenous nature worship. According to Mooij, this remained a problem of Christian missions even in his day.[52]

b. The mission of the VOC

In the beginning of the seventeenth century the Dutch appeared on the scene, posing a serious threat to Portugese hegemony in Indonesia. Their motives were similar: trade and evangelism. To strengthen their economic position, the Dutch East India Company (VOC) was established on March 20, 1602,[53] fully supported by the Dutch government. The Central Board of seventeen persons was chose from among the company members.[54] Although it was basically a trading company, it had its own armed forces and was able to declare and engage in war if necessary. The Central Board also had authority to make agreements with the "defeated" indigenous authorities, in this case, the Moslem sultans. On February 23, 1605, the Portugese bulwark in Ambon was successfully overrun, followed by Tidore on June 19 of the same year. Thus Portugese dominance came to an end and the VOC became the sole unshakable economic power in the area.

Conscious of it role as a Christian authority,[55] the VOC felt an obligation to carry out its mission according to Article XXXVI of the Belgic Confession, which stated, "... that they protect the sacred ministry, and

---

51. M.P.M. Muskens and Fr. Cornelissen, eds., *Sejarah Gereja Katolik Indonesia* I (Ende, 1974), p. 276.

52. Mooij, *Geschiedenis*, p. 8.

53. Ibid., p. 22; C.W.T. Van Boetzelaer, *De Protestantsche Kerk in Nederlandsch-Indië* ('s-Gravenhage, 1974), p. 1. Regarding the VOC, see "De Geoctroyeerde Oost-Indische Compagnie," *De Macedoniër* 8 (1890), pp. 55-167.

54. Regarding the Central Board of the VOC and their rights, see Mooij, *Geschiedenis*, p. 22.

55. As a Christian autority, the VOC opened its gathering with Bible reading and prayer. Examples of these prayers are noted in Van Boetzelaer, pp. 6-8; cf. Müller Krüger, p. 30.

thus may remove and prevent all idolatry and false worship, that the kingdom of antichrist may be thus destroyed and the kingdom of Christ promoted."[56] From this point of view, evangelization was the official task of the government. Accordingly, the slogan "*cuius regio eius religio*" (whose reign, his religion) was applied. In 1605, when the Dutch Admiral Matelieff captured Ambon, he left orders to convert the Roman Catholics to Dutch Reformed Christianity.[57]

The VOC held a monopoly in the three areas of trade (as the sole trading company), politics (as the sole authority), and religion (as the sole bearer of the Gospel). However, the Company was not without difficulties. Internally, the sincere interest of evangelizing came into conflict with political and economic interests. As a result, the sacred mission was often sacrificed for the sake of political power and commercial profit. From the point of view of missions, many agreements made with the sultans were improper. For example, one such agreement prohibited conversion from Islam to Christianity and closed the predominantly Moslem areas to Christian missions.[58]

56. Müller Krüger, p. 30. In connection with such duties, Pieter Both wrote the following instruction to "predikanten en schoolmeesters" as Governor General (Nov., 1609, Article 10):

"Bevordering van der bekeering van onchristenen en leering van derselver jonge jeugd, ten einde de naam van Christus verbreid en de dienst der Compagnie naar behoren mocht bevorderd worden." (The advancement of the conversion of non-Christians and instruction of these youth, in order that the name of Christ may be spread and the service of the Company may be advanced as is proper).

See Fischer, p. 4; A.M. Brouwer, *De Eerste Schreden* (Rotterdam, 1916), p. 25; I.H. Enklaar, *De Scheiding der Sacramenten op het Zendingsveld* (Amsterdam, 1949), p. 36.

57. Albert Hyma, *The Dutch Far East* (Ann Arbor, 1942), p. 70.

58. An example is the agreement made by Wolfert Hermanszoon on behalf of the VOC with the people of Banda, Moluccan Islands (1602):

"dat ieder zijn God zou dienen naar het geloof, dat God hem gegeven had, zonder dat de een den ander zou mogen haten of dit aanleiding zou mogen geven tot moeilijkheden, maar dat zij elkander met alle vriendschap zouden bejegenen en het overige Gode bevelen, die over 't geloof en 't gemoed rechter is en wezen zal." (... that each should serve his God, according to the belief that God has given him, without the one hating the other or this giving rise to difficulties, but rather, that they should treat each other with all friendliness and entrust the rest to God, who is and shall be the judge of belief and heart).

See Van Boetzelaer, p. 14; cf. "De Geoctroyeerde," p. 164. Müller Krüger views this "tolerant attitude" as the result of the political interest in maintaining peace and public order as well as economic gain, rather than religious tolerance in the true sense of the word; see Müller Krüger, p. 32.

As a result of such agreements, Christianity grew primarily in the regions where Islam had little or no foothold. In Java, South Sulawesi, South Kalimantan, and West Sumatra, areas regarded as solidly islamized Christian churches were established only in the large cities, i.e., Batavia (now Jakarta) (1619), Semarang (1750), Surabaya (1775), Ujung Pandang in South Sulawese (1669), and Padang in West Sumatra (1679). The membership of these churches was largely composed of the Dutch and indigenous people from the eastern part of Indonesia who worked in private and governmental offices.

As under the Portugese, mass baptisms were performed for political reasons under the VOC.[59] No religious instruction was given before baptism. The converts received incentive money as did the ministers.[60] The more people a minister baptized the greater the cash bonus received.[61] According to Van Boetzelaer, ministers received very small salaries which forced them to engage in trading, etc., for additional income. He maintained that such low incomes became the main reason behind the VOC's deterioration and eventual downfall on December 31, 1799.[62]

What were the consequences of such conditions for church life and mission? In 1705, a minister visited the Moluccan Islands and found not one regular church member from among the 3,298 baptized Indonesians. The Lord's Supper was not considered necessary and even preaching was considered meaningless for such "stupid Christians."[63] In their emotionally laden reports most ministers stated that paganism was still predominant in the life of the indigenous Christians. They called them "Christians by mouth," "rice Christians," "outwardly Christian," or "Christians without Christ like the Laodecian people."[64] It became the task of ministers to bring the life of the indigenous Christians into accordance with the Church Order of the *Indische Kerk* of 1643, which stated: "It is necessary to put the indigenous Christians under hard supervision in order to conform their life to the Dutch tradition."[65] The intention was to establish churches in Indonesia according to the pattern of the Dutch Reformed Church in the

---

59. Enklaar, *De Scheiding*, p. 37; Müller Krüger, p. 44.

60. Fischer, p. 4; cf. "De Geoctroyeerde," p. 166; Enklaar, *De Scheiding*, p. 37.

61. Stephen Neill, *A History of Christian Mission* (Middlesex, 1980), p. 224.

62. Van Boetzelaer, pp. 144-146; a saying was that VOC stood for *vallen onder corruptie* (Fall into Corruption).

63. Enklaar, *De Scheiding*, p. 40; Krüger, p. 44.

64. "De Geoctroyeerde," p. 66; cf. description of the disappointing spiritual life of indigenous Christians by Enklaar, *De Scheiding*, pp. 39-41; 62-65.

65. "het zal mede noodigh wezen, dat de Inlantse Christenen ingescherpt werden, dat haere habijte conformeeren naer de maniere van de Nederlanders," Van Boetzelaer, p. 47; Müller Krüger, p. 42.

Netherlands.[66] The result, however, was like the *Indische Kerk*, "a Western plant on Asian soil," as Mooij properly described it.[67] Nevertheless, most ministers continued to believe that the task of missions had to be accomplished. The alternative would have been to allow the people to become and/or remain Moslems, which would have meant a great loss of sympathy for the VOC among the indigenous population.[68]

However, during the period of the VOC, mission work was not entirely neglected. In its own way the VOC attempted to fulfill its mission task. It nurtured the *Indische Kerk* and functioned as her "foster mother" (*voedstervrouw*).[69] The VOC fully financed 254 ordained ministers and 800 "nurses" (*zieketroosters*).[70] By 1771, 43,748 people had been baptized in the eastern part of Indonesia. Among these, Ambon, with 27,311, and Sangir-Minahasa, with 12,396, recorded the greatest number of baptisms.[71]

c.   The mission of the *Indische Kerk*

After the Fall of the VOC, Indonesia was placed under the Dutch colonial government (*Bataafsche Republiek*, 1795). The first Governor-General from 1808 to 1811 was H.M. Daendels. His main task was to defend Indonesia from British attack. In the end he was forced to surrender power to the British Governor-General, Thomas Stamford Raffles, after the British defeated France and the Netherlands. During the period of British rule, from 1811 to 1816, the Dutch Missionary Society (*Het Nederlandsch Zendeling Genootschap*, founded in 1797, hereafter NZG) sent its first three missionaries to Java under the auspices of the London Missionary Society (hereafter LMS, founded in 1795). J.C. Supper went to Jakarta, G. Bruckner to Semarang, and J. Kam to Ambon.[72] The Indonesian Bible

66. Van Boetzelaer, p. 83; Müller Krüger, p. 38.

67. Mooij, *Geschiedenis*, p. 16; Van Boetzelaer characterized it as a "copy of the home church," Van Boetzelaer, p. 83.

68. Müller Krüger, p. 31.

69. Mooij, *Geschiedenis*, pp. 20-26.

70. Müller Krüger, p. 31; A.J. Rasker counted nine hundred *predikanten*, *De Nederlandse Hervormde Kerk vanaf 1795* (Kampen, 1981), p. 321.

71. Ibid., p. 44; cf. that already in 1727 there were 240 churches and schools, three hundred indigenous teachers, fifteen thousand regular church members, and five hundred thousand baptized members (mostly resulted from mass baptism); Rasker, p. 322.

72. Brückner (died 1856) was well-known as the first translator of the Bible into the Javanese language. Kam (died 1833) moved to Ambon where his work was very rewarding. He became the "apostle of the Moluccan Islands." On his way to Ambon he

Society, which played an important role in missions, was also established during this time (1815).

In 1816, Indonesia was again placed under Dutch rule as a part of the Kingdom of the Netherlands. King Willem I's desire to unite the existing denominations present in Indonesia (Lutheran, Remonstrant, Mennonite, and the Dutch Reformed) into one church was realized in 1835 with the formation of the *Indische Kerk*. This church was formally independent from any specific denomination and had its own confession.

In the Netherlands, the Ministry of Colonial Affairs was responsible for all matters related to church and mission. A committee was set up in the Hague on September 4, 1815, the *Haagsche Commissie*, to act as assistant to the Ministry of Colonial Affairs. It functioned as an advisory body, but had the right to select and examine missionary candidates. It also had the power to ordain missionaries and send them to the mission field.[73] In Indonesia, the Central Board of the *Indische Kerk* (*Bestuur over de Protestantsche Kerk in Nederlandsch-Indië*) was formed to be responsible for all matters regarding church and mission. The Central Board consisted of a chairman who was a member of the *Raad van Indië* (the India Council, a kind of parlaiment), a vice-chairman who was a minister in Jakarta, and three at large members who were prominant figures of member churches. In reality, the rights of the Central Board were very limited. They were able to do nothing more than give advice and make proposals to the government. Final dicision-making remained in the hands of the government, particularly the Governor-General.[74] The *Indische Kerk* was most dependent on the government in financial matters. Therefore, she remained in much the same position as the church was under the VOC.[75] Because the *Indische Kerk* was under the control of the government, she was unable to independently manage her life and work, especially in the area of missions. The major task of the ministers was reduced to taking care of the needs of their own church members.

The *Indische Kerk* in Purwareja, however, had a special relationship

stayed for a few months in Surabaya to revive the Christian community there. He worked together with an evangelist who later became known as *bapa* Johannes Emde. See I.H. Enklaar, *Joseph Kam: Apostel der Molukken* ('s-Gravenhage, 1963), pp. 28-30. Supper (died 1816) became the minister of a Malay-speaking church in Tugu and Depok (near Jakarta), and founder of a Bible society.

73. Cachet, *Een Jaar*, pp. 292-293.
74. Müller Krüger, p. 69.
75. T. Van Den End, "Dutch Protestant Mission Activity: A Survey," *Itinerario* 7 (1983), pp. 86-106; cf. Van Boetzelaer, p. 291, where he states that this church was a continuation of the VOC's mission, and p. 304, where he calls it a church without a mission.

with the indigenous Christian community in the surrounding areas. This community later became known as Sadrach's community, the major concern of this study. Purwareja, a military city, lies in the former Residency of Bagelen. During the nineteenth century, many military personnel, both Dutch and Indonesian, lived there.[76] Most of them were Christians formerly from East Indonesia who formed a small Christian community under the jurisdiction of the *Indische Kerk*. Purwareja, together with its neighboring city, Banyumas, belonged to the parish of the *Indische Kerk* in Semarang. Since they had no minister, the minister from Semarang regularly came to Purwareja and Banyumas to provide pastoral care and administer the sacraments. After 1857, Purwareja became the "preaching post" for the residencies of Bagelen and Kedu.[77] A small church building, accomodating one hundred persons, was erected in 1891. This church was primarily Western in its cultural makeup, its members being mostly Dutch. Like other *Indische Kerk* congregations, they generally paid little attention to the task of christianizing the indigenous people. This does not mean, however, that this church was not significant. Several members were actively involved in missions at their own initiative. C.P. Stevens-Philips, a lay person who was interested in missions among the indigenous people, began meeting with a small group of Javanese Christians in her home, as did the Brouwer family in Kutaarja, South Purwareja.[78] Others involved in mission work included two retired indigo workers, Schneider and Kielberg, and a retired military man, Van Holy.[79]

In the register of the *Indische Kerk* in Purwareja one can find a list of several Javanese baptisms which were recorded since 1851. The *Indische Kerk* ministers who performed these baptisms include Rev. Lammers Van Toorenburg and Rev. B. Braams (from the *Indische Kerk* in Samarang, 1851-1862), Rev. T.C.M. Hannegrat (Purwareja, 1863-1869), Rev. C.A.L. Van Troostenburg De Bruijn (Purwareja, 1869-1873, 1877-1878), Rev. Thieme (Purwareja, 1873-1877), and Rev. Petrus Heyting (Purwareja, 1879-1885). Heyting, in connection with his request to the government to appoint an associate minister for the *Indische Kerk* in Purwareja, wrote an important report on Sadrach's community in 1883 entitled, *Verslag van den toestand de verspreiding enz. der Inlandsche Christenen in de residentie Bagelen en aangrenzende gewesten* (*Report on the Origin and Spread, etc. of*

---

76. Cachet, *Een Jaar*, p. 254.
77. J. Mooij, *Atlas der Protestantische Kerk in Nederlandsch Oost Indië* (Weltevreden, 1925), p. 42.
78. L. Adriaanse, *Sadrach's Kring* (Leiden, 1899), p. 60.
79. Heyting, pp. 3-4.

Native Christians in the Residency of Bagelen and the Surrounding Areas).[80]

Through baptism, Javanese Christians became formal members of the *Indische Kerk*. However, they never became fully integrated into the church because of differences in social status, culture, and language. It was the opinion of the *Indische Kerk* that Javanese converts should be taken care of in a "special way." Two elders, J.C. Philips and A. Schneider were assigned to this task by the *Indische Kerk* in Purwareja.[81] For administrative purposes, Schneider was also appointed by the local government in 1877, as registrar for the Javanese Christians in Bagelen.[82] Despite these individual efforts, however, the mission endeavors of the *Indische Kerk* in Purwareja were severely limited due to internal ecclesiastical problems and governmental restrictions.

2. Christianization of the indigenous people by missionary organizations

The concept of separation of church and state became widely accepted in the nineteenth century, the impact of which greatly changed the life and mission of the church in the Netherlands and the Dutch Indies as well. The Dutch Reformed Church (*Nederlandsche Hervormde Kerk*, hereafter, NHK) lost its privileged status in the Netherlands. Neutrality now guided the Dutch government's policy in matters of religion. This new situation, coupled with the growing spirit of the Evangelical Revival, encouraged the establishment of various missionary organizations independent from the NHK. These organizations, initiated by individual Christians, aimed at awakening the awareness of groups of Christians for missions. They were involved in raising funds for mission work and in searching for, selecting, preparing, and sending missionaries to the mission field. They felt compelled to bring the Gospel to the entire world as Jesus commanded in Matthew 28, being convinced that God's shalom was only obtainable through the blood of Christ (see Col. 1:20). The missionary motto, *Vrede door het bloed der Kruises* (*Peace through the blood of the Cross*), became the personal motto of many Dutch missionaries. The race was on to find Christians willing to dedicate their lives to bring the Light to the "heathen."

The Dutch colonial government placed no prohibitions on the work of

---

80. Cachet, *Een Jaar*, pp. 273-274; Heyting, p. 2; J.D. Wolterbeek *Babad Zending in Tanah Jawi* (1939), p. 55. Heyting was born in Jakarta in 1842. He was a minister of the *Indische Kerk*, serving in several parts of Indonesia from 1874-1888. See C.A.L. Van Troostenburg De Bruijn, *Biographisch Woordenboek van Oost Indische Predikanten* (Nijmegen, 1893), pp. 184-185.

81. Cachet, *Een Jaar*, p. 277.

82. Heyting, p. 3.

non-Calvinistic and Catholic missionary organizations in the Dutch Indies. Our attention, however, will be limited to three Dutch Protestant missionary organizations which worked in Central Java during the nineteenth century.

a. The history, missionaries, and mission fields of *het Nederlandsch Zendeling Genootschap* (The Dutch Missionary Society)

The oldest missionary organization in the Netherlands, the NZG was founded on December 19, 1797, in Rotterdam[83] at the initiative of a Dutch missionary doctor, Johannes Theodorus Van Der Kemp (1747-1811). While Van Der Kemp was studying in London, he became acquainted with the LMS.[84] Upon his return home he, together with others who were interested in missions, founded the NZG after the pattern of the LMS. Like the LMS, the NZG was interdenominational and interconfessional, with a general Christian character.[84a] Its goal was the propagation of true Christianity based on the holy Scriptures and the Apostles' Creed. In a rather orthodox tone, this goal was formulated as "bringing Christ to people and people to Christ."[85] The NZG was independent from the NHK.[86]

The inspiration behind the formation of the NZG was similar to that of the LMS in terms of its eschatology, pneumatology, ecumenism, motivation, and concern for the enlightenment of the poor and uncivilized.[87] According to Boneschansker, the founders recognized signs of the coming

---

83. About the NZG, see further E.F. Kruijf, *Geschiedenis van het NZG en zijne zendingsposten* (Groningen, 1894); J.C. Neurdenburg, *De Christelijke Zending der Nederlander in de 17e en 18e eeuw* (Rotterdam, 1891); J.C. Neurdenburg, *Geschiedenis tegen over Kritiek* (Rotterdam, 1864); J. Craandijk, *Het Nederlandsch Zendelingsgenootschap in zijn willen en werken* (Rotterdam, 1869); J. Boneschansker, *Het Nederlandsch Zendelings Genootschap in zijn eerste periode* (Leeuwarden, 1987).

84. About Van Der Kemp, see further I.H. Enklaar, *De levensgeschiedenis van Johannes Theodorus van der Kemp Stichter van het NZG, Pioneer van de LMS onder Kaffers en Hottentotten in Zuid-Afrika 1747-1811 tot zijn aankomst aan Kaap in 1799* (Wageningen, 1972); *Life and work of Dr. J.T. van der Kemp 1747-1811, Missionary Pioneer and Protagonist of Racial Equality in South Africa*, trans. A.A. Balkema (Capetown, Rotterdam, 1988).

84a. "The Society wants to be viewed as a general Christian society that has as its only goal simply and sincerely to plant in people's hearts the true and actual Christianity as it is contained in the books of the Old and New Testaments and as it is expressed in the Apostle's Creed, without the addition of human doctrine," Graaf Van Randwijck, p. 69.

85. Craandijk, p. 9.

86. Van Boetzelaer, p. 202.

87. Boneschansker, pp. 53-59, 193.

of the Kingdom of God in the political, social, and ecclesiastical events of the time. The great moment had come for the propagation of the true Christian religion to all people (eschatology), motivated by love for Jesus and for the unconverted people of the world (motivation). New methods for bringing the Word of God were inspired by the Holy Spirit (pneumatology), and carried out by Christians of all denominations (ecumenism). Civilizing the "primitive" people overseas and bringing development and knowledge to the poor at home were major objectives (enlightment). Since Pietism played a significant role in missions at that time and the ideas of the Enlightenment were gaining much influence, the founders of the NZG were characterized by Boneschansker as "enlightened pietists" (verlichte piëtisten).[88]

Because of the openness of the NZG to all Christians regardless of their specific beliefs, serious difficulties developed. Theological thinking was increasingly influenced by the effects of the Enlightenment. What was called "liberal" on the one hand and "orthodox" on the other came into conflict in the NZG toward the second half of the nineteenth century.[88a] Friction within the NZG mounted. The liberals became more and more dominant in the organization resulting in the resignation of some of the orthodox members.[89] In an effort to resolve the internal conflict, an explanatory letter was circulated in which the original character of the NZG was emphatically restated.[90] Nevertheless, the appeal was unable to

---

88. Ibid., Proposal III.

88a. "Liberal" refers to those whose emphasis in missions was on "civilization and humanization through education," whereas "orthodox" refers refers to those whose emphasis was on "proclamation of Christ and conversion of the heathen." H. Berkhof, Sejarah Gereja [Church History], ed. I.H. Enklaar (Jakarta, 1967), p. 328; cf. Graaf Van Randwijck, p. 69, who shows how this theological dispute within the Dutch Reformed Church was echoed in the NZG. Regarding the theological dispute in the Dutch Refomed Church, see A.J. Rasker, De Nederlandse Hervormde Kerk vanaf 1795 (Kampen 1981).

89. Wolterbeek, p. 66; regarding such conflict, see I.H. Enklaar, "Groen van Prinsterer en het NZG," Aspecten van het Reveil (Kampen, 1980).

90. Craandijk, p. 14. Note 1 reads:

Wij kennen geen modern of orthodox of liberaal Genootschap. Wij weten alleen van een Genootschap, welks bestuurders en zendelingen zich ten doel stellen, uit liefde tot den Heer, de voorregten, die wij als Christenen genieten, over te brengen aan Heidenen en Mohammedanen. Wij wenschen de bestaande bepalingen te handhaven, maar achten daarbij de vrijheid zoo hoog, dat wij ze niet alleen aan onze leden laten maar dat wij ze ook voor elken bestuurder en elken zendeling eerbiedigen. Heet het thans, dat the Orthodoxen het Genootschap verlaten hebben. — wat toch slechts met eenigen het geval is, — wij zullen, indien noodig, ook andere rigtingen vrijheid laten van ons uit tegaan, zoodra zij den toeleg openbaren zich meester te maken van

prevent some members from leaving in favor of establishing their own mission organizations. The dominance of the liberals was short-lived, and already by the early twentieth century they had largely lost their influence.[91]

During the nineteenth century the NZG sent a considerable number of missionaries to different parts of the Dutch Indies. The first three missionaries were sent to Java in 1814, as was previously mentioned. In 1843, Jelle Eeltjes Jellesma (1816-1858) was sent to Seram on the Moluccan Islands, and from there moved to Surabaya. In 1848, he settled in Majawarna, which became the first significant congregation in East Java. He remained there until his death. T.A.F. Van Der Valk was sent to Surabaya in 1853. The following year, S.E. Harthoorn was sent to Malang and D.J. Ten Zeldam Ganswijk was sent to Kediri. All three missionaries represented the liberal segment (*moderne richting*) of the NZG.[92] In 1860, Poensen was placed in Kediri, and J. Kruyt in Majawarna, East Java. In the 1890's, the NZG sent the sons of J. Kruyt, namely, H.C. Kruyt to the Batak Karo people of North Sumatra in 1890, and A.C. Kruyt to the

het terrein, zoodra zij anderen willen verdringen. God sterke ons daartoe! Met Zijne bijstand twijfelen wij niet, of wij zullen ons Genootschap vrij houden van alle exclusivisme. Van eene vrije, ruime evangelieprediking, naar de behoeften der inlanders ingerigt, van deze alleen wachten wij de komst van het Godsrijk onder de volksstammen van Indische Archipel. Onze tijd geeft ruime stof tot nadenken, maakt dikwijls handelen moeilijk, maar niets is nadeeliger voor hem die daartoe geroepen is, dan bekrompenheid in het algemeen, en in dit bepaald geval in de opvatting der zending.

(We know of no modern, or orthodox, or liberal society. We only know of a society whose directors and missionaries, out of love for the Lord, have made it their goal to bring the privileges, which we as Christians enjoy, to the heathen and Moham-medans. It is our desire to maintain the existing conditions, but we esteem freedom so highly among them, that we give it not only to our members, but also respect that of every director and every missionary. Since it has been rumored that the orthodox have left the society — although this has been the case with only a few — we will, if necessary, allow yet other freedoms to originate with us, as soon as they [the orthodox] make plain their design to make themselves masters of the field, as soon as they want to push others aside — may God strengthen us thereto! We do not doubt that with His assistance we will keep our society free from all exclusivism. Through the free and abundant preaching of the gospel, directed toward the needs of the natives, and only through this, we await the coming of God's kingdom among the tribes of the Indies archipelago. Our times give much material for reflection, they often make dealings difficult, but nothing is more disadvantageous for the one who is called to missions than narrow-mindedness in general, and in this particular case, in the view of missions).

91. Graaf Van Randwijck, p. 884.
92. Wolterbeek, pp. 47-48, 60.

Toraja people of Central Sulawese two years later.

W. Hoezoo, as an example, was sent to Central Java in 1849, by the NZG. He lived in Semarang and studied the Javanese language under G. Brückner, the first NZG missionary to the area. Like the other missionaries, he did not gain many converts and was largely unsuccessful in his mission work.[93] Only ten out of the forty pupils he taught met the requirements for baptism. These ten were baptized on December 25, 1852. During the following years of Hoezoo's ministry only nine others were added to this number.[94] His standards for baptism were high. He was a "hard liner" who required converts to make a radical break with their culture. For example, circumcision was prohibited because it was considered a Moslem custom. Hoezoo was convinced that to permit circumcision in a predominantly Moslem culture like Java would be interpreted as a compromise with Islam.[95]

In the 1880's, Hoezoo had two congregations, one in Semarang with 160 members, the other in Kayuapu with seventy members.[96] Wolterbeek stated that Hoezoo's congregations lived in enmity with the surrounding Moslems,[97] probably because of their exclusiveness.

The writings of these missionary pioneers are valuable resources for deriving knowledge about the relationship between Javanese life and the mission of the NZG in the nineteenth century.[98]

b. The history, missionaries, and mission fields of the *Nederlandsche Gereformeerde Zendings Vereeniging* (The Dutch Reformed Mission Organization)

The original tolerance of the NZG to various theological positions caused a split in the 1850's with the result that three new missionary organizations emerged, which also worked in the Dutch Indies. The *Nederlandsche Zendings Vereeniging* (Dutch Missionary Organization) was founded on December 2, 1858, in Rotterdam, and chose West Java and South Sulawesi as its mission field.[99] The *Utrechtsche Zendings Vereeniging* (Utrecht

93. Guillot, *L'affaire Sadrach*, pp. 40-42; *Kiai Sadrach*, pp. 10-11; "Semarang," *De Macedoniër* 11 (1893), p. 173.

94. Wolterbeek, p. 50.

95. C.W. Nortier, *Van Zendingsarbeid tot zelfstandige Kerk in Oost Java* (Hoenderloo, 1939), p. 61; C.W. Nortier, *Tumbuh Dewasa Bertanggungjawab* [Growing Towards Responsible Maturity], T. Van Den End and P. Siahaan eds. (Jakarta, 1981), p. 68.

96, "Semarang," p. 173.

97. Wolterbeek, p. 50.

98. See the writings of Jellesma, Hoezoo, Ten Zeldam Ganswijk, Harthoorn, and Poensen listed in the bibliography.

99. Article 17 of its constitution shows that the NZV strongly opposed the liberal influence in the NZG. It reads: "De Vereeniging bestaat uit leden die erkennen dat de

Mission Organization) was established in Utrecht on April 13, 1859. It focused on the areas of Papua (now Irian) and Bali. The third organization, the NGZV, was founded on May 6, 1859, in Amsterdam. Its work was primarily carried out in Central Java.[100]

The unique character of the NGZV was clear from the beginning. A group of orthodox former members of the NZG orgnanized a committee to prepare for the establishment of a new missions organization. The committee consisted of six elected members: C. Schwartz, A. Ebing, I. Esser, N.M. Feringa, E.W. Heyblom, T.M. Looman, and J.De Neuville. They were given the special assignment of preparing a draft constitution for the new organization. The draft was then distributed in the end of May, 1859, to a wider circle. Many responded sympathetically to the draft. The proposed name of the *Nederlandsche Gereformeerde Zendings Vereeniging* was unanimously accepted. The basis and goal of missions were to conform to that name. As a Reformed organization, the Reformed Confession (*Gereformeerde Belijdenis*)[100a] was to be the solid base upon which the mission work would be carried out. An illuminating explanatory letter, it was stated that, "A Reformed mission organization can have no other foundation than the confessions of the Reformed church."[101]

The exclusive confessional character of the NGZV became more prominent in time. Membership was restricted to those who kept firmly to the "pure" Reformed faith. Such a restriction reflected the very firm attitude of the NGZV toward any form of liberal theology in regards to missions. This was re-emphasized in the aforementioned explanatory letter:

"Since we are convinced that Christianity itself is undermined through the denial of the divine authority of the Scriptures, the eternal and actual divinity of Jesus, the

Heere Jezus Christus hun volkomen Zaligmaker is, die dit in hunnen wandel toonen en verklaren niet te mogen samenwerken met degenen die zijne waarachtige en eeuwige Godheid loochenen." (The union consists of members who recognize that the Lord Jesus Christ is their perfect Savior, who demonstrate this in their lives, and who declare that they are not able to work with those who deny His true and eternal divinity). See Cachet, *Een Jaar*, p. 57; Graaf Van Randwijck, p. 72.

100. About some of the missionary organizations and their mission fields in Indonesia, see Cachet, *Een Jaar*, pp. 57-59; Wolterbeek, pp. 67-72.

100a. T. Van Den End, *Gereformeerde Zending op Sumba 1859-1972* (Alphen aan den Rijn, 1987), p. 71, n.3 explains that the reason the more general term "Reformed Confessions" was used in place of the usual mention of the Three Forms of Unity was because the NGZV was working together with the Free Scottish Reformed Church, which, of course, used the *Westminster Confession* as well.

101. Cachet, *Een Jaar*, p. 60; H. Dijkstra, "Overzicht van het Zendingsveld in Nederlandsch Oost-Indië, De Zending der Gereformeerde Kerken," *Nederlandsch Zendingstijdschrift* 8 (1896), p. 298.

atonement through satisfaction, and rebirth through the Holy Spirit, we cannot possibly work together with such as those who take this position.[102]

In other words, Reformed orthodoxy became the leading characteristic of the NGZV in its mission. Cooperation and compromise with liberalism was seen as an invitation to heresy which would ultimately result in the denial of the perfect redemptive work of Christ.

Putting this mission principle into practice was not easy for the NGZV in the early years. An immediate problem which came to the fore was the question of ordination. Who had the right to ordain and send missionaries to the mission field? The Dutch missionaries until that time were examined, ordained, and commissioned by the *Haagsche Commissie*.[103] Firmly upholding the separation of church and state, the NGZV viewed the *Haagsche Commissie* as a manifestation of governmental interference. The NGZV had no strong objection towards the right of the Commission to examine missionaries during the provisional time, but to entrust such a group with the authority to ordain was seen as biblically unfounded. The NGZV reserved ordination as the right of the church.[104] In 1880 this problem was finally solved when the local Reformed church in Renkum volunteered to act as the sending church.

The NGZV directed its full attention and activities to foreign missions. The Residency of Tegal in Central Java was chosen as its first mission field. An indigenous Christian community was already in existence through the work of two Javanese evangelists, Johanes Vrede and Laban, students of F.L. Anthing. This work was enthusiastically supported by the Resident of Tegal, A.A.M.N. Keuchenius, a close friend of Anthing. Like Anthing, he was one of the pioneers of the *Genootschap voor In en Uitwendige Zending* (Organization for Home and Foreign Mission, hereafter, GIUZ).[105] Contact with the Board of the NGZV was made through this organization.

---

102. "Daar wij overtuigd zijn, dat door de ontkenning van het Goddelijk gezag der Schrift, de eeuwige en waarachtige Godheid van Jezus, de verzoening door voldoening en wedergeboorte door den Heiligen Geest enz., het Christendom zelf ondermijnd wordt, kunnen wij onmogelijk zamen werken met de zoodanigen, die op dit standpunt staan." Cachet, *Een Jaar*, p. 60.

103. Cachet, *Een Jaar*, p. 265; about the *Haagsche Commissie*, see further Van Boetzelaer, pp. 286-288.

104. Cf. Cachet, *Een Jaar*, p. 268; Dijkstra, "Overzicht," p. 298.

105. F.L. Anthing, a lawyer and active lay evangelist in Semarang and Batavia, was one of the founders of the GIUZ (1851). This was the only missionary organization founded in Indonesia by lay evangelists for the expansion of God's kingdom in Jakarta and the surrounding areas (Article 1 of its constitution). It was conservative and orthodox in character, as is seen in Article 3 of its constitution: "Het Genootschap zal

In 1861, Aart Vermeer (1828-1891) was sent to Tegal as the first missionary of the NGZV. Vermeer began his career as an evangelist in Tiel, The Netherlands, and its surrounding areas. He was later examined and ordained by the *Haagsche Commissie* and was sent to Central Java as a missionary.[106] He worked in the Residency of Tegal until 1865, when he moved south to the city of Purbalingga in the Residency of Banyumas. While in Tegal he cared for a number of deserted Indonesian children in his home, for which he was not reimbursed by the NGZV. To generate additional income, he opened a small shop. The Board of the NGZV accused him of involving himself too much in worldly affairs and promptly fired him. He returned to the Netherlands in 1877, but soon went back to Purbalingga to continue his work independently. In 1887, he was reappointed by the NGZV and his reputation was restored as an NGZV missionary. He remained on the mission field until his death in 1891. During his work in these areas he managed to establish two small indigenous Christian communities in Tegal and Purbalingga.[107]

In 1865, when Vermeer moved to the city of Purbalingga, the NGZV sent H. Stove to Tegal as an associate missionary. He served for four years before leaving the mission field to enter government service.

The mission post in Tegal was not vacant long. In 1871, P. Bieger, an experienced teacher, came as Stove's replacement. He quickly mastered the Javanese language and received his missionary training under the leadership of Rev. H.W. Witteveen, founder and minister of the *Ermeloosche Zendingsgemeente* (Ermeloos Mission Congregation, the sending church).[108] After six years in Tegal, Bieger moved to the Residency of Bagelen to develope and nurture the indigenous Christian community there. In 1884, Bieger returned to the Netherlands and withdrew from the NGZV. He joined the NZG and worked for several years in Sabu on the

---

zich niet vereenigen met hen, die de waarachtige Godheid van onzen Heere Jezus Christus loochenen." (The Society shall not unite itself with those who deny the true divinity of our Lord Jesus Christ). See S. Coolsma, *De Zendingseeuw voor Nederlandsch Oost-Indië* (Utrecht, 1901); S. Coolsma, "E.W. King," *De Macedoniër* 3 (1885), p. 181; see also M. Lindenborn, *West Java* (Bussum, n.d.), pp. 119-122. The main concern of this organization was the christianization of indigenous people.

106. For the complete biographical data of Aart Vermeer, see Heyting, Appendix I.

107. During this twenty-five year service, Vermeer's congregation numbered about 750 people in three preaching posts, including forty to fifty children whom he nurtured. Cf. Dijkstra, "Overzicht," p. 302.

108. Several missionary graduates from the "Zendingschool" of Witteveen worked in parts of Indonesia. See further, "H.W. Witteveen," *De Macedoniër* 2 (1884), pp. 197-200; Cachet, Een Jaar, pp. 283-284.

Lesser Sundanese Islands, Madiun in East Java, and Semarang in Central Java until his retirement.[109]

H.F.W. Uhlenbusch was the fourth missionary sent by the NGZV to Central Java. He had formerly served as a missionary for the *Rheinische Missions Gesellschaft* (Rhineland Missionary Society), headquartered in Barmen, Germany. He arrived in Tegal in 1876, and worked as Bieger's assistant until Bieger moved to Bagelen. His work failed to progress, leading to frustration. Failing at both work and marriage, he became an alcoholic. In 1885, he was dismissed by the Board of the NGZV.[110]

The Residency of Tegal and the surrounding areas were once again without a missionary. The small Christian community, however, continued to be nurtured by a Javanese evangelist for almost five years. In 1890, R.J. Horstman was sent to Tegal by the NGZV. He had previously worked in the village of Kaliceret, Central Java, for six years as a missionary of the Neukirchen Missionary Society in Germany. Because of the erratic and meager salary he received from Neukirchen, however, he joined the NGZV in 1889. He was stationed in Pekalongan, a city east of Tegal.[111]

Jacob Wilhelm was sent to the city of Purworeja in the Residency of Bagelen, Central Java, in 1881. Born in 1854, he devoted his life to missions at the age of eighteen. He studied missions under Rev. J.H. Donner, the director of the *Zendingsschool* (Mission School)[112] for five years. Rather than receiving his ordination from the *Haagsche Commissie,* as was customary, Wilhelm was ordained by the Dutch Reformed congregation of Renkum which acted as the sending church.[113]

There was increasing awareness in the NGZV that educating the Javanese people was a vital means of mission. In response, the Board decided to commission a missionary with the specific task of establishing an education program. J.P. Zuidema, a former teacher, was appointed at

---

109. For biographical data of P. Bieger, see Cachet, *Een Jaar*, pp. 283-284; Dijkstra, "Overzicht," pp. 303, 305.

110. Cachet, *Een Jaar*, pp. 285-286; Dijkstra, "Overzicht," p. 303; Wolterbeek, pp. 109-110.

111. Dijkstra, "Overzicht," p. 313; Cachet, *Een Jaar*, pp. 295-296.

112. About J.H. Donner, see "In Memoriam Johannes Hendrikus Donner (18 October 1824-31 Augustus 1903)," *Het Mosterdzaad* 17 (1903), pp. 165-167; "Ds. J.H. Donner," *Heidenbode* 4 (1889), pp. 633-634; J. Van Der Linden, " Den Javanen een Javaan," *Licht stralen op den Akker der Wereld* (1947), p. 6 says that "J.H. Donner was a very influential figure upon his missionary students, and he loved much *Nederlandsch Oost Indië.*"

113. Cachet, *Een Jaar*, pp. 290, 298.

the November 8, 1886 Board meeting as a missionary teacher (*zendeling leeraar*). He was assigned to study both theology and the Javanese language before being sent to Purwareja, Central Java.[114] Together with Wilhelm, he established the Keuchenius School, named in honor of the Minister of Colonial Affairs who had a great concern for missions.[115] Zuidema's major tasks included managing and supervising the Christian schools, and training teachers, religious instructors, and indigenous helpers and evangelists. Zuidema dedicated his life to this work. Upon his retirement he returned to the Netherlands where he died on November 11, 1927.[116]

In the period from 1861 to 1894, the NGZV covered a large geographical area consisting of almost all of Central Java;[117] however, only seven missionaries had actually been sent out to work among the Javanese people. After June 1, 1894, the missions fields in Central Java became the responsibility of the *Zending van de Gereformeerde Kerken in Nederland*, the missionary organization which resulted from the union of *De Christelijke Gerformeerde Kerk* and *De Nederduitsche Gereformeerde Kerken* on June 17, 1892.[118]

c. The history, missionaries, and mission fields of the *Doopsgezinde Vereeniging tot Bevordering der Evangelieverbreiding in de Neder- landsche Overzeesche Bezittingen* (*Doopsgezinde Zendings Vereeniging*, The Dutch Mennonite Mission Society, hereafter, DZV)

The third pioneer missions organization in the Netherlands was the DZV, founded in 1847.[119] The Batak Mandailing people in South Tapanuli, Sumatra and the Residency of Jepara-Rembang in North Central Java were chosen as its area of focus in the Dutch Indies.[120] Pieter Jansz (1820-1904) was sent as its first missionary in 1851. He was a missionary

---

114. NGZV, Minutes, November 8, 1886 (Archives of the Dutch Reformed Missionary Society, Leusden).

115. About Keuchenius see "Het Aftreden van Minister Keuchenius," *De Mace- doniër* 8 (1890), pp. 169-177.

116. Cachet, *Een Jaar*, pp. 292-294; K. Van Dijk, "In Memoriam J.P. Zuidema," *De Opwekker* 75 (1932), pp. 561-569.

117. See map of the mission fields of the NGZV.

118. See "Nederlandsch Gereformeerd Zendingsvereeniging," *De Macedoniër* 11 (1893), pp. 271-274; and "Het Besluit van Generale Synode van Gereformeerde Kerken in Nederland in zake overneming van het werk der NGZV," *De Macedoniër* 11 (1893), pp. 275-276; cf. also T. Van Den End, *Gereformeerde Zending* p. 6.

119. Wolterbeek, p. 64.

120. About the work of the DZV see Theodoor Erik Jensma, *Doopsgezinde Zending in Indonesië* ('s-Gravenhage, 1968); Wolterbeek, p. 64.

teacher, and soon established a school for Javanese children in Jepara. Like other Dutch missionaries, Jansz was a "hard liner." He refused to baptize Kyai Ibrahim Tunggul Wulung, who went on to become a Javanese evangelist, because he felt that Tunggul Wulung lacked sufficient biblical knowledge and was deficient in the areas of Christian life and doctrine.[121]

Jansz's work produced few results. After three years of work he had only baptized five people. During the remainder of his stay only two were added to that number. After six years his congregation numbered only twenty individuals.[122] Frustrated by the lack of success, he turned instead to translating and writing. He completed the Javanese New Testament in 1888, followed by the Old Testament in 1893.[123] His well-known book, *Land Reclamation and Evangelism in Java* (*Landontginning en Evangelisatie op Java*) was published in 1874. In it he argued that land reclamation was the best method of evangelization. He envisioned several Christian villages and plantations emerging which would be accessible to Christians and non-Christians alike.[124]

---

121. A.G. Hoekema, "Kiai Ibrahim Tunggul Wulung (1800-1885): Apollos Jawa," *Peninjau* 7 (1980), p. 11.
122. A.G. Hoekema, "Pieter Jansz (1820-1904), First Mennonite Missionary to Java," *Mennonite Quarterly Review* 52 (Jan., 1978), p. 60.
123. Ibid., p. 73.
124. Land reclamation seems to have been a common method of evangelization during the ninteenth century. The idea behind the method was to build "Christian character" in the converts. The regulations to be met were written up as twenty-three articles, among which are the following:

— Alleen zij, die van erkend goed zedelijk gedrag zijn worden als opgezetenen van de onderneming toegelaten.
— Dengenen, die zich na hunne vestiging aan eenige grove misdaad schuldig maken, wordt het verblijf op het landgoed ontzegd.
— Het is den opgezetenen ten strengste verboden opium te smokkelen, te verhandelen, te bezitten of te gebruiken.
— Het is hun eveneens verboden sterken drank te gebruiken of te verhandelen.
— De opgezetenen verbinden zich, alle afgodische en bijgeloovige gebruiken te laten varen.
— Zij verbinden zich, zich van alle onzedelijkheid met name van overspel, te onthouden.
— Het is hun niet geoorloofd meer dan een vrouw te hebben.
— Het is hun ten strengste verboden hazardspelen te houden of er deel aan te nemen.
— Het is niet geoorloofd pand of woekerwinst te nemen of zich op eenigerlei wijze ten koste van anderen te verijken.
— Alle opgezetenen zijn gehouden, trouw de godsdienstige bijeenkomsten te bezoeken.

Like the congregation of Hoezoo in Semarang, the exclusive nature of Jansz's congregation was offensive to the people of the area. In 1859, it had only forty-two members. In 1863, a new Mennonite missionary, N.D. Schuurmans, was sent to assist Jansz in Jepara. In 1876, Jansz's son, Pieter Antonie Jansz, arrived in Jepara as the third DZV missionary. During the next twenty-five years, membership increased to 102 people. In 1881, the DZV was given a piece of land in Margareja by the government for cultivation. This land later became the center of the DZV's mission in the Residency of Jepara-Rembang. Mennonite missionaries were sent there in the late nineteenth century, but the number of converts remained very small.

3. Christianization of indigenous people by lay evangelists

The history of Christianity in Central and East Java[125] is marked by the existence of a number of small Javanese Christian communities. These communities resulted from the work of lay people and were established prior to the coming of the missionary organizations. Many Dutchmen and Euro-Indonesians retired in Central Java and dedicated the rest of their lives to Christ. Working on plantation staffs,[126] they came into contact

— (Only those who are of recognized good moral behavior are permitted as participants in the project.
— Permission to remain on the property is revoked for those who become guilty of some grave offense after their establishment.
— The participants are absolutely forbidden to smuggle, trade in, possess, or use opium.
— It is equally forbidden to use or trade in strong drink.
— The participants oblige themselves to give up all idolatrous and superstitious practices.
— They oblige themselves to refrain from all immorality, especially from adultery.
— They are not permitted to have more than one wife.
— They are absolutely forbidden to hold games of chance or to take part therein.
— It is not permitted to take property for usurious profits, or to enrich oneself in any way at the expense of others.
— All participants are required to faithfully attend all religious gatherings).

See "Jaarlijksch Overzicht van 't Zendingswerk in onze overzeesche Bezittingen," *De Macedoniër* 1 (1883), pp. 148-149.
125. About the history of Christianity in East Java, see C. Poensen, "Mattheus Aniep," *MNZG* 24 (1880), pp. 333-391; Cachet, *Een Jaar*, chapter IV: Adriaanse, *Sadrach's Kring*, pp. 5-28; C.W. Nortier, *Ngulati Toya Wening* (Bandung, 1928); Nortier, *Van Zendingsarbeid;* Nortier, *Tumbah Dewasa*.
126. These plantations produced commodity export items such as indigo, coffee, tobacco, and pepper as the realization of *Cultuurstelsel*, a policy which was introduced after the costly Javanese war led by Prince Dipanegara (1825-1830) from Yogyakarta.

with Javanese workers and farmers and became familiar with their lifestyle and customs. It was also customary for plantation owners to employ several Javanese workers for household tasks, as *jongos* (male servants) and *babus* (female servants). Motivated by missionary zeal coupled with piety, the "masters" introduced the Christian faith to their employees. By teaching them such things as self-discipline, personal hygiene, and morality, they attempted to "civilize" the Javanese people. The Javanese Christian communities which resulted became house churches (*huis-gemeente*). We will consider a few examples.

a. F.L. Anthing (1820-1883)

F.L. Anthing was a lawyer who practiced law in Samarang, Central Java. He felt a great burden for the evangelization of the Javanese people, and was convinced that the only promising approach was through native Javanese Christians. "Inlander moet worden gewonnen door den In-lander" (The native must be won by the native), he said, firmly. In Semarang he recruited several Javanese Christians to be trained as evangelists. In 1865, he was promoted to the post of Vice-Attorney General and moved to Batavia. In his home there he trained young people from East and Central Java, Sunda (West Java), Menado (North Sulawesi), and other areas for evangelism work. At least fifty people graduated as evangelists from the "Anthing Theological School." They worked in several places throughout the Dutch Indies,[127] including Central Java.[128]

After his retirement in 1870, Anthing dedicated all of his energies to mission work. According to his wife, he financed most of the mission himself,[129] although he did seek financial assistance from sympathizers in the Netherlands. In his final years he became affiliated with the *Aposto-lische Kerk* (Apostolic Church) and was appointed as an apostle in 1880. Three years later he was killed in a tram incident in Batavia. The congregations he established in the areas surrounding Batavia were known as the "Anthing Christian-Native Congregations" (*Anthingsche Christen-Inlandsche Gemeenten*). They were not affiliated with any particular denomination and grew rapidly during Anthing's lifetime.[130] Certainly

---

127. A.J. Bliek, "De Anthingsche Christen Inlandsche Gemeenten in Batavia's Ommelanden," *De Opwekker* 70 (1925), p. 282; Müller Krüger, p. 194.

128. Müller Krüger, p. 177.

129. P. Van Wijk, "Mr. F.L. Anthing en zijn werk te Batavia," *De Macedoniër* 3 (1885), pp. 28-33; cf. A.J. Bliek, "Een pionier in de Zending op west-Java herdacht," *MNZG* 67 (1923), pp. 298-308.

130. Cf. Coolsma, *De Zendingseeuw*, pp. 66-67; Bliek, "De Anthingsche Christen," pp. 278ff.; Müller Krüger, p. 194.

Anthing made an important contribution to the christianization of not only West Java and Batavia, but also Central Java through his theological training of indigenous evangelists.

b.   C.P. Stevens-Philips (1824-1876)

Christina Petronella Stevens, an Euro-Indonesian, was born on November 17, 1824. Her family was a "landlord" family in Yogyakarta. She married Johanes Carolus Philips, the head supervisor on an indigo plantation in the village of Ambal, near Purwareja. Brought up in a pious Christian family, Stevens-Philips became concerned about missions. When time permitted, she held Bible studies with her servants in the evenings. Sitting on a chair with her servants on a mat around her, she would explain the verses which the servants had recited.[131] In this way she introduced the Christian faith to the Javanese people. She also gave them religious instruction in the Apostle's Creed, the Ten Commandments, and the Lord's Prayer.

Stevens-Philips' first "pupils" were baptized in December, 1860, by Rev. Braams, a minister of the *Indische Kerk*. After her husband's retirement in 1864, the family moved to Tuksanga-Purwareja where she continued the work she had begun in Ambal. Through correpondence with Anthing, and Hoezoo and Poensen from the NZG, she attempted to find someone who would help her with the mission. Two Javanese evangelists were appointed to assist her: Abisai Reksadiwangsa from Jepara, North Central Java, and Tarub from Kediri, East Java.[132] In 1869, Sadrach also joined her in her evangelizing efforts.[133]

The house church of Stevens-Philips grew, attracting many Javanese people from the surrounding areas, including a Javanese regent and his wife.[134] In 1870, there were twenty-nine members.[135] Two years later this number rose to 183, and by 1873, membership had increased to 310 people.[136] Worship was conducted in the Javanese language and the sacraments were performed by the minister of the *Indische Kerk* in Purwareja. In 1873, Stevens-Philips became ill and was unable to work for the remaining three years of her life.

131. Adriaanse, *Sadrach's Kring*, p. 52.
132. Ibid.; Cachet, *Een Jaar*, p. 274.
133. Heyting, p. 2.
134. Ibid.
135. Adriaanse, *Sadrach's Kring*, p. 53.
136. Cachet, *Een Jaar*, p. 276.

c. J.C. Philips-Van Oostrom (1815-1877)

Johana Christina Philips was born in September, 1815, in Salatiga, the sister of Johanus Carolus Philips. She worked as a batik trader and thus employed Javanese servants and workers.[137] She taught those who showed an interest in the Christian faith. A problem soon arose because the Residency of Bayumas was without a minister to perform baptism for them. Philips-Van Oostrom contacted Hoezoo, who was unable to come to Banyumas due to the government restriction (RR. 123). The only way that he could help them was if they traveled the three hundred kilometers to Semarang. Nine individuals made the journey on foot and were baptized on October 10, 1858.[138] In the 1860's, baptisms were conducted in Purwareja by Vermeer.

When her workload increased, Philips-Van Oostrom received assistance from Johanes Vrede, a Javanese evangelist who received his training from Anthing[139] and had formerly worked with Hoezoo.[140] As in Purwareja, worship services were held in the Van Oostrom home in the Javanese language.[141] Philips-Van Oostrom died on January 11, 1877, leaving behind a vibrant Javanese Christian community.

d. E.J. De Wildt-Le Jolle (1824-1906).

E.J. De Wildt was born in the Netherlands in March, 1824. She married D.D. Le Jolle, a former cavalry captain of the East Indies Army, who was supervisor of a coffee plantation in Simo (near Salatiga). The couple moved there in 1853, and she began actively evangelizing her servants.[142] In 1855, ten were baptized by Hoezoo. The small group grew rapidly. A number of workers from the plantation and the nearby areas became interested in Christianity. Soon a full time evangelist was needed. Through correspondence with Jellesma in Majawarna, East Java, De Wildt-Le Jolle acquired the help of Petrus Sedaya, a Javanese evangelist trained by Jellesma.

In 1856, following the death of her husband, De Wildt-Le Jolle returned to the Netherlands. The fifty-member community she left behind faced serious difficulties because they no longer had the right to live on the

---

137. Coolsma, *De Zendingseeuw*, p. 151; Wolterbeek, p. 53.
138. Cachet, *Een Jaar*, p. 548; Wolterbeek, p. 54.
139. Wolterbeek, p. 89.
140. Adriaanse, *Sadrach's Kring*, p. 55.
141. Ibid., pp. 55-56; Cachet, *Een Jaar*, p. 553.
142. "Semarang," pp. 50-54.

plantation. With the assistance of Hoezoo, they were able to obtain a new village from the government. First called Nyemoh, it was later known as Wanareja. The evangelist, Sedaya, continued to work with them until the community was "adopted" by the *Ermeloosche Zendings Gemeente* under Rev. H.W. Witteveen. R. De Boer (1836-1891) was the first missionary to work there. After De Boer, the Neukirchener Mission gave assistance through a succession of missionaries. The missionaries of these two organizations eventually formed a local missionary alliance called the *Zendingsbond der Salatiga Zending*. In the Netherlands the *Vereeniging tot ondersteuning van de zendelingen der Salatiga-Zending op Java* (Society for the Support of Missionaries of the Salatiga Mission in Java) was established to raise financial aid for this missionary union, although according to this Society, missionaries were not paid with fixed salaries.[143] De Wildt-Le Jolle (then Van Vollenhoven through remarriage) was a board member of this organization.

e.   Tunggul Wulung (1800-1885)

Tunggul Wulung, a Javanese, was born in the village of Bangsa-Juwana as Ngabdullah (servant of God). He was also called Ibrahim, but his coworkers called him Tunggul Wulung.[144] In his early life he lived as a hermit and *guru ngelmu* (traditional Javanese religious teacher), practicing asceticism and meditation on the slopes of Mount Kelud in East Java. The nature of his introduction to Christianity is somewhat obscure since several differing versions exists. He did, however, have contact with various missionaries including P. Jansz, Hoezoo, Poensen, Jellesma, and Anthing. He studied under Jellesma, who baptized him in 1855.

During his stay in East Java, Tunggul Wulung visited Ngoro, Wiyung, Sidakare, and Majawarna, Christian villages which had been founded by Javanese evangelists, such as C.L. Coolen.[145] When he returned to North Central Java, he established the villages of Bondo, Banyutawa, and Tegalamba following this model. Tunggul's work was very successful. It is claimed that he once boasted, "In three days I can gain a greater number of

143. Ibid.; see Wolterbeek, pp. 218-245 for more about the Salatiga-Zending and its work in Central Java and regarding its establishment and constitution see, *Berichten van de Salatiga-Zending,* no. 1 (1891), pp. 3-6; no. 2 (1891), pp. 6-7; J.F. Bom Van Geel, *Overzicht van het ontstaan en de ontwikkeling der Salatiga-Zending* (Utrecht, 1911).

144. Tunggul Wulung was originally the name of a "general" who served as deputy to King Jayabaya of Kediri during the first half of the twelfth century. Because of the heroism of this "general" the name Tunggul Wulung might have been chosen; see Hoekema, "Kyai Ibrahim," p. 6.

145. Adriaanse, *Sadrach's Kring,* pp. 40-47.

people than Dutch missionaries do in thirty years."[146] Indeed, by the time of his death his church claimed 1,058 members, while P. Jansz claimed only 150 members after thirty-five years of work.[147] Perhaps in the face of such a contrast it is noteworthy that Tunggul Wulung employed "public debate" in evangelization (like the *guru ngelmu*) and *tembang* (Javanese poetry) and short Javanese prayers in worship.[148]

In conclusion, it is apparent that already since the second half of the nineteenth century several Christian communities existed in many places in Java. They were scattered Christian "enclaves" in the midst of the overwhelmingly Moslem environment. We can summarize them as follows.

First, the *Indische Kerk* was primarily Western in character. In Central Java, its congregations could be found in the urban areas of Semarang in the north and Purwareja in the south. Membership consisted of a small number of Europeans and Indonesians from outside of Java who worked for the government and on plantations. The focus of ministry was the pastoring of its members, with little outreach.

Second, the communities established by the various missionary organizations were exclusive in character. Placing their emphasis on pure teaching (*zuivere verkondiging*), they attempted to create confessional, denominational Christian communities. Because they implicitly demanded a radical break from the indigenous culture, their numbers remained small.

Third, the communities established by lay people and Javanese evangelists were integrative in character. Although these Javanese converts were baptized by ministers belonging to the other groups, they formed their own separate communities. Because they encouraged the Javanese to remain a part of their culture and society, these communities grew rapidly.

4. Obstacles to evangelization

In spite of the numerous missionary endeavors carried out in Central Java, by and large these efforts met with little success. The reasons for this was the fact that the nineteenth century Javanese context, as described in the preceding paragraphs presented a number of very real problems for missions.

During the nineteenth century the rural Javanese encounter with

---

146. "Jepara-Margareja," *De Macedoniër* 11 (1893), p. 89.
147. Ibid., p. 90.
148. Regarding short Javanese prayers and *tembang*, see Chapter III. section B1.

Western culture became more and more intense. In the seventeenth century Western contacts were made only through Javanese kings, and in the eighteenth century through regents, but in the nineteenth century direct contact with the village leaders and their people for purposes of labor and business became the norm.[149] This new situation brought the two cultures into a closer, more intense relationship. Not only did Western culture challenge the traditional Javanese culture, but Western Christianity threatened their religion as well.

The fact that the Javanese viewed the Dutch missionaries as part of the colonial regime obstructed the work of missions. The missionaries found themselves in an unavoidably delicate position.[150] Such negative feelings on the part of the Javanese, along with prejudice on the part of the Dutch missionaries, became serious considerations in mission work. It was not easy for the missionaries to put aside feelings of superiority in such a situation, since they came from the dominant party in a paternalistic relationship. On the other hand, it was difficult for the Javanese to overcome their feelings of inferiority. In other words, both sides found themselves "captive" to their respective positions in a colonial society. Although at times some of the missionaries attempted to distinguish themselves from their colonial-minded fellow countrymen, the Javanese were unable to avoid lumping all the Dutch together. To see the "different" Dutch, the ones who loved, took care of, and showed concern for the Javanese, was difficult. The result was a negative perception of the missionaries, and by extension, of Christianity.

Hoezoo noted that Christianity was seen as a foreign religion, the religion of the colonizing Dutch, who were seen as power hungry and extremely aggressive.[151] Jesus was nicknamed the "Dutch people's prophet" (*nabine Landa*). The Javanese leaders warned their people not to follow the missionaries (*aja melu-melu*).[152] Such warnings only served to strengthen negative perceptions of Christianity and prejudice toward the Dutch missionaries. The same attitude was prevalent among Javanese civilians (*ambtenaren*). They feared that if the missionaries were successful in christianizing them, they would also force them to become "Dutch" and discard their traditional culture.[153]

---

149. D.H. Burger, *Perubahan-prubahan Struktur dalam Masyarakat Jawa* [Structural Changes in Javanese Society] (Jakarta, 1983). p. 11.

150. Poensen, "Het Evangelisatie," pp. 410-413.

151. W. Hoezoo, "Evangelisatie op Java," *MNZG* 9 (1865), p. 34.

152. Ibid., p. 33.

153. Poensen, "De Javanen," pp. 132-133; cf. "Inlandsche Ambtenaren en Inlandsche Christenen," *De Macedoniër* 8 (1890), pp. 305-312. Such misunderstandings still

There was a growing perception among the Javanese that converting to Christianity meant buying into the colonizing structure. The Dutch were caricatured as desiring to build an empire for their own wealth and glory.[154] Such selfishness, according to Javanese Moslems, was an indication that they were *kafirs* (unbelievers) — "pork-eaters" and "uncircumcised" — who did not follow the example of obedient Abraham.[155] The fact that the Dutch drank alcohol and enjoyed dancing provided further proof of their "*kafir*-ness."[156]

The following story indicates the Javanese perception of the missionaries and Dutch people in general. As an oral tale, it was attractive to and easily understood by Javanese of all intellectual levels it quickly spread through the rural areas.

It is said that in the time when God decided to punish the world with a flood, in the days of Noah, there was a very big and tall man who was a close friend of Noah. His name was Ohnuk. The prophet Noah asked him to help take a very huge trunk, measuring 70 meters by 1.88 meters, from the nearby forest. When he asked his friend Noah why he needed such a large tree, Noah told him that the wood was to be used to build an ark for God who was going to send a great flood upon the earth. Ohnuk did not believe there was going to be a flood because it was still dry season, but he agreed to help, with one condition. Noah had to provide him with a dish of rice and an *emprit* (small bird) to eat. This Noah provided. After greedily eating the rice and meat, Ohnuk went into the forest to fetch the wood as promised. When he returned home with the intended trunk, the prophet Noah was very happy and appreciative of the good work Ohnuk had done.

God then commanded the prophet Noah to look for a wife for Ohnuk. This was an impossible task, since there was no single woman in the world to become the wife of the gigantic Ohnuk. But the prophet Noah persisted until he found a solution. He found a big white female buffalo for Ohnuk to marry. The buffalo became pregnant and delivered twins, a boy and a girl. The boy was named Onuk.

God finally delivered his promise and covered the world with a flood. The gigantic Ohnuk died, but the twins survived. After the flood they

existed until the beginning of the twentieth century; cf. H. Kraemer, "De Positie der Christen Javanen te midden hun volk," *De Opwekker* 69 (1924), pp. 313-326.

154. N.D. Schuurmans, "Nog eens, wat de Javanen zo als van ons denken," *MNZG* 32 (1888), pp. 355-358.

155. Hoezoo, "Evangelisatie," p. 34.

156. Schuurmans, "Nog eens," p. 355. Bodily contact between males and females during dancing was opposed by the Javanese *adat*. Therefore, Javanese dances like *tayuban* or *ronggengan* (erotic dances) were condemned by both the Javanese in general and the missionaries.

married and had a child. This child became, at last, the teacher of the Dutch people. Therefore, it is said that if a Javanese person converts to Christianity, the religion of the Dutch people, he becomes a follower of unbelieving Ohnuk's descendent who did not know God. He thus becomes *kafir*, an unbeliever.[157]

The "message" of the story was that the Dutch were not God-fearing people and Christianity was a false religion. The Javanese believed that those who converted to Christianity became Dutch members of a *kafir* nation.

Therefore, it was not surprising that the Dutch missionaries and Javanese Christians became the objects of insult and ridicule. Insults were supposedly circulated by the *santris*. For example, missionaries were scorned as "inspectors of the maize plantations."[158] Another insult was to call them "ei-panditas" (egg ministers) — white on the outside, but yellow on the inside — meaning that they were hypocrites like Balaam. Another satirical saying described Javanese Christians as "Landa wurung, Jawa tanggung" which means that they were neither Dutch nor Javanese.[159]

This perception, of course, brought further consequences. The gap between the Dutch missionaries and the indigenous Javanese prevented the integration of Christianity into Javanese life. In addition, an echo of the Crusades, which had for so long characterized the relationship between Christianity and Islam, still persisted in the attitude of some Dutch missionaries. The warring spirit characteristic of both sides continued. From the missionaries' point of view, Islam was a false religion. From the Moslem perspective, Christianity was corrupted by its falsified, inauthentic Gospel. While the Dutch missionaries considered themselves superior, the hajjis, *santris*, and *modins* considered themselves as *ummat Allah* (God's chosen people), and therefore superior to the uncircumcised Dutch.[160] Most of the missionaries regarded Islam as a real hindrance to their work, due to the way Moslems viewed the Christian religion. According to Islam, Mohammed was the final prophet, implying that Islam is the most perfect religion. It fulfills all previous religions, including

---

157. Poensen, "Een en ander," pp. 243-245; J. Kraemer, "Wat de Javanen zo als van ons denken," *MNZG* 32 (1888), p. 123.

158. The Javanese were familair with the Dutch who worked as inspectors on private and state owned coffee and indigo plantations, but since no maize plantations existed, this term was used to scorn the Dutch missionaries. Cf. "Oost Java: Majawarna," *De Macedoniër* 37 (1893), p. 118.

159. In Javanese thinking, Dutch meant being both white and Christian, while Javanese meant being both brown and Moslem. When a Javanese converted to Christianity, his skin remained brown, but he became a Christian like the white Dutch.

160. Hoezoo, "Evangelisatie," p. 34.

the religion of the prophet Isa (Jesus). The Gospel has been replaced by the Koran. The hajjis, *santris*, and other "fanatical" Moslems felt that they knew Christianity because it was included in the Koran.[161]

Islam, they believed, guaranteed not only eternal life, but also a good life in the present world. For proof, they pointed to the many regents (*bupati*) and other government officials who were Javanese Moslems.[162] Regarding eternal life, they believed that reciting *telekim* (prayers for the dead performed by a *modin* or other Moslem official)[163] at the time of the funeral guaranteed the journey of the dead to heaven, while the souls of the Christians and Dutch floated aimlessly after death.[164]

Wilhelm recorded that some village leaders threatened their people not to become Christian. They called Dutch Christianity *hagama tahi asu* (the religion of dog manure), or even *hagama tahi celeng* (the religion of pig manure).[165] Christianity was also often viewed as a religion which forced people to ignore the traditional heritage (*adat*). Such traditions as circumcision, *zakat-fitrah* (almsgiving), *slametan*, and *wayang* (shadow puppets), among others, had been handed down for generations and played a central role in rural communal life.[166] Conversion to Christianity meant leaving this way of life and adopting Dutch customs and lifestyle in its stead. It meant a denial of their "Javanese-ness" — a denial of their cohesiveness as a people. Therefore, Christianity was viewed as the destroyer rather than preserver of culture.

Another significant obstacle to missions was some of the Javanese "Christian" literature, which served to caricature Christianity rather than prepare the way for missions. In the nineteenth century many Javanese writings, containing more or less "Christian elements" were distributed. Most were probably written by non-Christians.[167] Written as both prose

---

161. Poensen, "Een en ander," pp. 194-195; cf. Hoezoo, "Evangelisatie," p. 34.

162. Poensen, "Een en ander," pp. 191-192.

163. *Telekim* is basically "een formulier van antwoord op de vragen die den doode omtrent zijn geloof door de grafengelen gedaan worden. Het is eene verbastering van het Arabische *telqin*. (a formula of response to the question addressed by the grave angels to the dead regarding their belief. It is a corruption of the Arabic *telqin*); Poensen, "Een en ander," p. 172, n. 1.

164. Ibid., 191.

165. Wilhelm, 1889, p. 49; 1890, pp. 124-125.

166. Poensen, "Een en ander," p. 196.

167. Van Akkeren points to "Serat Paramayoga" (written by the court writer Raden Ngabehi Ranggawarsita from the Mataram Kingdom, Central Java, in the nineteenth century) in which the coming of Christianity is inserted. According to Van Akkeren this writing shows a remarkable degree of "tolerance," a preparedness to integrate Christianity into Javanese society. He also mentions a Javanese writing that shows Christianity assimilated in such a way as to become unrecognizable. He writes,

and poetry in the Javanese language, these tales told about the prophet Isa, or Jesus. One example, noted by Poensen was the widely known "Serat Pataq" (The Letter of the Skull). It contained the story of the prophet Isa's discovery of the skull of the late king of Syam (Assyria). In a dialogue with Isa, the skull tells about his former life as a rich, powerful, and glorious king, but because he had no faith in God he had been placed in hell. For this reason "Serat Pataq" was sometimes called "Serat kabar naraka" (The Newsletter from Hell).[168]

Another Javanese story about Jesus can be found in part of the "Serat Anbiyo" (The History of Prophets), a well-known story read by Javanese people of all intellectual levels. Like other Javanese writings, it intertwined legend and myth. It included the stories of Jesus' birth, childhood, and miracles.[169] The "Archiring Zaman" (The Last Days), pictured Jesus as one of the *Mahdis* (messiahs), who, for a certain period, will come to rule with justice and wisdom.[170] "Hikajat" (History), written in the Malay language, described Jesus as an extraordinary man who had the ability to perform many wonders.[171] After performing many miracles, Jesus taught his disciples the following:

— Worship God and glorify Him as the Creator of the world and of heaven.
— Be thankful to God who always provides everthing.
— Give *sedekah* (alms or charity) to the poor *santris* in the form of food and clothing.
— Give funds for the establishment and maintenance of mosques.
— God will reward you in your present life and in the coming eternal world.

> Once Christianity had been introduced into the *desa* setting, it was laid open to the risk of being either lost or assimilated to such extent into all the social changes taking place as to become unrecognizable. And in fact there have been and are remnants of Christian influence, which, however interesting from the point of view of intercultural contact, cannot be considered as expressions of the faith of the Church.

See Van Akkeren, pp. 46-48, 150-151.

168. C. Poensen, "Een beschouwing van den inhoud van eenige voorname geschriften der Javaansche literatuur 'Serat Pataq'," *MNZG* 13 (1869), pp. 345-356; cf. also W. Hoezoo, "Nog eene legende over nabi Ngisa," *MNZG* 17 (1873), p. 266.

169. W. Hoezoo, "Het Javaansch geschrift 'Anbio' — geschiedenis van nabi Ngisa," *MNZG* 9 (1865), pp. 227-240. This story was probably written by an Islamic-oriented Javanese writer; cf. Koentjaraningrat, *Javanese Culture*, p. 333; *Kebudayaan Jawa*, p. 330.

170. W. Hoezoo, "Fragment van het Javaansch geschrift 'Achiring Zaman'," *MNZG* 13 (1869), pp. 307-312.

171. Hoezoo, "Nog eene legende," pp. 267-271.

It is clear from these teachings that although the story dealt with Jesus, its purpose was the propagation of Islam among the Javanese people.

Bieger mentioned two other stories. The first was entitled "Het bezoek der Wijzen uit het Oosten aan het kindeke Jezus" (The Visit of the Wisemen from the East to the Child Jesus), and the second, "Strijd van Hyang Jagad Nata met Kangjeng Nabi Ngisa" (The Struggle of the Great World King with His Majesty, the Prophet Jesus).[172] Unlike the previous stories, these two stories seem to draw more heavily on Javanese folklore and mythology. Jesus is pictured as God's chosen, a divine man, though His outward appearance is very much the same as an ordinary man. He was to be a great figure, even greater than the Javanese *devas* (gods). This was proven in the fight against Hyang Jagad Nata (God of the World). According to Bieger, these stories were told by Javanese parents to their children.

Although these stories might caricature Christianity and the person of Jesus, there is no indication of an attempt purposely to humiliate Jesus. Jesus is presented as a respected figure, a prophet with a unique birth, childhood, and life. He is recognized as Ngisa Rohullah (Jesus, the Spirit of God). Certainly the image of Jesus and his theological significance in these stories are, to a certain extent, different from what is portrayed in the Scriptures. Jesus is, however, recognized as a prophet who was seen primarily as a "herald of the coming" prophet, the greater Mohammed, who brought the true religion of God (*agama Allah*) to which all people would confess.

172. P. Bieger, "Javaansche Volksverhalen," *MNZG* 35 (1891), pp. 213-223.

CHAPTER II

SADRACH AND HIS COMMUNITY

In this second chapter we will begin by tracing the early history of Sadrach, a remarkable man and charismatic, indigenous leader of Javanese Christians, from before his conversion to his work as a Christian evangelist. Secondly, we will follow the development of his community from its first convert to its decline after his death.

A. Sadrach's Life from Early Youth to Independent Javanese Evangelist

1. Sadrach's early youth

The date and place of Sadrach's birth, as well as that of his parents, is unknown. Various reliable sources indicate that he was born around the year 1835, to a very poor village family, either near Jepara,[1] near Demak,[2] or in the village of Luring near Semarang.[3] All of these places are found in the coastal regions of North Central Java where Islam had its first foothold. Many devoted Moslem *santris* and hajjis lived in these areas.

Sadrach's given name was Radin, which, because of the "-in" ending, indicates in Javanese that he was of a rural background. This does not necessarily mean that his parents were so poor that they let the young Radin beg for food, as Adriaanse claimed.[3a] But Radin could have been a beggar as a student. It was a tradition for pupils of the Koran schools and *pesantrens* to "beg" as a part of the "curriculum." This was usually done on Thursday, as the Javanese word *ngemis* (begging), which is derived from *Kemis* (Thursday), shows. Begging in this sense was a way to raise funds for religious activities and charity work. It was viewed as the giving of alms, part of the Islamic obligations. This fund raising (not only

1. Adriaanse, *Sadrach's Kring*, p. 47.
2. Cachet, *Een Jaar*, p. 366; Wolterbeek, p. 94; Yotham Martareja, *Sejarah Adeging Greja Pasamuan Karangjasa* [History of the Establishment of the Christian Community in Karangjasa] (Karangjasa Documents, Karangjasa), unpublished mss.
3. Heyting, p. 2.
3a. Adriaanse, *Sadrach's Kring*, p. 47.

monetary, but also material, e.g., rice) was done house to house. Even *modins* were likely to have the right of "begging" and Moslems were persuaded to give by the saying: "Prayer brings man halfway to God, fasting to the gate of heaven, and the giving of alms opens its door."[4] Later on, Radin was adopted into a fairly wealthy Moslem family where he was raised according to the Javanese Moslem traditions. The practice of adoption into higher class families was common practice in nineteenth century Java. In Javanese it was called *nyuwita* (outright patronage), *ngenger* (patronage entailing some duties), or *magang* (apprenticeship), and was a form of apprenticeship. It was not done for economic reasons, but rather as a part of the traditional Javanese educational system.

2. Sadrach's education: Koran school and pesantren

Young Radin learned to read the Koran in a Koran school which also functioned as a "public school." He attended with other Javanese children ages six to ten. Reading the Koran, like circumcision, was mandatory and formed a part of one's Javanese identity. The school was informal and individual in teaching style. Lessons were given for an hour in the morning and usually in the evening as well, either in the home of the children's parents, in the *langgar*, or in the teacher's home.

The lessons taught in this school must not be compared with a "modern" school system with its fixed curriculum. The nature of the Koran school, as indicated by its name, was primarily religious. Emphasis was placed on memorizing and reciting the parts of the Koran which were considered necessary for ritual prayers used in religious ceremonies. Understanding the verses was not stressed at this early stage. In preparation for reading the Koran, the Arabic alphabet and basic grammar were taught. Upon completion of their study, a ceremony was conducted in which circumcision was performed on the "graduates." Girls were given lessons in the Koran in separate schools by female teachers.

The primary purpose of the Koran school was to prepare children to fulfill the minimum requirements of becoming "Javanese." The introduction of elementary Moslem teachings and Javanese obligations served to achieve that end. The basic requirements received in the Koran schools were enough, but those who were interested in further Moslem teachings could go on to study at a *pesantren* or with a Javanese *ngelmu* (knowledge) teacher.

Upon graduation from the Koran school, Radin became a Javanese

---

4. Regarding tradition of "begging" see J.F.G. Brumund, *Het Volksonderwijs onder Javanen* (Batavia, 1857), pp. 11, 22, 27; see also Poensen, "Een en ander," pp. 163, 167-168.

youth in the full sense. Rather than going directly to a *pesantren*, he first studied under a Javanese *ngelmu* teacher, Pak Kurmen, alias Sis Kanoman, in Semarang. How long he was a pupil (*murid*) of Pak Kurmen is uncertain, but in 1851, when he met Jellesma in Majawarna, East Java, he was still a *murid*.[5]

When Radin was approximately seventeen years old he went to East Java. He studied in various *pesantrens* there. In order to understand Radin's spiritual and educational development, one must also understand the *pesantren*.[6] The *pesantren* was basically a continuation of the Koran school. Its "curriculum," however, was broader and more profound. Stress was placed not only on memorizing and reciting the Koran, but also on exegesis of and commentary on the Koran and other Moslem books. Islamic obligations and teachings were also studied. The *santris* were trained to become intellectually independent.

The most significant element of the *pesantren* was not one of intellectual formation, but one of spiritual formation. Here students were equipped and prepared to enter into real society and life. The *santris* lived together in the same house complex (*pondok*) as the *kyais* and their families. Working in wet rice fields (*suwah*), taking care of cattle, cooking, and working parttime for the neighboring families were part of the training. In this way the *santris* experienced the hardships of life under a strict discipline, which forced them to develop individual initiative and creativity.

The *pesantren* was also a place where a sense of togetherness was developed — an important aspect of communal life. *Santris* came not only from the lower classes, but also from the middle and upper classes. The *kyais* treated them all equally, without discriminating between social classes. No distinction was made between rich and poor. All *santris* lived simply, and interpersonal relationships were made across class lines.

Thus one can see how Radin's personality was shaped by his Javanese Moslem education. While he was a *santri*, Radin met Jellesma, as was mentioned earlier, and may have also come into contact with some of the Javanese Christian communities in East Java. However, this first contact with Christianity did not yet lead him to conversion. Upon graduation from the *pesantren*, Radin returned to Semarang to live in a *kauman* (exclusive Moslem living area). He added the Javanese-adapted Arabic *Abas* to his name at this time, indicating that he was truly a *santri*.

---

5. Adriaanse, *Sadrach's Kring*, p. 48.

6. Regarding *langgar*/Koran school and *pesantren* of nineteenth century, see Brumund, *Het Volksonderwijs*, pp. 4-29; see Sartono, *Peasant's Revolt*, pp. 154-157; K.A. Steenbrink, *Pesantren, Madrasah, Sekolah* (Meppel, 1974), pp. 7-20.

3. Sadrach's conversion

An important event occurred after Radin Abas returned to Semarang. Once again he met his former Javanese teacher, Pak Kurmen. However, Pak Kurmen was no longer a *ngelmu* teacher. Having been defeated in public debate by Javanese evangelist Tunggul Wulung, he had become a Christian. Through Pak Kurmen, Radin Abas was introduced to Tunggul Wulung. This contact seems to have been decisive, and Radin Abas became seriously interested in the Christian faith. He was very impressed by Tunggul Wulung, and learned from him that to become a Christian did not necessarily mean leaving the Javanese *adat*. According to P. Jansz, Tunggul Wulung once affirmed his conviction that Javanese Christians should remain Javanese by stating that they must seek a Christ for themselves.[7]

During this period, Radin Abas also came into contact with Hoezoo. Adriaanse noted that when Radin Abas moved from the *kauman* to a small village outside the town, he regularly attended Hoezoo's church services, even though it was a walking distance of about five hours.[8] This was an indication of how seriously Radin Abas was interested in Christianity.

In 1866, Radin Abas decided to go to Batavia, accompanied by Tunggul Wulung, to meet Anthing. Anthing welcomed him warmly and accepted him as a helper. During his stay with Anthing, Radin Abas made the very important decision to be baptized. In preparation for baptism, he received religious instruction from Mattheus Teffer, a missionary of the NZG and close associate of Anthing.[9] On April 14, 1867, Radin Abas was baptized by Rev. Ader, the minister of the *Indische Kerk, Buitenkerk*.[10]

In keeping with the Roman Catholic and Protestant practice, Radin Abas took a Christian name, Sadrach, at his baptism. In the diary of Wilhelm of the NGZV, we read that the Javanese often combined their Javanese and Christian names. It is not known who chose the baptismal name "Sadrach" or why it was chosen,[11] but Sadrach himself consciously

7. Jansz's report of April 7, 1862 to the Board of the DZV as cited by Hoekema, "Kiai Ibrahim," p. 17.

8. Adriaanse, *Sadrach's Kring*, pp. 48-49.

9. Coolsma, *De Zendingseeuw*, pp. 838-840; Adriaanse, *Sadrach's Kring*, p. 50; Müller Krüger, p. 140; Guillot, *L'Affaire Sadrach*, p. 122; *Kiai Sadrach*, p. 61.

10. Adriaanse, *Sadrach's Kring*, p. 50; Heyting, p. 2.

11. For a possible explanation, see Guillot who interprets the name Sadrach from the perspective of his own thesis (that Sadrach's community was a social movement) by stating that, like the biblical Shadrach who struggled for recognition of his capabilities from Nebuchadnezzar, Sadrach, "while firmly keeping his Javanese identity, struggled for equal rights with the Dutch people," see Guillot, *L'Affaire Sadrach*, p. 126; *Kiai Sadrach*, p. 64

agreed to it and understood its meaning. The biblical character, Shadrach, is mentioned in Daniel 3 along with Meshach and Abednego. According to the story, these three men consistently kept their faith in the living God. They refused to worship the golden image of King Nebuchanezzar of Babylon, and were therefore cast into the fiery furnace. But the fire could not harm them because the saving power of God was with them. Even Nebuchadnezzar recognized this as the work of the Almighty, the God of these three faithful men. This was probably the reason why the name Sadrach was chosen. Radin Abas Sadrach would follow the example of the biblical Shadrach in becoming a defender of his faith at all costs.

4. Sadrach's work as a distributor of Christian literature

The *Indische Kerk* in Batavia had little desire for or intention of doing missions. Disappointed with this situation, several pious Christians, such as Anthing, Izaak Esser (Resident of Timor), Keuchenius (Resident of Tegal), and E.W. King established the GIUZ. Concerned for the spiritual welfare of the indigenous people, they focused their work on evangelization and the distribution of Christian literature. They employed a number of indigenous people who had been trained for such work, including Sadrach and Tunggul Wulung's son, Ibrahim. Tunggul Wulung himself also worked with them, though only for a few months.[12] This new job brought Sadrach into wider social contact with the Dutch lay evangelists.

Two prominent figures with whom Sadrach became more familiar with were King and Anthing. These two men are mentioned both in Sadrach's biography and in the history of the Karangjasa church written by Yotham while Sadrach was still living.[13] Like Anthing, King was a pious Christian who felt called by God to enter the ministry. An Euro-Indonesian, he was born on August 16, 1824, in Padang, West Sumatra. Before his conversion he worked in a trade office. Through his Scripture reading, he was struck by references to the cleansing power of Jesus blood.[13a]. Thus convicted, he left his work and went to Edinburgh, Scotland to study theology. Upon completion of his studies, he devoted his life to missions.[14] His Indonesian upbringing and his ability to converse in Indonesian (Malay) made King

12. Hoekem., "Kiai Ibrahim," p. 12.

13. Martareja, *Sejarah Adeging*; Yotham Martarcja, *Bab Anane Punjenengane Rasulku Jawa* (Karangjasa documents, Karangjasa), unpublished mss.

13a. Matt. 26:28; Rom. 5:9; Eph. 1-7; Heb. 9:14, 13:12; I Jn. 1:7, 9; Rev. 1:5, 5:9, 7:14.

14. King was a pioneer of church and Christian activities — founder of Rehoboth Church and Christian school in Batavia, founder and later secretary of the GIUZ; see Coolsma, "E.W. King," *West Java*, 3 (1885), pp. 177-197; Lindenborn, pp. 114-115.

akin to the indigenous culture and people. These were perhaps the factors which account for his close relationship with Sadrach. Sadrach's work for the mission society was promising and some of the local indigenous Christian communities grew extensively as a result.[15]

5. Sadrach's work with Tunggul Wulung

After a couple of years, Sadrach left Batavia for reasons unknown to return home to North Central Java. In 1868 he joined Tunggul Wulung and Pak Kurmen in developing Christian *desas* (villages) in Bondo. During that year, Sadrach made an "orientation tour" of several Christian *desas* in East Java, meeting with several Javanese evangelists who had already established such Christian colonies as a method of evangelization. During his travels, he visited and spoke with several Christian leaders, learning what he could about them and their communities, in what, in retrospect, was preparation for his next mission.

After working with Tunggul Wulung in Bondo for nearly one year, Sadrach decided to leave. Several reasons have been given for this decision. Cachet thought that a power struggle caused a conflict between Tunggul Wulung and Sadrach,[16] whereas Adriaanse blamed it on Tunggul Wulung's decision to take a second wife and Pak Kurmen's enslavement to opium, the two common spiritual diseases of that time.[17] Another reason offered by Yotham is more interesting since it gives us as a Javanese point of view.

According to Yotham's account, Sadrach left Bondo out of obedience to God's calling. It is told that one day Sadrach received a divine call (*wangsit*) to leave Bondo for a place unknown. Realizing that this was a call from God, Sadrach had no alternative but to obey. He was already settled in Bondo, having participated in the development of this Christian *desa* for nearly a year. Deep in his heart he was sad to leave, but he was not able to refuse the call. Finally, he wholeheartedly accepted God's call as the first priority in his life. Bondo, which had become a wealthy *desa* and a nice place to live, would have to be left behind. Sadrach, it is told, left Bondo with tears in his eyes, for the place where God would lead him.[18]

This story reminds us of Abraham, whom God called to leave his home to a place where God would lead him. Abraham faithfully obeyed as recorded in Genesis 12. Yotham's intention, like that of the biblical writer,

---

15. Adriaanse, *Sadrach's Kring* p. 51.
16. Cachet, *Een Jaar*, p. 364.
17. Adriaanse, *Sadrach's Kring*, p. 51.
18. Martareja, *Sejarah Adeging* and *Bab Anane*.

was to isolate the important point through this story rather than to tell the bare historical facts. He wanted to demonstrate Sadrach's obedient submission to God's calling, surpassing all human interests. Sadrach, after all, was the father of faith in the eyes of his community. Moreover, this form of story-telling was very attractive to the Javanese people and became an effective form of communication.

Although the historical motives lying behind Sadrach's departure for Purwareja were no doubt mixed, as they are in all historical decisions, there must also have been a dominant factor which ultimately became the decisive factor. Three persons have attempted to isolate that factor, giving rise to three distinct possibilities. Can one be isolated as the most plausible? It is difficult to do so because of the lack of sources. We must rely on the accounts, and inevitably, the interpretations of those who stand historically closest to these events. If we place this event in the chain of Sadrach's life, however, we may be able to at least postulate which of these interpretations seems most consistent with Sadrach's person and character.

The first interpretation attributes Sadrach's move to a quest for power. Sadrach was certainly a powerful man, and one might even say that he took steps to secure his power from the groping hands of others, but for Sadrach it was not a simple question of power. The Javanese view of power held that it was derived from God. It is highly unlikely that Sadrach would arrogate such power to himself. Unless he felt that he had personally been granted the charisma of leadership from above, he would never have dared to make such a bold start. A quest for power, in Sadrach's case must ultimately be explained in terms of his felt call.

So, too, must the second interpretation be viewed. If, indeed, Sadrach left for ethical reasons, namely, his opposition to polygamy and opium, how can these ethical impulses be explained apart from his conviction that he had been called by God? Certainly his opposition to these vices cannot be explained in terms of his Javanese background, for there they were not vices. It is only from the perspective of Sadrach's Christian identity that such an opposition makes sense. But we must go further, for even simple ethical opposition would not have been enough to cause Sadrach to depart. The Javanese sense of respect (*hormat*) would not have allowed such an affront to one's *kyais*. If Sadrach had left for ethical reasons, it would have taken more than personal opposition to empower his move. His opposition would have to be coupled with obedience to a higher authority. And here we must return once again to Yotham's attribution of Sadrach's move to the call from God.

Calls from God are hard to measure historically, but the human response to them is not. There is no doubt that Sadrach felt called. His courage in the face of stiff opposition manifests motives far deeper than personal ambition, and there is no reason to believe that the motivation was anything other than what he himself claimed it to be — a call from God. No doubt Cachet and Adriaanse may have isolated historical "facts," but have they isolated historical "truth"? We think not. In this instance, Yotham's explanation seems most plausible as the single decisive factor lying behind Sadrach's move.

Regardless of the reasons behind Sadrach's move to Purwareja, the fact remains that he thus began a new phase in his career. In Purwareja circumstances were such that, for the first time, he had the opportunity to become a fully independent Javanese evangelist comparable to the Javanese *kyaï*.

6. Sadrach's work with Stevens-Philips

There are several reasons that may account for Sadrach's involvements with Stevens-Philips. As was mentioned earlier, Stevens-Philips corresponded with Anthing, Hoezoo, and other missionaries to seek assistance in her mission work in Bagelen. It was via such correspondence that she found her helpers, and this may have included Sadrach.[19] Stevens-Philips was also well-known by Tunggul Wulung and his followers because several of her servants who came from North Central Java had studied under or followed Tunggul Wulung.[20] A third possibility may be the communication network which developed among Christian enclaves throughout Java, so that the need for indigenous helpers in mission work was met with relative ease.

Sadrach was welcomed by Stevens-Philips to work alongside her other two helpers, Abisai Reksadiwangsa and Tarub. Through the work of her helpers, Stevens-Philips' house church grew rapidly. Sadrach in particular demonstrated a great talent for evangelism. He possessed a special speaking ability which began to draw large crowds.[21] In his evangelizing, he employed the method of public debate used by Javanese gurus, who would challenge other gurus to a debate. The defeated guru submitted himself and his pupils to the winning guru to be his *murids*. Sadrach gained many converts debating Christian *ngelmu* with the Javanese gurus. Within

19. Chapter I, section B3b.
20. Adriaanse, *Sadrach's Kring*, p. 52.
21. Heyting, pp. 3-4.

a relatively short period he became a predominant evangelist, described by D. Pols as the great daring defender of "Javanese Christianity" like Tunggul Wulung, his guru.[22] Indeed, Sadrach became the Christian guru who gained *murids* be defeating other gurus in pubic debate. Further religious instruction was given to these converts by Stevens-Philips. Sadrach continued his former position as *guru ngelmu* even after he became a Christian.

Sadrach stayed with Stevens-Philips in Tuksanga, Purwareja for about a year before moving to Karangjasa, a village approximately twenty-five kilometers south of Purwareja.

B. Developing an Independent Javanese Christian Community

1. Background of the Residency of Bagelen and Karangjasa in the nineteenth century

Karangjasa was the first village where Sadrach independently established a local Javanese Christian community. Later in its development, Karangjasa became the headquarters of Sadrach's community from where the policies and strategies for mission activities were directed. It is necessary, therefore, first to say something about Karangjasa and the Residency of Bagelen.

The Residency of Bagelen lay in the center of the south coast of Central Java, between 109'21" and 110'11" east longitude and between 70' and 70'57" south latitude. It was bordered by the Residency of Pekalongan to the north, the Indian Ocean to the south, the residencies of Banyumas and Tegal in the west and northwest, and the Residency of Kedu and the Kingdom of Yogyakarta in the east.[23] In 1830, Bagelen, which had formerly belonged to the kingdoms of Surakarta and Yogyakarta, became a new residency through an agreement between the two kingdoms and the Dutch. The agreement was signed on June 22, 1830,[24] shortly after the Java War (1825-1830). In 1901, Bagelen became part of the Residency of Kedu.[25]

As a former territory of the kingdoms of Yogyakarta and Surakarta, its cultural life was largely influenced by the court, especially through the

22. D. Pol, *Midden Java ten Zuiden*, ('s-Gravenhage, 1939), p. 149.
23. At present Bagelen is no longer a residency, but a part of the Residency of Kedu, as is Karangjasa; cf. map of the NGZV's mission fields in Central Java; regarding Java in the nineteenth century, see P.J. Veth, *Java, geographisch-etnologisch, historisch* (Haarlem, 1896) and his *Aardrijkskundig-Statistisch Woordenboek van Nederlandsch-Indië* (Amsterdam, 1869).
24. "De Toestand," p. 65.
25. Ibid., p. 50.

lifestyle of the *priyayi gunung* (the local bureaucratic elite, appointed by the King to assure security and manage court affairs). These local Javanese nobility reflected the feudalistic mentality of the age. Their lifestyle was similar to that of the royal family.[26] Like a king who became the central figure for all his subjects, so the *priyayi gunung* became the central figures for the local people. Such a concentric pattern was very familiar to Javanese thinking. The King was placed at the center and was successively encircled by his *kraton* (palace), the *negara* (state), the *negari gung* (great state), and finally the *manca negari* (foreign country).[27] The relationship between the *priyayi gunung* and the local *wong cilik* was also patterned after the *kawula-gusti* relationship model. This hierarchical, feudalistic relationship gave much color to Javanese society, as well as its traditions and customs. The way to show respect to one's superiors, for example, was prescribed by tradition through such customs as kissing the foot and hand of a superior, bringing his or her umbrella, speaking in proper Javanese language, and mentioning his or her noble titles. All of these were practiced by the Bagelen people.

Bagelen measured 3,882 square kilometers with a total population of 238,767, or sixty people per square kilometer.[28] The land consisted primarily of low and high plains. The low plains included two large swamps, Rawa Mawar (165 x 6 km) in the east, and Rawa Tambakbaya (6 x 7,5 km) in the west. Along the low plains were several villages, including Karangjasa. During the dry season the plain was used to farm rice and coconuts, but during the rainy season some parts were constantly covered with water, making cultivation impossible.[29]

2. The initial steps to the vaccination affair

In order to get a clearer picture of the historical development of Sadrach's community, we will follow its development and Sadrach's role at each stage in chronological order. This period, from 1870-1933, began when Sadrach left Stevens-Philips in Tuksanga, Purwareja and moved to Karangjasa. In 1933, Sadrach's community was incorporated into the ZGKN which, in 1894, officially took over the responsibility for missions in Central Java from the NGZV.

The period from 1870-1882 will be divided into two parts, from 1870 until the death of Stevens-Philips on May 23, 1876, and from 1876 until

26. Cf. Moertono, p. 116.
27. Selosoemardjan, *Social Changes in Yogyakarta* (Ithaca, N.J., 1962), p. 24.
28. "De Toestand," p. 66.
29. Ibid., pp. 67-72.

1882 when Sadrach was detained for noncompliance with the government's regulation on vaccination.

a. Early development of the community (1870-1876)

Sadrach's decision to leave Stevens-Philips and her two Javanese evangelists was motivated by self-confidence and a spirit of independence, two
common characteristics of Javanese *kyais*. Sadrach's departure enabled
him to work more independently, no longer under the direction of Stevens-
Philips. Kyai Ibrahim who lived in the neighboring village, Sruwoh, was
the first to be converted by Sadrach's public debate method. Thereafter he
was Sadrach's faithful companion in his mission work. Sadrach's second
convert was the well-known Kyai Kasanmentaram, who was converted
after a debate which lasted for several days.[30]

   Other converts soon followed. Kyai Karyadikrama and Kyai Wiradikrama were brothers. Both were seekers after the truth as well as mystics.
A Javanese story tells of their conversion to Christianity. It was told that
after Karyadikrama married he remained in his village, while his brother,
Wiradikrama, moved to Banjur Mukadan (not far from Karangjasa).
There he married the daughter of the wealthy village leader. Wiradikjama
was later appointed as *carik* (secretary) of the village and became a
respected figure like his father-in-law. According to oral tradition among
Sadrach's community, their miraculous conversion happened this way.

   One day the first son, Karyadikrama, was meditating on the seashore of
the Indian Ocean. This ocean was very meaningful for the Javanese people,
who believed it to be the palace of the mythical princess, Nyai Rara Kidul.
While mediating, Karyadikrama suddenly heard a voice asking him to stop
meditating because that which he desired had been fulfilled. The voice
asked him to go to the north to meet *bocah angon* (a shepherd boy) who
would show him the truth. Karyadikrama went to the north as commanded. He arrived at a house, and was welcomed by Kasanmentaram, the
owner. After they had conversed for awhile, the *bocah angon* came to meet
with Karyadikrama, speaking of the Gospel (the truth). Karyadikrama felt
that this was the truth he had sought. Who was the shepherd? Sadrach,
who was called *bocah angon* by Stevens-Philips.

   The story continues with the meeting between Karyadikrama and
Wiradikrama, his younger brother, in Banjur. Karyadikrama told his
brother what had happened and what he had experienced. Wiradikrama
became convinced of the Christian *ngelmu* and together with his wife
converted to Christianity. He decided to move to Karangjasa, resigned

---

30. Adriaanse, *Sadrach's Kring*, p. 60.

from his job as *carik*, and left all his property. Giving up all his earthly possessions, he willingly dedicated his life to the newly found truth.

Naturally his father-in-law became angry with such a "foolish" decision, but Wiradikrama did not mind. Kyai Wirayuda, the father of the two brothers, was also very worried about his sons' conversion. They were the first Christian generation in Karangjasa, the founding fathers of the Christian community.[31]

All the *kyais* were taught by Sadrach himself, rather than going to Stevens-Philips for further religious instruction as had previously been done. Sadrach was now autonomous, although his relationship with Stevens-Philips continued. Sadrach considered Stevens-Philips his formal "protector," the "bridging figure" with the Dutch authorities, including the *Indische Kerk* and the Dutch missionaries. All of Sadrach's Javanese converts were baptized by the minister of the *Indische Kerk* in Purwareja as a result of Stevens-Philips' mediation.[32]

In Karangjasa and its surrounding areas, Sadrach gradually became an influential and respected guru with a "new *ngelmu*." He continued to engage other Javanese gurus in public debates and quickly gained many followers. Within a year the number of converts was close to a hundred. The need for their own church became urgent. In 1871, their first church was erected in Karangjasa. The converts could, for the first time, worship in Karangjasa instead of making the trip to Tuksanga every Sunday as they had done before.[33] According to oral tradition, as told by Yotham, the erection of the church was an astonishing event. It had been prophesied long before that a floating mosque (church) would be built without pillars in the depths of a swamp during the last days. People believed that the church erected next to Sadrach's house in Karangjasa was the fulfilment of this prophecy.[34]

Sadrach became a powerful guru, known not only for his ability in public debates, but also for his ability to control the devil and evil spirits. According to traditional Javanese beliefs, the places where these evil spirits dwelt, haunted places (*angker, sangar*) were dangerous and brought misfortune, sickness, and death.[35] Ceremonies were conducted by a *dhukun* to drive away the spirits in order to protect the people from harm. In Karangjasa, certain rice fields were regarded as *angker*. It was believed that those who dared to cultivate them would suddenly die. Therefore, they

31. Martareja, *Sejarah Adeging* and *Bab Anane*.
32. Adriaanse, *Sadrach's Kring*, p. 62.
33. Ibid., p. 63.
34. Martareja, *Sejarah Adeging* and *Bab Anane*.
35. Adriaanse, *Sadrach's Kring*, p. 68.

were called *sawah janda* (widowed rice fields).[36] Sadrach rented these fields and cultivated them without harm. As a result, people considered him invulnerable, a distinguished Javanese guru (*guru linuwih*). His converts viewed him as a gifted guru whom God had entrusted with a special ability or charisma for doing miracles and other wonders[37] which rendered evil powerless.

A short prayer asking for God's protection against *angker* was used by the followers of Coolen,[38] Tunggul Wulung,[39] Anthing,[40] and Sadrach.[41] Its content clearly indicates its rural origin. With slight variations, the basic prayer reads: "God the Father, the Son, and the Holy Spirit, neutralize the dangerous poison of plants so they become advantageous; render the spirits which haunt the soil and trees powerless. May the blessing of the Lord Jesus Christ give us prosperity. Amen."

Karangjasa soon became the gathering place for converts from different areas. There they met for worship and various other related reasons. Sadrach led the services in the Javanese language as he had done in Tuksanga. The spontaneous growth was reminiscent of the early New Testament church. The converts joyfully shared the Gospel, telling of their new experiences and faith to whomever they met. The greatest support came from the converted *kyais* who had the authority and influence to convince ordinary people to come to Christ. They became the backbone of the young Javanese Christian community.

Stevens-Philips, as leader of the Javanese community, frequently visited Karangjasa to preach and attend member gatherings. Upon request, she toured the villages with Sadrach to meet and converse with his *murids* face to face.[42] She visited Karangjasa regularly and made inspection tours with Sadrach until her illness in 1873.[43] A few months before her illness prevented her from working, they made a seventeen day inspection tour to the villages in the Residency of Banyumas (July, 1873). During this final tour, more than seven hundred people were baptized by A. Vermeer who, as before, had been invited to celebrate the Lord's Supper with the members.[44] Previously, C.A.L. Van Troostenburg De Bruijn had also

---

36. Ibid.

37. Ibid., p. 69.

38. Cf. W. Hoezoo, "Verslag over de gemeente te Majawarna," *MNZG* 7 (1863), p. 170; Nortier, *Van Zendingsarbeid*, pp. 5-16.

39. Hoekema, "Kiai Ibrahim," p. 14.

40. A.J. Bliek, "Anthing's Inlandsche Christen Gemeenten," *De Macedoniër* 29 (1925), p. 12.

41. Adriaanse, *Sadrach's Kring*, p. 70.

42. Ibid., p. 67; Wolterbeek, p. 103.

43. Cachet, *Een Jaar*, p. 279; Adriaanse, *Sadrach's Kring*, p. 66.

44. Adriaanse, *Sadrach's Kring*, p. 64.

performed several baptisms. On October 26, 1872, for example, he baptized 181 converts and on April 18, 1873, he baptized another three hundred ten.[45] According to Cachet and Adriaanse, membership increased rapidly. By the end of 1873, it had reached nearly twenty-five hundred, a fantastic result in the history of missions in Java, since these numbers had been achieved in only three years (1870-1873).[46] During that period, five churches were erected, in Karangjasa (1871), Banjur (1972),[47] Karangpucung, Kedungpring, and Karangjambu (all in 1873).[48]

This rapid increase in the number of Javanese converts produced resentment among the Dutch members of the *Indische Kerk*. They accused Van Troostenburg De Bruijn of spending too much time with the Javanese community and not enough time at his ministerial duties. This was probably the reason he was reassigned to the congregation in Semarang (April, 1873) and a few months later returned to the Netherlands on furlough.[49] His successor, Rev. Thieme, was forbidden by the church council to assist the Javanese Christian community.[50] This created many problems for the Javanese Christian community, and for Sadrach in particular, who had to look elsewhere for someone to administer the sacraments.

Another difficulty Sadrach faced during the illness of Stevens-Philips was the growing tension between himself and Vermeer. Sadrach's followers lived in many different places, including the Residency of Banyumas where Vermeer worked. Initially, Government Regulation 123, which restricted missionary movements,[51] applied only to Western missionaries and not to indigenous evangelists.[52] They were, therefore, free to go anywhere to evangelize. Vermeer accused Sadrach of territorial expansion. He sent a letter to Stevens-Philips' husband asking him to mediate the dispute. He was hesitant to get involved, however, so the conflict remained unresolved.[53] Sadrach took the initiative and sent his right-hand man,

45. Cachet, *Een Jaar*, p. 276; Adriaanse, *Sadrach's Kring*, p. 65.
46. Cachet, *Een Jaar*, p. 276; Adriaanse, *Sadrach's Kring*, p. 67.
47. Adriaanse, *Sadrach's Kring*, p. 63.
48. Ibid., p. 65.
49. Guillot, *L'Affaire Sadrach*, p. 159; *Kiai Sadrach*, p. 86.
50. Cachet, *Een Jaar*, p. 279; Adriaanse, *Sadrach's Kring*, p. 67; cf. Guillot, *L'Affaire Sadrach*, p. 159; *Kiai Sadrach*, p. 87.
51. See Chapter I, section A1.
52. This regulation was expanded to include the Javanese evangelists on April 26, 1886, by decision of the Dutch colonial government, Article 3, number 4. See Cachet, *Een Jaar*, p. 191.
53. Adriaanse, *Sadrach's Kring*, p. 72.

Markus Bangsareja, to meet Vermeer in Purbalingga in an attempt to negotiate, but without success. The resulting broken relationship had far reaching consequences for the community, since Sadrach could no longer ask Vermeer to administer the sacraments for his followers.

Sadrach and his followers were now completely isolated from the "Western church." The sacraments could no longer be celebrated since Sadrach himself felt that, as an unordained evangelist, he had no right to administer them. Consequently, for a number of years neither baptism nor the Lord's Supper were celebrated. It is, therefore, understandable that Sadrach was accused of disregarding the sacraments. Heyting reported that he prevented his followers from being baptized and that he had argued that it was unnecessary for salvation,[54] while Bieger stated that after being isolated, Sadrach had changed his mind about the necessity of the sacraments.[55]

It is difficult to believe that Sadrach completely rejected the sacraments, for he had highly appreciated them after his conversion. He himself was baptized and he also encouraged his followers to be baptized, either by ministers of the *Indische Kerk* in Purwareja or by the Dutch missionaries. More than likely Sadrach felt that although the sacraments were important, under certain circumstances, e.g., having no ordained minister, they were not absolutely necessary for salvation.

Because of the conflict between Sadrach and Vermeer, several rumors and accusations were circulated against Sadrach. Adriaanse indicated that the letter Vermeer sent to Stevens-Philips' husband asking him to act as mediator had also contained allegations against Sadrach. Thus it can be concluded that Vermeer and the people around him were one source of these rumors and accusations.[56]

As Stevens-Philips' illness progressed, the center of Javanese Christianity gradually shifted from Tuksanga to Karangjasa. Sadrach's role as the sole successor of Stevens-Philips became increasingly apparent. Although many of the Dutch missionaries viewed Sadrach as her shadow, it soon became clear that his career was built upon his own abilities. Sadrach was indeed not a helper, but a prestigious Javanese Christian *kyai*.

54. Heyting, p. 4.
55. Bieger's letter of May 21, 1882 as published in *Heidenbode* (Oct., 1882), p. 24; cf. Cachet, *Een Jaar,* p. 452.
56. Regarding accusations, see Chapter IV, section B.

b.   Sadrach's full independence as a Javanese leader and his connection with the vaccination affair (1877-1882)

By the time of Stevens-Philips' death, Sadrach's position as leader was secure and the community continued to grow. Sadrach easily overcame his "rival," Abisai Setradiwangsa,[57] to become Stevens-Philips' successor. Abisai had never achieved the same amazing results in his mission work, and therefore was not as well-known as Sadrach. According to Heyting, Abisai's knowledge of the Bible was better than Sadrach's, but he was not a talented preacher and did not draw large audiences. Sadrach's advanced achievement in evangelizing made Abisai jealous.[58] Abisai continued his work in Tuksanga, but with few results. The Javanese Christian community there did not develop. Van Troostenburg De Bruijn, who had returned to Purwareja for a second term as minister of the *Indische Kerk*, said that the membership had decreased to only ten people.[59] Although Abisai continued nurturing the congregation with the assistance of two elders, Johanes Karyadikrama and Markus Bangsareja, they produced few results.[60] Rather than working independently, Abisai kept in close contact with the Dutch missionaries and followed their mission policy.[61]

After the death of Stevens-Philips, Abisai found himself in an unfortunate situation. Cachet wrote that a year after her death both the house and the small church building were sold by her children who then moved to Salatiga. Even more devastating to the ministry, their one hundred forty copies of the Javanese New Testament were sold for the very low price of twenty-one guilders for the lot. Later they were resold for two guilders apiece.[62] The small community had nothing left. In 1878, shortly after this sad event, Bieger moved from Tegal to Purwareja and bought a house in Plaosan, a short distance outside the city. It had room enough to hold Sunday services, so the small community was prevented from dying out

---

57. Chapter I, section B3.
58. Heyting, p. 4.
59. Van Troostenburg De Bruijn, "De Zendingspost the Majawarna, *MNZG* 24 (1880), p. 12 n. 8; Adriaanse, *Sadrach's Kring*, p. 74.
60. Gereja Kristen Jawa Purwareja, "*Risalah Gereja Kristen Jawa Purwareja,*" [Treatise of the Javanese Christian Church in Purwareja] (Purwareja, 1976), p. 3.
61. In 1895, Adriaanse arrived in Purwareja as missionary of the ZGKN. He worked together with Timotius Reksadimurti (Abisai's son) who was appointed as *guru Injil* (evangelist) to "replace" his father after finishing his study at Keuchenius School; see ibid., p. 4. It shows that Abisai's son followed in his father's footsteps in becoming a paid evangelist. He also followed the missionaries' policy as had his father.
62. Cachet, *Een Jaar*, p. 286; Wolterbeek, p. 103.

completely. Due to the situation in Tuksanga, Abisai was in no position to challenge Sadrach's leadership.

Following the Javanese tradition, Sadrach changed, or rather added Surapranata to his name to indicate his new position. Surapranata literally means "he who has the courage to administer" (Javanese: *sura* = courageous/daring; *pranata/mranata* = to administer, to govern). Particularly in the past, names were a very important part of Javanese culture. The Javanese distinguish two different names: the "child name" — a name given to young children, and the "adult name" — the name adopted at the time of one's wedding, or, for the *priyayi*, when they were promoted to a higher function. The "child name" generally implies an expectation. Sometimes parents change the name of their children for various reasons. For example, if a child is always sick or suffers from a disease, etc., the parents might be advised by the *dhukun* to change the name of the child concerned. According to Javanese beliefs, the given name might be too heavy, and the child then becomes "overburdened."[63]

As a Javanese, Sadrach was committed to his own culture and traditions. As we have seen, he made additions to his name several times to mark the events he considered decisive. His "new" name, Radin Abas Sadrach Surapranata, revealed every important phase of his life, each with its own significance.

Cachet, however, misinterpreted Surapranata as "the Lord who governs," the highest name above all Javanese aristocratic titles. Such an interpretation indicates Cachet's ignorance of Javanese culture and tradition, and reveals his prejudice towards Sadrach. While it is true that *Sura* is the name of a Javanese *deva* (god), it is unreasonable, as far as Javanese culture and tradition are concerned, to conclude that Sadrach lifted himself above the Sultan and Sunan of the Yogyakarta and Surakarta kingdoms as Cachet claimed.[64] Javanese people are free to adopt any name, but no ordinary person would dare to take the name of the highest nobility for fear of being "overburdened" and "cursed" (*kuwalat*). The

63. Regarding Javanese names, see C. Poensen, "Iets over Javaansche Naamgeving en Eigennaamen," *MNZG* 14 (1870), pp. 123-216; Koentjaraningrat, *Javanese Culture*, pp. 236-237; *Kebudayaan Jawa*, pp. 238-239.

64. Cachet, *Een Jaar*, p. 336, n.: "Een der titels van Susuhunan van Surakarta, en van de Sultan Yogyakarta is *Panatagama*, Regelaar van den Godsdienst. Sadrach is aangenomen titel *Godheid die regelt*, verheft hem in eigen schatting, in het oog zijner volgelingen, dus boven de hoogste waardigheid onder de Javanen." (One of the titles of the Susuhunan of Surakarta, and of the Sultan of Yogyakarta is *Panatagama*, sustainer of religion. Sadrach has taken on the title "divinity who rules," which thus raises him in his own estimation, and in the eyes of his followers, above the highest rank among the Javanese).

proper interpretation is to understand the word *sura* as brave, daring, or courageous, as noted above. As such, *sura* is often used as a name for ordinary people. Adriaanse was quite right when he said that Sadrach was thus authorized and fully independent to govern and to administer all matters for the community.[65]

A name is believed to bring fortune as well as misfortune to its bearer. One's "adult name" in particular can be a legitimation of a new function and at the same time imply the expectation that the bearer carry out that new responsibility courageously. The name Surapranata should properly be interpreted in this manner, which is in keeping with the Javanese traditional values observed by Sadrach.[66] Hence, the name change was coupled with a conviction that Sadrach would be capable of performing his new function independently, risking all for the good of the community, which then numbered about three thousand individuals.[67] The name also indicated that he now had the right to do his new task, a task requiring bravery and courage.

As we have mentioned, spontaneity was a prevailing characteristic of the expansion of the community. The most effective means of communication in the rural areas during the nineteenth century was orally, through personal contact (*gethok-tular*). Before modern transportation and communication were developed, most inland areas of Java were isolated from the outside world. The only means of communication was through the people themselves. A primitive communication network was established via personal contact, so that even the remote areas were reached. Javanese *guru ngelmu* became well-known throughout Java by utilizing such communication in a system of *pagurons* (method by which *murids* were discipled). After a period of studying *ngelmu*, the *murids* returned to their own areas and became living witnesses of *ngelmu* and their guru.

A good illustration of this method is the mountainous village of Purba in the Residency of Pekalongan. Through the witness of Sadrach's *murids*, a small Christian community emerged. Although most of the inhabitants had never met Sadrach personally, they all recognized him as their guru.[68] This incredible phenomenon happened through the witness of two brothers, Sarta and Sarjan. These brothers were members of the Christian community in the neighboring village of Ciluluk, and regularly went to Purba to peddle their wares. In their contact with the people of Purba, they expressed their Christian faith without hesitation. They bore witness to

65. Adriaanse, *Sadrach's Kring*, p. 75.
66. Ibid., p. 76.
67. Ibid., p. 77.
68. Cachet, *Een Jaar*, p. 465.

Christ with modesty and honesty, which fascinated several of the people they met in Purba. Those who decided to join the Christian community first went to Ciluluk to receive Christian instruction from an elder there. Bieger came to baptize them, and a small group of Christians thus came into being. The group increased, and by 1891, when Cachet conducted his inspection tour in the area, the group had ninety members and five elders who represented the community at the annual meeting held in Karang-jasa.[69] It was by such means that Sadrach's community expanded. Within five years after Stevens-Philips' death, local Christian communities could be found in a number of villages in Central Java.

The rapid expansion of the community independent from Dutch control aroused the suspicion of the local government. Sadrach was, in fact, a very powerful figure and was thus regarded as a political threat to peace and public order in the region. It was the task of the government officials to keep an eye on indigenous mass movements which might become too political. Sadrach's community qualified as such in their opinion.[70] W. Ligtvoet, the Resident of Bagelen at the time, sought a way in which to place the community under the control of the Dutch officials, and, if possible, to exile Sadrach.[71] As the Resident responsible for the region, however, Ligtvoet was restricted to the use of law enforcement policies. Even though the government was restricted by law to remain neutral in all religious matters, he directly interfered without hesitation since he was of the opinion that if Sadrach could be replaced by a Dutch minister, the community would be more controllable. At the prompting of Bieger, the Board of the NGZV also decided that the community should be under missionary control. Bieger, who by that time had moved from Tegal to Bagelen, was considered by the NGZV to be the right man to be in charge of the "great mission." Several times Bieger met with Sadrach, attempting to persuade Sadrach to entrust the community to him. Each attempt, however, ended in failure. Bieger was very ambitious and had been attempting to take the leadership of the community away from Sadrach ever since his arrival in Bagelen.[72] When his attempts failed, he became impatient and accused Sadrach of disloyalty to the government.[73] Such charges were intended to give the government a legitimate reason to detain Sadrach and restrict his activities.

69. Ibid., p. 351.
70. Cf. Chapter I, section A1.
71. W. Ligtvoet to the Governor General, March 27, 1882 (National Archives Office, Jakarta).
72. Wilhelm, 1882, p. 14.
73. Adriaanse, *Sadrach's Kring*, p. 85; Van Der Linden, *De Javanen een Javaan*, p. 18.

In the meantime, Heyting (1878) had replaced Van Troostenburg De Bruijn as minister of the *Indische Kerk* in Purwareja. Since the names of the Javanese Christians who had been baptized in his church were listed in the register books, Heyting regarded them as official members of his church.[74] He, therefore, considered the possibility of incorporating the community into his church. Bieger argued that the community was the result of the diligent work of Stevens-Philips and her helpers and had developed outside the auspices of the *Indische Kerk*, and therefore, they should be under missionary (i.e., his) tutelage. A "competition" arose between Heyting and Bieger, each representing differing interests. Heyting represented the interests of the *Indische Kerk*, and indirectly those of the government, while Bieger represented his own high ambition of quickly and easily gaining a large number of "converts." The conflict was finally solved through compromise. Bieger accepted Heyting's offer to become an associate minister of the *Indische Kerk* in Purwareja. Together they agreed upon a plan to have Sadrach dismissed. Bieger would temporarily replace Sadrach as acting leader of the Javanese community until he (Bieger) was appointed as associate minister, at which time he would take the entire community with him into the *Indische Kerk*.

The plan, however, needed a legal basis and assistance from the government in order to succeed. These two respected ministers conspired to achieve their final goal; i.e., to purge an independent Javanese *kyai* who supposedly threatened the political stability of the region.

The solution came about quite by accident. At that time a smallpox epidemic broke out, and consequently, the government required all people to be vaccinated. According to Ligtvoet, Sadrach refused vaccination for religious reasons based on I Timothy 5:6-7 and II Corinthians 6:3.[75] The texts read:

I Tim. 5:6-7 "Ananging randa kang angalap sukane iku wus mati mumpung kauripan. Lha sira sakehing prakara iku, malah ajana **cacad** ing wong iku kabeh" (Javanese, 1829).
"Where as she who is self indulgent is dead, even while she lives. Command this, so that they may be **without reproach**" (RSV).

II Cor. 6:3 "Ingsun ora anyerikaken kalawan sawijining prakara supaya panyuwitaningsun aja **dicela**" (Javanese, 1829).
"We put no obstacle in anyone's way, so that **no fault** may be found with our ministry" (RSV).

---

74. Wilhelm, 1882, p. 9; Heyting, p. 8.
75. Ligtvoet, March 27, 1882; Heyting, p. 8.

The Javanese words *cacad* and *cela* can be interpreted to mean "physical scar." Since a vaccination usually leaves a scar on the body, Sadrach, according to Adriaanse, probably misunderstood these verses and used it to reject the vaccination.[76] This might have influenced some members of the community to refuse vaccination. Bieger himself objected to vaccination for religious reasons.[77] He believed that one should not avoid disaster from God and this might have influenced the people as well.

The accusations brought against Sadrach regarding vaccination were apparently an attempt to dismiss Sadrach from his position in the community. In his report to the Governor General, Ligtvoet acknowledged that he had detained Sadrach because his influence on the community was very strong and because he, Ligtvoet, wanted to limit that influence in the public's interest.[78] From this report it is clear that the Resident did not hesitate to interfere in church affairs, and all this in a country which had a policy of religious neutrality! Although Sadrach was not openly involved politically, his leadership and activities were viewed by the local colonial authorities as a political threat.

At the great gathering of elders in Karangjasa, held on March 15, 1882, Ligtvoet himself announced that Sadrach had been arrested. On the same occasion he appointed Bieger as the new leader of the Javanese Christians.[79] Sadrach was placed in prison where he remained for three weeks, after which he remained under "house arrest" at the home of Bieger for nearly three months. Since there was not enough evidence to warrant a trial, however, he was set free by decision of the Governor General on July 1, 1882.[80] Resident Ligtvoet retired early for reasons of "personal health" and Bieger returned to the Netherlands a short time later. He eventually left the NGZV to become a missionary for the NZG.[81] The drama was finally over and Sadrach and his followers could resume their work unhindered.

3. Enjoying cooperation with J. Wilhelm of the NGZV (1883-1892)

After his released Sadrach returned to Karangjasa. His prestige and

76. Adriaanse, *Sadrach's Kring* p. 102.
77. Bieger, Report to the Governor General, July 19, 1880 (National Archives Office, Jakarta); cf. W. Ligtvoet, Report to the Governor General, July 22, 1880 (National Archives Office, Jakarta).
78. Ligtvoet, Report, March 27, 1882.
79. Heyting, p. 9; Adriaanse, *Sadrach's Kring*, p. 177.
80. First secretary of the government to the new Resident of Bagelen, July 1, 1882 (National Archives Office, Jakarta); Wilhelm, 1882, p. 15; Heyting, pp. 2-3.
81. Heyting, p. 14; Adriaanse, *Sadrach's Kring*, pp. 113-115.

authority were unshaken. His leadership was unquestioned and he had even become more powerful in the eyes of the people. The vaccination affair turned out to be a blessing in disguise because, while he was detained in Bieger's house in Purwareja, he developed a friendship with J. Wilhelm. The friendship grew strong, and when Sadrach returned to Karangjasa the two men visited each other regularly.[82] Although from different backgrounds, the two men shared a kindred spirit, laying a solid foundation for the future of the community.

Wilhelm was the only Dutch missionary who was concerned about Sadrach's "misfortune." He alone attempted to understand the tragic affair from Sadrach's side. Deeply impressed by Sadrach, his diary entry of December 31, 1882 concludes with the statement that Sadrach was not guilty. He viewed the whole affair as a great mistake. He wrote: "My view is that Sadrach and the community are not wrong. The Lord has given him victory. The mistake is on the side of Ligtvoet, Bieger, and Heyting."[83]

On March 22, 1883, Sadrach came to Purwareja to ask Wilhelm to become the minister of the community. Wilhelm responded positively, without giving detailed reasons, convinced that his acceptance would be the way to develop the community. In the plenary meeting of elders held in Karangjasa on April 10, 1883, Sadrach informed them of the willingness of Wilhelm to work with the community.[84] Wilhelm was then unanimously accepted as their minister. A letter of appointment was written, signed by Sadrach on behalf of the twenty-six elders, representing twenty-two *mesjid* (mosque = local communities) with a total membership of 3,039.[85] On April 17, 1883, the elders again gathered. Wilhelm was also in attendance in his new role as minister. The group officially chose the name *Golongane Wong Kristen Kang Mardika* (The Group of Free Christians) for the community, and recognized Wilhelm as their only minister.[86]

The inclusion of the word *mardika* (free, independent) indicated that the independence of the community, which since the very beginning had been a prevailing characteristic, was to be maintained. All interference from the outside was to be rejected, whether from the government or from the *Indische Kerk* in Purwareja. Positively, the word *mardika* implied that the community had the right to express its faith freely, and to manage and organize itself in a way that was relevant to the context in which it

82. Adriaanse, *Sadrach's Kring*, p. 121.
83. Wilhelm, 1882, p. 17.
84. Wilhelm, 1883, p. 23.
85. Ibid., p. 27. On behalf of all the elders, Sadrach wrote a letter of call (*beroepingsbrief*) in old Indonesian (Malay). See Appendix II.
86. Wilhelm, 1883, p. 28; Adriaanse, *Sadrach's Kring*, p. 131.

Seated: Jacob Wilhelm, Sadrach Surapranata
Standing: Timotius Sitimurti, Musa Wirawijaya

operated. In short, the community possessed a freedom of which it could not be robbed — a freedom which was to be recognized by all.

It is likely that the word *mardika* was suggested by Wilhelm, who was familiar with the idea of freedom in the West. The principle of neutrality towards religion that had been adopted by the Dutch government left room for individual rights including freedom of religion. Such rights as determining one's own faith, expressing that faith in worship, teaching, and practices, and associating with others for religious purposes needed to be realized in Central Java, as they were in the Netherlands. The rights practiced by the Dutch had to be given also to the Javanese Christians. As a missionary, Wilhelm viewed such rights as mission principles parallel to the demands of human conscience. He was a very distinctive missionary who highly valued freedom and desired to echo it in his mission work in Central Java.

Sadrach certainly welcomed the principles Wilhelm supposedly suggested. As a *kyai* who lived and worked independently, however, these ideas were not something brand new to Sadrach. Like other Javanese gurus, Sadrach was very conscious of his Javanese background, and appreciated his own Javanese culture. For him, conversion to Christianity included the freedom to maintain Javanese culture and traditions, as he always reminded Javanese converts.[87]

A young, idealistic, and optimistic missionary, Wilhelm worked in cooperation with Sadrach using his own understanding of mission principles. He regarded Sadrach as a working partner in the full sense.[88] They worked not as supervisor and helper but as full equals.[89] This was a revolutionary attitude which had never before been practiced. The Dutch missionaries had a record of viewing themselves as superior to the "natives."[90] While the other Dutch missionaries regarded Sadrach as no more than a false prophet, Wilhelm viewed him as a colleague. He preferred to participate in the development of the community from "inside" rather than remaining aloof as an outsider. He attempted to bring the Dutch and Javanese worlds closer together. Like his Dutch colleagues, Wilhelm was critical of the Javanese people, but his criticism was always coupled with deepest concern and solidarity. Consistent with his principles, Wilhelm firmly stood to defend the right of the independence of the community.[91] Thus, Wilhelm distinguished himself from the others.

87. Adriaanse, *Sadrach's Kring*, p. 153.
88. Ibid., p. 127.
89. Ibid., p. 124.
90. Ibid., p. 125.
91. Wilhelm, 1883, p. 27; Adriaanse, *Sadrach's Kring*, p. 123.

Wilhelm's stance is reflected in his letter of April 17, 1883, which was sent to Governor-General F. Jacob (1881-1884). Its contents included the following:

— That the Javanese Christians, numbering three thousand, consisting of twenty-three rural local communities, never asked for incorporation into the *Indische Kerk* in Purwareja under the leadership of an associate minister.

— That the Javanese Christians rejected any form of religious suppression and would live, in addition to its right of religious freedom, in conformity with biblical truth.

— That the Javanese Christians wanted to remain as they were, an independent Javanese Christian community with the right to have its own guru.

— That the Javanese Christians freely elected their own guru in the person of J. Wilhelm, a missionary of the NGZV.

— That the Javanese Christians and their guru would not do anything that might cause public unrest or the like and, on the contrary, would maintain themselves as good citizens, loyal to the government of *Nederlandsch Indië*.[92]

Based on the above items, Wilhelm requested the government to reject any proposal that might be submitted by the *Indische Kerk* to incorporate the Javanese Christian community. In addition, he urged the government to recognize their rights and freedom.

These items were stressed again by Wilhelm in his letter of May 11, 1883, addressed to Rev. Heyting, who continually made attempts to incorporate the community.[93] Wilhelm sharply warned Heyting to discontinue with his insignificant attempts because the Javanese Christians had freely chosen their own guru, J. Wilhelm. He had whole-heartedly accepted the call, a fact that was demonstrated throughout his entire life.

The election of Wilhelm, of course, disappointed several people. Heyting lost the opportunity to incorporate the community. He never understood why Wilhelm, who was so young and inexperienced, had been elected. Heyting personally expected Bieger or Vermeer, both older and more experienced in Central Java, to be appointed. Heyting underestimated Wilhelm. He doubted Wilhelm's ability to convert Sadrach from his "false" ways.[94] He even speculated that Sadrach would influence

92. J. Wilhelm to the Governor General April 17, 1883, (National Archives Office, Jakarta); cf. Wilhelm, 1883, pp. 28-29.

93. Heyting, Appendix G; Cf. Wilhelm, 1883, pp. 31-32.

94. Heyting, p. 18.

Wilhelm and put him under his control.[95] Heyting was of the opinion that the election of Wilhelm was merely a strategy on Sadrach's part to achieve his ambition of keeping his position as long as possible.

Disregarding the speculations of his Dutch colleagues, Wilhelm continued to remain firm in his conviction. With great optimism he worked together with Sadrach. Both advocated freedom and independence in their own way. Sadrach, as *kyai*, taught in *pesantren* style, while Wilhelm, as missionary, taught in Western style. Both, however, highly valued independence as the right of every person.

The period of partnership was a rewarding one. As a Javanese familiar with Javanese culture and traditions, and as a former highly respected guru, Sadrach restricted his activities to evangelism for the expansion of the community. Together with other Javanese evangelists, he went to various villages, engaging in public debates with the influential *guru ngelmu*.[96] The results were remarkable, perhaps reaching the highest number of converts in the history of the mission to the Moslem world.[97] Wilhelm, on the other hand, concentrated on internal consolidation, reorganization, teaching, preaching, pastoring, and administering the sacraments.[98] He also translated the *Kort Begrip der Christelijke Religie voor hen die zich tot het Avondmaal willen begeren* [Short summary of the Christian Religion for those who wish to participate in the Lord's Supper], the *Nederlandsche Geloofsbelijdenis* [Belgic Confession], the *Heidelberg Catechismus* and the *De Kerkorde der Gereformeerde Kerken* into Javanese.[99] The translations were intended to be used as a church handbook to educate community members in the standards of the "true" church as Wilhelm perceived it — according to Reformed principles. He believed that by increasing their biblical knowledge, the life of the community and its members would be qualitatively improved. Hence, the main task of Wilhelm was improving the life of the community, i.e., shaping its Christian life.

The combination of the two talented and skilled leaders was a promising development in the life of the community. It is a great pity that this harmonious cooperation was brought to an end by the misguided recommendation of an outsider, unfamiliar with the situation, as we shall soon see.

95. Wilhelm, 1883, p. 25.
96. About public debate as a method of evangelization, see Adriaanse, *Sadrach's Kring*, pp. 211-212.
97. See statistical data in Chapter III, Section A3.
98. Adriaanse, *Sadrach's Kring*, p. 163.
99. See Wilhelm, 1887, p. 345 for his letter of May 23, 1887 sent to the Board of the NGZV.

4.   The relationship with the NGZV broken (1893)

As a missionary of the NGZV, Wilhelm regularly sent reports of his work in Central Java to the Board of the NGZV. The reports were intended to provide information to the missionary societies in order to draw attention to and support for the mission work. Wilhelm's work had been received with great enthusiasm by the missionary circle in the Netherlands. As a result, three additional missionaries were sent to Central Java for the "great harvest." Vermeer was reappointed as missionary in 1887, J.P. Zuidema was sent in 1888, and R.J. Horstman in 1889.[100]

During this period rumors about Sadrach and his "false" teachings once again began to circulate, fueled by conflicting reports from the missionaries. Confusion and uncertainty reigned among the Board members as negative reports increased. The promising work of Wilhelm was doubted by many. The person of Sadrach, his teachings, and Wilhelm's cooperation with him were the subjects of ongoing controversy. An onsite investigation, to be made as soon as possible, became the top priority. The minutes of the May, 1890, NGZV meeting indicate that the Board was commissioned to undertake an investigation in order to become better acquainted with the missionaries and the indigenous Javanese evangelists. They were also to assess the spiritual life of the Javanese Christian converts and familiarize themselves with any problems on the mission field.[101]

The *Nederduitsche Gereformeerde Kerken*[102] were planning to take over the responsibilities of mission work in Central Java from the NGZV.[103] Here also such an investigation was considered urgent. In the meeting of the provisional General Synod of the NGK, held at Leeuwarden in 1890, it was definitively decided to undertake an investigation. Frans Lion Cachet, minister of a congregation in Rotterdam, was chosen for the task.[104]

100. See Chapter I, section B2.

101. NGZV Minutes, May, 1890 (Archives of the Dutch Reformed Missionary Society, Leusden); "Inspectie reis," *Heidenbode* (June, 1890), pp. 124-125; Pol, *Midden Java*, pp. 153-154.

102. These were churches which in January, 1886, separated themselves from the NHK and called themselves "Dolerende Kerken" (*Nederduitsche Gereformeerde Kerken*); this historical event was called the *Doleantie*; see H. Berkhof, *Sejarah Gereja* [Church History], trans. and ed. by I.H. Enklaar (Jakarta, 1967), pp. 320-323; Rasker, pp. 171-190.

103. Mission delegate of the *Nederduitsche Gereformeerde Kerken* (appointed by the provisional Synod meeting of, June, 1888 in Utrecht) was charged with carrying out this plan by intensive discussions with the Board of the NGZV. It was hoped that the takeover would take place as soon as possible. See, *Heidenbode* (July, 1890), p. 138; Pol, *Midden Java*, p. 156.

104. *Heidenbode* (July, 1890), p. 139; Pol, *Midden Java*, p. 156.

Cachet, of Jewish origin, was an experienced missionary, having worked in South Africa among the "Kaffers" for fifteen years.[106] Because of his rich mission experiences, he was assigned to execute this important task by both the Synod and the Board of the NGZV, of which he was foreign secretary. He himself referred to the assignment as a *dubbele kwaliteit* (double capacity), an extremely difficult task which, Pol jested, far outweighed all the baggage he needed to bring with him for the inspection.[106] With a sum of more than ten thousand guilders provided by a business company for his living costs in the Dutch Indies, he was to carry out this very crucial mission.[107]

The instructions given by the Synod of the NGK were to investigate whether:

a) the communities in Central Java, consisting of converted Moslems and heathen, sufficiently displayed the image of the true Church of God,
b) the church offices were in conformity with the Word of God,
c) the Word of God was preached and the sacraments administered,
d) church discipline was exercised,
e) ecclesiastical ties were based on pure confession,
f) the church administration was in conformity with Reformed church order.[108]

The instructions from the Board of the NGZV were quite different from the above. They were to:

a) convey greetings of the Board to the missionaries and the community in Central Java, and
b) report on the properties of the NGZV in Central Java.

The Board also gave the mandate to:

— investigate the situation of the community and the execution of mission work in it,
— collect the missionaries' accounts of their work and draw conclusions from them,
— represent the Board to the government, the missionaries, and the community and take any necessary steps in all matters on behalf of the Board.[109]

---

105. See further, L. Wagenaar, "In Memoriam Ds. Frans Lion Cachet," *Heidenbode* (Dec., 1899), pp. 651-656.
106. Pol, *Midden Java*, p. 156.
107. NGZV Minutes, March 9, 1891 (Archives of the Dutch Reformed Missionary Society, Leusden). The company was *Factorij dere Nederlandsche Handelsmaatschappij*.
108. Nederduitsche Gereformeerde Kerken, *Acta Voorlopige Synode van Amsterdam 1892*, p. 22; Cachet, *Een jaar*, p. 834.
109. Cachet, *Een Jaar*, p. 306.

To get the maximum results for his investigation, Cachet toured several villages in Central Java, thoroughly examining and questioning the Javanese converts. Conversation was conducted in the Javanese language via a translator, who was either Jansz, Wilhelm, or the Javanese evangelist, Musa Wasman. Cachet's tour was completed within a year (he departed on April 9, 1891, and returned to the Netherlands on April 12, 1892), three months of which was spent traveling to and from the Netherlands.[110]

Cachet's concern for missions is evident by his willingness to make the very long journey to the Dutch Indies before the days of modern transportation, when one traveled such a distance at considerable risk. He was very committed to his task, even to the point of leaving his congregation for a year. Shortly after his return to the Netherlands, he presented a report of his investigation before the Synod of June, 1892. This gave him only two months to prepare.[111] Although he had only met with Sadrach once, for less than an hour, Cachet reported that Sadrach was neither a fanatic religious adherent, nor the proclaimer of a new religion, but merely a Javanese swindler who cunningly falsified Christian teachings in order to enrich himself materially and exalt himself socially. He concluded that all cooperation with him on the part of the missionaries was to be regretted. Sadrach's teachings, he claimed, were false, even outright lies when confronted with God's Word.[112]

Cachet was very disappointed in the situation of the community. The true churches he had imagined he would find did not exist. What he had found were, in his opinion, only groups of Javanese converts who lived in unchristian ways. They were led by "elders" who had only a very superficial knowledge of Christianity and who spread false teachings. He claimed that these groups could not be called churches in the true sense of the word, but only in name.[119] Cachet suggested that the NGZV cut off its relationship with Sadrach based on his conclusions: "For the glory of the Lord and out of love for the souls, even the soul of Sadrach, the Mission

---

110. Ibid., p. 875.

111. *Voorloopige Synode*, pp. 18-49. This report was developed into his thick book, *Een Jaar op Reis in dienst der Zending*, consisting of 879 pages, telling the complete story of his journey and inspection in Java.

112. *Voorlopige Synode,* pp. 46-49, Appendix IV, entitled "Dwaalleeraar in Bagelen;" Cachet, *Een Jaar*, p. 841.

113. Cachet, *Een Jaar*, p. 839. He wrote "dat de 'gemeenten' geen 'Kerken' konden heeten in de Gereformeerde beteekenis des woords, dat haar geestelijk toestand zeer gedroevend was." (that the congregation could not be called churches in the Reformed sense of the word, that her spiritual state was very saddening.); cf. Pol. *Midden Java*, p. 158.

should break from the lying Sadrach who has poisoned the life of the established 'Javanese Christianity' in which Christ no longer has a place."[114]

Since Sadrach had to be dismissed, in order to put an end to his missionary work, which was poisoning the mission fields of Central Java, Cachet requested the government to revoke Sadrach's *toelating als Inlandsche hulpzendeling* (permission to work as an evangelist, granted by the government according to Regulation 123).[115] The central government, however, rejected his request in July, 1892, for lack of just cause. It was the opinion of the central government that Sadrach was not an evangelist of the NGZV. Furthermore, he did not stimulate any social unrest, but rather took care of the Javanese Christians, a work which should be appreciated.[116]

The NGZV's actions against Sadrach drove almost all the Javanese Christians to Sadrach's side in the dispute. It was not surprising that from the total number of 6,374 converts, only about one hundred fifty sided with the missionaries and the other 6,224 continued to follow Sadrach as their guru and spiritual leader.[117] The *guru-murid* relationship between Sadrach and his followers was, in fact, stronger than Cachet had estimated. Unfortunately, the NGZV had not learned from the bitter experience of the failed attempt of Ligtvoet and Heyting to purge Sadrach ten years earlier. Now the mistake was repeated. Sadrach would not and could not be separated by force from his "children and grandchildren."[118]

It was not Sadrach but the NGZV who was almost driven out of Central Java. The NGZV's work of more than thirty years, including the nine years of Wilhelm was lost. The successor of the NGZV, the ZGKN, was forced to begin its mission from scratch. Wilhelm, who experienced a great deal of stress as a result of the accusations made against him, became seriously ill and died

---

114. Cachet, *Een Jaar*, p. 842; Adriaanse, *Sadrach's Kring*, pp. 319-320.

115. Cachet, *Een Jaar*, p. 841. About Regulation 123 see Chapter I, section A. Sadrach received his *toelating* on October 4, 1886. Extract from the Register of the Decisions of the Governor-General: license as missionary helper/native lay preacher: *Toelating* for Sadrach, No. 1/c, 4 October, 1886 (Karangjasa Documents, Karangjasa); His two deputies, Yohanes Kramawijaya and Markus Bangsareja, who played important roles in the development of Sadrach's community received their *toelatingen* on March 21, 1887; regarding Sadrach's deputies see Chapter III, section A.

116. C.C. Schot, "Iets over de vragen aan Indische Regeering om Sadrach in zijn arbeid te bemoeilijken en over Sadrach," *De Macedoniër* 11 (1893), pp. 13-22.

117. Pol, *Midden Java*, p. 172; Wolterbeek, p. 132. The number of one hundred fifty already included Javanese Christians under the leadership of Abisai Setradiwangsa, who was "pro-missionaries."

118. Adriaanse, *Sadrach's Kring*, p. 345.

on March 3, 1892, more than a month before Cachet returned from his tour.[119] Wilhelm's death left only two NGZV missionaries in Central Java — Horstman in Pekalongan, Residency of Tegal, and Zuidema in Purwareja. Horstman found his work difficult and unproductive. He took care of the existing Javanese Christian community but membership continually declined. In 1894, he left the field and returned home.[120]

5. Seeking a new partner and becoming the apostle of Java (1894-1924)

This second tragic event brought Sadrach a blessing in disguise, although he had to swallow a very bitter pill in the process. Sadrach, a highly respected Javanese *kyai*, with thousands of followers, had been deeply humiliated by his Dutch opponents. He did not collapse, however, and his

119. Cachet was a "unique" missionary with a special ability to interpret saddening events in a positive manner. His comments on the death of missionaries and their wives in Central Java reflect his convictions:

En zoo heeft ook onze Zending reeds hare beteekenisvolle graven in vier Residenties op Midden Java. The Muaratua, Tegal rust het gebeente van zuster Clara, de echtgenoote van zendeling Bieger. Op begraafplaats the Pekalongan is het graf van zuster Elise, de trouwe vrouw van zendeling Horstman; te Purbalingga-Banyumas is het graaf van eersten zendeling onzer veereneging br. Vermeer; en nu te Purwareja-Bagelen is onze zendeling Wilhelm ten grave gedragen! Die graven onzer zendelingen in de vier residenties, mogen ook ons een teeken zijn, dat wij een aanvang gemaakt hebben om dat land, in geestelijk zin, te veroveren, en roepen ons toe, dat wij den strijd daar tegen Mohammedanisme en Heldendom niet mogen opgeven tot dat de overwinning behaald is, en geheel Midden Java zich voor den Christus buigt." (And so, our mission already has her meaningful graves in four residencies of Central Java. At Muaratua, Tegal, rest the remains of sister Clara, the wife of missionary Bieger. In the cemetery at Pekalongan is the grave of sister Elise, the faithful wife of missionary Horstman; at Purbalingga, Banyumas is the grave of the first missionary of our organization, A. Vermeer; and now in Purwareja, Bagelen our missionary Wilhelm has been carried to the grave! Those graves of our missionaries in the four residencies can also be a sign for us that we have made start in conquering this land, in the spiritual sense, and they call out to us that we may not give up the battle against Mohammedanism and paganism until the victory had been won and all of Middle Java bows before the Christ.).

See *De Macedoniër* 37 (1893), p. 31. As a missionary who formerly worked in South Africa among the "Kaffers," Cachet was very impressed with missionary Krapf's strong witness. Krapf was convinced that the death of his wife in East Cental Africa was to open the way for success in mission work there. "Wat, naar den Mensch onmogelijk scheen, heeft de Heere heerlijk tot stand doen komen," (What appeared impossible to man, the Lord gloriously brought about), said Cachet, expecting the same to occur in Central Java. Clara Bieger died on September, 1871; Elise Horstman on December 12, 1891; Vermeer on October, 1891; and Wilhelm on March 3, 1892.

120. Wolterbeek, p. 131.

position became even more firmly established. His community separated completely from the small group of Javanese Christians who followed the missionaries, and soon became the largest Christian community at that time in Central Java.[121]

Such a large indigenous Christian community, however, found no favor in the eyes of the local government officials. According to Adriaanse, the local government had not yet completely given up on the idea of incorporation. The underlying motive was, of course, political. The final goal was to put Sadrach's community under the control of the government so that the threat of political instability in the region could be minimized.[122] The Resident, accompanied by his officials, made visits to several local Javanese Christian communities for that purpose. Specific steps were taken to bring about this goal. Among others, they included:

a) collecting data concerning the location of Javanese Christians and especially the elders and evangelists,

b) taking inventory of the local Javanese Christian communities for the report to the Central Board of the *Indische Kerk* in Batavia,

c) offering (financial?) assistance to these local communities,

d) systematically campaigning to urge the Javanese Christians to join the *Indische Kerk*,

e) and promising to appoint an associate minister to take care of them.

Unlike the similar unsuccessful endeavor of twelve years prior, a persuasive approach was used rather than force. Adriaanse described the efforts in these words:

> After the death of Wilhelm, the integration idea of 1882 remained. The goal was not to cut off the relationship between Sadrach and his followers by force (because Sadrach would certainly defend his position), but rather to bring Sadrach and his community under the authority of the Board of the *Indische Kerk*. One or more helpers would be employed and the present missionaries would be installed much as had been the case in the past with Bieger and Vermeer.[123]

Nevertheless, the local government and the *Indische Kerk* in Purwareja never achieved their goal. The Governor-General and the Central Board of the *Indische Kerk* in Batavia never agreed to the plan.

---

121. In 1895, the ZGKN counted seven thousand members; see N.D. Schuurman, "Staat der Zending in Nederlandsch Oost Indië anno 1895," *Nederlandsch Zendingstijdschrift* 8 (1896), p. 135. It can be ascertained that the total number included Sadrach's followers. The ZGKN, in 1923, counted only 4,023 members during the period from 1894-1923; see A. Merkelijn, "Enkele gegeven over Zendingsterreinen van de GKN over 1923," *De Opwekker* 69 (1924), pp. 158-159.

122. Adriaanse, *Sadrach's Kring,* p. 346.

123. Ibid., p. 347.

87

Sadrach Surapranata in front of his house

Sadrach, with *toelating* in hand, was free to move around the villages accompanied by his two trusted assistants, Yohanes Kramawijaya and Markus Bangsareja, making pastoral calls and evangelizing. He was still the central authority figure for his followers, and Karangjasa became the center of "Javanese Christianity." Now in his sixties, the age when the average Javanese begins to lose strength and vitality, Sadrach still worked energetically and remained an effective guru and *kyai*. Several groups of followers continued to emerge, for example, those in Kendal, Semarang.

A Javanese *guru ngelmu* who lived in the Residency of Bagelen converted to Christianity. He was not satisfied with the teachings given by Sadrach's assistant, and therefore went to Karangjasa to learn from Sadrach himself. After completing his study with Sadrach, he returned to his village bearing witness to the "new *ngelmu*" from Sadrach in Karangjasa. This guru had pupils in various distant places such as Kendal, Semarang, a coastal area in North Central Java. He also went there, witnessing to his "new *ngelmu*" before his pupils, teaching those who were interested. Thus, new groups of converts came into being who recognized Sadrach as their guru and *kyai* from whom they received the "new *ngelmu*," although they themselves never met Sadrach personally.[124] Several local communities emerged in this same way, which came as a great surprise to Cachet when he toured villages far from Karangjasa.[125]

Everything was going well. Pastoral visits and evangelization were being done and the number of converts was increasing, but the important element of the administration of the sacraments was still missing. Sadrach was very concerned about this problem and it was one of the reasons why he remained open to cooperation with the established church. Sadrach was actively seeking a new partner or partners to replace Wilhelm. At the same time, the ZGKN was seeking missionaries to go to Central Java. Cachet offered himself as a candidate, although his motives are unclear.[126] He declared before his congregation his desire to return to missionary service, not as a high-ranking mission official who would determine the future of mission work in Central Java, but merely as an ordinary missionary like the late Wilhelm. He, however, later withdrew his candidacy, probably due to his advanced age. He died five years later on September 27, 1899. Rev. L. Adriaanse from Zeist was accepted and sent to Purwareja (1894-1903) on November 9, 1894. He lived in the same house where Wilhelm had lived and died. He was the first *missionaire predikant* (ordained missionary) of

124. Ibid., p. 349.
125. Cachet, *Een Jaar*, pp. 358-360.
126. Pol, *Midden Java*, p. 168.

the GKN to be sent to Central Java after responsibility for the mission fields changed hands from the NGZV to the ZGKN.[126a]

Adriaanse was very concerned about Sadrach and his community. Before his departure he had carefully studied what had been happening with Sadrach and the mission work in Central Java. He planned to contact Sadrach upon his arrival. As he stated in the beginning of his book, he wanted to know exactly what happened in the so-called "Sadrach affair" because it would be very difficult to understand without knowing its history. Several of the questions involved touched on principles of mission methodology.[127] Adriaanse concluded that many of the judgments made regarding the affair were unfair and groundless. They were very often too Western in perspective, failing to take the Javanese context into account, partly due to a lack of accurate information. It was Adriaanse's intention to give more information about the mission history of Central Java by writing his book, *Sadrach's Kring*. He hoped that in this way those who were concerned about mission work in Central Java would get a more accurate picture of the situation.[128]

Like Wilhelm, Adriaanse was very sympathetic in his approach to Sadrach and the Javanese Christians. He made an effort to remain as positive as possible so as not to break open old wounds. Sadrach and Adriaanse visited one another in Karangjasa and Purwareja, and thus became better acquainted. Through his aquaintance with Sadrach, Adriaanse became more and more convinced that Sadrach was willing to live according to God's Word.[129] He realized that Sadrach was not a man who knew nothing about salvation as some had claimed, nor was he a man who claimed himself to be the incarnation of Christ, as others had accused.[130] Adriaanse underscored that the broken relationship between the NGZV and the Javanese Christians had originated from the NGZV's dominating attitude. He stressed that the Javanese Christian community was the result of Sadrach's work and that the Dutch missionaries' claim to the credit was imaginary. Adriaanse was also convinced that the community would welcome any missionary assistance if the Dutch missionaries did not try to control them.[131]

126a. See Chapter I, section 1b; Van Den End, *Gereformeerde Zending*, p. 6.

127. Adriaanse, *Sadrach's Kring*, p. v.

128. Ibid., pp. viii-xi.

129. L. Adriaanse to Deputaten voor de Zending op Midden Java ten Zuiden, July 2, 1897, as published in *Heidenbode* (Dec., 1897), pp. 369-371; Pol, *Midden Java*, p. 169; Wolterbeek, p. 262.

130. L. Adriaanse to Deputaten voor de Zending op Midden Java ten Zuiden, as published in *Heidenbode* (Jan., 1898), p. 418; Pol, *Midden Java*, p. 169.

131. Adriaanse's letter to Deputaten voor de Zending op Midden Java ten Zuiden, as published in *Heidenbode* (March, 1897), p. 370; Pol, *Midden Java*, p. 170.

Adriaanse was often invited by Sadrach to preach in Karangjasa. Sadrach was open to cooperation, and his concern for the sacraments was made evident when he himself asked Adriaanse to perform baptism for a number of his followers. Adriaanse did not refuse the request, but doubted the extent of their knowledge of Christian teachings. Taking great care not to be offensive, he required further religious instruction for those who were to be baptized. Musa Wasman, the Javanese evangelist who had accompanied Cachet as interpreter, now became Adriaanse's helper and was assigned to teach them.[132]

Adriaanse was extremely cautious in his relationship with Sadrach because he feared that he would meet the same tragic fate as Wilhelm. Therefore he consulted with the synodical deputies for the mission of the GKN in the Netherlands on every decision, especially during the time when Cachet was the foreign secretary and thus the decisive person with regard to mission policy.[133] As a result, any work which required quick decision-making was bogged down by bureaucracy. A typical example was recorded by Wolterbeek: Sadrach invited Adriaanse to preach in Karangjasa on May 17, 1896. However, this invitation first had to be cleared with the mission deputies of the GKN. A "preaching permit" was finally granted by the Board of deputies more than seven months later on November 23, 1896.[134] Clearly, the ZGKN played a decisive role in the mission policy of Adriaanse.

Adriaanse's relationship with Sadrach was not without reserve. The Dutch missionaries in general were concerned about the danger of syncretism. They believed that the greatest danger in missions was syncretism, and Sadrach was, in their opinion among those who bore this syncretistic stamp.[135] Adriaanse's reluctance to build a closer relationship with Sadrach and his suspicion of Sadrach's teaching soon became evident to Sadrach. Gradually he distanced himself from Adriaanse and no longer pushed for cooperation. The hopes of a working relationship similar to that with Wilhelm failed to materialize. Sadrach found himself unable to build a new relationship with the ZGKN.

Prior to Adriaanse's arrival in Purwareja, Sadrach had made contact with both the *Salatiga-Zending*[136] and the *Apostolische Kerk* in Magelang.

---

132. Ibid.
133. Wolterbeek, p. 262.
134. Ibid.
135. D. Bakker, *De Zending van de Gereformeerde Kerken* (Groningen, n.d.), p. 62; Wolterbeek, p. 263.
136. Regarding the *Salatiga-Zending* see Chapter I, section B3.

Contact with missionaries of the *Salatiga-Zending* actually began when Wilhelm was still alive. The contact was, however, mainly of a personal and informal nature. Some of the missionaries from the *Salatiga-Zending* attended the great annual gatherings in Karangjasa.[137] That Sadrach had a good relationship with them is evident in that he entrusted his followers in Kendal to the care of missionary Heller from the *Salatiga-Zending* in 1896.[139] Nothing more is known about this relationship.

Sadrach's relationship with the *Apostolische Kerk*, on the other hand, became more formal, leading to Sadrach's ordination as the apostle of Java. The *Apostolische Kerk* (which is regarded as a sect) was founded by the Scottish Presbyterian minister, Edward Irving. The sect is, therefore, sometimes called Irvingism,[139] although it was not officially established until 1835, a year after Irving's death.[140] The establishment of the *Apostolische Kerk* was initially a spiritual revival prompted by the feeling that the spiritual life of the established church had detoriorated. The members desired a community like that of the early church, filled with power, spirit, and various charismas, led by apostles who faithfully awaited the second coming of Christ. "Conventicles" began to flourish outside the official church, not only in England but also in Germany and the Netherlands. The Dutch "conventicles" were called *Katholiek Apostolische Gemeenten*. A disagreement on apostolic succession, among other matters, made a split inevitable. A new "denomination" emerged, calling itself the *Hersteld Apostolische Zending Gemeente* (1863). Apostle Schwartz, who ordained Anthing as an apostle in 1879, was a member of this group. His successor, Krebs, was regarded by other apostles as a *stam* (trunk, i.e. preeminent) apostle, and in 1897 he established the *Hersteld Apostolische Zendingsgemeente in de Eenheid der Apostelen* (hereafter HAZEA). The next point in the church's development was to organize the independent *apostolische gemeenten* at an international level.[141] From the

137. Some names from *Salatiga-Zending* who were present in the stated yearly meetings: Penninga and Stegerhoek, 1888; A. Jüngst and F. Kamp, 1889; see Wilhelm, 1888, p. 17; 1889, p. 88.

138. Adriaanse, *Sadrach's Kring*, p. 352.

139. I. Esser, "Apostolische Gemeenten of Irvingianen," *De Macedoniër* 2 (1884), pp. 165-167.

140. F. Boerwinkel, *Kerk en Secte* ('s-Gravenhage, 1959), p. 46.

141. For further elaboration on the *Apostolische Kerk*, see J.M. Köhler, *Het Irvingisme, eene historisch-critisch proeve* ('s-Gravenhage, 1876); Boerwinkel, pp. 45ff., especially regarding the *Hersteld Apostolische Zendingkerk*, *Hersteld Apostolische Gemeente,* and *Apostolisch Genootschap*; E.G. Hoekstra and M.H. Ipenburg, *Wegewijs in gelovig Nederland: Een alfabetische beschrijving van Nederlandse kerken en religieuse groeperingen* (Kampen, n.d.), pp. 19-24; M.J. Tang, *Het Apostolische Werk in Nederland* ('s-Gravenhage, 1982).

very beginning the office of apostle played a very important role. It was believed that the apostles were the legitimate leaders of the church from New Testament times until the second coming of Christ. The high position of the apostle is evident in the words of this song: "The office of the apostle is our rock on which we must build. He is today our God, the one in whom we trust."[142]

Mission work of the *Apostolische Gemeente* in the Dutch Indies began in the 1880's when pioneering missionary apostles (*apostel zendelingen*) arrived from the Netherlands. G.J. Hannibals and J.G.R. Jacobs led the small communities in Batavia and Cimahi. The community in Magalang was led by a Chinese apostle, Liem Cu Kim (1888). Sadrach came into contact with the Magalang congregation, and worshiped with them several times. This contact resulted in Sadrach's going to Batavia, accompanied by Yotham and Bangsareja, to be ordained by Hannibals as the apostle of Java. Upon his return to Karangjasa, on April 30, 1899, Sadrach celebrated his function of apostleship together with his community. During the special worship service, the Lord's Supper was served by Sadrach himself. He now had the right to administer the sacraments, a right he had desired and sought after for many years.[143]

Various reasons have been given for Sadrach's choice to become an apostle in the *Apostolische Kerk* based on differing interpretations of the facts surrounding the ordination. One view is that Sadrach feared that his leadership over his congregation would be forcefully taken away by the government, and his community would be incorporated into the *Indische Kerk* or taken over by missionaries of the ZGKN.[144] Another view is that Sadrach was convinced by Over, a Dutch soldier stationed in Magalang and an active member of the *Apostolische Kerk*, that some apostles in the Netherlands had received a revelation from God that Sadrach should be appointed as the apostle of Java. Others still said that since Anthing had also been ordained as an apostle in the *Apostolische Kerk*, Sadrach, even more convinced of the authenticity of the call, simply followed in the steps of his former teacher.[145] Yet another possibility is that Sadrach became convinced that the *Apostolische Kerk* was the true manifestation of the community of believers as later explained in the tract, "Is There Truth?"[146]

142. Boerwinkel, p. 50; "'t Apostel ambt is onze rots, waarop we moeten bouwen Hij is in 't heden onze God, waarop wij ons vertrouwen"

143. Pol, *Midden Java*, p. 172; Wolterbeek, p. 264.

144. D. Bakker, *De Zending* p. 93; Pol, *Midden Java*, p. 172.

145. L. Adriaanse to Deputaten voor de Zending op Midden Java ten Zuiden, as published in *Heidenbode* (Dec., 1899), p. 668; Wolterbeek, p. 263.

146. The tract, "Apa ada kebenaran itu?" (Is There Truth?) was written in the Malay language, published in Enkhuizen, center for HAZEA, at the time.

The pamphlet sharply criticized the established churches, claiming that the many splits and perversions were the result of church leaders living according to the flesh. It accused these leaders of trading the true salvation for a lie and living apart from true love. In short, there was no longer truth within the churches. The tract went on to claim that only an apostle could restore the churches from such a perverse situation.

It is possible that the simplicity of the *Apostolische Kerk* in regard to its organization, church offices (they did not require sophisticated theological education to be an apostle or church official),[147] order of worship, etc., were significant factors for Sadrach. Realizing that he himself was "uneducated" as were the members of his community, as the Dutch missionaries stated again and again, Sadrach found the *Apostolische Kerk* very appealing. The repeated humilitation of being suspected by the Dutch missionaries was another factor in his decision as he himself state:

> Earlier I got along well with missionary Wilhelm, but the Rev. Cachet came and split us apart. He wanted nothing to do with me; therefore, my heart was burning and when I came in contact with a Chinese Christian in Magalang, a student of Mr. Anthing, he advised me to join the Apostolic Church in Batavia.[148]

Internally, Sadrach's installation as an apostle brought no significant changes in the life of the community, however, externally it was very significant. The position of Sadrach and his community were strengthened. As a church leader, he now stood at the same level as others and his community was equal to those of other denominations. He was internationally recognized as an apostle[149] as stated in a *Legitimatie en*

---

147. *Anggaran Dasar Rumahtangga dan Syahadat Kerasulan Baru untuk para anggota dari Gereja Kerasulan Baru* [Algemene Huisregelen en Geloofsbelijdenis voor dienaren en leden der Hersteld Apostolische Gemeente in de Eenheid der Apostelen], (Bandung, 1966).

148. "Vroeger was ik goed met Zendeling Wilhelm, doch toen is Ds. Cachet gekomen en die heeft ons van elkaar verwijderd en wilde met mij niets te doen hebben en daardoor ben ik warm in mijn hart geworde en toen ik daarna in Magelang kwam bij een Chineesch Christen, een leerling van mijnheer Anthing, heeft die mij geraden, om mij aan te sluiten bij de Apostolische Gemeente in Batavia.

Adriaanse, *Heidenbode* (Dec., 1899), p. 715. The term " warm worden in het hart" is a Javanese/Indonesian expression "panas atine/ hatinya" which means "to become exasperated." Cachet's attitude towards him during the meeting in Karangjasa had been interpreted by Sadrach as humiliation; cf. Cachet, *Een Jaar*, pp. 368-372.

149. Portraits of Apostles from Germany, the Netherlands, Australia, Argentina, North America, Africa, and Indonesia/Java (Archives, Karangjasa).

Erkenningsbewijs (Letter of Recognition).[150] His status changed from a Javanese evangelist seeking sympathy and clemency from the Dutch missionaries to the respected Javanese leader of the greatest Javanese "church" of that time.

The ordination of Sadrach as apostle meant an end to the efforts of the ZGKN to revive cooperation with him. The end of the nineteenth and the beginning of the twentieth century was a difficult period for the ZGKN. These were years of challenge for missions in Central Java. A new mission approach (*kerkelijke zending*) which advocated the building of schools and hospitals as an auxiliary means of missions, especially in urban areas, in the hope that they would attract many, above all from into middle and upper classes, had by 1913 failed to produce satisfying results. More than fifty years after the NGZV began its work in Central Java the Mission claimed only 1,634 converts. Such poor results led to growing disappointment among the missionary societies in the Netherlands.[151] Some of the leading church figures, including Dr. A. Kuyper, suggested withdrawing from Central Java and directing mission work to non-Moslem lands in the hope of being more fruitful.[152] In other words, the mission work in Central Java was being questioned. It was in critical condition due to the lack of results. In contrast, Sadrach was reaching the peak of his career, winning a large number of converts. The suggestion to withdraw was rejected and the ZGKN continued working in Central Java.[153]

After becoming an apostle, Sadrach's contact with the Dutch missionaries was drastically reduced, as was that of his deputies. H.P. Igwersen, Adriaanse's replacement in Purwareja (1910), went to Karangjasa once to accompany a government official in interviewing Sadrach. He described Sadrach as "rather thin, but very tall, possibly well over seventy years old, but still energetic. He watched us through keen eyes under thick brows. A long but small grey beard grows on his chin."[154] This impression corresponds to the pictures of Sadrach often seen in missionary magazines.

150. Dated May, 1901 (two years after Sadrach's ordination) signed by J. Kofman Rz. (*voorzitter en apostel*, HAZEA) on behalf of the International Board of the *Apostolische Kerk* in Germany; see *Legitimatie en Erkenningsbewijs* [Legitimation and Recognition] issued by HAZEA in Enkhuizen, the Netherlands (Archives, Karangjasa, April, 1901).
151. Wolterbeek, p. 288.
152. Ibid., p. 289.
153. Dr. B.J. Esser, one of the missionaries working in Purbalingga at the time (1908), was the "defender" against the idea of withdrawing as is clear in his book, *De Goddelijke Leiding in de Zending, beantwoording der vraag of de Gereformeerde Kerken in Nederland een nieuw Zendingsveld in de "buiten-bezittingen" zullen zoeken* (Rotterdam, 1914).
154. P.H. Ingwersen, "Iets over Sadrach," *De Macedoniër* 19 (1915), p. 328.

Ingwersen was further impressed by Sadrach's strong personality. He described him as having a spiritually powerful appearance and strong disposition. According to him, Sadrach was energetic and a talented organizer, two characteristics, he said, the Javanese in general do not possess. He therefore concluded that Sadrach was possibly not really Javanese, but Chinese.[155] Ingwersen also wrote about Sadrach's Dutch assistant, Terburg.[156] Formerly a marine, Terburg was fired from his job over a mistake. He was in charge of correspondence with the *Apostolische Kerk* in the Netherlands, making contacts with government, officials etc. — a job more easily done by a Dutchman than a Javanese.

Ingwersen dwelt on Sadrach's advanced age of nearly eighty years. Perhaps Sadrach was already concerned about preparing a successor as leader of the community, although it may have been felt that such preparation was unnecessary since a charismatic leader like Sadrach was virtually irreplaceable and God would prepare such a leader in His time for the community. It appeared that Sadrach's main concern in his old age was that the unity of the community be maintained. The question was how to bring such unity into realization. As a Javanese guru, Sadrach appealed to the use of symbolism, an important aspect of Javanese culture. The symbol he chose was the *sapu* (brush of palmleaf ribs), which he made for each of the local communities. This was a very time-consuming task since there were more than eighty local communities at the time. He gave a *sapu* to every elder who came to him, and said that the community had to be united and strong like the *sapu*. The community is bound to each other, said Sadrach, like the *sapu*, namely, by Christ.[157]

It is difficult to know precisely what Sadrach intended by distributing the *sapus*, other than that he wanted them to function simply as the symbol of unity and strength, as claimed by his descendants.[158] But some of his followers interpreted it as more than a symbol, attributing a magical power to it. As a result, the *sapu* was never used for its usual function, but was treated as a precious heirloom from their admired guru. Regardless of how it may have been interpreted, Sadrach did something he considered good for his community. It was an important thing he could do to express his concern and hope at a time when he saw the end of his life drawing near.

On November 14, 1924, at an age of over ninety years, the great man in

155. Ibid., p. 331.
156. Ibid., p. 329, Ingwersen does not indicate how Terburg became Sadrach's assistant.
157. H. Van Eijk, "De Sadrach Gemeenten," *De Macedoniër* 38 (1934), p. 43.
158. Author's interview with Sadrach's great-grandsons, Supono and Suprapto Martasaputra, in Karangjasa, (February, 1986).

missions from Karangjasa, Radin Abas Sadrach Surapranata, died quietly in his home.[159] Sadrach's death and funeral were recorded by Rev. K. Van Dijk, an eye witness to the event.[160] There was no sign to indicate Sadrach's impending death. He had no serious illness. As was usual among elderly Javanese, Sadrach slept more often, especially the few days before his death. The woman who usually provided his food and took care of him was very surprised and a little frightened when she came into Sadrach's bedroom to awaken him, only to find him already dead. The news of his death spread quickly among his followers. They flocked to Sadrach's home to honor him for the last time. Among the distinguished guests who expressed condolences on the day of the funeral were the regents of Kutaraja and Kulon Praga (both relatives of Sadrach), missionaries Netelenbos and Van Dijk, missionary physician Dreckmeyer, and missionary teachers Harkema and Hooisma. The funeral was conducted by Apostle Schmidt from the *Apostolische Kerk* in Cimahi, West Java. It was apparent that Sadrach had been widely known and respected both inside and outside of his community.

6. Sadrach's community during the first decade after Sadrach's death (1924-1933)

The death of Sadrach naturally brought serious consequences to the life of the community, the most important of which, in our opinion, was the leadership crisis. Yotham Martareja, Sadrach's adopted son,[161] succeeded his father for eight years (1925-1933). At that time the community, consisting of eighty-six local communities,[162] experienced uncertainty over who was to be the leader and central unifying figure. There was obvious friction and division. Several figures claimed to be "the leader," but were not accepted by the entire community. The *sapus* that Sadrach distributed prior to his death were not powerful enough to protect the community from the threatening danger of disunity. This became clear during the first decade after Sadrach's death.

159. K. Van Dijk, "Sadrach's Kring na 1922," *De Macedoniër* 42 (1938), p. 266; Wolterbeek, p. 314.
160. Van Dijk, "Sadrach's Kring," pp. 267-268.
161. According to Wilhelm, Yotham was the son of Markus Bangsareja, Sadrach's deputy. When Yotham came to Wilhelm for schooling in 1887 he was ten years old. This means that he was born in 1877 in Karangjasa. See Wilhelm, 1887, p. 311.
162. Van Dijk, "Sadrach's Kring," p. 266.

a. Yotham Martareja, the half-hearted successor

Since Sadrach's marriage to a Javanese woman, Deborah, produced no children, they adopted a boy, Yotham, and a girl who later became Yotham's wife. Adriaanse conducted their marriage service in his church.[163] A little background information about Yotham might prove helpful.

Yotham studied at the Keuchenius School in Purwareja where Zuidema was supervisor. Adriaanse also taught Yotham in 1897, when Zuidema was on leave to the Netherlands. Since Yotham was primarily educated in a mission school, it influenced his attitude toward and understanding of Christianity. This clearly manifested itself in his leadership of the community.

Because of his educational background, for example, Yotham was not convinced about the authenticity of the office of apostle in the *Apostolische Kerk*. But as a son, he was cautious not to come into conflict with his father. According to Javanese custom, questioning one's guru or parents is considered a form of misconduct. Therefore, Yotham did not have the courage to discuss openly with Sadrach his views about the office of apostle.[164] As a graduate of the mission school, however, Yotham's understanding of Christianity might have been different from that of his father.[165]

After Yotham became leader of the community, Van Dijk visited him in Karangjasa (August, 1924). He got the impression that Yotham desired to resume contact with the missionaries.[166] Yotham was uneasy with the situation of the community and considered the idea of incorporating into the ZGKN for the sake of the future of the community. He vaccilated between following the path of his father's leadership or going his own way. He would "inherit" the largest Christian community in Central Java, the future of which lay with him if he was officially appointed as successor to Sadrach as leader of the community. Although he had been appointed de facto as "acting successor" by Sadrach shortly before his death,[167] the question of leadership was still a great burden to Yotham, for he realized that he was not capable of handling it, and the community was very needy, both materially and spiritually. Indeed, Yotham did not have Sadrach's self-confidence and was very pessimistic in his outlook. Ingwersen wrote the following about his impression of Yotham's personality:

163. Ibid.
164. Adriaanse, *Heidenbode* (Dec., 1899), pp. 667-668.
165. Van Dijk, "Sadrach's Kring," p. 271.
166. Ibid., p. 26.
167. Ibid., p. 268; Wolterbeek, p. 314.

The other thing that has been confirmed to us by the followers of Sadrach is that a successor has been appointed, but he does not look promising. Seeing his picture ... it is obvious that he is less talented. He looks quite different from Sadrach. His succession is possibly not disappointing for some, but those who know him personally — such as Zuidema, when he was a student at the Keuchenius School, and other missionaries who met him with the helpers at the mission fields of the *Utrecht Zendings Vereeniging* — view it quite differently. They are all of the opinion that Yotham — that is his name — is not the right man to assume leadership of the community, at least not in the same spirit and authority as Sadrach. He is modest and docile, better a follower than a leader.[168]

Based on this profile of Yotham, Ingwersen supposed that Sadrach's community would disappear in the near future.

It is true that a strong personality as well as leadership skills were very important for the leader of the community. The combination of both was the key to success. However, they were not the only factors. Many things were involved, both internally and externally. The circumstances and environment in which the community was living were significant considerations. At the time of Sadrach's death, Java was entering a new era. Modern education, science, and technology from the West were rapidly being introduced to Javanese life. These changes affected the Christian community as well. In the absence of a strong personality to lead them, the problem was how Sadrach's community could survive so that Ingwersen's "prophesy" might not be fulfilled.

Despite Yotham's uncertainty about the office of apostle, he half-heartedly accepted the position. A document written by Yotham, entitled "Saupama aku dadi rasul" (Supposing I were an Apostle) depicted Yotham's doubt.[169] In it he imagined how great and difficult the task would be. He would have to be faithfully committed to his work, living a life of good conduct and piety. Much church work needed to be done, which required a lot of money. Consequently, Yotham had very serious doubts. He wrestled with such questions. He felt incapable — in a dilemma. He felt that he could not meet the community's requirements either spiritually or materially. To become self-supporting was impossible for the community because it was poor. Financial assistance from the outside — from the church in Cimahi, or HAZEA in the Netherlands — could not be expected. Moreover, Yotham felt that he had not been equipped or prepared for the position. He was not a Javanese guru and was not acquainted with "Javanese-ness" like Sadrach had been.   Finally Yotham realized that to burden himself with all these thoughts would lead

168. Ingwersen, p. 288.
169. Yotham Martareja, *Saupama aku dadi rasul* [Supposing I were an Apostle] (Karangjasa Documents, Karangjasa).

to his death. He came to the conclusion "perlu opo nglakoni panggawe ora ngerti. Becik nurut kang wis tumitah gedhe katimbang tetruka, tanpa pawitan lan sangu" (It is purposeless to do incomprehensible work. It is better to follow what has been great than to pioneer with no capital or provisions).[170] This conclusion is puzzling, but may be a key to understanding what Yotham was wrestling with. It is our opinion that "kang wis tumitah gedhe" ("what has been great," or more literally, "what has been predestined to be great") points to the ZGKN, which at that time had become a "modern" enterprise — something "great" in Yotham's opinion. The rest of the sentence, "tetruka tanpa pawitan lan sangu" ("to pioneer with no capital or provisions," or more literally, "to start clearing a jungle for establishing a village with no capital or provisions/equipment"), points to the condition of Sadrach's community. In Yotham's opinion, the community lacked such basic tools as biblical knowledge, spiritual life, educated religious teachers and elders, and money. Yotham felt that to become an apostle would be to become a pioneer, like the first settler of a village who is unsuccessful because of lack of funds and equipment.

Yotham stood at the crossroads between the community as it had been under Sadrach and what it would be under his leadership. This document, if we have correctly interpreted it, reflects his dilemma between becoming an apostle or joining the ZGKN. Despite his inclination, Yotham decided not to join the ZGKN too quickly, because such an attitude would be seen as a betrayal of his father's trust, and would not gain support from the community. Rather, the situation developed in the following manner.

In March, 1925, about six months after the death of Sadrach, Apostle Schmidt came from Cimahi to ask Yotham if he was willing to be appointed as an apostle. Yotham did not answer immediately, but requested some time to consider the proposal. A few days later, Yotham wrote a letter stating his unwillingness to become an apostle for the following reasons:

— he doubted the continuation of the office of apostle
— he preferred the understanding of Christianity that he had learned at the mission school
— he intended to unite with the ZGKN for the sake of the future of the community.[171]

A copy of the letter was sent to the Dutch missionaries and was to be discussed in the meeting of April, 1925. But in the regular meeting of

---

170. Ibid.
171. Van Dijk, "Sadrach's Kring," p. 272.

Javanese elders on March 24, 1925, in Karangjasa, Schmidt asked who would be appointed as a successor to Sadrach. Yotham was unanimously appointed. Apostle Schmidt then said to him,

> You have heard them all choose you. You may not be the leader as they want unless you revoke the letter you wrote me. If you betray the teachings of Kyai Sadrach and you want to join the mission [ZGKN], they will not follow you and we will have to elect another successor. Therefore, I urge you to consider this seriously. Either you stand by your letter or revoke it and believe in the teaching of the *kyai*, being loyal to his example.[172]

Yotham had no time to ponder. He had to make a decision. He revoked his letter and reluctantly accepted the appointment of the elders. On the day of Pentecost, May, 1925, Yotham was ordained as an apostle.[173] Yotham's decision meant a continuation of Sadrach's leadership; therefore, no significant changes could be made in the life of the community. The official relationship with the ZGKN remained as before. The relationship remained open only on the level of individual personal contact.

It is surprising that Yotham made such a decision. We are tempted to inquire further as to why he relinquished his desire to unite with the ZGKN. Perhaps it reflected Yotham's docile personality as described by Ingwersen. Viewed from another perspective, however, it may have been a strategy to achieve the intended goal; namely, to incorporate with the ZGKN without a division within the community. Yotham's acceptance of the call was probably based on the following considerations:

— avoidance of a continuation of the leadership crisis,
— avoidance of the possibility of disunity among the community,
— strengthening of Yotham's position as a means of softening strong opposition and eliminating friction among community members.[174]

By following this strategy, Yotham expected to achieve his goal. Thus, his willingness to become an apostle was a means to an end rather than a rejection of his original goal.

In the opinion of the Dutch missionaries, some positive changes were made in the community under Yotham's leadership. They highly praised Yotham as a spiritual father who was, in many ways, "much better than

172. Ibid., p. 273.
173. Wolterbeek, p. 315.
174. The generation which experienced the tragic events of 1882 and 1892 in the relationship with the Dutch missionaries would gradually die out and be replaced by a younger generation more open to change. In addition, this younger generation would have no built up resentment and prejudice against the missionaries. Therefore opposition against Yotham's intention of incorporation with the ZGKN would gradually decrease.

Sadrach." He was not authoritarian, and therefore not blindly obeyed by the community.[175] The relationship with the missionaries was improved, and Yotham encouraged community members to take part in joint activities with the ZGKN, such as Sunday services[176] — something which would have been impossible under Sadrach's leadership. The missionary magazine, *Mardi Raharja* (published in Javanese), was circulated among the community. They utilized the mission schools and hospitals which had been established in the early twentieth century as the realization of the ZGKN's new mission policy.[177]

The relationship between the community and the ZGKN churches continued to improve on the local level, becoming more intense through joint activities. The two groups drew closer and closer. In places like Kebumen, Purwareja, Karangjasa, and Purbalingga, the community churches moved ahead on their own and incorporated with the ZGKN.[178] This was the result Yotham had hoped for. The incorporation process was evolving from the grass roots without a formal decision from the top.

b.   Yotham's definite decision to incorporate

Yotham's strategy was becoming clear. He had not given up his original goal. During his time as an apostle, he played an important role behind the scenes, quietly making contact with the missionaries via his helpers, and encouraging the community to build closer relationships with the ZGKN churches. Only the final step of full incorporation needed to be taken.

May 1, 1933, eight years after Yotham's installation as apostle, was a decisive day in the history of the community. Van Dijk welcomed Yotham and his colleague, Abraham Wangsareja, who had come to meet him. The two men came to inform Van Dijk that Yotham had definitely decided to incorporate the community into the ZGKN. The unbelievable decision, however, was not without risk.

Van Dijk was not in a position to act in response to Yotham's request; however, he did promise to inform the other missionaries and discuss the matter at their upcoming meeting. Some of the other missionaries were rather skeptical, but nevertheless, Yotham's intention was finally discussed in the meeting of May 15, 1933. The decision was made to:

— investigate the sincerity of Yotham's intention before taking further action;

175. Van Dijk, "Sadrach's Kring," p. 304.
176. Van Eijk, pp. 40-41.
177. Van Dijk, "Sadrach's Kring," p. 305; Wolterbeek, p. 301.
178. Van Dijk, "Sadrach's Kring," p. 305; D. Pol, "Sadrach Christenen," *De Macedoniër* 38 (1934), p. 347.

— set up an investigation committee consisting of three missionaries from Kebumen and Wanasaba with the tasks of discussing the matter with Yotham in more detail, representing the ZGKN in the upcoming elders meeting in Karangjasa, and assigning Yotham to inform local communities of the decision.[179]

From its decision, it is clear that the ZGKN was being very cautious. Their caution was due to several reasons. First, in dealing with church organization, everything had to be brought up and solved according to proper church procedures. Second, incorporation was not merely a matter of leaders, but touched the community at the grass roots level. Therefore a tour made by Yotham to inform the local communities about the issue of incorporation was regarded as necessary.

According to Van Dijk, Yotham informed the ZGKN that the community had eighty-six local communities with a total membership of 7,552.[180] The communities were distributed throughout nine areas in Central Java:

AREA	NUMBER OF LOCAL COMMUNITIES
Yogyakarta	20
Surakarta	14
Kebumen	12
Pekalongan	12
Banyumas	9
Magalang	7
Wanasaba	6
Purwareja	4 (including Karangjasa)
Semarang	2

Visiting each of these communities within a relatively short time was difficult task; Yotham, accompanied by Abraham Wangsareja, carried out the mission. In each community they met with the local elders and members, trying to convince them to incorporate. The advantages, according to Van Dijk, were the welfare of the community in terms of education in Christian truth, pastoral counselling, and spiritual growth, to equip the community of the saints in conformity with God's Word.[181]

During his tour, Yotham found that not all the local communities fully

179. Van Dijk, "Sadrach's Kring," p. 323.
180. Ibid.
181. Ibid., p. 380.

agreed with his idea. He often ran into strong opposition, sharp criticism, and even accusations. While these members still trusted Yotham as an apostle and recognized his leadership, they strongly rejected his intention of incorporation, regardless of the sincere motives lying behind it. When Yotham pointed out the advantages of education for their children in mission schools, health care from the mission hospitals, etc., they simply stated without argument that they did not need all those things. Their desire was to remain as they were and defend their freedom. Incorporation with the ZGKN meant giving up their freedom. They stood firm, challenging Yotham with the "ultimatum" of electing a new apostle if he incorporated.[182] Yotham was placed under severe psychological pressure. He was hurt by the accusation that he was selling Javanese souls to the ZGKN, as the following plea implies: "Father, you should not leave us, and not join the *Zending*. The *Apostolische Kerk* is the best place for us. Father, you must not sell our souls."[183]

There were, however, also local communities which fully supported Yotham. The local communities in Wanasaba and in the territory of the *Salatiga-Zending* (the northern parts of Central Java) supported Yotham, whereas the southern parts were under the influence of the opposition party lead by a certain Citrawirya. The reason behind this split between north and south was traced by Van Dijk back to the conflict between Sadrach and the NGZV. Although many of those who had directly experienced those events had reached an advanced age and others had already died, feelings of resentment and memories of the trauma were still alive among them. Since Sadrach had lived in Karangjasa, in the south, his personal relationship with and influence upon the life of the local communities in the south were far more intense than in the north. It is understandable, then, that the south rejected Yotham's decision. In contrast, the north had a less intense personal relationship with Sadrach and were not directly influenced by his conflict with the NGZV.[184]

The new mission policy, post-1913, of the ZGKN, which involved erecting schools and hospitals inside the "territory" of Sadrach's community may have contributed to the widening gap between the community and the ZGKN. Prejudice and resentment against the missionaries may have been built up as a result of these projects. In addition, at the end of Sadrach's life, when he was not able to make many pastoral calls due to his age, some members of the community "crossed over" to the ZGKN, though such action was prohibited by the leaders of the community.

182. Ibid., p. 326.
183. Van Dijk, "Sadrach's Kring," pp. 27-28.
184. Ibid., pp. 23-24.

According to Ingwersen, those who ignored the prohibition were fined 1.25 guilders as a form of compensation for the education in Christian *ngelmu* they had received from Sadrach and other *imams* (priests, i.e., leaders in the community).[185]

Through its new mission policy, the ZGKN became a modern, professionally managed enterprise. Mission schools and hospitals offered a better quality of life. Better education was a passport to enter the new age, an age of modernity and progress. Schools were becoming the only means by which people could gain the necessary tools to compete in such an age.[186] The indigenous Javanese in general welcomed this promising opportunity. It was possible for them to work in the hospitals and schools if they had enough education. If not, they could at least become a missionary helper (*hulpzendeling, guru Injil*) — a crucial position socially and culturally, which helped to bridge the gap between the missionaries and the Javanese.[187]

It was impossible to try to compete with the ZGKN in terms of funds, equipment, and skills. Sadrach's community would certainly be left far behind in such a competition. The community felt the presence of the ZGKN as a threat to its existence. There was something powerful, however, in the community which prevented its members from flocking to the ZGKN. What that "something" was is difficult to identify. Ingwersen speculated that it was the living promise of a future just and prosperous society where people would be free from compulsory service to the government, from the burden of taxes, from foreign influence — a society in which land would be distributed evenly among all people. These and

---

185. Ingwersen, p. 332.
186. Statistical data of mission schools and hospitals in South Central Java;

    a. schools (1925) — with Javanese language instruction-44, 3,256 pupils;
    schools (1938) — with Dutch language instruction-23, 4,430 pupils.
    b. hospitals (1938) — hospitals-9; *hulphospitals*-19; *polyclinics*-53; sanatorium-1; Dutch physicians-22; Javanese-4; Chinese-2; Dutch nurses-29; Javanese male nurses-179; Javanese female nurses-81; others-739.

Wolterbeek, pp. 320, 392.
187. In 1938 there were 126 helpers. See L. Adriaanse, *De Zendingsarbeid onser Gereformeerde Kerken onder de Javanen en Chinesen op oud den Java* (Zeist, 1940), p. 114. Indigenous helpers were regarded as necessary, and one missionary might employ ten to fifteen helpers. See "Methodologische Gedachten," *De Macedoniër* 2 (1884), p. 201-202; "De wijze van werken op Java," *De Macedoniër* 2 (1884), p. 264. They were as "oogen, ooren, handen van de zendeling" (eyes, ears, and hands of the missionary); see D. Crommelin, "De Inlandsche voorganger in de Oost Java-Zending," *Stemmen voor Waarheid en Vrede* (1913), p. 980.

other optimistic promises were still circulating throughout Sadrach's community.[188]

The promising schools and hospitals of the ZGKN were not enough to attract all the members of Sadrach's community, as was evident in Yotham's report. Yotham completed his tour within two months. He submitted his report at the great meeting in Karangjasa, on July 24, 1933, at which Bergema, Keuchenius, and Van Dijk were present as representatives of the ZGKN. The report listed the various attitudes found in the local communities:

1) local communities which definitely accepted the idea of incorporation — 31;
2) local communities which had not yet made any decision and asked for more time to consider the proposal;
3) local communities which definitely rejected the idea of incorporation — more than 40, about half of the total number;
4) local communities which were inclined to be "neutral."[189]

This, however, was not the final count. Some of the communities which had not yet made a decision were expected to join those who accepted the proposal.

Many factors, of course, influenced the process of decision-making, not the least of which was Yotham's leadership. He was not a person who was able to impose his own will upon the local communities. He could not persuade them in order to get full support. However, Yotham did not totally fail. Thirty-one local communities was not a small number. Had Yotham made this decision soon after the death of Sadrach, the result would have most likely been different and more disappointing to him. During his eight years in office he had paved the way to incorporation with the ZGKN with significant results. His goal, however, of bringing all the communities together as a united whole, had not been achieved. Yotham needed to approach the local communities which stood in opposition to his intention once again.

c.   The unavoidable division

Already prior to Sadrach's death the community was apparently threatened by divisiveness — a challenge Yotham faced from the very beginning of his leadership. Sadrach was probably aware of the growing tension and the

188. Ingwersen, p. 331. Regarding the characterization of religious movements of the nineteenth century, see Chapter I section A.
189. Van Dijk, "Sadrach's Kring," p. 56-57.

threat of the disintegration of the community after his death. Therefore, shortly before he died, he appointed Yotham as acting successor and made *sapus* as the symbol of unity — the unity he expected to be maintained.

Nevertheless, when Sadrach's death became imminent, several ambitious individuals began vying for position in the community. These individuals, of course, did not have the courage to oppose Sadrach's choice of Yotham as acting successor while Sadrach was still living. They waited for an appropriate time to make their move. They quietly gained a number of followers, especially among those who were dissatisfied with Yotham's leadership. After Sadrach's death the anticipated division manifested itself publicly with the appearance of two dissident figures, each of whom eventually led a portion of the community.

One of the figures was Raden Ngabehi Wijayasastra from Kranon, a village not far from Karangjasa. As early as one year after Sadrach's death he prepared to challenge Yotham's leadership.[190] In his opinion, Yotham was not the right man to succeed Sadrach, so he refused to recognize Yotham's leadership. Wijayasastra was a respected, well-educated man, formerly a station chief, but retired at the time. He was an aristocrat, having earned the high Javanese title of *Raden Ngabehi*. He and a few other unsatisfied individuals established a new group separate from Sadrach's community, in the year 1930.[191] Several community members from Purwareja, Kebumen, and Yogyakarta followed him. They called themselves the *Pasamuwan Kristen Jawi Netral* (the Neutral Javanese Christian Church), an independent group belonging neither to Sadrach's community nor to the ZGKN. Since Wijayasastra was not ordained, it is difficult to imagine how he organized his "church," especially with respect to administering the sacraments and exercising church discipline. Their organization was of the independent congregationalist sort, and they were introverted and seclusive in character. Later on, Wijayasastra considered the possibility of uniting with the ZGKN. In late 1934, several groups in Kebumen united with the ZGKN, followed by the groups in Purwasari, Palihan, Selong, and Kranon.[192]

The second primary leader to emerge was Kefas Citrawirya. Not much is known about his background, except that he was a farmer and could hardly read or write. He was an elder of the local community in Karangjasa where Yotham lived. He knew both Sadrach and Yotham personally. He had the high ambition of becoming an apostle himself, and since he probably knew about Yotham's plan for incorporation at a very early

190. Ibid., p. 20.
191. Wolterbeek, p. 346.
192. *Uit Purworedjo* No. 7 (1936), pp. 3-4; cf. Wolterbeek, p. 346, 361.

stage, he also had the ammunition he needed to achieve his desire. He actively encouraged the people to oppose Yotham, exposing the fact that Yotham would no longer be an apostle when he joined the ZGKN. He went to Magalang to meet Apostle Faasen from Cimahi, who at that time was visiting Liem Cu Kim there. Citrawirya sought support from Faasen and discussed the possibility of becoming an apostle, but nothing further was done. In fact, Citrawirya gained wide support among community members. His campaign to preserve Sadrach's community as it was was successful. Since his candidacy as the new apostle was not yet secured, he was reluctant to nominate himself publicly. Because he was less educated than Wijayasastra, his opponent, many people expected the latter to become the new apostle. Wijayasastra, however, was unwilling to accept the office.[193] Finally, after Yotham joined the ZGKN, Citrawirya was recognized as the apostle of the Javanese Christian community, and thereby inherited the tradition of Sadrach's leadership.

A third figure to emerge was Kramamiharja, however, because he did not have a significant number of followers, he failed in his attempt to oppose Citrawirya in 1934.

To summarize, Sadrach's community, the largest "church" in Central Java during Sadrach's lifetime, ended in an unavoidable division ten years after the death of its founder. Three communities resulted from the division. The community under Yotham united with the ZGKN in 1933. While thirty-one out of the eighty-six local communities initially moved with him, gradually the number increased until half of the total number of communities joined.[194] Obviously, this, segment of the community developed along the lines of the ZGKN mission policy. The community under Citrawirya remained in the *Apostolische Kerk*. This was initially the largest segment, but later decreased in number.[195] The *Pasamuwan Kristen Jawi Netral*, led by Wijayasastra, was the smallest group. This segment was similar to that of Citrawirya but without the office of apostle. In addition to these three main groups, a small number of members later united with the Roman Catholic Church.[196]

193. Van Dijk, "Sadrach's Kring," p. 25.
194. For local communities which united with the *Zending* in 1939, see Appendix III.
195. For local communities under the leadership of Citrawirya in 1939, see Appendix III.
196. Van Dijk, "Sadrach's Kring," p. 88.

Rev. Frans Lion Cachet, the mission inspector with "dubbele kwaliteit"

CHAPTER III

FEATURES OF SADRACH'S COMMUNITY

In this chapter we will describe in more detail the features of Sadrach's community and its unique character as shaped by Javanese culture. Our description will cover three areas: 1) organization, leadership, and membership; 2) worship, preaching, and rituals; and 3) spiritual life and the spirit of independence.

A. Organization, leadership, and membership

In this section we will discuss Sadrach's community as an "institutional church," especially with regard to its organization, leadership, and membership, which were closely intertwined. The rapidly growing membership, scattered through Central Java, needed an organization for both its leadership and general regulations. It will become clear, however, that Sadrach himself, due to his background as *guru ngelmu* and *kyai* intentionally did not concern himself with the institutional aspects of the community to a large extent.[1] His main concern was to spread the new *ngelmu* by teaching those who were interested. The community as such was more mystical in character, emphasizing spirituality more than the institution of the church.[2]

In order to better understand how these aspects gradually took shape, it is helpful to follow the history of the community in chronological sequence for each aspect. This history can be broadly divided into five main periods: during the life of Stevens-Philips, the period following her death, during

---

1. The Javanese *paguron* which emerged around a guru was basically a community of guru or *kyai* and his *murids*. Stress was placed on the idea of brotherhood. The bond between guru and *murid* was marked by a vow of faithfulness and obedience on the part of the *murids*. The community which resulted emphasized loving one another and encouraging solidarity among the members.

2. Cf. the two indigenous Japanese "churches," Mukyokai and Makuya Christianity (basically non-church movements, or churchless churches) which rejected all forms of institutionalized religious expression. See Carlo Caldarolla, *Christianity: the Japanese Way* (Leiden, 1979).

cooperation with Wilhelm, after the break with the NGZV, and the period following the break.

1. Organization

During its formative years under Stevens-Philips, the Javanese Christian community was under the auspices of the *Indische Kerk* in Purwareja. The Javanese members were, however, already independently conducting their own worship services. Beginning as a house church, the community grew outside the formal jurisdiction of the *Indische Kerk* and the mission church. Consequently, it was not patterned after the existing churches, but rather developed its own unique character. The small house church did not yet need much organization. Worship services were held regularly, but with no fixed order. Worship was informal, which encouraged the building of intimate personal relationships. Stevens-Philips was highly respected and became the central figure of the small community. According to Cachet, who saw things from his Western viewpoint, she was affectionately called "tante Pietje" and "grandmother," and some even viewed her as an incarnation of God.[3] In a sense, Stevens-Philips acted as guru and treated the members as *murids* and her "grandchildren." At this stage the community was a "primitive" model of the Javanese *paguron* system with very simple organization and leadership.

This basic model continued in the later development of the community with some adjustments made for its rapid growth. During the 1870's, Sadrach moved to Karangjasa to work semi-independently as *kyai* and Javanese Christian guru, and the community began to grow rapidly.[4] Nevertheless, he continued his relationship with Stevens-Philips, who acted as the "mediator" and "protector" of the community and became a symbol of unity. During this period Sadrach did not yet appear as the sole leader, but rather stood in the shadow of Stevens-Philips' greatness.

Following Stevens-Philips' death, the existing organizational model developed further. The number of converts increased and new communities were formed in several places. Because Sadrach was not able to directly handle the problems of each local community, he appointed local leaders to represent him. These were primarily chosen from among the first Christian generation converted by Sadrach, and were usually well advanced in years. They were called *sesepuh* (elder), *guru igama* (religious teacher), or *imam* (priest, *voorganger*), titles which were commonly used in the Javanese Moslem community. Their tasks dealt not only with spiritual

3. Cachet, *Een Jaar*, pp. 274-275.
4. Cf. the educational and spiritual background of Sadrach in Chapter II, section B.

matters, such as conducting religious ceremonies, but with all other needs of the community as well. They also represented the local comunities in public.[5] Each community had its own imam. When a community was without an imam it was Sadrach's responsibility to assign one from another local community or to appoint someone from within to become its imam.[6] Imam was an honorary office with no salary.

Each community was independent inasmuch as they had their own imam who was the leader who looked after the life of the local community. In addition to the imam, the local community also had a *carik* who was responsible for administrative matters. The independence of the local community did not, however, lead to disunity within the larger community. They were broadly united into one "big family" which transcended geographical boundaries. This was a significant achievement in light of the fact that, in the nineteenth century, poor transportation isolated Javanese villages almost completely. Many communities were located in the highlands and could be reached only by horse or on foot. Rivers were also a great natural hindrance to communication, especially during the rainy season. How these diverse local communities maintained their unity under such rural conditions is best explained by the following considerations.

Firstly, the Javanese *guru-murid* relationship, a prevalent characteristic of the community, was a significant uniting factor. Sadrach was known as a guru of a certain *ngelmu*, and like other gurus who formed groups of *murids*, this *ngelmu* spiritually united them. In fact, many outsiders viewed Sadrach's community as an ordinary *paguron*. Sadrach's *murids* were not seen as Christian converts who had established a unique and exclusive community similar to a mission church, but rather were considered indistinguishable from other Javanese communities.

In its early phase, Sadrach's community could be compared to the New Testament Christian community which initially was regarded as merely a new Jewish sect. Resident Ligtvoet once stated that Sadrach's community was a new sect of Christianity heavily influenced by Islam and comparable to a Moslem Javanese community.[7] The Moslems, on the other hand, regarded it as a new sect of Islam with a Christian color. This might account for Heyting's statement that Sadrach's community was greatly tolerated by the Moslems.[8] Furthermore, Adriaanse described Sadrach's community as being built upon the Javanese extended family system,

5. Heyting, p. 21.
6. Ibid.; Adriaanse, *Sadrach's Kring*, p. 80.
7. Ligtvoet, Report, March 27, 1882.
8. Heyting, p. 38.

emphasizing emotional and personal relationships.[9]

Like a Javanese guru, Sadrach became the uniting figure of his community. Solidarity and unity were built upon the awareness of having received the same *ngelmu* from the same guru (Javanese expression: "nunggal guru lan ngelmu"). In this connection, Heyting stated that the community was united as one body with Sadrach as its head.[10] His followers called him the "great shepherd" and "priestly teacher." Sadrach's position in such a relationship became a strong factor in maintaining the unity of the community.

Secondly, Sadrach's authority to appoint the local imams contributed much toward maintaining unity. In rural Javanese society, the founder and leader of the village usually had great power, and accordingly, special privileges. As founder of the community, Sadrach exercised his right to appoint the imams with caution. He took at least two things into consideration:

1) His personal relation with whomever he appointed. Because Sadrach knew his first converts the best, he was assured of their loyalty to him, and thus chose the local leaders from among them. Therefore, he knew that they would function as an extension of his own leadership.
2) The credibility of the candidate. Because the communities were small, the members were well-known to each other. Credibility was fairly easy to determine. Although community leaders were not formally elected, the wishes of the community were not difficult to ascertain. As a result, appointment by Sadrach simply "formalized" the will of the community.

Heyting reported that the imam was not necessarily a man from the local community.[11] This, however, happened only if the local community had no candidate. When the post was vacant, an imam from a neighboring community was assigned to take care of the community. This demonstrated the close connection between all local communities and simultaneously facilitated the maintenance of unity.

Thirdly, the regular meetings of elders and the annual meeting held in Karangjasa became substantial factors in maintaining unity. Since Karangjasa, where Sadrach lived, became the center of Javanese Christianity, these regular meetings greatly contributed to a feeling of unity and solidarity among the members. Elders from the local communities

9. Adriaanse, *Sadrach's King*, p. 91. Sadrach called his followers his "kinderen en klein-kinderen."
10. Heyting, p. 21.
11. Ibid.

attended the meetings which were informal and personal in character
—like those between gurus (local imams) and their upper guru (Sadrach).
The elders reported all the problems faced by the local communities, such
as relationships with the local authorities, the growth of the community,
building new churches, proposing candidates for imam, etc. In short, all
things dealing with the life of the community as a whole were discussed and
the problems tackled.[12] From these meetings the elders gained new insight
into the Christian community's life and a broader vision of what Christian
community meant. Geographical isolation was no longer a hindrance to
solidarity and unity. These regular meetings also provided solid evidence
that Sadrach was not only leader of the local community in Karangjasa,
with limited authority, but was recognized by all representatives as leader
of the whole community.

Later on these meetings gradually gained a place in the heart of the
community as the concrete expression of its unity. The annual great
gathering, called *kumpulan gedhe*, was not only attended by elders, but also
by other members who flocked to Karangjasa. Heyting compared
Karangjasa to Roman Catholic shrines, which attracted many pilgrims.[13]
A dimension of festivity was added to the extended meeting — the festival
of faith. Javanese Christians came to Karangjasa from all over, bringing
their own food for the three day festival. The program for all members
involved a worship service led by Sadrach followed by a common meal
eaten while sitting cross-legged on the floor. This was reminiscent of the
traditional Javanese *slametan*, the religious thanksgiving meal.

Fourthly, the unity of the community was maintained through the
teamwork of Sadrach's deputies. Sadrach did not want to work alone. He
was not a solitary fighter. He chose three men as his assistants, entrusting
them with certain responsibilities. Heyting mentioned three assistants:
Yohanes Kramawijaya, Markus Bangsareja, and Musa Wirawijaya,[14]
while Adriaanse mentioned only Markus and Yohanes.[15] Yohanes,
according to Heyting, acted as vice-imam, leading the community during
the time Sadrach was imprisoned. He was highly respected. Musa
functioned as *carik* for the community. All three men had a *ngelmu*
background and were converted by Sadrach. Yohanes had been a pupil of
the famous guru, Kasanmetaram. Markus, Yohanes's brother, had been a
follower of guru Wira Mohamad.[16] Yohanes and Markus were very often

12. Ibid., p. 22; Adriaanse, *Sadrach's Kring*, p. 79.
13. Heyting, p. 23.
14. Ibid., p. 21.
15. Adriaanse, *Sadrach's Kring*, p. 357.
16. Ibid., pp. 61-62.

mentioned in Wilhelm's diary because they worked closely with Wilhelm. They were among the twenty elders who approved Wilhelm's call as minister of the community.[17] Markus and Musa were evangelists, while Yohanes acted as the chairman of the elders in Karangjasa. Wilhelm noted that the three men were also members of the synod which consisted of seven people, and that Musa was its secretary.[18] In the official Almanac of 1891, all three were listed among the ten religious teachers. Yohanes and Markus were religious teachers from Karangjasa, and Musa from Karangtalun.[19]

It is clear from the above that the position of deputy was very important, recognized not only by the local community but by all the communities. Since they had worked with Sadrach from the very beginning, their leadership was widely accepted. Both individually and together they made many pastoral visits and did evangelism work. According to Heyting, their tasks as deputies were to encourage the followers to love their newly found faith, explain Sadrach's position on certain difficult matters, evangelize, assign mission territory, take care of the community's needs, look for candidates for local leader, and execute all decisions made in the elders meetings in Karangjasa.[20]

The local communities supported and benefited from such a system. Through the deputies, the members became better informed than they could from their local elders. Good communication was maintained between the local and "supra-local," periphery and center, through the elders and the deputies. A balance was maintained between the common interests of the community as a whole and the local communities. Each community, therefore, supported and at the same time benefited from the system.

The original structure of Sadrach's community can be summarized as follows:

1) The organization of the community grew up and developed along the lines of Javanese culture. Its structure was very simple — comparable to the *paguron* or traditional *pesantren* system. Personal and emotional relationships were emphasized, thereby focusing on the spiritual rather than the institutional aspects of church life. The community was fashioned after the familial model.

17. Wilhelm, 1883, p. 27.
18. Wilhelm, 1887, p. 394.
19. "Serat penanggalan ing taun agami Kristen 1891 kangge ing para golonganing tiyang Kristen ing tanah Jawi Tengahan," Almanac of 1891 (Archives of the Dutch Reformed Missionary Society, Leusden), p. 37.
20. Heyting, p. 22; cf. Adriaanse, *Sadrach's Kring*, p. 79.

2) The rising needs of the ever-growing membership demanded organization. As a result, assistants were appointed on the local level as imams. At the supra-local level three deputies were appointed, whose authority was accepted by all local communities.

3) The regular meetings were attended by all local leaders and any other members who chose to attend. These meetings also functioned to unite the community. Unity was maintained by the *guru-murid* relationship model, Sadrach's authority to appoint the local imams, the regular meetings in Karangjasa, and the teamwork of Sadrach's three deputies.

The involvement of Wilhelm in Sadrach's community brought significant changes to its organization. With his remarkable patience, Wilhelm gradually introduced Reformed church organization to the community. He never imposed his ideas nor made radical changes. His expectations were realistic, unlike his colleagues who expected Sadrach's community to become, in a short time, a Reformed church in Central Java. It was not surprising, therefore, that Wilhelm's involvement was viewed by many as meaningless, as evidenced in the tragic broken relationship between Sadrach's community and the NGZV. Wilhelm's unique characteristic was his deep concern and tolerance that made many of his colleagues, both in Central Java and in the Netherlands, impatient. In the next section we will examine how Wilhelm began to bring Sadrach's community into what the missionaries considered the "true church."

After Wilhelm became the minister of the community, the meetings in Karangjasa continued. Wilhelm regularly attended them in an effort to gain an indepth knowledge of the situation of the community. He also made several visits to local communities — *zendingsreis* (mission tour) as he called them.[21] During 1883, his first year as minister, he made two mission tours, thereby building more intimate relationships with members and increasing his knowledge of the local communities.

In his second year, he began a program of renewal. First, he formulated a confession (*belijdenis*) uniquely for the community. The final product consisted of five headings giving a basic understanding of the church, of the worldly government, and of the Christian attitude towards the government. The primary goal of the confession was to give guidelines to members who faced mistreatment at the hands of the local authorities because they were members of a Christian community.[22] According to the

---

21. Wilhelm, 1883, p. 38.
22. Wilhelm, 1883, pp. 35-36. The short confession consisted of five articles:

  a. We believe that Jesus Christ is our only master and head, that He caused His will

confession, the church is essentially a community of believers in which Christ Himself exercises His power and authority to govern His people as the head of His church. Therefore, earthly authorities, while deriving their authority from God, have no right to control His church. There is no obedience higher than obedience to God. Obedience to the government, therefore, was to be viewed in light of one's obedience to God.

Secondly, Wilhelm set up local and general church councils. Meeting with Sadrach and his deputy evangelists, Markus and Musa, from April 28 to May 1, 1884, in Purwareja, Wilhelm made the following suggestions for church organization which were subsequently adopted by the leaders:

1) Each community shall have its own council composed of its elected elders. One elder shall be elected as chairman responsible for meetings, worship, etc.

2) Each community and its council shall be placed under the guidance of the general council whose members are:

J. Wilhelm	minister
Sadrach Surapranata	evangelist
Marukus Bangsareja	evangelist
Musa Wirawijaya	evangelist
Yohanes Kramawijaya	elder
Ibrahim Admawijaya	elder[23]

Compared with the previous traditional organization this was not really new. Formalizing what already existed, however, was crucial as far as the institutional character of the church was concerned. The decision gave a "democratic" character to the existing organization. The council (*kerke-*

and doctrine to be written in the Bible, that every Christian congregation stands directly under His leading and, therefore, must remain free from every worldly constraint (Mat. 23:8, 10; Acts 20:28; Eph. 1:22, 23; Col. 1:18; 2:10).

b. We believe that all worldly governments are from God (Rom. 13:1-7).

c. We believe that worldly governments may not rule in the Christian congregation (John 18:36; Col. 1:13; Rev. 15:3).

d. We are completely prepared to honor and obey the Dutch Indies government in all things which do not concern our conscience our belief or religion, which do not bind or coerce our conscience, yes, in everything which is not contrary to God's Word.

e. We desire a teacher who is not dependent on the government nor on the Protestant Churches in the Dutch Indies but one who is in agreement with the will of the Lord (Mat. 20:18-20; Acts 20:28; I Cor. 12:28; II Cor. 3:5, 6).

23. Wilhelm, 1884, p. 49.

raad) took the place of the local community board, which had consisted of imam, vice-imam, and secretary. The difference lay in the fact that members of the *kerkeraad* were formally elected and its membership was open to more than three people. The general council filled the role that Sadrach and his three deputies had previously filled.

In addition to pastoral work and evangelization, there was a growing awareness that the needs of the poor should also be a responsibility of the community. To that end, in the meeting of June 30 to July 2, 1884, in Karangjasa, it was decided that every community should set up a rice barn (*lumbung miskin*) and raise money by placing a basket in the church.[24] It is not clear who managed this special task. Responsibility may have been added to the elders' task or given to an appointed individual. Wilhelm's diary gives no indication as to whom the task was assigned. Three years later, however, in his diary entry of August 20, 1887, the office of deacon was mentioned.[25] Until the office of deacon was established, it is likely that one of the council members was placed in charge of caring for the needs of the poor. In 1887, the office of deacon was added and the deaconate became an inseparable part of the community. Institutionally, then, Sadrach's community was equipped with the two offices of elder and deacon in addition to the teaching elder or minister in accordance with Reformed church organization.

Thirdly, Wilhelm established regional presbyteries or classes based on the geographical groupings of the community. This very important decision was made in the meeting of December 12 and 13, 1887.[26] Regional groupings were necessary due to the extension of the mission area into some residencies in Central Java, including the courts of Yogyakarta and Surakarta.[27] Seven classes consisting of forty local communities were established.[28]

24. Wilhelm, 1884, p. 52.

25. This is the first time Wilhelm noted the appointment of both elder and deacon. This occurred in the local community of Selong, Yogyakarta. Wilhelm, 1887, pp. 393-394.

26. Ibid., pp. 426-429.

27. In 1888 there were nine communities in the sultanate of Yogyakarta, with 1,013 members. Families numbered 230, living in 188 houses spread throughout sixty-one villages. These nine communities had fifty-five elders; see Wilhelm, 1888, p. 20. These numbers indicate tremendous growth because it had been only one year before that the communities in Yogyakarta had had their chairman, secretary, and preacher recognized by the Resident; see Decision n. 1548/TB, November 30, 1887 (National Archives Office, Jakarta). Javanese noble Josef Natataruna was chairman, Harjasentana was secretary, and Wilhelm was preacher; see Wilhelm, 1887, p. 430.

28. Names of the communities in each classis:

Yogyakarta: Selong, Yogyakarta, Kebonagung, and Prangkokan

After 1887, regional classis meetings were attended by representatives of the local communities in the region, representatives of other classes, and synodical representatives. These classis meetings were held in addition to and eventually replaced the regular elders meetings which were held every thirty-five days in Karangjasa.

Wilhelm took an active part in the elders meetings by leading the opening service and preaching before the gathering.[29] He also took part in the preparation and organization of the meetings. During 1886, the number of regular elders meetings was reduced to six. One great gathering, celebrating the day of Pentecost, was also held, combined with a thanksgiving festival celebrating the renovation of the church building in Karangjasa. This great gathering was also called the mission festival (*zendingsfeest*).[30] During 1887, six elders meetings were held and the second mission festival was celebrated, again over Pentecost, on May 28-30.[31] In 1888, five elders meetings were held and one great gathering on October 20-23.[32] In 1889, only one meeting was recorded, held on October 11 and 12, called the *kumpulan gedhe*.[33] Since Wilhelm's diary ended in

Purwareja: Purwareja Jelok, Bulu, Slewah, Benca, and Sapuran
Karangjasa: Karangjasa, Awu-awu, Banjur, Pagedangan, Pamrihan, Kedungdawa, and Jatisari
Kedungpring: Kedungpring, Karangpring, Karangpucung, Sampang, Pondok, and Kedungwaru
Purbalingga: Purbalingga, Grujugan, Bojong, Panusupan, Karangjengis, Muara-tua-Tegal, and Pangantulan
Bendawuluh: Bendawuluh, Pungangan, Telagaabang, and Gajahmungkur
Derma: Derma, Purba, Ciluluk, Prata, Jambangan (Gunungsari), Bandar-Kajen, and Gintung; Wilhelm, 1887, pp. 428-429.

29. Wilhelm, 1885, p. 115.
30. This great festival took place on June 12, 1886. It was attended by 345 people from thirty-one communities. One cow and six sheep were slain. Wilhelm preached from Exodus 20:24, "In every place where I cause my name to be remembered I will come to you and bless you." Vermeer was also present. See Wilhelm, 1886, pp. 218, 220.
31. Attended by 474 people. Wilhelm preached twice, on Matt. 19:4-6 and II Cor. 3:17-18. During the service five people were baptized, one of which was Josef Natataruna. See Wilhelm, 1887, pp. 348-351.
32. Attended by 408 people from fifty-three communities, including 142 elders. Missionaries Penninga and Stegerhoek from the DZV in Salatiga, and Zuidema and Vermeer from the NGZV were also present. Community statistics at the time were: 5,025 members, fifty-three communities, two hundred elders, 285 villages. Wilhelm preached on Matt. 6:13 for the opening service. See Wilhelm, 1888, p. 17, 20.
33. Attended by 204 people from sixty communities. Vermeer, Zuidema, and Wilhelm from the NGZV, Jungt and Kamp from the DZV in Salatiga, and L.S. De Bruyn, minister of the *Indische Kerk* in Purwareja were present. Wilhelm preached on Phil. 2:1-15 for the opening service. The Lord's Supper was served at the meeting. See Wilhelm, 1889, p. 87, 89.

August, 1890, no further data is available.

From these records we can draw the following conclusions:

1) One of the meetings held by the community each year in Karangjasa was considered very special. It was called *kumpulan gedhe* and it can be compared to an annual synod meeting. Based on Wilhelm's diary, this meeting had been held since 1886. At the first gathering, thirty-one local communities were represented. In 1887, thirty-three communities were represented, in 1888, fifty-three communities, and in 1889, sixty communities.[34] The fifth meeting was not recorded by Wilhelm, but Adriaanse noted that fifty-five local communities were represented. The sixth, in 1891, was attended by representatives of seventy-two communities.[35]

2) The grouping of local communities into classes in 1887 meant that clasis meetings were held in each region on fixed Javanese days.[36] Therefore, the frequency of the general elders meetings in Karangjasa was reduced and eventually replaced altogether by the classis meetings.

3) Wilhelm's efforts to organize Sadrach's community as a regular institutional church was successful in many respects. The center of authority had been shifted from Karangjasa to the regional and local communities. These classical and local meetings point to a structure of church organization that came closer to Reformed church structure. The authority of each local community was stressed rather than the strong center in Karangjasa. Adriaanse claimed that Wilhelm had successfully altered the structure away from centralization and toward decentralization, a structure much nearer to Reformed principles.[37]

---

34. Ibid., p. 88.
35. Adriaanse, *Sadrach's Kring*, p. 269; Almanac of 1891, p. 67.
36. Almanac of 1891, p. 30. The Javanese calendar has only five days (*sepasar*), namely, Paing, Pon, Wage, Kliwon, Legi. Usually these are combined with the international system, Sunday, Monday, etc., so one ends up with Sunday-Paing, Monday-Pon, etc. Each combination reoccurs in thirty-five days (*selapan*). According to Javanese belief, certain days are considered best for certain kinds of work and for bringing good fortune. The fixed Javanese days used for classes meetings as stated in the Almanac were:

Bagelen	Rebo Wage	(Wage Wednesday)
Banyumas	Rebo Pon	(Pon Wednesday)
Yogyakarta	Selasa Wage	(Wage Thursday)
Kedu	Rebo Pon	(Pon Wednesday)
Pekalongan	Kemis Legi	(Legi Thursday)
Tegal	Kemis Legi	(Legi Thursday)

37. Adriaanse, *Sadrach's Kring*, p. 355.

Pol, therefore, could consider Sadrach's community a Reformed church in Java.[38]

There is no doubt that Wilhelm introduced new elements in terms of church organization. Administrative reforms also took place. Each community was given its own register book to manage community life as much as possible act the local level. This type of organization was new and alien to the rural Javanese population who were accustomed to a system where authority and power were concentrated in the hands of the leader. As a result, the introduction of the new system of organization did not reduce Sadrach's position. He remained as guru and *kyai* for the Javanese Christians. This became clear when the relation between the community and the NGZV was broken. The community quickly resumed its old organization in keeping with Javanese tradition. The incorporation into the *Apostolische Kerk* allowed the old system to remain intact with Sadrach acting as apostle. The role of Sadrach as the "central" figure did not diminish.

2. Leadership

During her lifetime, Stevens-Philips was the central figure in the community. Soon after her death, however, Sadrach emerged as the sole leader, taking responsibility for the whole community. As we have seen, he then entrusted certain responsibilities to his three deputies. They, together with Sadrach, became the "Central Board" of the community. They were the policymakers and had the right to make all final decisions. On the local level, the imam was the sole leader, assisted by the *carik* and sometimes by the vice-imam.

The community was characterized by the Javanese *guru-murid* relationship model. Such a relationship is not to be compared with oppressor and oppressed; rather, an imam was basically independent, having authority over his local community. Only his guru was considered superior to him. Wilhelm compared the position and role of the imam with that of the bishop in the early church. He compared the structure of Sadrach's community to the episcopalian system where one bishop is recognized as superior.[39]

This Javanese "episcopalian" model was based on the Javanese extended family system, a system where the father, as leader of the family,

38. Pol, *Midden Java*, p. 152.
39. Wilhelm, 1886, pp. 282-283.

plays the dominant role. His words, therefore, are to be obeyed, but the other family members still have the freedom to express their opinions and make suggestions. On the other side, the leader gives room for the various opinions of the "children." He hears suggestions with patience and wisdom. His attitude is one of tolerance and his approach is persuasive (*momong*) and accomodative (*momot*). This is the original traditional Javanese leadership model.

One may well ask how Wilhelm fit into this leadership model, and how the community dealt with two leaders from different backgrounds and different styles of leadership. For this purpose three sources are available which represent different perceptions. The first, Wilhelm's diary, of course represents his perception. The second, the report of a Controllor in Karangkobar, written on May 31, 1883, is based on interviews with some of the local community leaders, and therefore represents the viewpoint of an ordinary member.[40] The third, the Almanac of 1891, basically supports Wilhelm's view.

When the *algemeene kerkeraad* (general synod) was formed in April, 1884, Sadrach ranked second after Wilhelm on the list of its seven members. This did not mean, however, that Sadrach lost his position as community leader. According to the list, he is named as one of the Javanese evangelists with the status of "helper" like the other evangelists. Sadrach accepted this position without question. According to Guillot, there are two reasons why Sadrach agreed to this. Firstly, Sadrach agreed to cooperate with the missionaries on the condition that they would not dismiss him from his position as *kyai*. Sadrach, of course, understood Wilhelm to have no such ill intentions. Secondly, Sadrach's followers wanted cooperation with Wilhelm. To refuse meant the threat of losing many followers. Therefore, according to Guillot, Sadrach preferred to work with Wilhelm who continued to acknowledge him as guru.[41]

It is our opinion that Sadrach was unconcerned about his formal position. Debating one's formal position is the business of those who are familiar with more complex organizational systems in which specialization occurs. As a Javanese *kyai* and guru whose credibility, power, and authority did not depend on his formal position as defined on paper, Sadrach did not pay much attention to such formalization. His position as *kyai* and guru was not the result of an election or by a letter of decision or appointment, but rather was achieved through the gradual informal recognition granted him by his followers. The position of *kyai* and guru did not require formal recognition even from the government. From this point

---

40. Heyting, Appendix F.
41. Guillot, *L'Affaire Sadrach*, p. 239; *Kiai Sadrach*, p. 140.

of view, it is understandable that Sadrach accepted the position which was given to him. The "sophisticated" church organization introduced by Wilhelm was not threatening or restrictive to his authority as *kyai* and guru.

Wilhelm, too, noted in his diary that Sadrach was listed second after him among the seven members of the "Synod of the Javanese Christian Church" held in Central Java in 1887. Wilhelm was listed first as teacher, and the rest were all elders: Sadrach Surapranata, Yohanes Kramawijaya, Markus Bangsareja, Ibrahim Admawijaya, Timotius Sitimurti, and Musa Wirawijaya, who was the *carik*.[42] In other words, on paper Sadrach's formal position was merely that of a helper to the Western missionaries.

The second source, however, gives quite a different picture of Sadrach's position. This view indicates Sadrach's position and leadership in practice rather than on paper. I.G. De Wolff Van Westerrode, the Controller in Karangkobar, Banyumas, wrote his report about Sadrach's community in the following villages: Batur, Pekasiran, Karang Tengah, Grogol, Aribaya (all in the District of Batur), Penanggungan, Kubang, Bantar, Pager Gunung, Pandansaren, Sibebek (District of Karangkobar), Bendawuluh, and Sigelok (District of Banjar). The report consisted of seven pages depicting the perception of Sadrach's community, at least in these regions. Of special interest is the section dealing with the members' attitude towards Sadrach's authority and leadership.[43] Stefanus Suradikrama (Panus), who was the *carik* and vice-imam of his community, represented his fellow Christians in an interview with the Controller. He stated that Sadrach was the main shepherd (*opperherder*) of the community and Wilhelm was the second, under Sadrach. Wilhelm was Sadrach's helper in the areas of biblical exegesis and administration. If they had a difference of opinion, Sadrach was the one they obeyed.[44]

This report, in contrast to the previous view, clearly shows that Sadrach held the highest position. Wilhelm was not "above" but "under" Sadrach. Nevertheless, the community was to obey him as the second shepherd because he had been appointed by Imam Sadrach. The report also spoke of the authority of Wilhelm within the community. He was not able to work effectively unless Sadrach supported him as the minister of the community. The position itself was meaningless without Sadrach's support. Again, it is evident that in the eyes of the people it was not the formal structure but the authority of Sadrach that was significant. Their respect for Wilhelm lay in

42. Wilhelm, 1887, p. 394.
43. Heyting, Appendix F, pp. 5-6.
44. Ibid., p. 6.

the fact that Imam Sadrach "has appointed him, therefore we obey."[45] Although Wilhelm was more educated and better equipped for church leadership, Sadrach's position as *kyai* and guru was not to be underestimated.

Adriaanse also discussed the position of Sadrach and Wilhelm. He claimed that as "his teacher, the founder of the community, Sadrach is higher than Wilhelm, but Wilhelm has something more because he is a Dutch minister."[46] According to Adriaanse, the "something more" that Wilhelm possessed was his ability to act as mediator between the community and the colonial government. Such a role was very important and much easier for a Dutch person to carry out. Because the community often ran into difficulty with the village leaders and other authorities, Wilhelm's specific function as mediator was very advantageous. Wilhelm noted several occasions where such a role was urgently needed.

That Sadrach's words were obeyed rather than the commands of the local authorities is demonstrated in the following event. The local authorities in the District of Batur called a meeting to be held on May 4, 1883. The purpose of this government-sponsored meeting was to investigate the situation of the indigenous Christians in the region, and discuss their incorporation into the *Indische Kerk*. Heyting, from the *Indische Kerk* in Purwareja, would also be present at the meeting. The community members, however, refused to attend. Stefanus Suradikrama considered the meeting meaningless and said that many members did not come because they already had their own church. But the real reason for their refusal was their loyalty to Sadrach as their shepherd whom they should obey. Since the meeting was held without notifying Sadrach first, Stefanus had the right to forbid the members from attending. The prohibition was based on his interpretation of John 10:1-5, which reads,

> Truly, truly, I say to you, he who does not enter the sheepfold by the door but climbs in by another way, that man is a thief and a robber, but he who enters by the door is the shepherd of the sheep, to him gatekeeper opens; the sheep hear his voice, and he calls his own sheep by name and leads them out. When he has brought out all his own, he goes before them, and the sheep follow him, for they know his voice. A stranger they will not follow, but they will flee from him, for they do not know the voice of strangers (RSV).

Stefanus interpreted the relationship between the sheep and shepherd from his Javanese perspective, a relationship comparable to that between *murid* and guru. Stefanus was of the opinion that in matters of religion, community members must be obedient to their spiritual leader, like *murids*

45. Ibid.
46. Adriaanse, *Sadrach's Kring*, p. 165.

to their guru. Had the meeting been previously approved by Sadrach, most members would have attended.

The extent of Sadrach's influence upon his followers can be seen in the following excerpt from the interview.

> Controller: If the elected shepherd is blind and brings the flock to a dangerous place and then falls down into the ravine, will the flock follow?
>
> Stefanus: Yes, the flock will follow him until death.
>
> C: Do you obey all of Sadrach's commands?
>
> S: Yes, we do.
>
> C: If Imam Sadrach asks you to go to Surabaya, do you go then?
>
> S: Certainly.
>
> C: If an official asks you to go somewhere, will you go?
>
> S: Yes, if Imam Sadrach does not forbid us to go. If he forbids, we will not go, but Imam Sadrach gives us freedom to obey the government except in religious matters. Imam Sadrach once said, 'If I prohibit you to do anything, do not do it, but if I do not forbid you, you are free to do it.' And it is clear that Imam Sadrach has forbidden us to take part in religious gatherings led by another shepherd. I will forbid the members to attend such a meeting.[47]

These answers reflect not only Stefanus's opinion, but that of most members. It is clear, therefore, that Javanese leadership remained the model within the community.

A third source of information is the Almanac or calendar of 1891, which was circulated among the community. According to the list in the Almanac, there were four missionaries of the NGZV and ten Javanese evangelists working in Central Java.[48] All missionaries were called

---

47. Heyting, Appendix F, pp. 4-5.
48. Almanac of 1891, pp. 36-37.

The four missionaries were:

bhagawan A. Vermeer	— Purbalingga
bhagawan J. Wilhelm	— Purwareja
bhagawan J.P. Zuidema	— Purwareja
bhagawan R.J. Horstman	— Pekalongan

The ten Javanese evangelists were:

kyai Sadrach Suprapranata	— Karangjasa
mas Yohanes Kramawijaya	— Karangjasa
mas Markus Bangsareja	— Karangjasa
mas Musa Wirawijaya	— Karangjasa

bhagawan, a Javanese title which at that time was still used. The word *bhagawan* referred to a distinguished figure who had perfect *ngelmu* and wisdom whose advice was willingly accepted as good for all. Perhaps it was the Javanese translation of *dominee* (minister), which at present is translated *pandita*. The word *bhagawan* as the title of the missionaries presented the image to the Javanese people that the missionaries were outstanding people who had a higher spiritual position in the community because they possessed a superior *ngelmu* or "theology." Javanese evangelists, on the other hand, were called guru. Although guru was considered a high position, it was lower than *bhagawan*. Sadrach ranked first among other Javanese gurus with the specific title of *kyai*.

Another Javanese word used in the Almanac is *pangirid*, a translation of the Dutch *oudste* or *ouderling* (elder), or perhaps *voorganger* (leader).[49] The word *pangirid* was used for the man who led a group of people in a procession. His main task was to be responsible for the procession, not only to give direction, but also to encourage and motivate the participants during the long and exhausting journey so that each member reached the final goal. The use of this word indicates how the Javanese perceived the position of elder.

As soon as a small Christian community was established, one or more persons were appointed as *pangirid* for the care of the members. One *pangirid* was chosen as *sesirah* (head), and another as *carik*. According to Wilhelm the *sesirahing para pangirid* (head of the *pangirids*) was responsible for conducting worship services.[50]

We can summarize the question of leadership in Sadrach's community as follows:

1. The leadership and organization of Sadrach's community went hand in hand. In the first phase, when the *paguron* system, the traditional Javanese *pesantren*, was the model in Sadrach's community, the leader became central. Distribution of power beyond the leader was virtually unknown. A traditional Javanese leader was regarded as divinely appointed, and his leadership can best be described as single-handed. In

mas Ismael Admawijaya	— Kedungpring
mas Petrus Slamet	— Purbalingga
mas Timoteus Sitimurti	— Purwareja
mas Soleman Harjaminarsa	— Yogyakarta
mas Yokanan Karyabangsa	— Bendawuluh
mas Lion Thomas	— Pekalongan

49. Wilhelm, 1889, p. 63.
50. Wilhelm, 1890, p. 118.

Sadrach's community, such leadership was personified at the "supra-local" level by Sadrach and his three deputies, and at the local level by the imam, vice-imam, and secretary.

2. The Reformed church organization, based on the prebyterian model which was introduced by Wilhelm, naturally revised the system of leadership, at least on paper. The three offices of minister, elder, and deacon gave Sadrach's community shape as an institutional church. Power was distributed through the synod and classes. This structure, however, failed to take root. In reality, Sadrach remained the main authority.

3. The use of the Javanese terms *bhagawan*, guru, and *pangirid* in the Almanac of 1891 may be viewed as an attempt to indigenize the Reformed leadership structure in the initial phase. The translator's purpose in using these terms was to provide a Javanese understanding of Christian leadership.

3. Membership

The foundation of Sadrach's community lay in the rural population. To a certain extent it was similar to other rural religious movements of the nineteenth century and shared in their basic characteristics: a mass movement with a charismatic leader, nativistic, and messianic-millenarian. These characteristics attracted the rural people, and also often evolved into protest movements.[51]

The growth of Sadrach's community can be attributed to several factors. First, various government regulations such as the *Cultuurstelsel* and taxes imposed by the colonial government were an economic burden to the Javanese people, particularly the peasants.[52] In their economically depressed situation, the people usually sought a messianic leader who would bring liberation, justice and freedom. Religious movements provided the means by which to express their hopes by making optimistic, often utopian promises. Proclaiming Jesus Christ as the messianic *ratu adil* seems to have been an attractive element in Sadrach's *ngelmu*. In addition, the emphasis on spirituality and the continuation of Javanese *adat* in the life of the community also contributed to its appeal.

The spontaneous growth of the community was accelerated by debate and the discipling system, the specific method of a *guru ngelmu* in proclaiming the Gospel. Because Sadrach began his mission by christianizing Javanese *guru ngelmu* and their *murids*, the number of converts

---

51. Chapter I, section A.
52. "De Toestand," pp. 77-78 explains twelve different taxes imposed on the people.

quickly increased. Although they were primarily from the peasant class, this does not mean that they were only from poor families. *Kyais* and *guru ngelmu* were a highly respected rural elite group. One can assume that positions of local leadership, especially in the early stages, were filled by the *guru ngelmu* whom Sadrach converted. Because of the spontaneity of this system, even the most isolated mountainous villages could be reached by the Gospel.[53]

The growth of Sadrach's community can be traced through four stages. The period from 1870-1885 was a time spectacular growth. On February 6, 1871, Van Troostenburg De Bruijn of the *Indische Kerk* performed twenty-one baptisms, and another seventy-five at the end of the year. On August 15, 1872, thirty-nine people were baptized, and on October 20 of the same year, 188 more were baptized. In April of 1873, about three hundred ten baptisms were performed. Therefore, within three years already over six hundred thirty people had been baptized.[54] Seven local communities existed in 1873, with two church buildings and a membership of 1,464.[55] Vermeer performed over one thousand baptisms at the request of Stevens-Philips, so that in 1874, membership had increased to about twenty-five hundred with five church buildings in Karangjasa, Banjur, and Jambeyan.[56] Three years later membership had grown to over five thousand people.[57] Members lived in approximately two hundred different villages,[58] spread over the three residencies of Bagelen, Banyumas, and Pekalongan.[59] In 1882, Bieger baptized 1,089 people in Bagelen and five hundred forty in Pekalongan, for a total of 1,629 baptisms.[60]

From 1884 to 1893, membership was still increasing. Data is available from Wilhelm's diary and the missionary magazine, *Heidenbode*. When Wilhelm began his work, Sadrach's community had 3,039 members in twenty-five local communities. Members could be found in 117 villages in the Residency of Bagelen, thirty-four villages in Pekalongan, and sixteen villages in Banyumas.[61] In 1886, there were thirty-one local communities

---

53. Some of these places were visited by Cachet on his investigative tour, namely, Derma, Ciluluk, and Purba, located in the mountainous area of the Residency of Pekalongan; Cachet, *Een Jaar*, pp. 437, 449, 465.

54. Adriaanse, *Sadrach's Kring*, p. 63.

55. "Bagelen," *De Macedoniër* 8 (1890), p. 215.

56. Adriaanse, *Sadrach's Kring*, p. 67.

57. Ibid., p. 93.

58. Heyting, p. 47.

59. Heyting, Appendices A, B, C, D, include detailed statistical data of Sadrach's community and the missionary group; Cf. Appendix III.

60. Heyting, p. 13; Wilhelm, 1883, p. 22.

61. Wilhelm, 1883, pp. 27-28; Adriaanse, *Sadrach's Kring*, p. 163.

and in 1887, about thirty-three spread over the five residencies of Bagelen, Banyumas, Pekalongan, Tegal, and Yogyakarta.[62] In 1888, fifty-five local communities numbered 5,648 members. They were led by two hundred fifty elders and were distributed among 285 different villages. In 1889, Wilhelm recorded sixty local communities, 5,937 members and 371 villages; in 1890, seventy communities, 6,794 members, and 411 villages.[63]

The statistical data recorded by missionaries after 1894 is more sketchy since they had no direct contact with Sadrach's community. The separation from the NGZV, however, seemed to have had no impact on its growth. The community continued to expand to include almost all the residencies of Central Java, with a total of seventy local communities.[64] The two Javanese kingdoms of Yogyakarta and Surakarta had also been reached by the Gospel, and several small communities had already emerged. While a few of the members were from the noble class, the basic rural character of the community did not change.

The fourth period after Sadrach's installation as an apostle was characterized by further growth. Two sources of membership records are available from Sadrach's descendents. The one records annual increases in membership from 1907 to 1929.[65] The second contains more detailed statistical data, including the names of the leader of each local community.[66] From these sources the following data can be obtained:

— the smallest number of baptisms occurred in 1907, with only forty-nine baptisms, and the largest number in 1928, with 787 baptisms.

— the total number of baptisms in the twenty-three year period (1907-1929) was 6,779.

— in 1907, the second source recorded a membership of 2,735, a number drastically reduced from the near seven thousand membership of 1890. This would seem to mean a drastic loss of members in a seventeen-year period.

According to Guillot, the decrease in membership was caused by the fact that Sadrach was already aging and therefore was not able to make the

62. *Heidenbode* (April, 1889), p. 74; "Van ons Zendingsveld in Indië," *Heidenbode* (March, 1891), p. 229.
63. Wilhelm, 1889, p. 87. Data on Sadrach's community in Wilhelm's diary of 1890 is comparable to data found in the Almanac which is more detailed; Almanac of 1891, p. 67; Cf. Appendix III.
64. Adriaanse, *Sadrach's Kring*, p. 356.
65. For annual number of baptisms during the period 1907-1929 as stated in the document from Karangjasa, see Appendix III.
66. For data on Sadrach's community in 1907 with the list of local leaders as stated in the document from Karangjasa, see Appendix III.

adjustments necessary to deal with the changing world.[67] This conclusion, however, is questionable since the other source recorded an average of 208 baptisms each year between 1907 and 1929. In 1924, the year of Sadrach's death, a record high of 512 people were baptized. Adriaanse as well noted that separation from the NGZV had no great effect on Sadrach's community, and, in fact, some communities had even been established in the Kingdom of Surakarta.[68] Van Dijk, who worked in Wanasaba and Kebumen, two areas where many of Sadrach's followers lived, stated that the community consisted of eighty-six local communities several years before Sadrach's death.[69] When Yotham Martareja expressed his desire to incorporate with the ZGKN in 1933, the community consisted of 7,552 members and eighty-six local communities.[70] J.C. Rutgers estimated that Sadrach's community had about twenty thousand members in the year of Sadrach's death.[71]

In light of the above data, it is difficult to believe that Sadrach's community experienced such a drastic loss of members. It is more likely that the data used by Guillot did not include the full membership. This is indicated by the fact that the twenty-eight villages mentioned were located in only the two residencies, of Bagelen and Banyumas. However, in 1891, Sadrach's community had spread into the six residencies of Bagelen, Kedu, Banyumas, Tegal, Pekalongan, and Yogyakarta,[72] joined by the Kingdom of Surakarta in 1898. We can conclude, therefore, that Sadrach never lost a large number of followers. He remained the *kyai* and guru of a large and growing community until his death.

For many years Sadrach was the unchallenged leader of the Javanese church, which showed remarkable growth in the rural environment. Yet, toward the end of his life the community began to decline in certain areas, partly because of missionary policies, but partly because Sadrach was, to a certain extent, unable to answer the questions of those members, especially of the younger generation, who were becoming more and more modernized and westernized as a result of rapid urbanization. The community as a whole, however, continued to flourish. When, after Sadrach's death, he

67. Guillot, *L'Affaire Sadrach*, pp. 281-282, 325; *Kiai* Sadrach, pp. 169-170, 200.

68. Adriaanse, *Sadrach's Kring*, p. 356.

69. Van Dijk, "Sadrach's Kring," p. 266.

70. Ibid., p. 323; the local communities were distributed throughout the residencies as follows: Yogyakarta-20, Surakarta-14, Kebumen-12, Banyumas-9, Magalang-7, Wanasaba-6, Purwareja-4, Pekalongan-12, Semarang-2; cf. Pol, "Sadrach Christenen," p. 347.

71. Jacqueline C. Rutgers, *Islam en Christendom* (The Hague, 1912), p. 239; cf. Van Eijk, p. 39.

72. Almanac of 1891.

was not succeeded by a charismatic leader to hold the community together, the community could no longer resist incorporation into a church that was more "advanced," i.e., adjusted to the modern times.

B. Worship, preaching, and ritual

Sadrach's community had its own style of worship and system of rituals which were closely tied to the existing Javanese tradition. There was no uniform pattern since every local community, under the supervision of the imam, was free to conduct religious ceremonies and services in its own way. There were, however, similarities which we will identify by examining some of the sources available.

1. Worship

a. Church buildings

As has been mentioned, the expansion of Sadrach's community was rapid and spontaneous. In areas where small groups of converts existed, simple churches were built as soon as possible to serve as the center for evangelism and community life. In this way the community was unified. Such a feeling of unity was crucial since they lived amid a great non-Christian majority. This served as one means of developing a basic sense of togetherness and self-confidence in the Christian community.

The church was usually built from material found in the village: the roof from sedge grass and palm leaves, the walls from bamboo, and a floor of hard-packed dirt. The building was very simple and similar to the *langgar* which could be found in every Javanese village. The wealthier communities generally built better buildings, comparable to the *mesjid*, or mosque, in the village. The traditional *mesjid* in the rural areas was a simple structure similar to the common house — an open building with a three-tiered roof and a wide veranda.[73]

The church building was called a *mesjid*, which indicated that they were still integrated into the life and heritage of the Javanese community. In addition to a church bell, they continued to use the drum like that of the *mesjid* as the call for worship. Some churches used a *kentongan* (hollow tube) made of bamboo or wood, which was normally used to sound an alarm or give a special sign to the villagers, especially during the night. In

73. About Javanese mosque, see further H.J. De Graaf, "De Oorsprong van der Javaansche moskee," *Indonesia*, vol. I (1947-1948), pp. 289-306.

some churches a small table was used as a pulpit. The Scriptures were laid on the table much like the Koran was in the Moslem service. The worshipers sat on the floor which was covered with a rough woven mat or plaited palm leaves.

The church was erected in the imam's yard both for practical reasons and as a "theological" acknowledgment that the imam was the central figure in the life of the community. His role was like that of a Javanese guru or *kyai* among his followers and *santris*.

The church in Karangjasa, which was erected in Sadrach's yard, was more unique. This church, built in the old rural mosque style, was erected in 1870, and was since renovated several times. A large renovation was completed on June 12, 1886, followed by an official ceremony which coincided with the mission festival. According to Wilhelm, about 345 people attended.[74] The church had a three-tiered roof and a *cakra* (a disc with several protruding arrows)[75] on the roof in place of a cross. As the greatest church in Sadrach's community, it symbolized the unity of the communities throughout central Java.

b.   Clothing used during worship

The members of Sadrach's community knew nothing of Western dress such as suits, neckties, trousers, and hats. Rather, they wore their own Javanese clothing which consisted of a sarong or piece of batik (Javanese print cloth), a *surjan* (shirt), and a small head-cloth. The men were required to remove their head-cloth during the worship service, but in certain areas the women were required to keep their heads covered with a small white cloth.

Heyting, familiar only with the Christian tradition, compared the head covering to that of the Roman Catholic nun.[76] He related its use to Paul's insistence in I Corinthians 11:1-15 that women wear a veil.[77] Horstman and Vermeer supported Heyting in this interpretation. Adriaanse, however,

74. Wilhelm, 1886, p. 218.
75. This arrow was a weapon of Sri Kresna; see Chapter V, section B.
76. Heyting, p. 25.
77. These verses offer advice on the proper dress of men and women. I Cor. 11:4 reads: "Any man who prays or prophesies with his head covered, dishonors his head," and verse 7 says: "for a man not to cover his head, since he is the image and glory of God" (RSV). Women, in contrast to men, must be veiled, as suggested in verse 5: "but any woman who prays or prophesies with her head unveiled dishonors her head —it is the same as if her head were shaven," and verse 6: "for if a woman will not veil herself, then she should cut off her hair; but if it is disgraceful for a woman to be shorn or shaven, let her wear a veil" (RSV).

had a better explanation since women were not required to cover their heads in all areas but only in those regions where Islam was still strong, such as in Pekalongan and the northern coastal areas.[78] Adriaanse correctly maintained that, rather than being a Christian custom, the head covering was a continuation of an old Javanese Moslem tradition.[79] Because they lived in Moslem territory, these Christians were reluctant to give up this common tradition because it would distinguish them from their fellow villagers. This was important because they lived in the context of a closed rural society in which a sense of community rather than individuality was emphasized.

c. Worship services

Worship services were held every Sunday and on the special holy days of Christmas, Passover, Ascension Day, Pentecost, and New Year's Day. Services were held twice every Sunday, at 9:00 am. and 4:00 p.m. This was possible since Sunday was not a compulsory work day.[80]

It was the task of the imam to conduct the services and prepare the liturgy. Cachet noted that there was no fixed liturgy in any given local community, and the liturgy varied from place to place.[81] There was some continuity, however, since the elders discussed worship as a part of their regular meetings in Karangjasa. According to Adriaanse, Sadrach composed a handbook for services as a practical guide for his followers. Unfortunately, no copy exists today. This handbook contained the Lord's Prayer and the Ten Commandments along with the summary of the Law as found in Matthew 22:37-40. It also included prayers for both individual and communal use.[82] This was particularly useful for rural community members who were generally less educated, and therefore found prayer difficult. Memorizing prayers, however, was familiar to them since it was a Moslem custom as well.

Although worship varied from place to place, a typical worship service probably used an order of worship similar to the one recorded by Heyting.[83] This type of worship service was most likely more common in

78. Adriaanse, *Sadrach's Kring*, p. 360.
79. Ibid.
80. Originally compulsory work for the government was to be carried out by Javanese Christians on Sunday along with their fellow villagers. Later on Christians were exempted from this Sunday work, but were required to make up the time on another day. See Wilhelm, 1885-1890; Heyting, p. 33.
81. Cachet, *Een Jaar*.
82. Adriaanse, *Sadrach's Kring*, p. 362.
83. Heyting, p. 26.

communities whose members were somewhat educated. Men and women sat separately. When the imam, followed by the elders, entered, all the men stood up. Together they recited the Lord's Prayer or another opening prayer, after which everyone sat down. At this time the offering plate was passed.

The official worship service then began with the imam offering a prayer of thanksgiving followed by a Javanese hymn. Two Scripture readings were read with singing between them. In the morning service the readings were taken from the New Testament and from the Old Testament in the evening service. Either a short exposition of the text or a personal testimony by the imam followed. The service closed with more congregational singing.

A similar worship service was recorded by Adriaanse.[84] In his account, the members, especially those who came from distant places, gathered on the veranda of the imam's house before the service for something to drink. Before worship, while standing at the door of the church, they softly recited a short prayer of confession. Then they proceeded to the pulpit area where they placed their offerings in a box and said a prayer of thanksgiving before going to their seats.[85]

The imam began the service with an individual prayer or the Lord's Prayer, followed by congregational singing. This was followed by the Ten Commandments and the summary of the Law. Sometimes the Apostles' Creed was recited at this time. The Scripture was read from the New Testament in the morning and from the Old Testament in the evening, with singing during the interval between readings. The sermon was often based on personal experience rather than an exposition of Scripture. Worship was closed with a prayer of thanksgiving, followed by the blessing.[86]

These two accounts of worship vary only slightly. The similar elements are prayers, songs, Scripture readings, a sermon of sorts, and the offering. It is noteworthy that Heyting did not mention the use of the Ten

---

84. L. Adriaanse, "Syncretisme", pp. 362-363.

85. Example of thanksgiving prayer: "Lord the Father, the Son, and the Holy Ghost; we, men and women, are strengthened in our love to You. Have mercy on us, praise be to You. Be with us, oh God, the eternal Father. Amen"; Adriaanse, *Sadrach's Kring*, p. 382.

86. Example of individual prayer before worship: "Oh my Father, Lord God the Father, I am a sinner, forgive my sin. Amen." Prayer for offering: "Oh God my Father, I offer this money which is to be the offering to You, God the Father. Amen"; ibid., pp. 359-360. Prayers which, according to Adriaanse, were composed by Sadrach in the formulary booklet were in short form. They were easy to memorize and were intended for use by community members, most of whom were simple peasants.

Commandments and the Apostles' Creed. These accounts serve as an indication of the variety of liturgy found throughout the community. The absence of a fixed liturgy allowed for flexibility, since rigid liturgical formulas would have been contrary to the nature of the community. Another reason for the differences between these two accounts may be that Adriaanse wrote sixteen years after Heyting, during which time the liturgy may have developed somewhat. Adriaanse's account was written after Wilhelm had been working with the community for ten years, and had probably influenced the liturgy to a certain extent.

Sadrach's community was only one of many rural Javanese Christian communities in East and Central Java. Contact between these communities was maintained through the indigenous evangelists. Through this contact, Javanese Christianity took on its own unique character.[87] Before beginning his own community, Sadrach himself had made several tours to Javanese Christian communities in East Java. He had been very much impressed by Coolen's community among others, and seems to have derived some aspects of the liturgy used by Coolen's community.[88]

At the beginning of the worship service in Coolen's church the members all rose when Coolen entered. He began the service with a personal prayer and then invited the congregation to sing. The *pengandelan* (creed) was recited in unison, followed by the Scripture reading. Sometimes the reading was followed by a short exposition, but often not. After the Scripture reading the *gaiban* (communal song) was sung. Worship was concluded with a prayer of thanksgiving offered by Coolen, followed by the *pepujan* (Lord's Prayer) in unison.[89] After the service a *wayang* performance was held on the veranda of Coolen's house.

The Creed and Lord's Prayer were arranged in Javanese *tembang* (a particular musical form found only among the Javanese and Sundanese) by Coolen himself.[90] The creed was adapted to the Moslem *syahadat*:[91]

---

87. Coolsma, *De Zendingseeuw*, p. 189.
88. Adriaanse, "Syncretisme," p. 331; cf. Chapter II, section A.
89. Nortier, *Ngulati*, pp. 52-56.
90. The Creed in Javanese *tembang* arranged by Coolen was as follows:

Sun angandel marang Allah sawiji anglangkungi kwasanipun,
kang waged nyipto langit lan bumi,
sawijining Yesus Kristus putra kasih Gusti kulo,
kang nampani roh kang suci,
lair saka prawan Maryam,
pasrah bawah Pontiyus Pilatus,
sarta den prapat pinatenan,
lan den pendem ambles dateng naraka,

Sun angandel Allah sawiji,
Lha illah lha illolah,
Yesus Kristus ya Roh Allah.
Kang nglangkungi kwasaniput,
Lha illah lha illolah,
Jesus Kristus ya Roh Allah.

[I believe that God is One.
There is no God but God.
Jesus Christ is the Spirit of God,
Whose power is over everything.
There is no God but God.
Jesus Christ is the Spirit of God.]

telung dinane purna gesang
muluk menyang swarga laya kesuma,
lungguh asta tengening Allah,
inggih ngriku pinangkane ngadili pati lan urip.

Sun angandel sajeroning mahasuci lan sadaya mesjide kristen
rukune tyang alim,
kasapuran ing durakane,
sarta urip saking duginge,
urip sadaya salaminipun. Amin.

This is the complete creed in the form of Islamic *syahadat* which Coolen arranged for worship. Translated literally it reads:

I believe that God is one whose power is great
who is able to create the sky and world,
the only Jesus Christ, beloved Son, my Lord,
who receives the Holy Spirit
born from virgin Mary,
surrendered under Pontius Pilate
and was punished with the death penalty,
and was buried, descending to hell,
the third day perfectly alive,
ascended to the quite flowery heaven,
and sits beside the right hand of God
from where he comes to judge the dead and alive.

I believe in the Most Holy and all the Christian community
communion of the saints,
covered from his wickedness
and alive from the flesh
all alive forever. Amen.

Nortier, *Ngulati*, p. 10.

91. Ibid., p. 55.

It is important to note the phrase "Yesus Kristus ya Roh Allah, [Jesus Christ is the Spirit of God]" which is parallel to the Moslem understanding in the Koran of "Isa Rohullah [Jesus, Spirit of God]." Van Akkeren preferred to translate this phrase as "Jesus Christ and the Spirit of God" since Coolen intended this phrase to bear witness to the doctrine of the Trinity.[92]

The Creed was also used during the Thursday evening gatherings (*dzikiran*).[93] The phrases "Lha illah lha illolah, Yesus Kristus ya Roh Allah" were repeated, beginning in a soft voice. The volume gradually grew louder, accompanied by hand-clapping and head movements from side to side and up and down, alternately. The emotion grew more and more intense until finally a state of trance or mystical union was induce. *Dzikir* was one of several traditions which were preserved to become a part of Javanese church life.[94]

According to Adriaanse, Sadrach learned the *tembang*, among other things, from his visits to East Javanese communities.[95] Heyting pointed out that, in addition to the *tembang*, the tradition of evening gatherings for fellowship, prayer, and singing was also practiced in Sadrach's community.[96] Already during the time of Stevens-Philips, her pupils gathered in the evening for Scripture reading and religious instruction in *tembang*.[97] According to Van Troostenburg De Bruijn, this was called "Rerepening Tiyang Kristen" [Song for Christians].[98]

92. The word Rohullah is an additional name of Ngisa, taken from Koran Sura 4:169 *wa rohun minhu* (spirit from Him, namely, God). As a surname, it explains who Ngisa is, thus His name means that he is the spirit of God. In the Javanese translation, "kang anduweni roh saka Allah" this means "he who has spirit from God." This does not point to the third person of the Trinity. Therefore, "Jesus Kristus ya Roh Allah" is better translated as "Jesus Christ is the Spirit of God," in accordance to Moslem background. See W. Hoezoo, "Bijdrage tot de kennis van de Bijbelsche Legenden der Mohammedanen," MNZG 9 (1865), p. 236, n. 3.

93. Such fellowship (*dzikiran*) was usually done by *santris* on certain occasions an also by *abangans* in ceremonials meals for the commemoration of the dead. See Koentjaraningrat, *Javanese Culture*, p. 364; *Kebudayaan Java*, p. 363.

94. Poensen defined *dzikir* as "zekere godsdienstige handeling doorgaans voorname-lijk bestaande in het herhaalde uitroepen van den naam Allah," MNZG 24 (1880), p. 115. *Dzikir* is only one out of several preserved traditions which have influenced the life of the Javanese church. Regarding traditions in Javanese congregations in East Java, see C. Poensen, "Matius Aniep," MNZG 24 (1880), pp. 333-391.

95. Adriaanse, *Sadrach's Kring*, p. 52.

96. Heyting, p. 26.

97. Adriaanse, *Sadrach's Kring*, p. 52.

98. Van Troostenburg De Bruijn, "Zendingspost Majawarna," MNZG 24 (1880), p. 4.

In the Almanac of 1891, three different types of *tembang* were used for the Ten Commandments, the Apostle's Creed, and the Lord's Prayer. Another five types were used for special prayers: opening prayer, morning prayer, prayers before and after meals, and evening prayer. The following examples provide insight into the worship of Sadrach's community.

1)   The Ten Commandments[99]

Tembang Kinanti contained eighteen verses. Verse one was an introduction in which the writer reminded the readers of the time when God gave these commandments to Israel on Mount Horeb. It read:

1.   Nyawa ulun kang den emut maring Hyang kang Maha Widhi, ingkang angagem kamulyan rikalanya karsa paring, dawuh pepakene ngarga, Horeb den ajrih kang suci.
[My soul should remember Hyang Kang Maha Widhi, Who dressed in glory when He gave the Commandments on the mountain, Horeb.]

"Hyang kang Maha Widhi" was originally the Balinese title for God, but was also used by the Javanese to mean the One Who Knows All. In the following verses "Yehuwah" and "Allah" were used as names of God.

2.   Wondene dedawuhipun kadya kang kocap puniki, ingsun iki Yehuwah Hayang, myang ratunira kang uwis angluwari sira saka, ing kanistan nulya ngirid
[That His Commandments are as spoken, I am Yehuwah Hayang, your King, Who brought you out from evil and accompanied you]

3.   Metu sing panguwasanipun iblis marmanya sireki, Ywa nganggep Allah liyannya, kejabanya ingsun iki sira aywa samya karya, ukir-ukiran utawi
[Out from the power of Satan; therefore, you should confess no other God besides me, and you should not make graven images]

Other verses used "Maha Mulya Gung" (the Most exalted) and "Gusti" (his Majesty) to refer to God, for example:

17.   Duh ingkang Maha Mulya ung mugi karsa apeparing, sih welasan dateng kita, kang supadi dasih neki sageda darbeni sedya, netepi dateng saliring,
[The Most Exalted should be willing to give His loving grace to us, in order to enable us to have courage to do all this faithfully,]

99. Almanac of 1891, pp. 91-95.

18. Dedawuh Gusti puniku mugi karsa aparing, kekiyatan anggen kita, anglampahi mijil saking panrimah tuwin pracaya mring Yesus Kristus jeng Gusti.

[Those commands of the Lord, He will willingly give us the capability to obey them out of heartfelt thanks and belief in Jesus Christ, the Lord.]

Verses four through sixteen were comparable to Exodus 20:4-17 and need no further comment. Throughout the text titles from both a Hindu and Moslem background were used for God.[100]

2) The Creeds[101]

Both the Niceno-Constantinopolitan and the Apostles' Creeds were in the Almanac of 1891. The first was written as prose with the phrase, "ingkang jumeneng ratu adil, kratonipun tanpa wekasan [Who became the just king, whose kingdom is eternal]" referring to Jesus.[102] The Apostles' Creed, however, was written as a Javanese poem, *tembang Macapat*, consisting of four verses, accurately translating the content of the Creed. These two creeds were widely known in Sadrach's community. The reference in the first to *ratu adil* was attractive to the Javanese Christians, while the poetic form of the second made it relevant and easy to recite.

3) The Lord's Prayer[103]

The Lord's Prayer was composed in *tembang Pucung* consisting of seven verses. Its content was similar to Matthew 6:9-13. The word *rama* was used for God, meaning "Father."

4) Opening Prayer for worship[104]

The *tembang Dandang gula* was used as the opening prayer and consisted of three verses. Verse one asked for God's blessing and illumination upon the community as they prepared for worship and hearing the Word of God. Verse two asked the Holy Spirit to guide the preacher. Verse three closed

---

100. Regarding Javanese titles for God, see Poensen, "Bijdragen," p. 190; Cf. Hadiwijono, p. 164.
101. Almanac of 1891, pp. 95-97.
102. Regarding Jesus proclaimed as *ratu adil,* see Chapter IV, section B3.
103. Almanac of 1891, pp. 97-98.
104. Ibid., pp. 98-100.

the prayer with the hope that the words that they hear might strengthen the faith of the listeners and make them obedient to God.

5) Morning Prayer[105]

The morning prayer contained sixteen verses set to the *tembang Maskumambang*. The contents were varied, including thanksgiving and intercession for oneself, one's neighbors, and the government.

6) Mealtime Prayer[106]

The prayer before meals used the *tembang Mijil*, while the prayer after meals used the *tembang Megatruh*. Each consisted of four verses. Both were prayers of thanksgiving to God for his care and included a blessing especially for the poor.

7) Evening Prayer[107]

The fourteen verse evening prayer was similar in content to the morning prayer, including intercession and thanksgiving.

The emphasis on individual piety can be seen in these prayers. Such things as good conduct, obedience, faithfulness to God's call, and focusing on the life beyond rather than on this earthly life (which also constitute the ideal Javanese life) are evident throughout.

The use of the *tembang* for communicating the Gospel was significant. *Tembang* had been used in Javanese literature for centuries and was a very popular form of communication. It was used primarily for moral-ethical teaching, particularly in classical Javanese literature.

Tembang was divided into three major groups with variation in each group: *Macapat, Ageng*, and *Madya* or *Tengahan*. The *Ageng* and *Madya* were commonly used for the *bawa swara* (introductory melody) in a complete *Gending* (Javanese instrumental and vocal combination). The *Macapat*, however, was the most common and required no instrument.

On special occasions, such as childbirth or circumcision, a *tukang maca* (professional reader) was invited to recite literary works which contained moral teachings.[108] The meeting was usually held in the evening and was

---

105. Ibid., pp. 100-102.
106. Ibid., pp. 103-105.
107. Ibid., pp. 105-108.
108. Koentjaraningrat, *Javanese Culture*, p. 212; *Kebudayaan Jawa*, p. 225.

accompanied by a discussion time (*sarasehan*). The *Macapat* was thought to be the most effective means for communicating moral teachings in public during such occasions. As result, it was used most often by the Javanese evangelists for proclaiming the Gospel.

2. Sadrach's preaching: the triumphant Christ and Christian obedience.

Due to the absence of the sacraments within Sadrach's community for a certain period, preaching and personal witness were of special importance. To a certain extent, we have only a limited report of the content of Sadrach's preaching, but we may gain some insight into how Sadrach and other imams witnessed to Christ, and who influenced them in that respect. First, the preaching of the Javanese evangelists who preceded Sadrach will be discussed. These evangelists worked in East Java in the Christian communities which Sadrach visited.

Harthoorn, of the NZG, reported that the Javanese evangelists often compared the risen Christ to the prophet Mohammed in their preaching. Soleman, for example, emphasized that Christ was greater than Mohammed. In one of his sermons he said,

> Granted,Mohammed had some power...., it must still have been far inferior to that of Christ. Mohammed can only hear if the face is turned toward the east when praying; Christ, however, has the power to hear no matter how one twists or turns, to the east or west, north or south. Thus, Mohammed only has power in the east, but Christ in the east, west, north, and south. Is Christ not, then, greater than Mohammed? Granted, Mohammed was someone. That is natural. But ask a *santri* once if Mohammed ascended into heaven. What does he answer? Maybe? What maybe? We have certainty. Our Savior ascended; we know the day — forty days after his resurrection. And that is certain because the eleven — the eleven, and not the three or four, which would have otherwise been enough — the eleven disciples saw it. And now the *santris* say, maybe he ascended. But where is that "maybe" written? It is nothing but a pretext. Brothers, *Mohammed is in Arabia, the dead Mohammed is there! Christ, the living Christ is in heaven.* Brothers, take this to heart so that you are not moved, but stand firm in the faith![109]

It is clear that Soleman's Moslem background influenced his understanding of Christianity. He frequently compared his faith before and after his conversion — his faith as a Moslem and his faith as a Christian. His newly found faith, he claimed, was not only different, but greater and higher than his old faith. This lay in the fact, he believed, that Jesus was greater than Mohammed. He was no ordinary prophet, but a powerful prophet who had been raised from the dead, defeating the powers of death, which no other prophet had done.

---

109. As quoted in Harthoorn, "Iets over den Javaanschen," p. 207, emphasis ours.

The claim that Jesus was the risen, living, and powerful prophet meant that his followers were required to faithfully obey Him in all areas of life. Therefore, Christian obedience, as expressed in *good works*, was also stressed by the Javanese evangelists. Albertus, the Javanese helper of Jellesma, preached the following about Christian obedience based on I Timothy 6:14-15.

> ... Timothy, who was instructed from his youth in the Scriptures, who outshone many others in piety. If such a word was directed toward him, it would certainly be good for us to listen. And what was commanded to him? What do we read? That he keep this command! What command? We read in verse 11, 'Pursue righteousness, godliness, faith, love, endurance, and gentleness.' And how must this command be kept? 'Without spot or blame.' What does that mean? I will clarify it with an example. If you were ordered by the national government to carry out a certain task, for example, to work the coffee plantations in the hills, then you would comply with the order because the command comes to you from the highest government, because you have no choice, because you must. Now, if you keep this command because it has come to you from a higher authority, then you don't keep it without spot or blame. You can only keep this command without spot or blame when love dwells in your heart. And for how long must we keep this command thus? One day? One month? One year? It says: '... until the appearing of our Lord Jesus Christ.' And when will that take place? In two years? Oh, then this would be an easy command! If that were so, then you could live for awhile yet, like one year, as you pleased, and then begin to keep this command! But that's not the way it is brothers! That time cannot be determined. Therefore, without ceasing, we must always keep this command of the Lord. And what will then happen at that appearing? Then he will show himself as the blessed and only powerful Lord, King of Kings and Lord of Lords. The Kings and Lords of this earth are knaves compared to him. It will be manifested to all who he is. Now His glory is still a hidden glory. The Mohammedans do not believe in Him because His glory cannot yet be seen with this, the carnal eye; now it can only be seen with the eye of the Spirit. Blessed is the one who has already come to know Him as He is. The revelation of His glory will cause him no fear. No, only joy![110]

The is that the followers of Christ must be obedient to Him during this interim period between His first and second coming. At the consummation of time, when Christ comes again, everything will be made perfect.

Another Javanese evangelist, Paulus Tosari,[111] preached with similar emphases. Paulus had been a *santri* before his conversion to Christianity. For the Christian, he claimed, human destiny was certain. Unlike that of the *santri*, Tosari's experience confirms,

---

110. Ibid., pp. 208-209.

111. Kyai Paulus Tosari was a well-known Javanese evangelist in East Java (1813-1882). For more about him see C. Poensen, "Paulus Tosari," MNZG 27 (1883), pp. 283-333; Nortier, *Van Zendingsarbeid*, pp. 26-33; Mardja Sir, *Kyai Paulus Tosari* (Jakarta, 1967); R. Soedibjo Meriso, *Paulus Tosari, pemrakarsa pembangunan gedung greja Majawarna* (unpublished mss., 1975).

Whether God will condemn is uncertain; whether God will reward, is uncertain: man does not know. [When I] became a Christian, and later a minister, I did not dare say: Who knows? It is uncertain. Nor did I then dare to give the assurance that he who believes is saved, because I thought, who knows? It is uncertain. But now I know that these things are thus, and I am certain of it, because the Lord Jesus has said it. Now I repeat it without tiring, so that people may be converted.[112]

Tosari also preached about what Christians must do during the interim, until Christ comes again. Preaching on Matthew 13:47-52, he said,

The Lord Jesus has not spoken thus in order to make us afraid. He has not come to make us afraid; no! But to push us to self-examination and self-testing. And all you who are here now, examine yourselves! Young and old, male and female, examine yourselves. Soon will come the time when you will be examined on the great day which is to come. But don't postpose it until then. For, the one who thus neglects himself is not good, not virtuous, not decent, not religious, not Christian! Christian does not mean going to church and *kumpulan* (a special evening house-gathering): rather, it is a daily self-examination of how we stand in relation to God. He may, of course, come to church, the one who neglects this; there he is separated from the righteous. In verse 51, the disciples answered yes, and when they said yes, they meant yes. That doesn't mean that they gave the right answer, but that they had laid it up in their hearts and lived according to it. And you, would you just say yes and not do accordingly? That is not the custom of Christians. Their yes is yes, no, no; anything more than this is from the Evil One. Otherwise the world would be more upright than they, for the world says no and it is no.

He continued with his interpretation of verse 52.

The Lord speaks of learning, but of what learning? There are different sorts of learning and knowledge: that of collecting and compiling, that of being clever. The learning of the world gives no advantage; it works death, for it is written: 'I will destroy the wisdom of the wise, and the intelligence of the intelligent I will frustrate.' The learning from God, on the contrary, is profitable for all things: it teaches us to understand the heart, to recognize and detest sin and evil, to leave the world, to boast in Christ, to live and die in God. Brothers, if we seek that wisdom, we will be happy.[113]

As a result of his wanderings through the villages in East Java before and after his baptism, Sadrach became familiar with the teaching and preaching of the evangelists and leaders of the Christian communities located there. It is likely that he was interested in their preaching of the risen Christ as well as their emphasis on good conduct as the expression of Christian obedience. Like Sadrach, the first generation of Javanese evangelists were from a Javanese Moslem background. To a certain extent, then, Sadrach followed his "predecessors" in focusing his preaching on the risen Christ and Christian obedience.

112. Harthoorn, p. 204.
113. Ibid., pp. 201-202.

As has been mentioned, Sadrach utilized the method of public debate with Javanese *guru ngelmu* in his evangelizing. One famous guru from the Residency of Kedu, Kyai Sejawiguna, was defeated by Sadrach in a debate.[114] Sadrach convinced Sejawiguna by claiming that Mohammed's teaching was false. Unlike Jesus, Sadrach argued, Mohammed was an ordinary man like every other man. His body had already decayed and had not been not raised from the dead. Therefore, he could not be the Savior who could save all sinners. In Sadrach's argument we can hear an echo of the preaching of the evangelists from East Java.

Beginning with an understanding of Jesus as an extraordinary prophet based on His resurrection, Sadrach moved on to his second emphasis —obedience to the most powerful prophet by following His example. At the Synod meeting of 1889, Sadrach preached on Christian obedience based on Matthew 13:34-35, 47-48. He emphasized the fact that our works will bear fruit insofar as we faithfully obey Christ's commands and example.

> The Lord spoke *through* parables, and revealed through them many hidden things of the Kingdom of God. Here we read what the outcome will be in the great harvest for the work of the brothers who desire to walk in the footsteps of the Lord. Although it appears that in the outcome many evil ones have been gathered, yet their work overall is not in vain.

> We arm ourselves at all times with the full armor of God, so that we are always competent in our work, and can resist all evil. We count on the fact that the hostile heart will strive against us in our preaching, with old, delapidated, unwieldly weapons. Fear not, believe in the Lord's help, and be assured that the net will be filled.[115]

At the Synod meeting of the following year, Sadrach preached on the same topic, using Matthew 28:18 as his text. He stated that Jesus, who has power in heaven as well as on the earth, has commanded His disciples, that is, all Christians, to preach the Gospel. This great command must be

114. Sejawiguna was a well-known Javanese *kyai* who was converted by Sadrach, and received his religious instruction from Wilhelm. He was baptized on July 5, 1890, and took on the Christian name Elia. See Wilhelm, 1889, pp. 99, 106, 111, 113, 130, 139. Frans Van Lith, S.J., a Roman Catholic missionary (1863-1926) who worked in Central Java in Muntilan, stated that Kyai Sejawiguna became leader of Sadrach's community in Bintaro (near Muntilan). Sadrach came to Sejawiguna's house very often to conduct Sunday services which were often followed by conversation between Sadrach, Sejawiguna, and Van Lith, who also attended services at times. This was told in Van Lith's brochure, "Kyai Sadrach: Eene les voor ons uit de Protestansche Zending van Midden Java" as quoted by J. Weitjens, S.J., "Pastoor van Lith mengenai Kyai Sadrach" [Pastor Van Lith on Kyai Sadrach], *Orientasi* 6 (1974), pp. 183-202.

115. Wilhelm, 1889, p. 93; "Van ons arbeidsveld in Indië," *Heidenbode* (Feb., 1890), pp. 74-77; cf. Cachet, *Een Jaar*, p. 371, n. 1; Adriaanse, *Sadrach's Kring*, p. 228.

obeyed without fear. He said, "We are all obligated, with reverent obedience, to fulfill the commands of our Lord Jesus Christ, for all power in heaven and on earth has been given to Him."[116]

For Sadrach, obedience to Christ meant first of all obedience to His teachings — His *pranatan* (law) — which needed to be a part of the Christian's daily life. This is evident in the following account recorded in Wilhelm's diary. Wilhelm had received a distinguished guest, Raden Mas Kapiten Natataruna, an aristocrat from Yogyakarta. He had been attracted by Sadrach's preaching and had expressed a desire to become a Christian. Before going to see Wilhelm, Natataruna had visited Sadrach a few times in Karangjasa. Sadrach had asked him to go to Wilhelm in Purwareja for religious instruction. To that end, Sadrach wrote to Wilhelm, introducing Natataruna. In the letter, Sadrach wrote, "mau menurut pengajaran Kristus, yaitu Tuhan Jesus punya pranata" (Natararuna will obey and follow Jesus' teachings, because it is the law of Jesus).[117] Natataruna's desire to become a Christian was above all interpreted by Sadrach as a willingness to obediently obey Jesus' teachings, namely, His *pranatan*.[118]

In conclusion, the distinctive and basic Christian doctrine of the resurrection of Christ became the main theme of the preaching of Javanese evangelists in the nineteenth century, including Sadrach. Jesus was presented as the risen and living Christ, the most powerful and extraordinary prophet, the triumphant Christ. Because Jesus was recognized as powerful and superior, His commands were to be obeyed and His example followed. Thus, Christian obedience became the second emphasis of preaching. Sadrach remained faithful, however, to the pillar of the Christian faith in his preaching: as Paul stated in his letter to the Corinthians, "If Christ has not been raised, then our preaching is in vain and your faith is in vain" (RSV).[119]

3. Rituals

To understand the use of ritual in Sadrach's community, it is important to note that the members of the community did not live apart in exclusive

116. "Van ons Zendingsveld in Indië," *Heidenbode* (March, 1891), pp. 229-230; Adriaanse, *Sadrach's Kring*, p. 228.

117. Wilhelm, 1887, p. 314.

118. *Suprapranata*, the additional name Sadrach took after becoming a fully independent leader (see Chapter II, section B2) might be interpreted, in this connection, as implying that Sadrach was really concerned about moral discipline by fulfilling *pranatan*.

119. I Cor. 15:14.

communities, but rather lived in the villages alongside their Moslem neighbors. Therefore, their lifestyle could not easily be distinguished from other Javanese. Heyting noted that the manners, traditions, and customs observed by Sadrach's community were much the same as those observed by the Javanese Moslems.[120] The differences and similarities are best seen through a comparison of the two traditions. This comparison will be restricted to the religious rituals performed at the critical stages of a person's life, such as marriage, pregnancy, childbirth, circumcision, and death.

a. Rituals concerning marriage

A Javanese Moslem marriage was performed by the *pengulu* (Moslem marriage official)[121] in a mosque or in the bride's home. The ceremony was called *akad nikah*, and in it the groom presented a sum of money and the Koran as a token of marriage. Before the *pengulu* and the witnesses, the couple pronounced the *syahadat* as a personal confirmation of and commitment to their faith. The wedding then continued in accordance with the traditional Javanese custom.[122]

Rather than using the Javanese Moslem wedding ceremony, the members of Sadrach's community created their own. When a couple planned to marry, notice was given in advance to the imam so that preparations could be made. The ceremony was performed during a church service and was open to all members, who were expected to attend to ask God's blessing on the couple. The imam conducted the service which began with prayer and an opening song. The Scripture reading was taken from Ephesians 5:22-33, with an emphasis on love as the basis of marriage. The marriage form, which included a short explanation of the meaning of marriage, was read. The imam then questioned the couple about their promises to each other and commitment to God. After the imam blessed the couple the Creed was recited. The service was concluded with a prayer of thanksgiving. Following the church service, the traditional Javanese customs were observed.

In the early stages of the community, Sadrach performed all marriage services. Later on, however, this task was assigned to the imam of each

---

120. Heyting, p. 30.

121. In Coolen's community, *pengulu* was adopted for the office of religious teacher of the community (*pamulang*). Like in a Moslem community, the *pangulu* of Coolen's community also performed marriages in addition to teaching new converts. The other office was *pinisepuh* (elder). See Nortier, *Ngulati*, pp. 56-57.

122. Adriaanse, *Sadrach's Kring*, p. 369.

community.[123] They were also assigned the task of registering all marriages, births, deaths, divorces, and marital reconciliations.

b.   Rituals concerning pregnancy, childbirth, and circumcision

In Javanese society the first pregnancy was considered an important event, since it was an indication that one's lineage would continue. Through pregnancy a woman was spared the shame of infertility, an accusation that could lead to divorce or polygamy on the part of her husband. Because great care needed to be taken for the first pregnancy, the woman was required to abstain from certain foods and drinks, as well as work that might endanger her or her child. *Slametan* was observed in the fifth month (*nglimani*) and the seventh month (*mitoni/tingkeb*) to guard the baby from evil spirits. Sometimes it was also done in the nineth month to honor the "twins brothers" (*slametan memule sedulur*). The placenta was considered the "younger brother" and the amniotic fluid was considered the "older brother" which would protect the spirit of the child.[124]

In Sadrach's community this custom was preserved, but in simplified form. The expensive Javanese feast and various *sajen* (offering meals) were omitted. Instead, a small reception was given for the neighbors. At the reception, the imam, on behalf of the host, gave a short introduction about the purpose of the gathering followed by a prayer of intercession and thanksgiving. A meal was prepared, but much of the food was taken home by the guests.[125]

According to Javanese custom, *slametan* was observed several times for the birth of a child. Within the *santri* circle, when the child was seven days old, *slametan* was held for naming the child and for the first haircut. During the celebration, called *kekah* (*aqiqah*), a cow and sheep were slain as an offering and the meat was brought to the mosque to be distributed to the poor. The *abangans* had a similar ritual when the child was five days old (*sepasar*). When the child was thirty-five days old, the same *slametan* was made (*selapanan*). This was the beginning of a series of *slametans*

123. Heyting, p. 31. Horstman noted that in the area of Pekalongan, the imam performed weddings in a very simple way. After reading I Cor. 7:1-16, the couple had to promise to love one another by answering these questions:

— Do you promise to love your wife, when she is sick you will not leave her?
— Do you promise to obey your husband, and when he is sick you will not leave him?

See R.J. Horstman to F.L. Cachet, June 30, 1892 (Archives of the Dutch Reformed Missionary Society, Leusden).
124. Koentjaraningrat, *Javanese Culture*, pp. 353-354; *Kebudayaan Jawa*, p. 351.
125. Adriaanse, *Sadrach's Kring*, p. 382.

celebrated on the third (3 x 35 days), fifth (5 x 35 days), and seventh (7 x 35 days) "birth days" which were considered crucial. The ritual on the seventh "birth day" was called *tedak siti* (touching the ground) when the child was permitted to step on the ground for the first time, symbolizing the first stage of learning to walk.

Circumcision was an important ritual for both the *Islam santri* and the *Islam abangan*, although it was not one of the five Moslem obligations. In the Shafi'i school, however, it was not only considered *sunnah* (the example of Mohammed), but was also an obligation. This may have been due to their theological understanding of Sura 4:125 in which God commanded His people to follow Abraham's "religion," even though circumcision was not specifically mentioned. The *santri* Moslems viewed circumcision as *adat* which ought to be fulfilled as a profession of the Moslem faith, while the *abangan* Moslems considered it an initiation into adulthood. Some of the words used for circumcision are *sunat*, *sunnah* (the example of Mohammed), *khitan*, *tetak*, and *supit* (to cut).

The age at which a child should be circumcised varied. The *santri* considered the ritual a sign of Islam, and therefore performed it at the age of seven days. Others circumcised babies at the age of forty days. Most, however, performed the ritual between ten and sixteen years of age. A symbolic circumcision, called *kafud*, was also performed for females. A piece of saffron was placed over the vagina. A female *dhukhun* performed the ritual by slitting the saffron as a symbolic circumcision. Usually this was done when a young girl had her first menstrual period. It was accompanied by another ritual, *kramas* (hair washing). From this point on she was expected to drink Javanese *jamu* (herbal medicine) for health and beauty.[126]

While not all these rituals were performed in Sadrach's community, some were maintained with minor changes. It was customary for parents to bring their children to the church at the age of forty days to be presented to God.[127] The imam used flower petals to sprinkle water upon the child's head in the name of the Father, Son, and Holy Spirit. During the ceremony the *dupa* (clay pot in which incense was burned) was lit and a communal song in Javanese *tembang* was sung. Following the service, a common meal, similar to the Javanese *kenduren* (religious meal) was provided in the home of the imam to give thanks to God. Circumcision was never abolished from the life of the community despite the missionaries' strong opposition to it.[128]

126. L.T. Maijer, *Een Blik in het Javaansche Volksleven* II (Leiden, 1897), p. 392; Koentjaraningrat, *Javanese Culture*, p. 361; *Kebudayaan Jawa*, p. 359.
127. Cf. Luke 2:21. Jewish tradition is also observed by Jesus' parents.
128. Chapter IV, section B3.

c. Rituals concerning death

The following dialogue between a *modin* and a Christian concerning death and funerals indicates some of the Javanese beliefs on death and the afterlife.

'If you become a Christian, when you die you will be buried like a dog or a cat because no one will pray for your soul and no one will sacrifice a cow or a sheep for you,' says a modin. He then continues, 'Prayer is crucial for lifting the gate of heaven, and the slaughtered animal will bring you across the *wot ogal-agil* (swinging bridge). Then you will safely enter heaven.' 'How clever is the animal which has the ability to bring the dead to heaven!' answers the Christian with surprise.[129]

This story indicates the Javanese concern with the journey of the soul to its eternal resting place. There was a common belief among the Javanese that the soul of the deceased wandered about in the area of the house where it had lived. Because the spirit did not leave immediately, *slametan* was held several times during the first three years to commemorate the phases of the spirit's journey. Each was conducted by a *modin* and involved the sacrifice of several cows and sheep.[130] *Slametan* was made in the evening of the day of the funeral (*ngesur tanah*), on the third day (*nelung dinani*), the seventh day (*mitung dinani*), the fortieth day (*matang puluh*), the second anniversary (*mendak pindo*), and the third anniversary (*nyewu*) of death.

Slametan was required to help the soul on its journey to heaven. For those whose *amal* (good deeds) was not sufficient, the journey was very difficult. Before entering heaven, the soul had to pass over a bridge called *wot ogal-agil* by the *abangan*, and *siratul-mustakim* by the *santri*. The bridge was believed to be constructed of one-seventh of a female hair. Under the bridge was a deep crater filled with molten magma.

The funeral was conducted by the *modin* either at the home of the deceased or at the graveside. Each step was a significant part of Javanese belief and custom. The body was laid in a north-south position until it was buried, at which time it was laid facing west, toward Mecca. The *modin* recited special prayers when the body was washed, when it was brought from the house to the grave, and when it was placed in the grave. The coffin was decorated with flowers.

In Sadrach's community the imam conducted the funeral, usually according to the *pranatan* which had been issued by Sadrach as a guide. According to Adriaanse, Christian funerals were very similar to the existing Javanese custom.[131] The use of prayers, flowers, and a kind of

---

129. "Jepara-Puntjel," *De Macedoniër* 1 (1883), pp. 145-146.
130. Description about *slametan* for the dead, see Koentjaraningrat, *Javanese Culture*, pp. 364-366; *Kebudayaan Jawa*, pp. 362-363; Geertz, *Religion of Java*, pp. 68-76.
131. Adriaanse, p. 378.

slametan as a commemoration of the dead were all similar. It was the opinion of the Javanese Christians that this ritual was preserved to counter the accusation that Christians were buried like dogs.[132]

The prayers used for Christian funerals were recorded by Adriaanse. Their Christian character is obvious. As well as serving as a means of "transferring" the soul to heaven, these prayers were essentially a doxology to God, the origin of all to Whom all will return.

> 1) For the dead the necessity is gone to face either East or West, North or South. He has now left this world and has become perfect. This is my purpose in praying to you, oh God. I submit the soul of the dead to the Almighty, the One who has decided. Amen.

> 2) Oh God, our Father, we present this soul to be with You. May it come into Your sacredness. we submit the body and soul which is still in the world to Your hands, that the soul may return to its origin. Amen.

> 3) Oh Lord God, Who is in heaven, in Your Essence are capability, name, and reality from Whom is the mortal life of man, Who is the source and origin of the world; the world is mortal but You are the eternal God. Amen.[133]

d.   Rituals concerning land cultivation and farming

Land and its cultivation were central in the life of the rural Javanese because of their total dependence on it. A *sedekah-bumi* (offering for land) was held annually at the home of the village leader or in the graveyard where the founder of the village was buried. This *slametan* was called *bersih desa* (to clean the village), and was celebrated to cleanse the village from evil, disaster, and misfortune.[134] It was a large festival in which all the villagers took part, and was usually accompanied by an all night *wayang* performance and a *tayuban*, an erotic dance feast.

The members of Sadrach's community held their own annual festival during the time for planting crops rather than joining in the village celebrations.[135] The members gathered in the church where the imam conducted a worship service based on Genesis 1. The service centered around God's creation and his command to mankind to cultivate His creation. Psalm 104, which depicts the greatness of God as Creator, was sung as the communal hymn. Following the service, a large feast was held on the veranda of the imam's house. Food was brought by the members and prayers of intercession and thanksgiving were offered by the imam.

132. Ibid., p. 379.

133. Ibid., p. 378.

134. Ibid., pp. 374-375; Van Akkeren, pp. 13-14; *Heidenbode* (February, 1889), pp. 76-80.

135. Adriaanse, *Sadrach's Kring*, p. 375.

Ceremonies were also conducted at the time for ploughing the *sawah* (wet-rice fields) and at harvest time.[136]

e. New Year celebrations

In Javanese Moslem tradition, *Idhul Fitri* (*Lebaran* — to finish; i.e. the day after fasting) was a solemn celebration. After the month-long fast of Ramadan was over, Moslems gathered in an open square to celebrate with *sholat Ied* (communal prayers). God was thanked for helping them successfully pass the physical and spiritual exercises during the past month. They celebrated because their faith had been refreshed and strengthened, their solidarity with the poor had been increased, and they were better equipped to continue their earthly lives and surrender themselves in obedience to God. Reconciliation to God and to one's neighbors was another important aspect of the *Lebaran* festival. Traditionally, the younger approached the older; for example, children to parents, pupils to teachers, subordinates to superiors. In this way harmony in social relationships was restored.

The coming of the New Year was also clebrated in Sadrach's community. On New Year's Eve, and again on New Year's Day, the members gathered in the church for worship. The New Year's Day service was followed by a *bujana pirukunan* (meal of reconciliation), served in the imam's house.[137] The specific character of the *Lebaran* was thus preserved. The period between Christmas and New Year's Day became a period of celebration and reconciliation for community members, during which time they paid visits to one another.

f. Miscellaneous rituals

Various other Javanese traditions were preserved in Sadrach's community, including rituals for healing, driving out evil spirits from humans or places, and prayers for neutralizing poison. When a Javanese family requested such a ritual, the *modin* conducted the *slametan* and sacrificed an animal. Before being slaughtered, the animal was sprinkled with water over its entire body. The head and neck were covered with a piece of white cloth to symbolize the purification of its soul so it would not become a wandering spirit. As he pronounced the prayer, the *modin* slaughtered the animal. The head was completely cut off after the *modin* was sure that the animal was already dead.

This custom was performed in a similar manner in Sadrach's com-

136. Ibid., p. 384.
137. Ibid., p. 373.

munity. The prayer, recited by the imam, was as follows:

> I present a cow to be slain, which is clean. As I speak, the knife cuts the artery and throat. May the bad smell go and the good taste remain; may its soul return to Your heaven together with its skin, flesh, bone, and marrow; indeed the strongest elements of good taste remain and is really delicious. Oh God, You are God. Amen.[138]

It was believed that if a cow was slain and eaten by man the cow would return to heaven. That is why the confusing phrase "may its soul return to Your heaven together with its skin, flesh, bone, and marrow" was included The prayer indicated their view that cattle were living things and therefore ought to be treated with "honor."

It is important to note that not all Javanese Moslem rituals were acceptable for use in Sadrach's community. Sadrach selected the ones which that were appropriate.[139] Two types of rituals in particular were not observed in the community, the first of which was the *slametan* to honor the spirits of the dead. This ritual was performed by the Javanese during the month of Sya'ban. A visit was made to the graveyard to bring flowers and burn incense. Each family made an offering meal. Sya'ban was the month of "spirit" and therefore was also called Ruwah (from *ruah*, which means spirit). A *slametan* to honor the dead, especially prophets, was also held during the month of fasting on the 21st, 23rd, 25th, 27th, 27th, and 29th days of the month.

Another group of rituals rejected by Sadrach were those public celebrations which were closely bound to Islam. The *slametan suran*, which was held in the month of Sura (Muharam), commemorated the death of Husein, Mohammed's grandson, who had died on the 10th of Muharam, 680 AD, as a martyr during the war in Carbella. Another ritual, Muludan, held on the 12th of Mulud (Rabi'ulawwal), celebrated the birth and death of the prophet Mohammed. *Slametan barakah* (blessing or grace) was celebrated on the 15th of Ruwah, which was believed to be the night in which Allah decided who would die within the year. During that night the *abangans* celebrated by staying awake until very late, while the *santris* would go to the mosque to recite the Koran. The ascension of Mohammed was celebrated on the 27th of Rajab by the *santris*, and was also an optional ritual for the *abangans*.[140]

The effort of the members of Sadrach's community to christianize the Javanese Moslem rituals is impressive. Because Javanese customs were

138. Ibid., p. 388.
139. Ibid., pp. 385-387.
140. For a description of Javanese Moslem rituals which already became "public" (not only observed by the *santris*) see Koentjaraningrat, *Javanese Culture*, pp. 267-371; *Kebudayaan Jawa*, pp. 366-370.

necessary in the context of village communal life, they made a noble attempt to remain within their Javanese heritage without denying their new faith.

C. Spiritual Life and the Spirit of Independence

This section deals with Sadrach's community as a community of believers who demonstrated signs of new life. The prevailing characteristic of this new life was their spirit of independence.

1. The spiritual life of Sadrach's community

a. A community of new life

Conversion is not only a matter of individual transformation, but is also one of community life. Those who convert to Christianity are expected to associate with others of the same faith — to join a community of new life. This faith-based community appears in concrete form in worship and other collective activities, in its prayer and doxology to God. Were these same ingredients present in Sadrach's community? As one eyewitness described them, "those Christians get together with other fellow villagers during the night, praying and singing."[141]

We can imagine the transition from the old community of *murids* to the new community of believers in Christ. There was certainly discontinuity. The atmosphere of *ngelmu* with its rigid *rapal* (chanted formulas) was transformed into an atmosphere of worship, prayer, and fellowship. They were no longer pupils of a Javanese guru, but pupils of Christ, gathering for worship. *Rapal* was replaced by prayer, *dzikir* with spiritual songs, and *kesaktian* (the power of invulnerability, usually sought through *ngelmu*) by the yearning for God's grace. Autosoterism and justification by works was replaced by faith in the redemptive work of God through Christ. In this way, life in *ngelmu* (self-oriented) was gradually transformed into life in Christ (self-denying).

This new life was manifested in the willingness of the community members to contribute money for erecting their own churches. The travel costs of their imams, who attended the meetings in Karangjasa once every three months, were also financed by their contributions. All this was done with joy. Heyting, who interviewed several members of Sadrach's community from several different locations, always received the same answer,

---

141. Heyting, p. 20.

that they were satisfied with their newly found faith.[142]

Other manifestations of this new life appeared in the area of morality. Missionaries of the past century described certain "moral diseases" which threatened Javanese life, namely, gambling, polygamy, and opium.[143] Gambling brought economic ruin. Friendships and family life were broken down. Divorce and polygamy also resulted.

The status of Javanese women was very low. They were treated like a commodity to be bought and sold, to be used and disposed of if one did not like them anymore. Underage marriage was common among the villagers, and another contributing factor to divorce. Furthermore, out of frustration and economic stress, young widows would leave their villages. Some became *tledek* or *tandak* (erotic dancers) in *tayuban* or *ronggeng* (public performers).

The third public disease, opium, also caused serious damage among the people. Missionaries compared its use with alcoholism in Europe, which also caused poverty and moral degradation.[144] It brought with it a great loss of both physical and spiritual life.[145] The missionaries felt that it was their moral duty to fight against such a situation. They campaigned against the use of opium by publishing tracts and advertisements in missionary magazines of the 1880's.[146] They wanted the "Opium pacht in Nederlandsch Indië" (opium lease in the Dutch Indies) abolished. Ironically, the "Christian" Dutch government made no attempt to prohibit opium abuse. Economics took priority, and millions of guilders were flowing into government coffers each year as a result of the opium trade.[147]

Because the missionaries had the best interests of the indigenous people in mind, they often came into conflict with the government. In such situations of conflict, however, their "prophetic" calling all too often yielded to the political and economic will of the government.

Sadrach was also concerned for the life of his community. Like other gurus and *kyais*, he emphasized individual piety and living an upright life.

---

142. Ibid., p. 30.

143. See Poensen, "Javaansch als mensch," pp. 26-74, 113-151; D.J. Ten Zeldam Ganswijk, "Iets over de Javanen in Betrekking tot de evangelieprediking in Oostelijk Java," MNZG 1 (1857), pp. 89-121; S.E. Harthoorn, "Iets over de Javaanschen Mohamedaan en de Javaanschen Christenen," MNZG 1 (1857), pp. 183-212.

144. Poensen, "De Javanen," p. 176.

145. "Banyumas-Bagelen," *De Macedoniër* 2 (1884), p. 172.

146. Some pamphlets as stated in the *Heidenbode* read as follows: "De opium pacht valt in een doorboorden buidel," "In de opium pachtrolle staan geschreven: zuchting, ach en wee," "Opium pacht noch opium regie, maar stuiting van 't kwaad." For more on the same subject, see H.B. Breijer, *De Opium en de Zending* (Arnhem, 1887).

147. "Uit Indië," *Heidenbode* (August, 1889), pp. 1-7.

Sadrach himself was known by many for his upright conduct, and no doubt exerted considerable influence on the life of the community. In this way, the community became an effective missionary witness among their non-Christian Javanese fellows. Heyting and Adriaanse both bore witness to the fact that Sadrach strongly opposed polygamy as well as prostitution. He even consistently prohibited the traditional feast which was accompanied by *tayuban*.[148] In general, members of Sadrach's community did not participate in gambling, polygamy, or the use of opium.[149] According to Heyting, most of the leaders of the villages where the community was established were satisfied with the conduct of the Christians, and Christians often composed the best element of the village.[150] Controller De Wolff Van Westerrode, who had direct contact with members of Sadrach's community, said that they never lied, but fulfilled their obligations to the government without grumbling. Nor did they demand special rights because of their Christianity, but maintained good relations with their Moslem neighbors.[151]

The impression is left that the life of the community was marked by simplicity, modesty, and honesty. These traits were inherited in part, no doubt, from such pious lay evangelists as Stevens-Philips, and from the *guru ngelmus* and *kyais*, ex-mystics like Sadrach and his fellows, who emphasized good conduct in accordance with the Javanese ideal life. This in turn was strengthened by the fact that they constituted a Christian minority living among the overwhelmingly Moslem majority. In this they remind us of the early Christian community, who lived in an overwhelmingly non-Christian world. Heyting and the goverment officials concluded that although the average member of Sadrach's community had little knowledge of Christian doctrine, they were well aware of Christian obligations.[152]

The community was well aware that as followers of *ratu adil*, Jesus Christ, they were to be obedient to His commands. Javanese evangelists and imams considered the Ten Commandments to be the *ngelmu* of *ratu adil*, which should be obeyed. Members practiced a simple form of thinking, and were more interested in concrete and tangible practical matters than in abstract doctrinal matters. They emphasized what was done more than what was thought. This does not mean, however, that they did not understand the central teachings of Christianity. They knew very

---

148. Heyting, p. 31; Adriaanse, *Sadrach's Kring*, p. 436.
149. Heyting, p. 33; Adriaanse, *Sadrach's Kring*, p. 436.
150. Heyting, pp. 32-33.
151. Ibid., Appendix F.
152. Ibid., p. 34.

well that Jesus was the great imam who died on the cross and was raised again for human redemption. They acknowledged the Lordship of Jesus, whom they perceived as a living prophet, who gives assurance of eternal life. They considered the *ngelmu* taught by the *ratu adil*, Jesus, superior to all other *ngelmu*.[153]

Another striking feature was the contrast drawn by the members between their former lives as Moslems and their present and future lives as believers in Jesus. The old faith was compared with the new. They pointed out how they knew only a little of Islam and its traditions because the *santris* and the imams never explained what Islam was. As Moslems they knew nothing of Islamic teaching, but after becoming Christians, they knew who they were. They now pronounced their prayers from the depths of their heart. They had not adequately understood the Koran, but now they could read the Scriptures. They asked themselves, what have we to do with the Arabic language? Islam may meet the needs of those who understand the language of the Koran, but we appreciate the Scriptures more, because they have been translated into our own language.[154]

In conclusion, we can say that there was a demonstrable link between the Christian faith the members of Sadrach's community embraced and the new life which they led.

b.   Developing new life through church discipline

Church discipline was also exercised in Sadrach's community. Problems relating to the life of the community were discussed every three months at the regular elders meeting in Karangjasa. This included problems relating to church discipline.[155] This indicates an effort on the part of the community to develop their new life on the basis of Christian teaching and the Ten Commandments, although this may have been carried out at times in a rather legalistic fashion. The "spiritual diseases" mentioned above were not tolerated within the community. Heyting's report that the performance of *wayang* was prohibited on the basis of Christian teaching is embarassing if true. Heyting reported that when a circumcision feast was held at which *wayang* was performed by a Christian *lurah* (village head), it was viewed as an offense requiring discipline, a violation of Christian teaching. While the circumcision was tolerated, *wayang* was not.[156] The *lurah* received a harsh warning from Sadrach himself.

153. Ibid., p. 37.
154. Ibid.
155. Wilhelm, 1883, p. 319.
156. Heyting, p. 31.

Members who married non-Christians, especially Moslems, before the *pengulu*, and those who were absent from Sunday worship any length of time without notifying the imam (violation of the fourth commandment), were considered apostates, and were accordingly excommunicated unless they confessed their "sin." All members who were found to be violating God's law (church regulations) were handled in the same way, regardless of position. An example of this is related by Adriaanse, who told of an imam who was engaging in trade throughout the week, including Sundays. He was also a lover of *wayang*. The case was brought before the elders meeting and discussed. It was decided that the imam should be given a warning. After the imam had ignored several admonitions, he was dismissed. A new imam was then appointed and the Sunday service was moved to the new imam's house.[157] Another example is the case of Kasanmunadi, whose son married a Moslem girl before he had made his profession of faith. Although Kasanmunadi was a close friend of Sadrach's, and had cared for him when he was in prison,[158] he was not exempted from church discipline. Wilhelm reported that Kasanmunadi had to confess his "sin" of permitting his son to marry a Moslem, and was not permitted to serve as elder for one year.[159]

The procedure of church discipline was not, however, arbitrary. Sadrach was the dominant figure, of course, and was highly respected. The guru and *kyai* was always like a father to his followers, so it is not surprising that problems were usually brought to Sadrach for advice, and were discussed by the imams in the regular elders' meetings. If the problem was crucial and needed immediate attention, Sadrach himself went to the village to assist the local imam in finding a solution. Such cases, however, were very rare. Sadrach had no ambition to make the community revolve around himself, or to be involved in every aspect of its life. When he was involved, however, he would warn the errant member three times. He acted in all things like a father toward his children. Persuasion was considered more important than punishment. This procedure was also applied to imams who erred. Before dismissing an imam, several attempts were made to pastorally counsel him. Excommunication was only the final step taken against members who were absolutely unresponsive. When someone was excommunicated, this was publicly announced in the worship service, and notice was given to the *lurah*. Such a notice was necessary for administrative reasons in matters such as compulsory work, and *zakat* or *fitrah*.[160]

---

157. Adriaanse, *Sadrach's Kring*, p. 392.
158. Heyting, p. 9.
159. Wilhelm, 1889, pp. 55-56.
160. *Zakat fitrah* is the fourth Islamic obligation (*rukun Islam*) in the form of monetary

The community was always open to those who confessed their sins. Such persons were accepted into or reunited with the community, an action representative of reconciliation with God and neighbor. For this too there was a specific procedure and ceremony. For example, a special worship service was held, usually on Saturday night, for the rehabilitation of an imam.[161] An imam who had been assigned at the elders' meeting in Karangjasa lead the worship. Community members and imams from neighboring communities were invited to attend. A metal bowl filled with water and flower petals, and a zinc box containing the Scriptures were placed in front of the pulpit. The repentant imam and his wife were strategically seated in the front. The worship leader would begin by announcing to the members of the audience the purpose for which they were gathered, and the audience was asked to witness the event. The leader then asked the imam to stand and addressed several questions to him concerning his recommitment to the new life and obedience to God. A hymn was then sung in Javanese *tembang*. James 5:8-20 was read, with special focus on verses 19 and 20: "My brethren, if anyone among you wanders from the truth, and someone brings him back, let him know that whoever brings back a sinner from the error of his way will save his soul from death and will cover a multitude of sin" (RSV). Afterwards, the leader would ask the community if they were willing to accept the confessing imam and his leadership. The leader then took the metal bowl and lifted it while holding the Scriptures in the other hand. He then said, "May the water of cleansing of the Holy Book be with you." The metal bowl was given to the imam and the leader said, "Wash your face with this water in order to release you from sin." The service was closed with another song and a blessing. The next day, the reconciled imam led the worship service, and a reception was held at which a large meal was served for all members. Like the Javanese communal meal, this was intended to act out the reconciliation in a concrete way.

A few more examples will show that church discipline in Sadrach's community was carried out in all seriousness, based on Christian principles.[162] The sacredness of marriage was stressed and was given much attention by the members. There was essentially no single justifiable reason for divorce or polygamy, not even infertility. If a woman had been deserted by her husband, however, she was allowed to remarry. Mixed marriages

---

contributions for special purposes, e.g., the poor. In Central Java among the Javanese *abangan, zakat fitrah* is collected yearly in the end of the fasting month of Ramadan.

161. Adriaanse, *Sadrach's Kring*, pp. 393-394.
162. Ibid., p. 395.

were permitted between Christians and non-Christians if they were performed in the church.

A polygamous Moslem who converted to Christianity was not required to divorce his wives. Nor was the Moslem wife of a polygamous husband required to leave her husband. If, however, he or she wished to divorce, there was no objection. The reason lying behind this is rather interesting. A spouse who did not convert to Christianity was considered to be dead. This was probably based on Romans 7:1-3:

> The law is binding on a person only during his life. Thus a married woman is bound by law to her husband as long as he lives; but if her husband dies, she is discharged from the law concerning the husband. Accordingly, she will be called an adulteress if she lives with another man while her husband is alive. But if her husband dies, she is free from the law, and if she marries another man she is not an adulteress. (RSV)

Death in these verses meant physical death for Paul. The members of the community, however, understood it to mean spiritual death, and used it to justify divorce in such cases. Thus several cases were reported by Adriaanse in which wives, some with children, were abandoned because they would not become Christians. Although this is tragic, such a misinterpretation is understandable because Paul made it sound as though the decision to stay or to leave an unbelieving spouse was up to the individual (I Cor. 7:15a). We must concede, however, that the spirit of Paul's advice was quite the contrary (I Cor. 7:15b-16), and that Paul actually preferred that those who were married remain so.[163]

What conclusions can we draw concerning the spiritual life of Sadrach's community? It was a community that strove to make the new life it had received manifest in its daily life. There was an awareness of their minority position in society, and as a result, they attempted to remain above reproach through moral self-discipline and compassionate church discipline. It was for these reasons that they were praised by government officials as the best element of their communities.

2. The spirit of independence (keberdikarian)

Keberdikarian (from berdirdiatas kaki sendiri), literally, "to stand on one's own feet," was a prominent feature of Sadrach's community from the very beginning. This spirit originated from the culture of the Javanese rural village, which had been self-supporting since ancient times. In this section we will examine how this spirit of keberdikarian found expression in the life of Sadrach's community.

---

163. I Corinthians 7:12-16.

As noted, *keberkidarian* was a distinctive feature of Javanese rural life. Those who seriously observed Javanese rural life in the past century discovered this spirit among the people. Poensen never tired of stating how independent the Javanese peasants were.[164] The founding fathers of the Javanese villages cleared the jungles and established farming communities with great courage and heroism. New independent villages continued to emerge in Java well into the nineteenth century. The founders of the village continued to hold a special place in the hearts of the villagers. Their graves usually became the object of veneration. Such veneration functions as form of spiritual unity among villagers even today.

There were also several Christian villages established in East and North Central Java in the past century as the result of the pioneering efforts of Javanese evangelists. Jansz was a great proponent of establishing Christian villages as a form of evangelizing. His book, *Landontginning en evangelisatie op Java* (Land Reclamation and Evangelization in Java) was published to promote this method of evangelizing. This method was successful, of course, only so long as there was still uncultivated land to reclaim, as was the case, in the nineteenth century. Jansz may have been inspired by the success of Coolen, who established a prosperous Christian village in Ngoro, which attracted many of the non-Christian Javanese from the surrounding area.[165] There can be no doubt that the success of such a method was due in part to the sense of self-sufficiency it provided to its participants, and to the exemplary perseverance of the leaders.

Javanese villages were basically independent, self-supporting, and self-governing in internal affairs. Village life was communal in nature, based on solidarity, harmony, and cooperation between members. According to Burger, this spirit of *gotong royong* (concerted action), significantly colored rural economic and social life. In Javanese rural society, where the role of money was not yet decisive, the economic system was not regulated in a business-like fashion, but was based on mutual help and loyalty to the village leader. Entrepreneurship was not yet known among the villagers.[166]

The independence of the villages is best seen in the system of land ownership. According to Poensen, there were two different types of ownership: communal and individual. The communal system of collective, village-owned land, was found primarily in Central Java. Each member of the village had an equal right to cultivate the land as regulated in the village gathering.[167] Cultivation rights were usually restricted to village in-

164. Poensen, "Javaansche Desa," p. 73.
165. Van Akkeren, pp. 55-68.
166. Burger, p. 14.
167. Poensen, "Javaansche Desa," p. 97.

habitants to insure the welfare and independence of the village. However, people who lived outside the village could sometimes farm part of the land for a rental fee.[168]

Although the wet-rice fields had been very important to the villagers for many years, they were not the only source of income. The mixed gardens around the village houses (*pekarangan*) and the dry fields (*tegalan*) were two other sources of income. A large variety of crops could be raised in these areas. If the rice harvest failed, it was possible to live off the harvest from the *pekarangan* and *tegalan*. Koentjaraningrat noted that several crops, such as cassava, soybeans, corn, and peanuts had been used by Javanese farmers since the early nineteenth century as a substitute source of income in case of a rice failure. After the economic depression of 1885, growing these crops was encouraged by the colonial government to increase food production.[169]

Among the farmers were some who engaged in small trade — buying merchandise in one place and selling it in another, going from village to village. Others owned simple stores (*warung*) and sold various everyday items.[170]

This brief survey clearly shows the spirit of independence among the villagers. Van Akkeren concluded that, from earliest times, the Javanese village had been the bearer of social and economic autonomy.[171]

Sadrach and his community lived in such an environment. As has been noted, they lived among the villagers rather than in separate communities. Like their neighbors, most members of the community earned their living from farming or small trade.[172] They were simple villagers who were satisfied with their life. Modernity had not yet reached the villages, and money was not a determinative factor. Sadrach's community was generally self-supporting apart from the villages.

The spirit of independence was also reflected in the life of the leaders. Sadrach's deputies, Yohanes, Markus, and Musa, all ex-*guru ngelmu*, were never paid for their work in the community. They each had their own occupation, either as farmer or small trader. The imams, as well as the other church officials, worked as farmers.[173] This was probably a continuation of the Javanese *guru ngelmu* and *pesantren* tradition in which spiritual work was highly appreciated but could not be a fulltime, paid job.

168. Brumund, "Het Landbezit," pp. 87-88.
169. Koentjaraningrat, *Javanese Culture*, p. 175; *Kebudayaan Jawa*, p. 185.
170. Poensen, "Javaansche Desa," p. 55.
171. Van Akkeren, p. 5.
172. Heyting, p. 28.
173. Ibid.; see also, L. Adriaanse to Deputaten voor de Zending op Midden Java ten Zuiden, Dec. 1, 1896, *Heidenbode* (March, 1897), pp. 268-271.

In the Javanese *pesantren*, the *kyai* was not paid but was motivated in his work by believing that it was a good deed which would reap benefits in his future life and in the hereafter. Material contributions, however, were not rejected, especially in the area of religious education.[174] The *guru ngaji* (teacher of Koran recitation) was also unpaid.[175] It was customary, however, also in Sadrach's community, for the members to make voluntary contributions to their leaders as "presents."[176]

Adriaanse told a moving story that demonstrates the spirit of independence in the community. The event occurred shortly after Cachet's departure from Central Java. Wilhelm, who spiritually suffered greatly from Cachet's decision, made a visit to Karangjasa to see Sadrach. He wanted to know Sadrach's personal opinion about his staying in Central Java, even though the NGZV was forcing his return to the Netherlands. Sadrach assured Wilhelm that both he and the community were still willing to have Wilhelm be their minister and that they would provide him with a place to live.[177] Such an offer demonstrates Sadrach's independence and self-confidence in finding a solution to Wilhelm's problem.

The independence of the community was also seen in their concern for the poor.[178] Motivated by the spirit of *gotong-royong*, the community members raised funds to rent a piece of land from a former indigo plantation for an extended period of time, which was then distributed to the needy. They were able to erect simple houses and grow crops for a living. Twenty families were helped in this way — a group large enough to constitute a small Christian village. According to the land ownership and land use regulations of the time, the use of land for such resettlement was permitted by the government.[179]

The economic life of the community was also discussed at the regular elders' meetings in Karangjasa. Very needy members were given financial aid through a special fund collected by the local communities. A basket was placed near the pulpit or front door of each church during worship services so that members could contribute to the fund. Another cooperative organization which provided funds, called *Sinoman* (literally: youth),[180] was used for those who needed capital to start a small business.

174. Zamaksyari Dhofier, *Tradisi Pesantren: suatu study tentang pandangan hidup Kyai* [*Pesantren* Tradition: A Study of Kyai's Life-View] (Jakarta, 1985), p. 24 n. 15.

175. S.A. Schilstra, "Langgar en Pesantren," MNZG 37 (1893), pp. 325-336.

176. Heyting, pp. 21, 28, 30, 52.

177. Adriaanse, *Sadrach's Kring*, p. 326.

178. Ibid., pp. 428-430.

179. Cf. Poensen, "Javaansche Desa," pp. 98-99; Brumund, pp. 47-104.

180. According to Koentjaraningrat, this was a youth organization for boys, originally in the education field. For girls it was called *biyada*. Today these two youth

Unlike the financial aid fund, funds received through *Sinoman* were to be paid back at a low rate of interest. Through the use of this method, it was hoped that community members could avoid borrowing from Chinese usurers.[181] It not only provided for material goods, but also aided in developing a sense of Christian community.

This kind of cooperation was not new. In the village community in the Residency of Bagelen, of which Karanjasa was a part, such cooperation had existed for a long time. Called *grojogan* in Javanese, it included various activities such as hoeing, planting rice seedlings, and weeding the rice fields. In its original primitive form, cooperation involved setting up a rice barn (*lumbung-padi*) in which part of the harvest was stored in the event of a poor harvest the following year. New seedlings for the coming season were also stored there.

Finally, it is important to see how the community itself understood its independence as reflected in its name, *Golongane Wong Kristen kang Mardika*, and its minister (*pandita mardika* — free minister). What was their intention in including the work *mardika* in its name? To answer this question, it is necessary to look at the history of the community from the very beginning. In its formative years, the community developed around independent lay evangelists, and were thus separate from the *Indische Kerk* and the NGZV. When Wilhelm was the minister, they cooperated with the NGZV, but were not officially a part of the mission organization. The members never stopped thinking of Sadrach as their leader during this time.

Thus the word *mardika*, as understood by the community members, also meant total economic independence. A respected member boldly stated the following in a converstation with the Dutch Controller:

Member: '... J. Wilhelm calls himself a *pandita mardika* because he is free and does not depend on the government or any organization for his salary.'

Controller: 'How does he live if no one pays him?'

Member: 'He does not necessarily worry about his living. When he agreed to become the minister of our church he knew he would receive no salary and trusted in God to give him what he needed. In addition he has the *right to trade*.'

Controller: 'Why did you not recognize Bieger as your minister? Was he a *pandita mardika*?'

Member: 'Certainly not, because he received a salary form the government.'[182]

organizations are still found only in the traditional parts of Banyumas and Bagelen, and are considered conservative and unprogressive. See Koentjaraningrat, *Javanese Culture*, p. 199; *Kebudayaan Jawa*, p. 211.
181. Adriaanse, *Sadrach's Kring*, p. 429.
182. Heyting, Appendix F, emphases ours.

It is also obvious that the idea of a paid minister was foreign to Javanese thought. Although Wilhelm received a salary from the NGZV, the members of the community were unaware of it. In Javanese thought, no one who was involved in spiritual or religious work was professionally employed for that purpose. They were to support themselves by farming or trading, as the conversation above implies. They were to stand on their own feet economically, as exemplified in the lives of Sadrach and the leaders of the community, in which the spirit of independence was heavily emphasized.

Sadrach Surapranata with his "big family"

CHAPTER IV

ISSUES RAISED AGAINST SADRACH AND HIS COMMUNITY

Sadrach's encounter with the Dutch missionaries produced several areas of controversy within the Reformed mission circle. Although the personal ambitions of some of the missionaries added to the problem, the major cause lay deeper, in the gap between the Javanese and Dutch socio-cultural and political backgrounds. This gap was much wider in the nineteenth century than it is today, and frequently caused prejudice and misunderstandings among members of the two groups.

In this chapter, the viewpoint of the Dutch missionaries will be presented, particularly of those who accused Sadrach of misusing his authority, utilizing a leadership style contrary to Calvinistic principles, spreading false teachings, and developing a Javanese rather than a Christian community. In an effort to understand the origin of these accusations, the mission theology which characterized Reformed mission activity in the nineteenth century will also be discussed. It will become obvious in our discussion that some accusations were quite ethnocentric and sometimes even politically motivated. Our attention, however, will focus on those accusations related to confessional aberrations, since they were, in our opinion, the predominant ones.

A. The Mission Theology of the Reformed Mission and its Implementation

From the outset, the intention to create and maintain theological orthodoxy was the specific mark of the Reformed missionary activities[1] in Central Java. The "Three Forms of Unity" of the Reformed Churches in the Netherlands[2] formed the confessional basis of missions, but to translate this into missionary practice was often difficult. While it was clearly stated

---

1. Regarding the establishment of the NGZV, see Chapter I, section B2.
2. The Three Forms of Unity, consist of:

   a. *Heidelberg Catechism* (1563)
   b. *Nederlandsche Geloofsbelijdenis* (Belgic Confession) (1561)
   c. *Canons of Dort* (1618).

in the constitution of the NGZV that its mission was to be Reformed, such principles were not easily realized. The problem of missionary ordination, for example, revealed how certain basic questions concerning church and mission were seen from the Reformed theological standpoint — questions of what Reformed mission really was.

Like a child learning to walk, with no concrete guidelines and experiences at the beginning phase, the NGZV carried out its mission through a process of trial and error.³ Therefore, the need for more detailed and concrete guidelines for missions based on Reformed principles was urgent. Both the Board, as policymakers on the homefront, and the missionaries in the field needed direction in carrying out their tasks. To clarify these issues, we will follow the development of mission theology within the Reformed churches insofar as it was related to missions in Central Java. The contributions of a handful of Reformed mission theorists set the direction taken by the NGZV to build a distinctive theology of missions.

Twenty years after the establishment of the NGZV there seemed to be a growing consciousness that the church was the organization primarily responsible for missions,⁴ as C.H. Koopman implicitly asserted.⁵ Koopman, a member of the NGZV Board (1879), emphasized that missions was God's will and command. God himself was the sender and entrusted the task of missions to His church. In this way the church became a missionary church.' Until the church was able to fulfill the obligation herself, missionary organizations like the NGZV were needed, but simply as "tijdelijke plaatsvervangster der Kerk" (a temporary substitute for the church). Koopman was of the opinion that the goal of missions was "zielen voor Christus te winnen" (to win souls for Christ) for the glory of God. He characterized missions as the work of faith. God Himself was the sender who should be obeyed. Missions, he felt, was the working out of God's promise, and the way to demonstrate love to those whom we ought to love.

J.H. Donner, the director of the mission of the *Christelijke Gereformeerde Kerk* and a member of *de Deputaten Synode van de Gereformeerde Kerken tot de Zending onder Heidenen en Mohammedanen* (1892), ela-

3. Graaf Van Randwijck characterized nineteenth century missions as "de tijd niet van zendingsbeleid, maar van improvisatie" *Handelen en denken, in dienst der Zending* ('s-Gravenhage, 1981), p. 408. This general observation seems to be valid to a certain extent for Reformed missions in its early stages as carried out by the NGZV.
4. The *Christelijke Gereformeerde Kerk* had already, since 1860, considered missions the official task of the church; see Van Den End, *Gereformeerde Zending*, p. 5.
5. C.H. Koopman, "Aan het Hoofd bestuur der Nederlandsche Gereformeerde Zendingsvereeniging;" C.H. Koopman, "Letter to the NGZV Board," *Heidenbode* (August, 1878), pp. 14-15; also in *Heidenbode* (September, 1878), pp. 17-18.

borated on the goal of missions by asking what the message of missions to the heathen was. According to him, the Lord had entrusted the church with "de volheid van de bedeeling en bediening des Evangelies in Christus Jezus" (the fulness of the dispensation and ministry of the Gospel of Jesus Christ) which was to be brought to the heathen.[6] He claimed that while it is true that the church of Jesus Christ must proclaim the Word of God, the good news of reconciliation and peace, light and life in Christ, it also had the responsibility of administering the sacraments as a means of strengthening the new and abundant life of Christian community among the community of converts. In contrast to the liberals[7] who stressed education as a prerequisite for doing missions, Donner recognized only the powerful, continuing work of the Holy Spirit in mission activities by which the Gospel obtains access to the human heart. He feared, however, that mission work among the heathen was largely influenced by the spirit of the age (*rijdgeest*), which was viewed as a great danger for missions. He therefore advocated that God's Word be proclaimed as cleanly and purely (*louter en zuiver*) as possible. He was convinced that the power of God's Word and the Holy Spirit always preceeded mission work. On this point Donner certainly defended the orthodox principles and methods of the Reformed mission, and disagreed with those who emphasized "civilization of the heathen through education" as part of their mission.

D.P.D. Fabius (1851-1931), Professor of State Law since October 21, 1880 at the Free University in Amsterdam,[8] spoke of the significance of the Reformed faith as the solid basis of missions.[9] While it was not the intention of missions to dwell on dogmatic differences nor to introduce the heathen to theological disputes, he insisted that the Reformed confessions were significant for mission work among the heathen. He advocated equipping missionaries with a specifically Reformed understanding of the sacraments, general and special revelation, and church order, since he felt that a proper understanding of these things could have a great impact upon the spiritual life of the converts. For this reason he, like Donner, stressed purity (*zuiverheid*) in the proclamation of the Word of God. Unity and cooperation with other missionary organizations was desirous, but was to be tempered with the caution the the solid Reformed basis of mission not

6. J.H. Donner, "Wat moet de Zending de Heidenen brengen? *Het Mosterdzaad* (June, 1882), pp. 81-84, (July, 1882), pp. 97-100; cf. Van Den End, *Gereformeerde Zending*, pp. 83-85.

7. Regarding the "liberal" segment, see Chapter I, section B2.

8. J. Stellingwerff, *Dr. Abraham Kuyper en de Vrije Universiteit* (Kampen, 1987), p. 114.

9. NGZV, Minutes, June 15, 1882 (Archives of the Dutch Reformed Missionary Society, Leusden), Van Den End, *Gereformeerde Zending*, pp. 85-86.

be yielded or sacrificed for such purposes. Such a statement reveals the emphasis on maintaining orthodoxy and the exclusive character of Reformed missions.

Abraham Kuyper, a member of the NGZV, was appointed as its advisor in 1871.[10] During the missionary conference held in Amsterdam in 1890, he spoke on the theological basis of missions among the Jews, the Moslems, and the heathen, as well as on missionary methodology. The summary of his address was published in the form of twenty-seven theses.[11] He understood missions as flowing from the sovereignty of God — it is the command of God. Doing missions is obedience to God's command, like Jesus the Son who himself was the "missionary" of the Father, obediently doing what his Father commanded. Similarly, the church, as the primary bearer of missions, must be obedient to Christ's command. According to Kuyper, "every creaturely mission is only a reflection, representation, or instrument of the one principle mission, that of the Son by the Father." He went on to say that,

— The Incarnation was the coming of the Son into the world so that He Himself, in His own person, might carry out the first stage of His mission.

— The mission of the evangelists and apostles, like that of the prophets, did not replace Christ, but was an instrument in His hand, and distinguished itself from every subsequent mission in that it applied to the ecumenical church of all places.

— The Holy Scripture itself is the permanent and enduring revelation of the mission of Christ on earth, and His commission to the world.

— Christ carries out His mission through all ages in the local church through His servants of the Word. This mission is directed toward all the baptized, as baptized, and therefore as those incorporated into the Covenant of Grace.[12]

Regarding missions among the Moslems, Kuyper stated that,

Likewise, the mission among the Mohammedans should not direct itself toward the individual, but must turn itself against Islam as such. Let it lock onto the anti-pagan efforts of Islam, as well as onto the true elements which still remain in their confession of Moses and the Christ; let it, moreover, attack the parasitic plant which has overgrown and choked the true confession under the confession of Mohammed

10. NGZV, Minutes, October 15, 1871 (Archives of the Dutch Reformed Missionary Societ, Leusden); Van Den End, *Gereformeerde Zending*, p. 81, n. 1.

11. "Zendingcongres," pp. 89-92; A. Kuyper, *Historisch Document*, J. Bootsma ed. (Utrecht, 1940), pp. 1-20; see also NGK, *Acta van het Zendingcongres* (Amsterdam, 1890), pp. 2-11.

12. "Zendingcongres," p. 90; Kuyper, p. 2.

and the Koran; reprove the Moslem for his piously dressed sensuality; restore the Law and Gospel in their purity and fulness; and replace the essence of Islam with the essence of the Christian religion.[13]

Kuyper's understanding of missions among the heathen, unlike the mission to Islam where the approach seemed to be more "positive," was not directed toward the seeking out of true elements in the existing religious structure, but was rather dedicated to its elimination. He felt that the mission to the heathen should be directed toward the achievement of four goals, namely,

— to overthrow idols
— to lead the idolaters to Holy Baptism in order to reveal the church of Christ among their people
— to bring this revelation of the church of Christ into relation with the mother church
— to remold the heathen culture into a Christian form.[14]

In contrast to the existing system where mission work was carried out by missionary organizations independent of the church, Kuyper advocated what is called "kerkelijk zending" (ecclesiastical mission). He was of the opinion that missions should become a part of the regular church structure with the local church bearing responsibility for mission work. The door was also open for local churches to carry out its mission work cooperatively.[15]

Regarding mission methodology, Kuyper felt that the proclamation of the Gospel to the heathen and to Moslems must

...direct itself toward the special nature of the people among whom it works, especially the extent of their idolatry; and furthermore, it must give complete freedom to the confession of Christ, in order that, as soon as it leads to a particular church formation, it may take on that unique form which pertains to the mode of existence of such a people.[16]

This proposal was then elaborated by asking whether the goal of missions should be to establish an annex of the sending church among other peoples or simply to bring them the commission of the Lord and to leave the form of the church to God's leading. Kuyper noted that the absolute form of the church insisted on by former generations, who thought that those who had been converted should be gathered into

13. "Zendingcongres," p. 90; Kuyper, p. 7.
14. Ibid.
15. "Zendingcongres," p. 91; Kuyper, p. 13; for further elaboration on church missions in practice, see W.H. Gispen, "Kerkelijke Zending in de practijk," De Macedoniër 8 (1890), pp. 280-297.
16. "Zendingcongres," p. 90; Kuyper, p. 13.

churches which were modeled as closely as possible after the mother church, was now considered wrong. He, therefore, proposed that diversity of confession and worship was possible, and that since Scripture gave no specific instructions for such things, a wealth of variation according to time, circumstance, cultural character, etc. was even to be desired so long as it conformed to scriptural principles.[17] Therefore, we may conclude that Kuyper had a certain sensitivity to contextualization.

Kuyper's distinction between mission work among the heathen and among Moslems was relevant for the mission work in Central Java since the Javanese were considered Moslem. In Kuyper's opinion, each group had its own "capital sin," that of the heathens being paganism, and that of the Moslems being sensualism. This was clear in his statement quoted above, that the mission among the Moslems had to be directed against Islam per se rather than toward individuals. He went on to say that the sin of the Mohammedan is sensuality, and that mission must attack this sensual essence with the authority of the law of the spiritual life since Christ preaches a spiritual life over against the sensual. Therefore, Christian missions calls Moslems as well as heathens to conversion.[18]

On the occasion of the same missionary conference, Cachet, who then became the leading member of the NGZV Board as secretary for foreign affairs,[19] spoke enthusiastically about "The work of the Reformed churches currently being carried out by the mission in the Indies."[20] His enthusiasm was expressed by his statement that,

> In every *dessa* [village] where believers live, not only is the light of the Gospel *enkindled*, but that light becomes a *source of light*, a focus of light in an ever widening circle. Through the cohabitation of Christian natives with non-Christians the Gospel is gradually propagated; and the greater the expanse over which the Christian communities are preached, the greater may be the expectation that the entire region will be evangelized, for if they let its light shine, as must be expected, its adherents will be able to be called true Christians.[21]

17. Kuyper, p. 14.
18. Kuyper, p. 10. Cf. D. Bakker, who, in a speech about mission work among the Moslems, said that although Islam was monotheistic, working among the Moslems was not redundant. He stated,

> First of all, because although they believe in one God, they do not believe in that One God as He has revealed himself in the Holy Scriptures. They reject the Son and the Holy Ghost and cannot, therefore, come to a knowledge of salvation in their religion (John 3:36). In the second place, because their monotheism is mixed with all sorts of heathen idolatry, as can be seen in their worship of the black stone, the grave of Mohammed, and such." See D. Bakker, *De Zending*, p. 9.

19. Cf. Chapter II, section B3.
20. NGK, *Acta Zendingcongres*, pp. 50-64.
21. Ibid., p. 54.

Recognizing that Christian congregations had been established in Central Java, he further insisted that

> Each of these congregations has been established, as much as possible, according to Reformed order, with elders as overseers, and as such they are to be distinguished from "mission posts" or "mission stations," because the organization, by the very nature of things, has never been the responsibility of the NGZV, and certainly is not now. But none of these native churches has its own pastor and teacher yet.[22]

In his speech he compared mission work to fishing based on Jesus' statement in Mark 1:16: "Follow me and I will make you fishers of men" (RSV). According to Cachet, the proclamation of God's Word to the heathen was to be done in such a way as to open their hearts to the Gospel, thereby leading to conversion. In addition to the Gospel, "fishing" also included medicine and education which functioned as auxiliary equipment to missions. He was of the opinion, therefore, that, in addition to theological education, missionaries should have a working knowledge of medicine and education. Proclaiming the Gospel, healing the sick, and educating the heathen were inseparable means of doing missions, means which Cachet confirmed had been employed by the NGZV from the very beginning.[23] Drawing from Cachet's description, it is our opinion that the auxiliary equipment to missions might become the attracting "bait" in the hands of the "fishermen," and the "basket" in which the fish were collected was, of course, the church — the community of believers into which converts were to be incorporated.

Like Kuyper, Cachet also made a theoretical distinction between missions among the heathen and among Moslems. He said that,

> The less a heathen people has come in contact with Mohammedanism the sooner it is receptive to the Gospel. And also the reverse, the more a people has fallen under the influence of Mohammedanism, the less the Gospel finds entrance. The history of both Mohammedanism and the mission to Mohammedan lands clearly demonstrates this. Christianity has known no more stubborn enemy than the heathens who have become followers of the false prophet. Mohammedanism stifles every germ of yearning after tolerance or forgiveness, and tramples the conscience.[24]

---

22. Ibid., pp. 54-55. It is worthy to note here that Cachet, who initially recognized the indigenous Christian community as "Inlandsche Kerken" drastically changed his mind and later renounced it. Quarles Van Ufford notes that this change was not occasioned by new insight gained from his investigation. To the contrary, Cachet had formulated this denouncement and recorded it in his diary while his vessel was still enroute to Batavia. Therefore, Quarles Van Ufford concludes that Cachet came to Central Java not to foster cooperation with the "Inlandsche Kerken" but to end it. See P. Quarles Van Ufford, "Cycles of Concern, Dutch Reformed Mission in Central Java, 1896-1970," in *Religion and Development*, ed. P. Quarles Van Ufford and M. Schoffeleers (Amsterdam, 1988), p.. 78.

23. NGK, *Acta Zendingcongres*, p. 56.

24. Ibid., p. 53.

Furthermore, Cachet felt that

> Mohammed is the idol of the Mohammedans and fatalism is their fetish. Mohammedanism has never been anything other than a hindrance and a stone of stumbling for the spread of God's kingdom among the heathens. And there is no increased gains to expect for the Gospel from the — mostly forced — conversion of the heathen peoples to Mohammed. And so, it is to be considered a gracious leading from the Lord that although the Javanese has accepted Mohammedanism, he still has not become a Mohammedan.[25]

Cachet also stressed the establishment of the institutional church in his lecture. He said,

> ...the primary purpose was always the preaching of the Gospel to the heathen and Mohammedans who had been brought to the churches which gathered in accordance with the Reformed order; these churches meet together on a classical level, and are served, temporarily, by the missionaries, not as their permanent shepherds and teachers, but as advisors.[26]

He concluded the lecture with the statement,

> Wonderful will be the day when a Javanese from among the Javanese, a delegate of the Javanese churches, takes a seat here in the synodical meeting of our Reformed churches, and our churches will be represented at the general gathering of the Javanese Reformed churches.[27]

From this overview of the development of the theology of missions in Reformed circles of the nineteenth century, it is clear that emphasis was placed on the establishment of the institutional church on the mission field. For example, in a report of Mission Day, held in Leiden on September 4, 1883, and sponsored by the *Zending of the Christelijke Gereformeerde Kerk*,[28] the first point of the agenda reads "To what extent can the Reformed principles of church government, worship, and discipline be applied within the church of the heathen?"[29] It is evident here that institutional church planting was the main concern of the Reformed mission. The report goes on to state that missionaries must not only proclaim the Word of God, but also establish God's church in the heathen world. In order to achieve this goal, the primary question became that of the most effective mission method. A related question arose from the

25. Ibid.

26. Ibid., p. 56.

27. Ibid., p. 64.

28. The churches which separated from the *Nederlandsche Hervormde Kerk* in the *Afscheiding*, 1834, and united under the name of the *Christelijke Gereformeerde Kerk* in 1869; see Berkhof, p. 317-318; for more about the *Afscheiding* see Rasker, pp. 55-70.

29. *Christelijke Gereformeerde Kerk,* "Verslag van de Zendingsdag van de Zending der Christelijke Gereformeerde Kerk te Leiden op September 1883," *Het Mosterdzaad* (October, 1883), pp. 148-158; cf. Van Den End, *Gereformeerde Zending*, p. 89.

complaint by some of the Reformed constituency that missionaries gave too little attention to Reformed principles, and rather carried out their mission according to their own personal views, feelings, and inclinations.

In the nineteenth century, the missionaries' sole criteria for determining truth and untruth, especially with regard to "paganism" was according to "their own" Dutch Reformed standards. We have already seen how Cachet applied such ethnocentric standards for measuring the life of the Christian community in Central Java (1891). The side effect of using "their own" standards as the only norm was that most missionaries possessed an impatient and intolerant attitude toward that which they considered to be idolatrous and paganistic. Unfortunately, indigenous culture in its totality tended to fall into these categories. Accordingly, it is obvious that in practice, mission work among the heathen and Moslems did not differ. Both heathen and Moslems were considered pagan. Such a view continued even into the early twentieth century.

We may conclude, therefore, that the NGZV, as a Reformed missionary organization in the nineteenth century, attempted to developed a distinct mission theology based on the Reformed faith.[30] In practice, emphasis was placed on individual conversion, in spite of Kuyper's admonitions to the contrary — converting the heathen and bringing them into the institutional church. Conversion included the transformation of paganistic lifestyles to a higher Christian morality. The sacraments, administered by the ordained missionaries, were also stressed. Reformed mission figures such as Kuyper insisted that doing away with idolatrous and paganistic lifestyles and customs was a prerequisite for baptism into the institutional church. The goal of missions was the establisment of Reformed churches on the mission fields as the true church of Christ. In this spirit the NGZV carried out its mission to Central Java.

It was only in 1896 that the Middelburg Synod made an important decision regarding what we would today call contextualization. We regard this decision as a step by Reformed missions toward the encouragement of contextualizing indigenous Christian communities, although in reality on the mission field it was still considered questionable. The decision reads,

> Our Reformed Churches in the Netherlands possess a Western, and to a certain extent, also a national character, which also is in the form of the confession, and even in the language and choice of words. Inasmuch as God has not created all peoples the same but has created the Javanese different than us — Eastern in his way of thinking, completely different in his level of development, and with a different past — the

---

30. A more complete and detailed formulation of Reformed mission based on the Reformed faith was made at the Middelburg Synod (1896) and published as "Rapport in zake de Zending," *Heidenbode* (Sept.-Oct., 1896), pp. 203-218.

demand may never be made that he accept our forms, but the Eastern form of song, prayer, and confession, which pertains to his existence must well up from the very bosom of the converted portion of the Javanese.[31]

B. Accusations Against Sadrach and his Community and the Resulting Theological-Missiological Issues

In this section the accusations against Sadrach and the community as recorded in various sources will be delineated and elucidated and the issues which arose from them will be discussed.

1. Accusations as recorded in various sources

The accusations against Sadrach and the community will be discussed chronologically in two time periods: before the vaccination affair (1882), and after the affair, when Wilhelm was "employed" by the community as minister.

a. Accusations brought against Sadrach and the community before the vaccination affair

According to Heyting's report (1883), the following nine accusations were brought against Sadrach:

1). He displayed marks on both hands which were supposed to prove that he was the Christ.
2). He once suddenly made himself invisible after church and after four days he reappeared just as suddenly, an event which his followers attributed to supernatural forces.
3). He allowed himself to be called not only imam, which means spiritual lord, but moreover *bapa, kayai, tiyang sepah, gusti,* and even *raden mas ngabehi Surapranata* (the one who is courageous in the appropriation of authority).
4). He and his followers gave the appearance of a distinguished *priyayi* and his

---

31. Onze Gereformeerde kerken in Nederland bezitten een westersche, en ten deele ook een nationaal karakter, dat ook in de vormen der belijdenis, en tot in taal en woordenkeuze uitkomt. Overmits nu God niet alle volken eender schiep, maar den Javaan anders dan ons, oostersch in wijze van voorstelling; hem op geheel anderen trap van ontwikkeling plaatste; en hem een ander verleden gaf, mag nimmer de eisch gesteld, dat hij onze vormen overneme, maar moet uit den boezem zelf van bekeerde deel der Javanen, die oostersche vorm voor lied, gebed en belijdenis opkomen, die bij zijne existentie past.

Kuyper, p. 35; see "Rapport in zake de Zending," p. 212.

panakawans (attendants thought to possess divine wisdom) when they traveled.

5). On certain occasions, he allowed a white *payung* (umbrella) to be held over his head.

6). He received the hand and foot kiss.

7). He allowed the tails of his garment to be carried by *embans* (female attendants whom only the Javanese nobles possess) when he went to the bathroom.

8). He had several weapons in his house, at least when he assumed the leadership of the community.

9). He pressured every new convert to purchase a *keris* (dagger) which he had blessed.[32]

These nine accusations may be summarized as follows.

— Sadrach claimed himself to be the Christ (accusation a).

— He aggrandized himself (*zelfverheffing*) to the level of a Javanese aristocrat by using Javanese aristocratic titles (*raden mas ghabehi* and *gusti*) and following aristocratic customs (accusations d and g). At least he regarded himself as a highly respected Javanese, full of wisdom, as demonstrated by his use of honorable Javanese titles (accusation c).

— He pretended to have supernatural powers (accusation b).

— He was a rebellious political leader as demonstrated by his possession of "many" weapons (accusation h).

— He enriched himself personally by selling "blessed" daggers (accusation i).

These accusations in turn led to further accusations. The accusations recorded in Wilhelm's diary reveal the same basic themes.[33] According to Wilhelm, they were formulated by Van Troostenburg De Bruijn, Schneider, Abisai, and Bieger in their efforts to replace Sadrach as leader of the community. His diary reads:

> In a few meetings held with Sadrach, Bieger demanded from him the complete surrender of the community, and that he give up all rights and duties given to him by Mrs. Philips, and that he either withdraw or return to Japara. Sadrach was not the type to obey immediately, which had the result that Bieger called in help from both European and native officials and composed nine accusations with Rev. Van Troostenburg De Bruijn and Schneider and Abisai, with the hope of rendering him harmless. These accusations, however, contained not-a-one that made him politically dangerous, at which the government could intervene.[34]

According to Wilhelm, Bieger, aided by government officials and the three men mentioned in his diary, attempted to take leadership away from Sadrach. The reasons for the conspiracy were recorded in his report to the

---

32. Heyting, p. 5; see also Bieger's letters of March 28 and July 1, 1878, *Heidenbode* (Oct., 1878), pp. 21-22.

33. J. Wilhelm, *Aantekeningen* (Archives of the Dutch Reformed Missionary Society, Leusden, n.d.), pp. 13-15.

34. Wilhelm, 1882, pp. 14, 22.

Board of the NGZV dated May 21, 1882, where he stated that the Javanese Christians were like small children and, therefore, the need for further education and guidance was urgent. Although they had a good grasp of the core of the Christian message — salvation only through the blood of Christ — Bieger maintained that their knowledge of the Word of God was insufficient.[35] Vermeer, on the other hand, interpreted Bieger's attempt more broadly. He saw it as a means of restoring Dutch influence over the Javanese Christian community; an influence which he felt was still necessary.[36]

b. Accusations after the vaccination affair

Three sources exist which record the accusations brought against Sadrach and the community after the vaccination incident, namely, the accusations recorded by Uhlenbusch, the correspondence between Wilhelm and Horstman, and the accusations recorded in the minutes of the *Algemeene Vergadering der Gemeenten* held in Purwareja.

Uhlenbusch's article, "Sadrach in Bagelen," contained various accusations against Sadrach. Since he was of German origin and upbringing, Uhlenbusch's writing was colored by his cultural context. His cynicism was apparent. He wrote:

> That conceited Sadrach left for Karanjasa, which he compared to Rome, in order to get away from all Hollanders and their authority since he was a European-hater, missionaries not excepted. He established himself there as someone who viewed himself as exalted over everything, and who, through his daring, had climbed up to [the position of] superior of all communities; he who stocked his house with all manner of weapons as though he were an old Knight of the Rhine; he who boldly allowed himself to be called *gusti*, the highest title the Javanese language has for a mortal beside the title of God and Jesus Christ; he who pretends to be, as it were, a second Christ, stigmatized by the five stigmata of the crucified Christ. For we [Uhlenbusch!] do not consider Sadrach's case one of an eccentric thought, imagination, fancy, idea, etc., but view it as a cunning trick on his part in order to appear as an impressive person or a miraculous creature. Thus, like a noble knight, nobleman, prelate, and even as a holy martyr, albeit without blood, we behold his majesty, his holiness, his innocent martyrdom, sitting under his canopy, surrounded by his humble subordinates, mas Johanes, mas Jasu, mas Markus, etc. Why not Balaam as well? Sadrach is also an ardent follower and worshiper of the teaching of a blissful kingdom at the end of the world. His views, with respect to that, are very fleshly and sensual, and above all, revolutionary. That Sadrach himself will then reign is easy to read between the lines, even though the name of Jesus is used.[37]

---

35. See P. Bieger to the Board of the NGZV in *Heidenbode* (Oct., 1882), p. 24.
36. Adriaanse, *Sadrach's Kring*, p. 286.
37. W.H.F. Uhlenbusch, "Sadrach in Bagelen," *De Opwekker* (Oct., 1884) as cited by Adriaanse, *Sadrach's Kring*, pp. 172-173.

The theme is similar to that found in the accusations recorded by Heyting and Wilhelm. A new element is the accusation that Sadrach claimed to be a just king (*ratu adil*), coming in a blissful kingdom. Uhlenbusch also explicitly accused Sadrach of being a European-hater who desired to drive out all Dutch people and undermine their authority, including the missionaries.

The accusations recorded by Horstman are the most complete and detailed. Parts of his correspondence with Wilhelm are pregnant with accusations. In his letter of July 19, 1890, he defined Sadrach's Christian *ngelmu*. Included were the following elements.

1). that Sadrach was the Christ, was to be called *Gusti* was born of the virgin Mary, and bore the stigmata in his hands and feet.

2). that Sadrach was established in Karangjasa, whence he ruled over all Java. His duties included the appointment of Dutch missionaries — Vermeer, Horstman, Zuidema, and Wilhelm, and their dismissals —Bieger and Uhlenbusch.

3). that the elders of the churches and the Dutch missionaries were obliged to come to Karangjasa once every year in order to worship and sacrifice in the *mesjid*. Each household was to set aside one penny per day for the occasion, or, if that was not feasible, to empty the church's poor box.

4). that the Christians who were faithful in this were permitted to keep their *jimatsrapal* (amulets), *japa* (formulas), and *ngelmu*, as well as the customs of circumcision, *sedekahs* (common meals), *sesajen* (offering meal), etc. without guilt. They were no longer required to go to Mecca since the *mesjid* was now at Karangjasa.

5). that the *ngelmu sejati* (true and noble knowledge), church books, etc. which were composed by Sadrach and distributed by the Dutch missionaries, were supplements to the *Injil* (the Gospel).

6). that before marriages and baptism, the Dutch missionaries and elders first had to ask Sadrach for his permission and would then receive assurances of his favor and blessing (for a fee).

7). that churches and missionaries who did not agree with these things were to be regarded as non-Christians who were to be neither trusted nor recognized.[38]

In order to convince Wilhelm of the truth of these accusations, Horstman sent another letter, dated July 27, 1890, which included yet more accusations. In it, Horstman recorded the following teachings which had been attributed to Sadrach.

---

38. R.J. Horstman to J. Wilhelm, July 19, 1890 as cited by Adriaanse, *Sadrach's Kring*, pp. 249-250; cf. Wilhelm, 1890, p. 142.

There is but one God; and Mohammed is his prophet, therefore, use the name of Kangjeng (his majesty) Mohammed with honor. After him, God sent Jesus, His son; he lived, suffered, and died, and ascended to heaven, in order to come again as *Roh Allah* (Spirit of God). He remained for awhile in Africa, and now lives in Java under the name of Sadrach Surapranata, who himself says that he is the *ratu adil*. It is proof enough that no one knows his father and mother and that every one knows that he came from Demak, the place of the *ratu adil*. For now, Karangjasa is the designated place to which also all those who are truly Christians go at least once a year in order to bring tribute and honor... Jews are Javanese and the Javanese language is the language of the Jews in which the Gospel of *Roh Allah* was given. Therefore, Arabic is superfluous and the Koran is no longer necessary. The Javanese have been placed under the rule of the whites because the missionaries must come from the whites, who will crown the *ratu adil* when the time comes. They come together with Sadrach every year at Karangjasa in order to worship him and also to wait for instructions from God.[39]

Horstman also noted that in addition to *kangjeng*, Sadrach was called *ratu adil, panutan, gusti,* and *bapa*. As frequently as once a month, envoys from every community went to Karangjasa to obtain Sadrach's advice, blessing, help, and favor. Honor was shown by kissing Sadrach's big toe as well as doing the *sembah* (ritual bowing). When the *pandita* was not able or willing to help in a particular matter, the people would go over his head to the "*gusti* in the South." Sadrach had already driven away seven Hollanders who refused to recognize him. He commanded that Javanese Christians be free from obligatory work on Sundays, and decided that they did not have to pay the *pitra* (alms), demands which the government obeyed. whatever power his *rasuls* (white *panditas*) had, came from him. Their primary task was to maintain the suppression of the communities, whereas the task of teaching was delegated to his Javanese helpers, like Musa. Sadrach had prophecied that Hebron, another Javanese helper, would be the next teacher for Semarang, Pekalongan, and Tegal.

Naturally, Horstman pointed out, the Hollanders understood little of this affair — they were only tools. His accusations continued. The Javanese who do not recognize Sadrach as *ratu adil* were considered Pharisees despite their baptism. No fellowship was to be maintained with them — no greetings, no shaking of hands. *Panditas* who worked against the situation were dismissed by Sadrach as was the case, Horstman claimed, with Bieger, Uhlenbusch, and Vermeer. The last was reappointed because he repented, judging from his reception by Sadrach. That the communities were required to show their gratitude to Sadrach went without saying. Before marriages, his favor was requested and paid for. If Sadrach threw a wedding for one of his *anak angkat* (foster children), a

---

39. R.J. Horstman to J. Wilhelm, July 27, 1890 as cited by Adriaanse, *Sadrach's Kring*, pp. 253-255.

messenger went through all the communities for *sahosan* (tribute), which brought in a good amount of money. In addition, at the major gatherings some communities collected tribute per household, others paid in goods. Anything which did not come from Sadrach was not good and could not be trusted. No one was baptized without first visiting Sadrach. Horstman concluded that "the whole thing is a mixture of Javanism, Islam, and Christianity."[40]

The correspondence between Horstman and Wilhelm continued even during Cachet's inspection tour of Central Java. Over a two year period, they engaged in a polemical debate about Sadrach's authority and teachings, each party trying to convince the other. In October, 1891, when Cachet was already in Central Java, Horstman once again wrote Wilhelm in an effort to convince him that the accusations against Sadrach were true. In this letter, Horstman formulated the accusations in a more systematic manner and went a step further in stressing that he was truly convinced of their authenticity and validity. The accusations included in this letter were:

1). Sadrach was a fraud who presented himself as the Christ (*ratu adil*) and allowed it to be preached that his kingdom had come and that Karangjasa was the true Mecca. These teachings were derived from the fact that, supposedly, his origin was unknown, his person immutable and immortal, his exaltation and position were the highest, his influence and power in material and spiritual matters were unlimited, and his residence was situated in the place prophesied by the Javanese prophets.

2). It was claimed that the Christian Scriptures and some of the Javanese *ngelmu* contained prophecies concerning his coming, and thus could be said to contain his teaching. For this reason the Lord's Prayer, Apostles' Creed, and Ten Commandments were taught even though many pagan customs and teachings were retained.

3). Sadrach's envoys and executives were the white *panditas* since they came to Java by God's command under the leadership of white rule. Their purpose and destiny was to anoint, the *ratu adil* at some time in the future. These envoys were cared for, led, appointed, and when necessary, dismissed, by Sadrach, which is why they obeyed him, carried out his will, and honored him. Naturally, the Javanese teachers and instructors, elders, and members did the same.

4). Not only Java, but soon the whole world would follow and serve this king. The rapid advance of Sadrach's teaching in Yogyakarta, Kedu, and the proclamation of "that teaching" throughout the world were proof of this.

40. Ibid.

5). No one could come to that *ratu adil* unless he was led under the *watu tumpang* (holy stone) and over the *wot ogal-agil*, which were none other than Sadrach's heretical teachers. Approaching the *ratu adil*, therefore, required payment.

6). Those who came to the *ratu adil* received forgiveness of sins, blessing, and benevolence, which could be obtained for circumcisions, baptisms, marriages, and other necessary occasions after the payment of money or other goods.[41]

An attempt to end the controversy surrounding these accusations was made at the annual *Algemeene Vergadering der Gemeenten*, held on December 16-19, 1890.[42] All of the NGZV missionaries were present except, ironically, Horstman, but they were unable to reach agreement. An unsuccessful attempt was made to condemn Sadrach as a heretic, and no alternate solution was found. The significance of this meeting is that the accusations against Sadrach, which were clearly formulated and discussed, were made "official." They can be summarized as follows.

1). Christians were to regard the Imam Sadrach as the Lord himself, and his mother as the virgin Mary. The stigmata on his hand and feet were offered as proof for this claim.

2). Sadrach was established in Karangjasa from where he reigned over all Java like a king.

3). Sadrach claimed authority to appoint the missionaries, elders, pastors, and president-elders of the church. He also claimed authority to dismiss them. Once a year the elders and missionaries were required to appear in Karangjasa in order to fulfill their pledge either by sacrifice or payment in the *mesjid*.

4). Every household was required to raise *zakat* of one penny per day. If a community was unable to raise the required amount, they were obliged to take it out of the poor boxes.

5). The preceding year, two missionaries from Semarang had appeared in Karangjasa as representatives of the Christians of Semarang in order to bring their reverent tribute to the *gusti*, Imam Sadrach. They thereupon entered the *mesjid* in order to bring their promised offering or to pay their pledge.

6). Sadrach interpreted the *Injil* in his Catechism, church books, and the like, and it was the missionaries' duty to distribute them.

7). According to Sadrach's command, marriages and baptisms were the

41. R.J. Horstman to J. Wilhelm, October, 1891 (Archives of the Dutch Reformed Missionary Society, Leusden).

42. This was an ordinary Synod meeting. Fifty-five local communities were represented by one hundred members; Adriaanse, *Sadrach's Kring*, p. 269.

work of the missionaries and the elders, but they were first compelled to ask for permission in Karangjasa. Blessings, obtained through the influence and power of Imam Sadrach's prayers, were purchased at that time.

8). Every Christian who obeyed these things was permitted to use *jimats* and to continue with their own *nglemus* and *japamantra*, as well as the practices of circumcision, *sedekah, sesajen*, and the like.

9). Javanese Christians were not required to go to Mecca because the temple of God, it was claimed, was in Karangjasa. Whoever did not agree with this were not to be called Christians and could not be trusted.[44]

The accusations brought against Sadrach during the fifteen year period before and after the vaccination affair[43] can be categorized as follows:

1). Accusations dealing with the person, authority, and influence of Sadrach. Included here are the accusations that Sadrach aggrandized himself by using Javanese aristocratic titles and by changing his name. In the opinion of the missionaries, he had too much authority and his influenced was unchecked. Such authority was viewed as contrary to Reformed principles in addition to posing a political threat to peace and public order.

2). Accusations dealing with Sadrach's position. According to the missionaries, Sadrach misused his position for personal profit by collecting money from Javanese Christians.

3). Accusations dealing with Sadrach's claim to be *ratu adil*. Included are his claims to possess supernatural powers and to have received the stigmata.

4). Accusations dealing with Sadrach's teachings. Sadrach was accused of lacking proper knowledge of the Bible and Christian teachings. His teachings were thought to be false because he mixed religious elements from Javanism, Islam, and Christianity.

2. Elucidation of the accusations against Sadrach

In order to put the accusations brought against Sadrach in proper perspective, it is important to realize that Sadrach and some of his teachings were sometimes misunderstood by his followers as well as by the Dutch missionaries. To see how these misunderstanding occurred we must refer to the reconstruction of the Javanese rural situation in the nineteenth century.

---

43. Adriaanse, *Sadrach's Kring*, pp. 270-271.
44. See also a summation of the accusations recorded by Cachet, *Een Jaar*, pp. 364-368.

It has been mentioned that in the rural areas of Central Java news circulated quickly, primarily through oral communication which was the only effective means of communication at the time. The rural people in general were uncritical listeners and myth and legend easily crept into their "news." Certain rumors, misunderstandings, and unconfirmed news stories were not distinguished from truth.[45] Since similar circumstances prevailed in Sadrach's case, rumors and misunderstandings gave opportunity for accusations to arise. Wilhelm, who was aware of this situation, urged his fellow missionary, Horstman, to be critical in what he heard about Sadrach and warned him against too quickly believing what people said about him. Wilhelm wrote, "I fear that they have gotten you all wound up and that you can now very easily get the people to say what you want, because a Javanese catches our drift so quickly. I advise you to carefully ask those who have something to say against Sadrach from whom they have heard it."[46]

This letter is only one among many in which Wilhelm urged Horstman to be careful about making judgments based on hearsay alone. That aspects of Sadrach's teachings were misunderstood by some of his followers as well as by the missionaries is evident. We will discuss these objections and the way in which they were misunderstood, below.

1). The accusation that Sadrach claimed to be Christ himself, or the expected *ratu adil* who would rule Java and the entire world, was described by Wilhelm as a serious problem. He agreed that to identify Sadrach as *ratu adil* and Christ was a distortion of the message of God. His letters to Horstman make clear, however, that he was never convinced that Sadrach himself made such claims. He discovered that two of Sadrach's followers, Jakub Tumpang and Jirmija Wiratikta, were circulating this false teaching. He wrote,

> The worst among them [the false brothers] is a certain Jirmija who has done and taught evil things. His every movement has been watched the last two years. From the foregoing it will be clear to you that it is oh so dangerous to accept accusations against Sadrach when false brothers, above all Jirmija, have made them up."[47]

In his reply to Wilhelm, Horstman mentioned the punishment of these "false brothers." He felt that their false teachings needed to be spelled out in detail, and the nature of their blasphemy made plain.[48]

---

45. See Chapter I, section A.
46. Wilhelm to R.J. Horstman, July 26, 1890 as cited by Adriaanse, *Sadrach's Kring*, pp. 256-257.
47. Ibid.; Wilhelm, 1890, p. 143.
48. R.J. Horstman to J. Wilhelm, September 19, 1890 as cited by Adriaanse, *Sadrach's Kring*, p. 265.

When Wilhelm first heard that Sadrach was claiming to be *ratu adil*, he met with Sadrach in July, 1890, to ask him about the matter. Sadrach maintained that he had never made such a claim. Still concerned, Wilhelm went to Karangjasa the following month to discuss the matter with church members and elders, but found no indication that Sadrach had made such a claim.[49] Wilhelm pursued the issue until he located the source of the false teaching. In a classical meeting in Purwareja on October 13, 1890, the guilty party acknowledged and confessed his sin.[50]

2). Sadrach was also accused of self-aggrandizement, since he used several Javanese aristocratic titles and practiced such aristocratic customs as handkissing and being sheltered by an umbrella. Such accusations were indicative of the influence of the court tradition upon the life of the common people. This accusation, therefore, must be viewed in light of the fact that the Residency of Bagelen, where most of Sadrach's followers lived, formerly belonged to the kingdoms of Yogyakarta and Surakarta and were largely influenced by the court tradition.[51] The images of the king, princes, and other aristocrats were vividly imprinted on the minds of the common people. The use of Javanese aristocratic titles and the practice of aristocratic customs, therefore, may have been the result of such images. In addition, in the nineteenth century, as was previously mentioned, the entire life of the Javanese people was still overwhelmingly marked by feudalism and, accordingly, the court tradition was still regarded as the ideal.

The palace was not only the center of the government, and therefore the source of regulation and power, but it was also the center of life for all people.[52] The common people perceived the king, princes, and members of the royal family as supernatural, possessing special powers. As such they often became figures of myth and legend. Because of this perception, anyone who demonstrated special talent, regardless of origin, was quickly associated with the royal family. From this point of view, it is understandable that Sadrach was seen as an aristocrat since he demonstrated special abilities. In the Javanese rural context of the nineteenth century, Sadrach could easily have become a legendary and mythical figure who had supernatural powers and was able to perform wondrous deeds.[53] It

49. Wilhelm, 1890, p. 142.
50. Adriaanse, *Sadrach's Kring*, p. 267.
51. See Chapter II, section B.
52. Ibid.
53. This has also been the case with Islam in Java — the first nine Moslem missionaries (*walisanga*) were perceived as extraordinary saints with supernatural powers. They became figures of myth and legend.

was claimed that he could "disappear" and heal illnesses with his urine, among other things. In addition, the other titles which Sadrach was accused of using, such as *bapa,* imam, *panutan, tiyang sepuh*, and *kyai,* were used for respected Javanese leaders. From this point of view it is understandable that Sadrach, originally an ordinary man from the "little people," was accused of pretending to be a Javanese aristocrat.

3). Sadrach was accused of making his village, Karangjasa, a type of Mecca or Rome, to which Javanese Christians, elders, and white *panditas* made a pilgrimage every year to honor Sadrach and bring "tribute." It is true that Karangjasa became the center of Javanese Christianity after Sadrach moved there. The annual great gathering and the *zendingsfeest* had been held there since 1885. These gatherings were attended by representatives of the *Salatiga-Zending* and elders of the local communities, as well as by the NZGV missionaries.[54]

4). Sadrach was accused of misusing his authority by arbitrarily dismissing missionaries Vermeer, Bieger, and Uhlenbusch and by reappointing Vermeer after he confessed his "sin," when in fact, missionary Bieger returned to the Netherlands shortly after the tragic vaccination affair, Uhlenbusch was dismissed by the Board of the NGZV for ethical reasons (alcohol-related), and Vermeer was dismissed for his "worldly" involvement in setting up a small shop in Purbalingga. Ten years later the Board of the NGZV restored Vermeer to his position as missionary, which he obediently filled until his death.[55]

5). Sadrach was accused of being a powerful leader whose voice was obeyed by the government. The accusation claims that the government lifted its requirement of compulsory service on Sunday because of Sadrach's command. It was, in fact, Wilhelm who became the protector and defender of the rights of the Javanese Christians. His diary serves as evidence that he filled the role of rescuing them from difficulties with the government.[56] Wilhelm was very concerned about the social problems faced by the Javanese Christians, especially when they were treated unjustly by government authorities.

6). Sadrach was accused of misusing his position to enrich himself by collecting tribute and money for various favors. Adriaanse denied that Sadrach collected money for his personal interests. The money he collected was intended for *diakonia* and the socio-economic improvement of the

54. See Chapter III, section A.

55. Regarding missionaries Bieger, Uhlenbusch, and Vermeer, see Chapter I, section B.

56. Wilhelm, 1888, pp. 5, 22, 24-25; 1889, pp. 35, 38, 43-44, 49, 63, 78, 83, 85-86, 95-96.

community.[57] Adriaanse pointed to serveral "pilot projects" carried out by Sadrach for the community as evidence of Sadrach's concern for the social and economic welfare of his followers.[58] Furthermore, Adriaanse repeatedly bore witness to the fact that Sadrach was an economically independent guru. While he sometimes was offered a gift from his followers as a token of appreciation, he never extorted money from them.[59]

In conclusion, it is worthwhile to note the opinions of three of Sadrach's contemporaries. Heyting, who was familiar with the Javanese Christian community and the vaccination affair, concluded that:

1). Sadrach successfully achieved his ambition to be regarded as an extraordinarily holy man.

2). Sadrach had great authority, and his influence upon the community was nearly unlimited. This was in contradiction to the Calvinist understanding of the position of minister within a congregation.

3). Sadrach did bear the name Raden mas Ngabehi Surapranata.

4). Sadrach issued regulations as though he had the right to act as the government.

5). Sadrach had misused his position to enrich himself.[60]

From the beginning, Wilhelm doubted that all the accusations could be substantiated. He was convinced that the accusations both before and after the vaccination affair indicated an attempt to oust Sadrach from a leadership position. Like Bieger, Horstman believed that the Javanese, including Sadrach, needed to be led, and were out of place in a position of leadership, as indicated by a letter to Wilhelm in which he wrote,

> We know all too well that our little Javanese, since they are still children, continually need to be under supervision. Perhaps after a century or so we will be able to make them like European Christians who have been under the influence of God's Word and Spirit for centuries. This also goes for Sadrach, of course, who, although he is somewhat more advanced, still will need much supervision, admonition, leading, and direction, etc.[61]

Horstman's real motive in writing to Wilhelm was to topple Sadrach from his "throne." It was Adriaanse's impression, after carefully observing the situation between Sadrach and the Dutch missionaries, that the issue lay more in the question of power than in Sadrach's teachings. He wrote, "I am of the opinion, as you have already read between the lines,

57. Adriaanse, *Sadrach's Kring*, pp. 425-431.
58. See Chapter III, section C2.
59. Adriaanse, *Sadrach's Kring*, p. 426.
60. Heyting, p. 6.
61. R.J. Horstman to J. Wilhelm, September 7, 1890 as cited by Adriaanse, *Sadrach's Kring*, pp. 263-264.

that the struggle between the missionaries and Sadrach is not over some item of doctrine, but over who will be the boss."[62]

Aside from the theological and missiological issues raised through these accusations, it is also apparent that Sadrach and his teachings were very often misunderstood by a number of the Javanese Christians. Some of Sadrach's followers even went so far as to deliberately misinterpret his teachings for their own interest and profit. As a result, misunderstandings multiplied as these "stories," were "spiced up" and circulated from village to village. The NGZV missionaries also misunderstood him, partly because they were unable to grasp the very core of certain Javanese customs. Some, however, intentionally misinterpreted Sadrach's teachings and utilized the existing misunderstandings and "stories" to level accusations against him. The real objection of the Dutch missionaries to Sadrach and his community thus became more complex.

C. The Theological and Missiological Issues Arising from the Accusations

1. The Objection to Sadrach's great and "unlimited" authority

The Dutch missionaries regarded Sadrach's authority as unlimited. They saw him not as the respected leader of the community but felt that he was being venerated, like a cult object. Cachet thus interpreted the name Surapranata as "Divinity who rules" (*Godheid die regelt*) and judged that because of Sadrach's unlimited authority, he had replaced Christ's position in the community, and concluded that Christ "has no place" within the community.[63] Cachet was convinced that a true Christian leader, as a servant of God, could not exercise the kind of unlimited authority that Sadrach possessed, leading him to question Christ's *position* there.

Heyting characterized Sadrach as "living law" (*levende wet*)[64] and his will "was considered a holy law by his followers, to which they owed unconditional obedience."[65] Heyting also questioned whether Sadrach's authority in the community could be justified. It was his opinion that the title "great shepherd" (*gembala agung*), which the members of the community used for Sadrach, was not a title which should be used for a true Christian leader. Heyting described Sadrach's authority as "such power, an *imperium in imperio* [kingdom within a kingdom],"[66] and felt

62. Adriaanse, *Sadrach's Kring*, p. 89.
63. Cachet, *Een Jaar*, p. 361.
64. Heyting, p. 24.
65. Ibid., p. 41.
66. Ibid., p. 43.

that it was a political threat to the Dutch colonial government. Acting more as a minister of the government than of the church, he offered the solution of installing an assistant pastor in the *Indische Kerk* in Purwareja with the special assignment of "pastoring" (controlling!) the Javanese Christian community.

Heyting also compared Sadrach's authority within the community to that of the Pope. He compared Karangjasa, the center of Javanese Christianity, to Rome, the center of Roman Catholicism. He referred to Sadrach as the Javanese Pope who exercised "papal authority" over his community.[67] Uhlenbusch also used the images of the Pope and Rome in his discussions of Sadrach's authority. He rejected Sadrach's authority on the grounds that such unlimited authority was unacceptable and intolerable in the church.[68]

Horstman's objections were similar. It is clear from his correspondence with Wilhelm that he was strongly opposed to Sadrach. He viewed Sadrach not only as a false teacher, but also as a man whose authority was damaging to his fellow Javanese. He viewed the movement within the Javanese Christian community as "undoubtedly on the way to Rome."[69] Therefore, Sadrach had to be removed from a leadership position at all costs. "Sadrach must be led, but may not lead," he wrote to Wilhelm.[70]

It is clear from the above discussion that the Dutch missionaries were very opposed to Sadrach's authority. Heyting viewed the problem from both a theological and political point of view,[71] while the others regarded it as a theological issue only. Their concern as Reformed missionaries was to keep the Reformed faith at the center of their work. Their consideration of the similarities between Sadrach's authority and that of the Pope's is indicative of this concern.

Heyting's assessment of Sadrach's authority was based on the Calvinist understanding of church office, in this case, that of minister. He claimed that Sadrach had "assumed an air of authority over his community which, all other considerations aside, is simply contrary to our Calvinistic principles, with regard to the relationship a minister ought to have with his followers."[72] Office bearers were to be servants of God. He concluded, therefore, that because Sadrach's authority was contrary to that of a

---

67. Government decision No. 5, April 10, 1884 (National Archives Office, Jakarta).
68. Uhlenbusch as cited by Adriaanse, *Sadrach's Kring*, pp. 172-173.
69. R.J. Horstman to J. Wilhelm, January 4, 1891 as cited by Adriaanse, *Sadrach's Kring*, p. 277.
70. Ibid.
71. Government decision No. 5.
72. Heyting, p. 6.

servant, it was unjustifiable. According to Reformed principles, which was the sole theological norm used by all the missionaries, "As for ministers of God's Word, they have equally the same power and authority wheresoever they are, as they are all ministers of Christ, the only universal Bishop and the only Head of the Church."[73] Furthermore, regarding authority and church offices, "The Church of Jesus Christ knows no hierarchy, no person exercises authority over another person, and no office is higher than another office. For, there is but one authority in the Church, namely that of the Word; and there is but one Head of the church, namely Jesus Christ."[74] In light of these Reformed principles, upon which their mission work was founded, it is understandable that the Dutch missionaries raised questions regarding the nature and extent of Sadrach's authority within the community.

2. The objection to the Javanized character of Sadrach's teachings

On September 3, 1890, Wilhelm sent Horstman a letter informing him that the false teachers within the community had been discovered in the persons of Jakob Tumpang and Jirmija Wiratikta.[75] Horstman, however, was not satisfied with this answer and remained fully convinced that Sadrach was the primary source of the heresy. Horstman concluded that since both of the accused men were followers of Sadrach and had learned Christianity from him, he was ultimately the source of their false teachings. In his reply to Wilhelm he began with the question, "Did Jacob [Tumpang] also learn such things about Sadrach, and Jirmija [Wiratikta] too?"[76] In other words, he firmly held to his conclusion that Sadrach was the source of the heresy and false teachings which were circulated among the Javanese Christian community. He denounced these false teachings in another letter to Wilhelm,

---

73. Board of Publications of the Christian Reformed Church, *Belgic Confession* in *Ecumenical and Reformed Confessions* (Grand Rapids, 1979), Article XXXI; cf. A. Kuyper's keynote speech, Proposition II (alle zending door creaturen is slechts afschaduwing, representatie of instrument voor de eenige principiele zending, die van den Zoon door den Vader), and Proposition VI (de zending der Evangelisten en Apostelen was niet, gelijk die der Profeten, plaatsvervangend, maar instrumenteel in de hand van den Christus...), "Zendingcongres," p. 90; Kuyper, pp. 1-2.
74. *Belgic Confession*, Article XXXI.
75. J. Wilhelm to R.J. Horstman, September 3, 1890, as cited in Adriaanse, *Sadrach's Kring*, p. 263; see also p. 184.
76. Horstman to Wilhelm, September 7, 1890.

After the discovery of the truth of these accusations, we wrote to the communities that these false, dangerous, godless, and anti-Christian teachings must not be tolerated because they conflict completely with God's Word and Will as revealed to us. The above named Sadrach is a man who was born at ..., to ..., his profession is ..., he lives at ....[77]

In their polemical correspondence they continually tried to convince one another of their error. Horstman even accused Wilhelm of having viewed things from Sadrach's perspective for so long that he was unable to be objective about his false teachings. He offered Wilhelm the following advice, "I advise you, however, if you want to get to know the state of affairs in your communities, that you not look at things through Sadrach's eyes; the man is deceiving you and is supported in this by his followers. It is brotherly advice I am giving you, in love."[78] Despite Horstman's stubbornness, Wilhelm would not give in. He tried to see the situation objectively, and act as much as possible according to God's will and word. He pleaded with Horstman,

Ever since my arrival on Java I have allowed myself to be led by love, and have never looked at things through another's eyes; not through the eyes of a colleague, and even less through the eyes of Sadrach or any other guru. I try to see things through the eyes of God's Word and Will, to be led by God's Spirit, and to practice daily self-denial.

That the people believe many vile things about Sadrach even though Sadrach never taught such things can be understood now that the false teacher has been found. That you insist on believing that Sadrach teaches such things cannot be allowed. You can err just as well as Sadrach can lie. In Purwareja there is a pious man that has learned that Dr. Kuyper works through a satanic spirit — many believe this. Is Dr. Kuyper then a servant of Satan? There are people at Pekalongan who have been taught by Jirmija that Sadrach is the *ratu adil*, yes, Christ in person. Must Sadrach therefore himself teach (or learn from himself) such things?[79]

The two missionaries debated from different standpoints. In Horstman's opinion, false teachings, heresies, lies, and any form of paganism needed to be done away with at the source. Since he viewed Sadrach as the source, the solution was to remove Sadrach from his position. Wilhelm, on the other hand, viewed such drastic measures as vain.[80] Horstman was

77. Horstman to Wilhelm, September 19, 1890.

78. R.J. Horstman to J. Wilhelm, January 4, 1891 as cited by Adriaanse, *Sadrach's Kring*, p. 277.

79. J. Wilhelm to R.J. Horstman, January 16, 1891 as cited by Adriaanse, *Sadrach's Kring*, p. 279.

80. Regarding their different views and strategies for missions, see J. Wilhelm to R.J. Horstman, September 25, 1891, and Horstman's reply to J. Wilhelm, October, 1891 (Archives of the Dutch Reformed Missionary Society, Leusden).

convinced that such paganistic practices needed to be fought against at all costs. He wrote,

> How else could it be possible that, for example, here an 'elder' is a *dhukun sunat*, there another practices a *ngelmu dowa* for healing the sick, and in yet another place, another flees to the *deva* for a fruitful harvest or the rapid birth of his child? This all is not occurring in some corner, but before the eyes of heathens, Christians, and missionaries."[81]

His "mission strategy" for countering such practices was delineated in the same letter.

> It is now abundantly clear that things cannot go on this way and that all these things must be brought to an end first of all by the missionaries. We may have no part in the sins of others. We must bear witness against these shameful things (idolatry), we must let Christians know that we completely and totally detest such things. The missionaries must decisively and definitely demand of Christians that they cast aside all such blasphemous and scandalous practices and obey God's Word alone.[82]

Although Wilhelm took Horstman's accusations into account, he felt that it was wrong to generalize. While some paganistic practices remained in the community, not all the Javanese Christians followed them, and he was disheartened that Sadrach was blamed for them all. Wilhelm was saddened by the letter of the NGZV Board, dated November 12, 1889, in which the accusations against Sadrach's teachings as "impure" were stated. He responded with these words:

> That which was said about Sadrach saddens me. He is accused of preaching Javanism.... It was further said that Sadrach mixes strange teachings with the preaching of the Word. The Board certainly has written this on the basis of the word of someone who either does not know what he is talking about or who keeps company with unsuitable persons. For, the one who preaches God's Word must direct himself to the unique nature of the people, must lock onto that which is anti-pagan, that is to say, onto the true elements in their religion, which clearly indicate that the people have descended from ancestors who received divine revelation. For all the uninitiated, thus, sound preaching will have the appearance of strange teachings mixed in with the proclamation of the Word. Before anyone can be believed in this matter he must first show that he is familiar with the religion, the social circumstances, and the language of the people.[83]

The basic problem with Sadrach's teaching was his mixture of Javanism and the Gospel — a mixture of "alien teachings and God's Word." In other words, the Dutch missionaries considered Sadrach's teachings to be syncretistic. The view that his teachings were Javanized with an Islamic flavor was underscored by Horstman in his letter of July 27, 1890, in which

81. Horstman to Wilhelm, October, 1891.
82. Ibid.
83. Wilhelm, 1890, pp. 109, 127.

he stated, "... the whole thing is a mixture of Javanism ... Mohamme-danism, and Christianity."[84] It is, therefore, not surprizing that those who felt responsible for the mission work in Java, namely, Zuidema, Horst-man, and Cachet, came to the conclusion that Sadrach's teaching were nothing but "poison for our mission fields,"[85] and "... in connection with our mission, it is extremely damaging for our mission work and dangerous for the mislead souls."[86]

It is clear from our description that the missionaries' accusations against Sadrach's teaching relate to three major themes; namely,

— Christ was understood and proclaimed as *ratu adil* and *panutan*.
— The Gospel was understood and proclaimed as *ngelmu*.
— Javanese *adat* was preserved in the life of Sadrach's community.

From the missionaries point of view, coming from a theological back-ground in an orthodox, Reformed faith,[87] such teachings were theolo-gically unjustified. Their measuring stick was always "the purest procla-mation" and "the purified contents of Scripture." The theological propositions behind these three objections will be summarized below.

a. Christ understood and proclaimed as *ratu adil* and *panutan*

Proclaiming Christ as *ratu adil* and *panutan* was considered theologically improper because, from a Reformed perspective, it distorted the teaching of God's kingdom as proclaimed by Christ and disregarded Christ's role as mediator for human redemption. Thus the missionaries felt that the very core of Christology was threatened to a certain extent. *Ratu adil*, also called *Erucakra* (Master of the *cakra*) or *mahdi* (the one who will come), functioned in Javanese belief also as a moral teacher. He was very often linked to a legendary, mythical figure who was himself an incarnation of *deva*, coming into the world as a human being for a certain period of time in order to bring order to a chaotic situation. When his divine mission was completed, he would return to heaven.[88] The kingdom in which *ratu adil*

84. Horstman to Wilhelm, July 27, 1890.
85. J.P. Zuidema to the Board of the NGZV, *Heidenbode* (July, 1897), p. 323; Adriaanse, *Sadrach's Kring*, p. 314; cf. Cachet, *Een Jaar*, p. 842.
86. Cachet, *Een Jaar*, p. 841.
87. See Chapter I, section B2.
88. For further elaboration of *ratu adil* and *mahdi*, see J.M. Van Der Kroef, *The Javanese Expectation: Their Origin and Cultural Context in Comparative Studies in Society and History*, Supplement I (New York, 1959), pp. 299-323; Andre Corsini Harjaka Hardjamardjaja, *Javanese Popular Belief in the Coming of Ratu Adil, a Righteous King* (Rome, 1962); W. Hoezoo, "Achiring Zaman," *MNZG* 27 (1883), pp. 1-42.

was to reign was understood by the missionaries, Uhlenbusch for example, as merely "a sumptuous kingdom" with a "very fleshy, sensual, revolutionary" character.[89] Such a kingdom was basically contrary to the perspective of God's kingdom as eternal and spiritual in character.

The opposition of the missionaries, however, lay not so much in the different nature of the two kingdoms as in the nature of *ratu adil* and his mission, which they perceived as being very different from that of Christ. According to the *Belgic Confession*, "Jesus Christ... is the only begotten. Son of God, begotten from eternity, not made, nor created (for then He would be a creature), but co-essential and co-eternal with the Father, *the very image of his substance and the effulgence of his glory*, equal unto Him in all things."[90] He is truly God and truly man (thus against docetism). The Javanese *ratu adil,* on the other hand, was simply a perfect person, although he might be bestowed with divine characteristics and be an extraordinary man. The Dutch missionaries felt that proclaiming Jesus as *ratu adil* and *panutan* would have far reaching consequences with regard to the doctrine of the redemptive work of Christ as the once-for-all atonement for the liberation of man from the forces of sin. Article XIV of the Belgic Confession, entitled "The Creation and Fall of Man, and his Incapacity to Perform What is Truly Good," indicates that man, although created according to the image of God, is incapable of doing good works to attain his salvation because he has sinned.[91] Man is justified, therefore, not by good works, but by faith.[92] "Salvation consists in the remission of our sins for Jesus Christ's sake," and is obtained through grace alone, and not by works.[93] The missionaries viewed the Javanese *ratu adil* as one who pointed out the way of salvation, whereas Jesus Christ was himself the way. Thus, Cachet concluded that Sadrach and his fellow Javanese evangelists did not proclaim the crucified Christ, the perfect Redeemer, but rather Javanism.[94]

b.   The Gospel understood and proclaimed as *ngelmu*

The Dutch missionaries rejected the proclamation of the Gospel as *ngelmu*

89. Uhlenbusch, as cited by Adriaanse, *Sadrach's Kring.*
90. *Belgic Confession*, Article X.
91. Ibid., Article XIV.
92. Ibid., Article XXII.
93. Ibid., Article XXIII.
94. Cachet, *Een Jaar*, p. 371, n. 1. It is worthy of note that on July 12, 1890, Wilhelm preached Jesus as *ratu adil* based on I John 5:1: "Jesus Kristus nabi kita kang luhur, pantawis kita kang sejati lan ratu kita kang adil lan langgeng" (Jesus is our exalted prophet, the true mediator and the eternal just king); see Wilhelm, 1890, p. 141. Cf. *Almanac of 1891,* pp. 71-89, where *ratu adil* is adapted for evangelization.

based on their understanding of what *ngelmu* was. They felt that the concept of *ngelmu* was inseparably associated with Javanism, the combination of native religion with Hinduism, Buddhism, and Islam. *Ngelmu*, in this context, includes the ability of humans to manipulate supernatural forces in the visible world — divine power which influences human life through fortune or misfortune — and direct it toward human interests.[95] *Ngelmu pasek* is dominated by elements from native religion, Hinduism, and Buddhism, and *ngelmu santrian* has an Islamic character. Both, however, deal with the question of the essence of life, union with the Absolute (mysticism), and supernatural powers (magic).[96] The missionaries viewed *ngelmu* as nothing more than speculative, superstitious religious knowledge characterized by mysticism, magic, and syncretism. With such an understanding of *ngelmu*, their objection to its use in evangelism and in the life of the Christian is understandable.

Horstman was very vocal in his opposition to the use of *ngelmu*. He saw no benefit in its use because, in his opinion, it was superstitious. Javanese gurus who practiced *ngelmu* were merely misleading the people, and advancing their own interests. The Gospel, he felt, was the Light which was diamatrically opposed to darkness. Compromise was out of the question. The Gospel's purpose was to liberate people from satanic forces such as those found in Javanese *ngelmu*. He was shocked and grieved that such practices were not only observed by "lay" church members, but by "elders"; not only in the "corner," but in full view of Javanese *kafirs*, Christians, and, above all, missionaries! He was appalled to discover that in Pekalongan and the surrounding areas elders were acting as *dhukun sunat* (one who performs circumcisions) and *guru ngelmu*, healing the sick by pronouncing *rapal*, and worshiping *devas* for a good harvest, safe childbirth, and other worldly purposes.[97]

In his October, 1891 letter to Wilhelm, Horstman reaffirmed his stand that Javanese Christians had to be confronted with an alternative. They needed to choose between Yahweh and Baal, between Christ and Balaam. A strong warning had to be given to the Javanese Christians — they needed to abandon their superstitious and idolatrous practices. Since they were not able to understanding the Word of God, they needed to recognize the position of the missionaries as the only ambassadors of the Highest King

95. For more about *ngelmu* see S.E. Harthoorn, "De Zending op Java," *MNZG* 4 (1860), pp. 105-137, 212-252; Poensen, "Een en ander;" C. Poensen, "Bijdrage tot de Kennis van Godsdienstige en zedelijke toestand," *MNZG* 9 (1865), pp. 333-357; Poensen, "De Javanen," pp. 123-216.

96. Cf. Chapter I, section A2.

97. Horstman to Wilhelm, October, 1891..

(God). They needed to believe, obey, and do what the missionaries preached, commanded, and instructed.[98]

Horstman's rigid attitude is representative of the view of the NGZV Board as well as of most of his contemporaries, as is evident in Cachet's conclusions from his inspection tour. D. Bakker, missionary to Central Java for the ZGKN, the successor of the NGZV, was of the same opinion as the NGZV missionaries in his attitude toward *ngelmu*. He saw no value in *ngelmu* for evangelization. He felt that it was impossible to proclaim the Gospel as *ngelmu* because, in his opinion, they were not only different, but essentially contradictory. *Ngelmu*, as defined by Bakker, was nothing more than a secret teaching which was believed to bring good fortune.[99] It dealt with magic, the spirits of darkness, and was syncretistic in character, mixing elements from animism, Hinduism, Buddhism, and Islam. He also believed that in *ngelmu*, the living God, the Creator whom man should worship, was replaced by creatures, and therefore be described in one word: idolatry.[100]

Contrary to *ngelmu*, the Gospel is the liberating force of God which judges man for worshiping creatures and evil spirits. The Gospel could not, in Bakker's thinking, be regarded as *ngelmu*, even true *ngelmu*. The Gospel centers on the crucified Christ, not on the fulfillment of human fancies as does *ngelmu*.[101] It must be fully proclaimed even though it becomes "foolishness, and a stumbling block for the gentile." According to Bakker, the Gospel demands radical faith, conversion, repentance, and rebirth.[102] It must not be proclaimed in a compromising manner — one cannot put new wine into old wineskins. For Bakker, proclaiming the Gospel as *ngelmu* was self-deception, darkening the very core of the Gospel itself and leading astray those who hear such a proclamation.[103]

M. Lindenborn, director of the mission house of the *Nederlandsche Zendings Vereeniging* (hereafter NZV) and a contemporary of Bakker, was also involved in the *ngelmu* issue. His views of *ngelmu* and of the indigenous culture in general, however, were more moderate than Bakker's.[104] As a director who was responsible for missionary training, he

---

98. Ibid.

99. D. Bakker, "Theologische Opleiding," p. 322; D. Bakker, "Nationaal Christendom," p. 290.

100. D. Bakker, "Nationaal Christendom," p. 298.

101. Ibid., p. 292.

102. D. Bakker, "Theologische Opleiding," p. 324.

103. Bakker's view seems to be a continuation of the NGZV's emphasis on proclaiming the Gospel as *louter en zuiver verkondiging*, as was previously mentioned.

104. Their polemic appeared in D. Bakker, "Theologische Opleiding," pp. 321-327; D. Bakker, "Nationaal Christendom," pp. 289-301; M. Lindenborn, "Nationaal

paid close attention to indigenous cultures in an attempt to find cultural elements which could be utilized in evangelization and the expression of Christianity. His starting point was that every nation or country, like an individual, has its own identity composed of its cultural and national character, which makes it distinct from every other nation or country. This "national" identity is God-given and should not be taken lightly. Rather, it should be preserved and developed. According to Lindenborn's understanding of the Great Commission, missions really meant education —"... teaching them to observe all that I commanded you" (RSV).[105] Educating the Christian community or church toward maturity was impossible without an appreciation of the identity of the people. He concluded, therefore, that "since a people is a personality, with its own character, and since the distinction between the races and peoples is neither incidental nor sinful, the mission is not permitted to kill the unique nature of the people."[106]

In Lindenborn's opinion *ngelmu* was part of the cultural character of the Javanese and, therefore, a part of their "national" identity. He argued that the magical element in *ngelmu* was not essential, and that the mystical element was the most crucial. He defined *ngelmu* as "the knowledge which is power, and which is obtained through mystical union with the guru, whose word alone is power for those who are united with him and do that which he commands."[107] He went even further to say that *ngelmu* might contain many points of contact with the Old and New Testaments, e.g., John 1:12; 15:7; 17:3, etc. He put forth the question: Is it not possible to proclaim the Gospel as *ngelmu*?

The theological and missiological problem of *ngelmu* was not restricted to the NGZV in Central Java, but was faced by NZV missionaries in West Java as well.[108] Since both of these mission groups separated from the NZG, and were both of a conservative, orthodox character, a comparison of their views may lend insight to the problem in Central Java.[109] H.C.G. Rutting of the NZV, acknowledged that proclaiming the Gospel as *ngelmu* was very attractive to the Javanese and drew large audiences in the early stages. He witnessed the emergence of several Christian communities as

Christendom op Java," *Stemmen voor Waarheid en Vrede*, 59 (1922), pp. 529ff.; M. Lindenborn, "Evangelie en *Ngelmu*," *MNZG* 60 (1916), pp. 249-269.

105. Matthew 28:20.

106. Lindenborn, "Nationaal Christendom," pp. 536-537.

107. Ibid., p. 644; Lindenborn, "Evangelie en *Ngelmu*," p. 266.

108. Bliek, "De Anthingsche Christen," pp. 333-334; C.J. Hoekendijk, "Evangelie en *Ngelmu*," *MNZG* 61 (1917), pp. 25-26.

109. See Chapter I, section B. About *beginselen* of the NZV, see NZV, *Toelichting der Bepalingen van de Zendingsvereeniging te Rotterdam* (Rotterdam, 1861).

the result of such methods. He observed, however, that if the continuing practice of *ngelmu* was permitted in the life of the community, the members were not directed to the basic message of the Gospel. Genuine faith and a Christian lifestyle did not develop and the congregations, accordingly, became weak.[110] Like Bakker, Rutting understood *ngelmu* to be only a medium of contact with the world of magic and spirits through fixed *rapal* and *sarana* (formulas for action). *Ngelmu* which does not have contact with the world of magic and spirits should not, in Rutting's opinion, be called *ngelmu*. He further argued that the *form* of *ngelmu* cannot be separated from its *content*. While they can be distinguished, they are, in essence, inseparable. It is impossible, he believed, to empty the contents of *ngelmu*, thus leaving the capsule to be filled again with new content — that of the Gospel. He thus rejected *ngelmu* for evangelization and stood firm on his belief that it was better to lay a strong, solid foundation for a new building, for the building depends on that foundation to resist attack.

Another NZV missionary, C.J. Hoekendijk, was more positive in his view of *ngelmu*. He argued that as long as *ngelmu* was only a form by which to proclaim the Gospel but did not change the Gospel's central message, it could be employed. The central message included the theological understanding of the person of Christ, his redemptive work, reconciliation of sinners with God, conversion, and rebirth. The outward expression of the Christian faith lies in the cultural field, and should, therefore, be adapted to the native culture. Hoekendijk compared the outward expression of Christianity to clothes. The kind of clothing one wore could be freely chosen according to the will of the wearer, depending on his size. Goliath, he pointed out, would not have been defeated if David had worn Saul's armor; likewise, heathenism and Islam will not be defeated if "Eastern" Christianity is clothed in Western dress.[111] The puzzling question, however, remained: What was Eastern clothing? While Hoekendijk had no quick answer, his experience in missions led him to conclude that the missionaries and their indigenous helpers on the mission field should establish a regular conference where *ngelmu* and other problems could be discussed.[112] *Ngelmu* presented a real problem for the missionaries, on the one hand; yet on the other hand, it was effective and relevant for the Javanese. Therefore, it had to be taken seriously into account as a tool for evangelism.

In reality, *ngelmu* is much more than a knowledge which deals only with magic and superstitions as many missionaries perceived it. It is, rather, as

110. H.C.G. Rutting, "Evangelie en Elmoe," *De Opwekker* 60 (1917), p. 307.
111. Hoekendijk, pp. 18-20.
112. Ibid., p. 21.

broad as life itself. The most basic and crucial element is the mystical by which, according to Javanese understanding, one may approach and grasp the great mystery, the Absolute, God. Through these mystical experiences one's religious and spiritual life is enriched. To define *ngelmu* as only magic and superstition, therefore, is to significantly limit its scope, and thus, its use in missions. To narrow the meaning of *ngelmu* in such a way is to severely limit access to the Javanese world of thought.

In summary, some of the missionaries viewed *ngelmu* merely as the use of magic and communication with the spiritual world. As such, it was to be rejected as superstitious and syncretistic. Others, however, were more moderate in their assessment and attempted to find the possible significance of *ngelmu* for doing missions.

c. The preservation of Javanese *adat* in the life of Sadrach's community

The problem of Javanese *adat* in the life of the Javanese Christians came to the fore as soon as Dutch missionaries came into contact with Sadrach's community. The missionaries saw nothing of value in the practice of *adat* and demanded that the converts abandon such practices. The Javanese, on the other hand, viewed *adat* as something very precious which deeply influenced all of the Javanese society.[113] The Javanese refused to believe that *adat* enslaved them, and therefore constantly battled against the missionaries' judgment. Bakker expressed the missionaries' position when he wrote, "Javanese *adat* is completely idolatrous and must therefore be replaced by Christian traditions and customs, no matter how great a struggle this may produce."[114]

Like Horstman, the other missionaries considered Javanese *adat* to be "paganistic and superstitious," in other words, nothing short of idolatry. The Dutch missionaries who emphasized "pure and refined proclamation" could not imagine that the Javanese converts were truly Christian unless they gave up their *adat*. Such a view was commonly adopted by missionaries in the nineteenth century. In contrast, Sadrach and his fellow Javanese evangelists had great appreciation for their own culture. They were of the opinion that becoming Christian did not entail having to abandon Javanese *adat* as their cultural heritage and identity. In conformity with this opinion, Adriaanse noted Sadrach's insistence that Javanese converts remain Javanese.[115] Sadrach and his followers became defenders and advocates of the preservation of *adat*. The community

---

113. Wilhelm pointed out the strength of *adat* in Javanese life; see 1889, p. 40; 1890, p. 119; see Brumund, *Het Volksonderwijs*, p. 39; Cachet, *Een Jaar*, p. 339.

114. D. Bakker, *Verhoudingen*, p. 57.

115. Adriaanse, *Sadrach's Kring*, p. 153.

members observed *adat* without hesitation, although with some adaptation to the Christian faith.[116] Members of the community were acutely aware of *adat* as a part of Javanese life which functioned to enrich the spiritual life of the community. This awareness was further strengthened by the fact that they considered the preservation of *adat* as a regulation issued from Karangjasa[117] and, therefore, worthy of observance.[118]

To better understand the missionaries' point of view regarding *adat*, we shall use the disagreement over circumcision in Wilhelm's diary as a case study of the missiological problem of *adat* in general. This example also serves to convey the position of the Javanese Christians toward *adat*.[119]

Circumcision became an issue in Sadrach's community because of the case of a respected Javanese aristocrat, Natataruna. According to Wilhelm, Natataruna was "Raden Mas Josef Suryahasmara, captain of the Yogyakarta legion, son of Pangeran Ario Natakusuma, Major Adjutant, and grandson of Kangjeng Gusti Pangeran Hadipati Pakualam I."[120] Natataruna was a new convert, a respected man both inside and outside the Christian Javanese circle. He was the first aristocrat to be converted by Sadrach during Sadrach's evangelization "campaign" in Yogyakarta. His further religious instruction, however, was received from Wilhelm.[121] Natataruna was very important in Wilhelm's opinion, as evidenced by the many references to him in Wilhelm's diary.[122] Both Wilhelm and Sadrach seemed to have known him well.

After being taught in the Christian faith for a certain period, he, together with other Javanese converts, was baptized on May 30, 1887. According to the custom, he added a Christian name, Josef, to his own name at the time of his baptism.[123] He was actively involved in church activities in the Residency of Yogyakarta, and served for a period of time as "president" of the Javanese Christian communities there.[124] His first son, Raden Mas Tengku Nataadmaka, who was baptized in March, 1889, became the first Javanese theological student and was sent to the Netherlands to study theology. Upon his return to Central Java he was to become a candidate

116. Chapter III, section B2.
117. Adriaanse, *Sadrach's Kring*, p. 154.
118. Ibid., p. 382.
119. Regarding the question of circumcision among the Sundanese (West Java), see W. Mintardja Rikin, *Ngabersihan als knoop in de tali paranti* (Meppel, 1973).
120. Wilhelm, 1887, p. 350.
121. Chapter III, section B.
122. Wilhelm, 1887, pp. 312, 345, 350, 364, 430, 446; 1888, pp. 9, 28, 29, 30; 1889, pp. 38, 39, 60, 81, 87.
123. Wilhelm, 1887, pp. 350-351.
124. Ibid., p. 430.

for the ministry[125] but, unfortunately, he died in the Netherlands.[126] Because of Natataruna's position as a Javanese noble and his role in the Javanese Christian community, his view on circumcision and the problem it created had a great impact on the life of the Javanese community.

Wilhelm recorded in his diary a letter he received from Natataruna on December 21, 1888, informing Wilhelm that he was planning to have his eldest son circumcised.[127] The letter included an invitation for Wilhelm to come to Yogyakarta. While the reason for the invitation was not explicit, Wilhelm replied by sending a cable of refusal. His message represented the stance of the NGZV missionaries on circumcision. He wrote: "Natataruna, Yogyakarta. A Christian is not allowed to have his son circumcised. If he does so, it means he breaks he law and God will send His wrath on him. J. Wilhelm."[128] The word Wilhelm chose to use for circumcision was *menyelamken* (corruption of *meng-Islam-kan*), which means "to islamize" rather than "to circumcise." The general understanding among the Javanese was that circumcision meant islamization —a ritual confirmation of the Moslem faith. Wilhelm did not feel the need to include any argumentation against circumcision in his cable, and felt that by pointing out that it was violation of divine law and would awaken the wrath of God, Natataruna would reconsider and not go through with the circumcision. Unexpectedly, however, Wilhelm received a speedy reply on December 22, 1888. Natataruna wrote:

"To Mr. J. Wilhelm, Minister in Purwareja. I have received your cable and I understand its meaning. Herewith I confirm that I do not islamize my son, but will only have him circumcised. The reason is because I am Javanese. Even more, all the Christians in Yogyakarta have their sons circumcised. My wife and I send our greetings. Raden Mas Kapitein Yosef Natataruna.[129]

Natataruna's reply indicates that he first considered himself a Javanese, but was also conscious of his Christianity. Most Javanese regard circumcision as affirmation of *syahadat*, but others view it primarily as a sign of one's Javanese identity. This is clarified by C. Albers, a NZV missionary who worked in Meester Cornelis (presently Jatinegara, near Jakarta), who said, "Many Javanese have their child circumcised, not first of all intending to make them Moslem, but rather to take part in an ancient

125. Wilhelm, 1889, p. 57.
126. Ibid., p. 99. In the meeting of the Board of the NGZV, September, 1894, Cachet, as Tengku Nataadmaka's foster parent, informed them of Tengku's death; however, the date of death was not noted; see NGZV, Minutes, September 14, 1894 (Archives of the Dutch Reformed Missionary Society, Leusden).
127. Wilhelm, 1888, p. 28.
128. The original cable was written in Malay (old Indonesian). Ibid., p. 28.
129. Ibid., p. 29.

tradition by which, as they say, the child becomes a Javanese; not a Moslem, but a Javanese."[130] Natataruna belonged to this group and claimed that circumcision had nothing to do with Islam. Therefore, the distinction between "islamizing" and "circumcising" found in his letter is legitimate. He had the courage to abandon Islam, but refused to deny his Javanese identity.

Natataruna serves as a representation of Sadrach's community with regard to circumcision. "Remaining Javanese" and "preserving *adat*" became watchwords for Sadrach and the other evangelists. They saw no contradiction between being truly Christian and truly Javanese at the same time. For them *adat* was not a hindrance nor a danger to their newly found Christianity, even though the missionaries opposed them.

The "Natataruna affair" caused unending controversy among the missionaries of the NGZV. In a missionary meeting held in March, 1889, the issue was raised and Wilhelm was accused by Vermeer and Zuidema of being too "weak" in his stance towards paganistic practices such as circumcision.[131] They attributed his permissiveness to Sadrach's control.

To determine whether these accusations were well-founded, we must first understand what Wilhelm did to deal with the situation. Wilhelm's cable makes clear that he firmly rejected Natataruna's plan to have his son circumcised. Natataruna, however, went ahead and carried out his plan. In an attempt to understand the situation, Wilhelm researched the Javanese view of circumcision. He found, as did Alber, that in the Javanese context circumcision is the fulfillment of *adat*. He did not deny the fact that many Javanese, especially among the *santris*, also claim circumcision as a Moslem rite, but an increasing number of educated Javanese Moslems viewed circumcision as an obligation apart from its religious significance. In addition, circumcisions were performed almost everywhere in the world, not only in Moslem countries, and even appeared in the Scriptures. As Wilhelm argued, it was not regarded as a sacrament by the Javanese Christians.[132] Thus, through his experience with Natataruna, Wilhelm finally reached an understanding of the Javanese view of circumcision.

His arguments, however, were not convincing to his colleagues. Conflicts between the missionaries over this issue as well as how to view *adat* in general grew more intense. Wilhelm continued in his attempts to convince his fellow missionaries. He wanted Natataruna himself to testify

---

130. *Overzicht van de zesde zendingsconferentie van Nederlandsch-Indische Zendings-bond gehouden te Batavia en te Depok van 26 Augustus-8 September, 1889* (Rotterdam, 1889), p. 76.

131. Adriaanse, *Sadrach's Kring*, p. 222.

132. Ibid., pp. 222-223.

as to why he had had his son circumcised. To that end, he requested Natataruna to write a "letter of testimony." In conjunction with Natataruna's letter he also planned to send a second letter written by another party stating that circumcision was not Islamic *syariat*. With these two letters in hand, Wilhelm fully expected the controversy to draw to a close. His letter to Natataruna reads as follows:

> I request that you write a letter in which you acknowledge having Tengku circumcised. I need such a letter to enable me as soon as possible to discuss the problem so that, hopefully, an agreement can be reached. The testimony must consist of two separate letters. The first should be your testimony concerning the circumcision — why you did it. Was it the fulfillment of Islamic law, or simply an outward, physical sign? The second letter must be written by someone else, stating that circumcision is not an Islamic obligation, and that the circumcision of Tengku does not mean that he has been islamized. I hope that you will reply as soon as possible, and that Tengku will be able to return to Purwareja.[133]

Wilhelm's efforts failed completely. Even with Natataruna's letter of testimony, the controversy could not be resolved. It is possible that the missionaries were afraid of making the wrong decision. Or, it could be an indication of the dependence of the missionaries on the Board of the NGZV, which determined most of the mission policies. This problem was, in fact, referred to the Board in the Netherlands for resolution.[134] The decision would be followed by all the missionaries on the field. In its meeting of May 27, 1889, the Board of the NGZV reached the unanimous decision that circumcision was to be combatted by all missionaries.[135]

The reasons behind this decision are easily traced to the NGZV's intolerant attitude toward Javanese culture and belief. They accepted the judgment that paganistic practices were evident in the life of the Javanese Christian community, such as "circumcision and whatever is done in the name of *adat* and religious obligation." All of these customs and beliefs were to be rejected because they were against Reformed principles.[136] This decision of the NGZV reflects the attitude which it held throughout its history — an attitude of intolerance toward non-Christian cultures. Such an attitude was reflected by its missionaries in Central Java, especially in their strong opposition to the preservation of Javanese *adat* in Sadrach's community.

In conclusion, we would like to distinguish between the two types of

---

133. Wilhelm, 1889, p. 39.
134. Ibid., p. 59; Adriaanse, *Sadrach's Kring*, p. 22.
135. NGZV, Minutes, May 27, 1889 (Archives of the Dutch Reformed Missionary Society, Leusden).
136. "Uit Indië," p. 3; cf. Kuyper's view on missions among the heathen which were previously mentioned.

charges brought against Sadrach and his community. The first type we will call "unfounded" charges. These are charges which were based on rumor and innuendo and were uncritically accepted and propagated by the missionaries. In some instances, this was simply the result of their lack of knowledge and understanding of the Javanese cultural context in which they worked. In other instances, however, there appear to have been vested interests at work — the desire to remove Sadrach from his position within the community was motivated not by true concern for Javanese Christians, but by political concerns and personal ambition.

A second type of charge we will call "founded" charges. These charges were sincere concerns based on specific missiological issues which arose as a result of the missionaries view of Western Christianity as the norm by which Javanese Christianity must be measured, and to which Javanese Christianity must conform. Ultimately these charges boil down to a basic difference of opinion on the nature and use of contextualization in mission practice. Whereas Sadrach and his community saw contextualization as the vital means by which the Gospel was communicated to the Javanese soul, the Western missionaries saw it is compromise, or even worse, syncretism. The inevitable result was conflict — the growing pains of pioneer missionaries working in an age of improvisation.

CHAPTER V

THE SIGNIFICANCE OF SADRACH'S CONTRIBUTION TO THE CONTEXTUALIZING EFFORTS OF THE CHURCH — A SUMMATION

In this final chapter we shall review the material presented to establish the validity of our original hypothesis that Sadrach's achievements, though often misunderstood, were an early example of genuinely contextualized Javanese Christianity and, therefore, of singular importance for the history of the Javanese church. It has been made evident that Sadrach developed an indigenous Christian community which manifested itself through its organization, leadership, teachings, and traditions. Sadrach developed a style of leadership and form of community which were not only rooted in and inspired by traditional Javanese values and customs, but were also critically corrective of those same values and customs. Sadrach's task was made all the more difficult by the Dutch missionary context in which he worked, a context which was not supportive of the concept of an indigenous expression of Christianity. It is our conclusion that Sadrach provided an expression of the Christian faith which lay close to the heart of his people, commended itself to their minds, corresponded to their sensibilities and experiences, and spoke effectively to their needs and expectations, their hopes and aspirations. In this concluding chapter we will draw together and review the evidence which has been presented in support of this thesis.

A. The Independent Leadership of Sadrach

Sadrach's religious and educational background, as well as the historical development of his community must first be understood in order to get a proper perspective on the community and its problems. The growth of Sadrach's leadership corresponded to the growth of his community. The conclusions drawn by Cachet were regarded by Adriaanse as imbalanced and one-sided because he ignored the Javanese realities of culture, education, economics, and history, and viewed the situation only from a

Western, Dutch perspective.[1] In contrast, the inception and development of the community is better understood when it is viewed from the perspective of Sadrach's personality and leadership *as a Javanese*. Adriaanse and Van Lith, for example, were very impressed by Sadrach's personality and self-confidence. In contrast to the "childish dependence" of most of the Javanese with whom the Dutch missionaries dealt in the nineteenth century, Sadrach was an exception, an outspoken exponent of what lay beneath the tranquil Javanese surface.[2] His educational background and his position as a *guru ngelmu* and *kyai* were significant factors in the formation of his personality and leadership.

As a result, Sadrach worked independently. He never worked under direct supervision for long periods of time, even during his "apprenticeship" under Anthing and Stevens-Philips. He never became a professional evangelist, nor dependent on any organization for his salary,[3] but remained unpaid — a system which he also developed in his own community. Sadrach's independent style of leadership was an important factor in the formation of the independent spirit of his community as well.

Already during Stevens-Philips's lifetime, Sadrach had moved away from the Philips home to become an independent evangelist and to establish his own Christian community. His methods of evangelism and community development were thoroughly Javanese. Using the Javanese *kyai* method, he engaged his opponents in debate, winning them for the Christian faith. Rather than consigning them to Stevens-Philips for instruction, however, Sadrach himself took over the responsibility of preparing them for baptism, leaving only the act of baptism itself to Vermeer or the ministers of the *Indische Kerk*.

While his position was highly admired by his followers, the Dutch missionaries refused to recognize it. They preferred to consider Sadrach a follower of Stevens-Philips and an ordinary evangelist's helper like the other missionary helpers, when in reality his authority went far beyond

1. Adriaanse, *Sadrach's Kring*, p. vi.
2. "Childish dependence" is a term used by such missionaries as Harthoorn, Poensen, and Bakker among others to describe the character of the Javanese people. Although this represents a typical colonial view of the indigenous people, it is of particular interest for us, having come from an indigenous Javanese background, since it helps us understand the way in which the Dutch missionaries treated the Javanese people and carried out their sacred mission among them. Such judgments are, of course, generalizations, and therefore a partial misjudgment of the real situation. What the missionaries saw as dependence was, in fact, a misunderstanding of the Javanese emphasis on respect and politeness.
3. Adriaanse, *Sadrach's Kring*, p. 61.

what the Dutch missionaries had imagined. The attempts to incorporate Sadrach's community into Dutch organizations and churches by separating Sadrach from the community failed, due largely to their misunderstanding of this fact.

Finally, it can be seen from its historical development that Sadrach's community developed free from missionary influence, especially during the crucial period of its formation, when its unique character took shape. The role of the *Indische Kerk* and the Dutch missionaries during this period was confined to the administration of the sacraments. The role of Stevens-Philips, in contrast, served to encourage Sadrach's independent development. As an Euro-Indonesian, she could understand the Javanese culture and was sensitive to the Javanese context. As a lay person who trusted Sadrach, she could work with him without suspicion. As a woman, she could work with Sadrach as an equal partner rather than as a superior and subordinate. Rather than viewing Sadrach as a rival, she stimulated Sadrach's development according to the Javanese system.

We can conclude, therefore, that Sadrach's personal background in the *pesantren*, and as a *guru ngelmu* and *kyai* were contributing factors to the independent spirit and self-confidence with which his community was formed. This was significant for the growth of Sadrach's community, which stood in vivid contrast to the missionary churches. His leadership was uniquely Javanese, and therefore his community became a uniquely Javanese expression of Christian community.

B. Sadrach's Community, Rooted in the Context

Sadrach's response to the Gospel was, as we have seen, from within the Javanese context. Therefore, his message was more easily understood, learned, and communicated, and was effective in drawing new converts. A review of the correlations between Sadrach's community and its Javanese context will demonstrate how the community was rooted in its environment — the key factor behind the community's growth.

1. Sadrach's community and the rural environment

Contact with Western civilization in the rural areas of Java did not occur until the second half of the nineteenth century. Even then it was not prevalent, and did not change the closed and isolated character of the rural community. Contacts with the cities, the centers of progress, were almost absent, and the poor transportation system hindered efforts of communication. Villages were (and often still are today) linked by "mouse tracks" which could be passed only on foot, and filled up with mud during the rainy season.[4] The Javanese and Dutch officials who toured these areas were carried on a *palanquin* (a carried chair). When Cachet made his tour, it was reported that he was offered such a mode of transportation by the Javanese.

The economic and cultural gap which was (and to a lesser extent still is) evident between the rural and urban people was expressed in the great (court) tradition and the little (common, peasant) tradition.[5] Sadrach's community was composed primarily of the little tradition of the peasants. The education provided through the Koran schools and *pesantrens* was religious in nature.[6] Western education and technology had as yet made no inroads into the rural community. "Profane" knowledge was not a part of the "formed curriculum." This does not mean that Javanese youth were uneducated. Rather, they were educated through an informal system which was more conducive to the needs and conditions of rural life. A system of apprenticeship was used to learn necessary skills from parents or other experienced adults. Through this apprenticeship young people were prepared to take an active part in Javanese social life.

Most of the Dutch missionaries, however, failed to understand this educational system and viewed the Javanese villagers as primitive and uneducated.[7] Their conclusions were based on the fact that when Western education was introduced in the rural areas there was little response. Overlooking and underestimating the informal indigenous education system, they claimed that Javanese children preferred to sit on a buffalo's back for the whole day rather than sitting in school for two or three hours.

As leader of the community, Sadrach was concerned about the education of its youth as well as the improvement of the economic situation. He initiated a *pesantren* style of education in the community which was supported by Wilhelm who recommended that the NGZV support these schools.[8] This simple education system was expanded and

4. At the time of our visit to Karangjasa in February, 1986, the road connecting this village was unpaved. It is somewhat difficult to reach during the rainy season because most of the road is covered with water and mud. Conditions in the nineteenth century, of course, were no better.

5. Koentjaraningrat, *Javanese Culture,* p.vii; *Kebudayaan Jawa,* p.2.

6. Chapter II, section A. Regarding Javanese education in the nineteenth century, see W.A. Knibbe, "Onderwijs en opvoeding der Javaansche bevolking," TNI 11 (1849), pp. 275-288; Van Der Chijs, pp. 212-323; W. Hoezoo, "Uit de Inlandsche School op Java," MNZG 17 (1873), pp. 48-55.

7. Chapter I, section A.

8. Chapter II, section B.

was reported on the annual synod meeting in Karangjasa.[9] When Zuidema came to Central Java in 1888 as a missionary teacher, he was surprised to find an existing education system. Because of his unfamiliarity with the *pesantren* system, however, he found the schools to be very "primitive," and had difficulty appreciating this traditional form of education.

In the area of economics, Sadrach utilized the cooperative method which already existed among Javanese village communities, by which members could borrow a small sum of money for setting up a small business. He also initiated the raising of funds to purchase land for distribution among the needy members of the community.[10] Through these activities Sadrach fulfilled his role as *kyai* as one who concerned himself with both the spiritual and physical life of his *murids*. Thus, informal personal relationships, which were a very important aspect of community life, were strengthened between he and his followers.

Sadrach's leadership style was tailored to the rural context. Rather than emphasizing the individual, the development of the village collective life was stressed. The preeminence of communal life over individual interests was characteristic of the Javanese village community from of old, and those who placed their individual interests first were considered deviant, sometimes to the point of exclusion from the community. The spirit of *gotong royong* was based on the principle of reciprocity, exchanging service for service, which was central to village life.[11] Such a societal structure required a unique type of leadership. The leader not only needed to delegate tasks and responsibilities, but also needed to function as a symbol of communal life. He functioned as *primus inter pares* (first among equals), uniting the community as its adhesive leader. Sadrach became this type of charismatic, informal leader, uniting the Javanese Christian rural community under his leadership. Without this type of individual leadership, the community could not exist.

In Javanese society a charismatic leader also became widely known through his extraordinary abilities as *dhukun*, exorcist, and *guru ngelmu*. The oral communication system which was utilized tended to integrate myths and legends from the court tradition into the history of gurus and *kyais*. The circulation of these stories was vital to the success of the leader. Sadrach, too, became the subject of this type of story, and thus

9. The meeting was held on October 20-23, 1888, in Karangjasa. At the time there were nine schools with 175 pupils (7 female); cf. Wilhelm, 1888, p. 20.

10. Chapter III, section C.

11. Van Akkeren, p. 22.

became widely known after the fashion of a traditional Javanese religious teacher.[12]

The NGZV missionaries, however, rejected this type of leadership arrangement for the community. They became irritated with the total dependence of the community members on their leader. In their opinion such a concentration of power was dangerous because of its arbitrariness and possible misuse. They feared that such a leader could become dictatorial, the sole figure who could make all decision and laws for the community based on his own will with no restrictions. Such great authority, they felt, was beyond the limits of human authority, and could not be possessed by a servant of God. Such unlimited authority was in God's hand alone, and was a threat to public life when claimed by mortal man.

Their argument appears to be based on the twin pillars of Calvin's ecclesiology: the sovereignty of God and the equality of believers. It is not surprising, therefore, that Heyting viewed Sadrach's leadership style as being contrary to the principles of Calvinism.[13] Cachet also opposed it, pointing to the titles attributed to Sadrach by his followers as indicative of an authority that was unacceptable in the church.[14] D. Bakker went as far as to say that Sadrach became so central in the life of the community that he replaced Christ as the center.[15] In contrast, Adriaanse, who knew Sadrach personally, was more moderate in his judgment. He understood that noble titles were used by the Javanese to show respect, and included such figures as the Dutch officials and missionaries. This did not mean, however, that the Javanese regarded them as *devas*, or gods.[16]

It is our conclusion that at the time the Dutch missionaries in general misjudged and misunderstood the significance of the role of Javanese leaders in their communities. Because of their Western, individualistic approach, they failed to understand the communal aspects of traditional Javanese society. They overlooked the fact that Javanese leadership was charismatic in nature. A leader was not voted in by the people, but rather gained his position by divine ordinance.[17] Authority was viewed as coming "from above," entrusted to the person by God. Such authority was to be used for noble purposes for the good of all people. In Javanese thought, God was the sole possessor of authority and power. It was His

---

12. Chapter II, section B.
13. Chapter IV, section C.
14. Cachet, *Een Jaar*, pp. 841-842.
15. D. Bakker, "Nationaal Christendom," p. 299.
16. Adriaanse, *Sadrach's Kring*, pp. 397-398.
17. Chapter III, section A.

to delegate or take back if it was used for self-interest. When a Javanese leader misused his power, his authority gradually decreased and the gift of healing was lost. As a result, he lost the trust of the people. However, as long as the authority was used for good, the charisma remained with the individual. Therefore, what was seen as arbitrariness among the missionaries was viewed by the Javanese as a gift from God.

A second misunderstanding on the part of the Dutch missionaries was the strong characteristic of fatherliness in Javanese leadership. This characteristic "forced" a leader to act as a *bapa* (father) to his followers, treating them with love as his children and grandchildren, thus making it difficult to misuse his authority and power.[18]

2. Sadrach's community and the Moslem environment

Because Sadrach's community was basically rural, its members largely came from a Moslem *abangan* background. Therefore, *adat* remained an important part of the community's life. Sadrach placed a high value on *adat*, viewing it as a precious inheritance to be preserved. Becoming a Christian did not mean having to abandon one's *adat*, a view which contrasted sharply with that of the Dutch missionaries and also of the Javanese population of the time.[19] Rather than placing Javanese *adat* in conflict with Christianity, Sadrach preferred to approach the differences as a *Javanese*, and attempted to harmonize as much of the Javanese culture as possible with Christianity, incorporating many of the Javanese Moslem customs into the life of the community. The accomodation to traditional Javanese customs and rituals which resulted prevented Sadrach's community from being cut off from the Moslem Javanese community at large.[20]

In his efforts to harmonize, Sadrach took over many elements of the *Islam abangan*, for example, the *paguron* educational system, the *guru-murid* relationship, and the use of local gurus to function as imams of local communities. He also maintained such Moslem customs as separate seating for men and women in church, and the use of the veil, and continued to use the terms *mesjid* for church and *imam* for its leader

18. Chapter IV, section B. The very common title, *bapa*, was also rejected by the missionaries, which indicates their lack of knowledge regarding the core of Javanese culture.

19. A radical break from Javanese culture was implicitly and indirectly demanded by the Dutch missionaries. This perception prevailed among the Javanese people; chapter I, section B 4.

20. Chapter III, section B; Bakker, "Onze Zendingsterrein," p. 364.

which led Uhlenbusch to label the community "Mohammedan Christianity," and Bakker to call it "a heathen Mohammedan religion in Christian clothing."[21] Sadrach was not, however, uncritical in his use of Javanese *adat*. He carefully selected those traditions which were capable of being "christianized." As a general rule, this meant selecting those customs which were not closely bound with Islam;[22] that is, the customs which, as the result of a long historical process, had become disassociated from their original religious meaning.[23] It is clear, therefore, that while Sadrch's community provided room for *adat*, this was done with great care and a critical eye. Charges of "syncretism," therefore, were and are unjustified.

A good example of Sadrach's use of Javanese *adat* is the church building in Karangjasa.[24] The building was built on the pattern of the Javanese mosque, yet the symbols were reinterpreted in a uniquely and completely Christian way. The three-tiered roof was a symbol of the Holy Trinity. The *cakra*, which replaced the Moslem crescent, was itself taken from Javanese lore,[25] and was reinterpreted to symbolize the power of God's Gospel to pierce even the most obstinate of human hearts. The "accuracy" of these interpretations is not the issue here. What is significant is the fact that Sadrach's community made the attempt to appropriate existing Javanese symbols for Christ, and thus, to make the Christian faith more communicable and intelligible to their Javanese context. It was, indeed, an early effort at indigenization.

In contrast to the *santris*,[26] Sadrach's community was more accomodating and open to the existing culture, as were the *Islam abangan*. As has been noted, many of the customs of the *abangan*, such as burning incense and sprinkling water with flowers, became a part of the ceremonial and ritual life of Sadrach's community.[27] The community appeared, therefore, to have the same attitudes as the *abangan*. Van Akkeren, in his

21. Bakker, "Onze Zendingsterrein," p. 364.

22. Chapter III, section B.

23. Some Indonesian sociologists and cultural anthropologists distinguish two categories of *slametan* — sacred (closely bound to religious ceremonies) and secular. See Bachtiar, pp. 86-87; 90-93; see also Koentjaraningrat, *Javanese Culture*, pp. 350-351; *Kebudayaan Jawa*, p. 347.

24. Chapter III, section B.

25. The *cakra* was the weapon of Sri Kresna, incarnation of the mighty Wisnu. He was a consummate politician, diplomat, and strategist of war, and the most intellectually brilliant on the Pandawa side. He made final victory possible for Pandawa. For a short description of *wayang* figures, see Benedict R.O.G. Anderson, *Mythology and the Tolerance of Java* (New York, 1965).

26. Regarding *santri*, see Chapter I, section A.

27. Chapter III, section B.

study of indigenous churches in East Java, distinguished between those Javanese Christians who were deeply rooted in the wet rice background, as were the *abangan*, and those who viewed Christianity as something which would always remain a stranger in the midst of Javanese culture, as did the *santris*.[28] Just as two types of Islam existed in nineteenth century Java, by analogy we can also speak of two types of Christianity. *Kristen abangan* refers to the expression of Christianity which was more closely bound to the culture. This form of Christianity was developed by the Javanese evangelists. The second type, *Kristen putihan*, as developed by the missionaries, was an expression of Christianity which was suspicious of Javanese culture. In the early phase of mission history in Java these differences were expressed in the terms *Kristen Jawa* (Javanese Christianity) and *Kristen Landa* (Dutch Christianity).[29] Sadrach's community might best be described as *Kristen Jawa "abangan."*[30]

3. Sadrach's community and the age of feudalism-colonialism

Rather than eradicating the Javanese feudal structure, Dutch colonialism served to strengthen it by supporting the ruling Javanese nobility as agents of the Dutch colonial government. The nobility remained in office and furthered the aims of colonialism. The "caste" system remained intact.

Although Sadrach came from the lowest class in Javanese society, he was able to rise above the miserable conditions to become the leader of thousands of rural Javanese. He was socially elevated through the "merit" of Christianity, thus breaking the chains of a feudal and colonial society. He approached the Dutch authorities and the Javanese nobility walking rather than crawling, and was seated "on a chair" among them, a position not accorded to the common man. This incredible achievement was sometimes misunderstood by the Javanese who viewed him as a Javanese nobleman or a supernatural figure who bore various aristocratic titles. This was also misunderstood by the Dutch missionaries who accused him of arrogating to himself honors above his position.

Sadrach's consciousness of emancipation for the indigenous common people was a precious attribute in nineteenth century Java. He provided an example of social and political liberation for the community without resorting to social protest and political activism, as was so often the case

28. Van Akkeren, p. 148.
29. Chapter I, section B.
30. Chapter III, section B.

in religious communities of the time.[31] Guillot correctly perceived that Sadrach's self-confidence and independence, which sometimes appeared arrogant and unbending, became an important factor in holding the loyalty of his followers.[32]

This, however, was not the sole factor in Sadrach's appeal. His followers were impressed with his unique personality as were some of the missionaries, such as Adriaanse, Van Lith,[33] and Kraemer,[34] who saw him as having great potential. In a society where the vast majority of the Javanese had little opportunity to develop their personal identity, self-confidence, intellect, and initiative, indigenous Christian figures like Sadrach became bearers of the liberating message for thousands of "mute" Javanese common people.

In this connection we can also see the political implications of Sadrach's proclamation of Jesus Christ as *ratu adil*,[35] which served to awaken the awareness and hope for emancipation among the Javanese population. The nature of Sadrach's community and his own rise to prominence served as an implicit political critique of the existing feudal, colonial structures. Nevertheless, Sadrach must first of all be seen as a religious leader rather than as a political leader who consciously directed

---

31. Chapter I, section A. Especially regarding religious revivalism, which became a widespread phenomenon in the latter part of the nineteenth century in Java, see Sartono, *The Peasants' Revolt*, pp. 140-147; cf. Sartono, *Ratu Adil*, pp. 9-36.

32. Guillot, *L'Affaire Sadrach*, pp. 326-327; *Kiai Sadrach*, p. 201.

33. As Van Lith said, "Hij stak een hoofd uit boven al zijn rasgenoten, letterlijk en figuurlijk" Weitjens, p. 190.

34. H. Kraemer was impressed by the person of Sadrach. He described him as:

> Een man van temperament en durf, van zelfbewustzijn en besef van eigen aard en eigen recht. Een ongewoon verschijnsel in het woestijn-stille Java dier dagen: een man die zich dorst te poneeren tegenover de vertegenwoordigers van het machthebbende volk: Wat zou hij in dezen tijd anders beoordeeld zijn dan vroeger toen alleen maar intuitive geesten als Wilhelm daarin iets diepers en edelers konden zien dan aanmatiging en hoogmoed. [A man of temperament and daring, of self-awareness and understanding of his own nature and right; an unusual phenomenon in the wilderness-silent Java of those days; a man who longed to set himself in opposition to the representatives of the ruling people. How differently he would be judged now than earlier, when only intuitive souls like Wilhelm could see something deeper and more noble in him than pretentiousness and arrogance.]

H. Kraemer, "Nationaal Christendom op Java," *De Opwekker* 70 (January, 1925), pp. 103-112.

35. Jesus as *ratu adil* was used by the Javanese Christian church in Central Java in church songs under the title "Gusti Jesus Ratu Adil," *Kidung Pasamuwan Kristen Jawa*, no. 139.

a people's movement against the Dutch colonial government in order to achieve a particular political goal.

The ability of Sadrach's community to remain close to Javanese culture is particularly significant in light of the fact that Christianity, in nineteenth century Java, was generally perceived as a colonial religion. The missionaries were viewed as part of the colonial regime, and Christianity was a foreign agent with a Western stamp.[36] This kind of cultural imperialism led to cultural alienation in most cases, but Sadrach's community was able to overcome these negative associations in order to present Christianity in a new and more "Javanese" light.

C. Contextualization and Deficient Implementation of Reformed Mission Strategy

The Gospel which came to Indonesia was in the form of Western Christianity, bound to Western culture. Despite the sincerity of the missionaries, they seemed unable to present the Christian message without simultaneously imposing their own culture upon the indigenous people, whether consciously or unconsciously. The problem of spreading Western culture along with Christianity has been an enduring problem in missions, for conversion involves not only a change from one religion to another, but always entails cultural critique and change as well. The result of cultural alienation, which occurs when indigenous people are uprooted from their culture through conversion to Christianity, has been common throughout the history of missions.

In the nineteenth century the opinion was prevalent that to employ local cultural elements would be to darken or even falsify the genuine Christian message, producing a pseudo-Christianity at best. Western missionaries were quick to raise the warning at the first indication of syncretism, and often accused indigenous Christians of being paganistic and superstitious.[37] On the other hand, there was a feeling among the indigenous people that Christianity implied westernization. This feeling was not unfounded since in the past the two undeniably went hand in hand. Bavinck, for example, acknowledged that missions was more often damaging to than upbuilding of the indigenous culture.[38] He felt that the time had come to seriously study the relationship between Christianity and culture. He recognized the naïveté of missionaries in their previous

36. Chapter I, section B 4.
37. Chapter I, section B.
38. Bavinck, "Zending en Cultuur," p. 63.

attempts, and advocated that missions should be constructive rather than destructive of culture. Christianity, according to him, should lay the basis for cultural transformation in order to form a new culture, namely, a Christian culture with an indigenous character.[39]

This understanding of missions as the transformation of indigenous cultures, however, was not yet a major concern of missionaries in the nineteenth century.[40] Most missionaries of that time preferred to impose Western culture rather than stimulate cultural transformation. Church planting was understood as simply the extention of the church of the homeland, as is clearly seen in the mission of the VOC and the *Indische Kerk*.[41] According to Brouwer, mission was understood as:

... simply, to be able to bring Western ideas to the East, and to be able to teach our psalms, prayers, compendium, and catechism there. ... A simple sharing of the fact of salvation and instruction in doctrine there is able to turn the Indonesians into good Christians. ... Simply, to be able to bring to the East the church order and organization just as it is found here, and especially, the Western Reformed faith.[42]

Justus Heurnius (1587-1651), who served as missionary to the Dutch East Indies, is cited by Brouwer as stating that "the church in the East must be like that in the West, also in regard to form and organization.[43]

Although written two centuries previously, a similar spirit was still evident in the nineteenth century, as can be seen in the work of the NGZV missionaries.[44] The 28th Annual report of the NGZV (April, 1889) stated

39. Ibid., p. 62.
40. It was only in the first half of the twentieth century that missionaries such as Schuurman, Bavinck, and Kraemer gave serious attention to Javanese culture in their pioneering work. See A. Wessels, "Op weg naar een contextuele missiologie," *Religies in Nieuwe Perspectief*, eds. R. Bakker *et al.*, (Kampen, 1985), pp. 109-136. The several important works of these three missions figures include: B.M. Schuurman, *Pambiyake Kekeraning Ngaurip* [Uncovering the Mystery of Life] (Bandung, 1968); Bavinck, *Christus en de mystiek van het Oosten;*); H. Kraemer, *The Christian Message in the Non-Christian World* (London, 1938); H. Kraemer, *De strijd over Bali en de Zending* (Amsterdam, 1933).
41. Chapter I, section B.
42. "... eenvoudig de westersche voorstellingen in het oosten te kunnen overbrengen, en hier onze psalmen, gebeden, kortbegrip, en chatechismus te kunnen laten leren, ... daar eenvoudig mededeeling der heilsfeiten en onderricht in geloofsleer kunnen maken, de Indonesiërs to goede Christenen... de kerkorde en organizatie zoals zij hier gevonden werd, in zonderheid ook de westersche gereformeerde belijdenis, zonder meer te kunnen overbrengen naar het oosten." Brouwer, pp. 106-107, 109, Lindenborn "Nationaal Christendom," pp. 531-532.
43. "... dat kerk in het oosten ook wat vorm een organizatie betreft aan die van het westen gelijk moet zijn." Brouwer, p. 42; Lindenborn, p. 532.
44. Chapter I, section B; Chapter IV, section A.

that, regarding the organization and state of the native congregations, the indigenous churches needed to be directed toward independence following the spirit of Reformed principles, taking into account the national character, language, and customs of the Javanese people.[45] On the surface, such a statement looks very promising with regard to contextualization. However, the actual result on the mission field was quite different from the stated formulation. A further statement in the Annual Report gave room for such an occurrence. The Report went on to declare that the mission churches should be Javanese Reformed churches. The *Heidelberg Catechism* was to be used for religious instruction, and the *Belgic Confession* was to be the confession of faith. In addition, public worship services were to follow the Reformed order of worship as far as possible.[46]

The ZGKN, which took over the mission work of the NGZV, used a similar approach to missions, as was evident by their assignment to Cachet. He was to investigate whether:

> ... indeed, the churches which have gathered from among the Mohammedans and heathens sufficiently display the image of a church of Christ; whether the offices are established in accordance with the Word of God; whether the service of the Word and sacraments are maintained; whether church discipline is exercised with authority; whether her church relations rest on true confession; whether the administration of her church life agrees with the principles of Reformed church administration.[47]

During his final days in Central Java, Cachet summoned the missionaries for the instruction "to work toward the institution of congregations after Reformed principles."[48]

The understanding of missions which developed within the Reformed Churches in later stages indicated a growing consciousness of the need to consider the character, needs, circumstances, and culture of the indigenous people,[49] even though this understanding was often neglected

45. NGZV, *28th Jaarverslag* (April, 1889), p. 3 as quoted by Bakker, *De Zending,* p. 89.

46. Ibid., p. 90.

47. "... metterdaad de kerken uit Mohammedanen en Heidenen vergaderd, genoegzaam de ware gestalte van eene kerken Christi vertoonen, of er ambten zijn ingeseld naar den woorde Gods, of de dienst des woords en der sacramenten wordt onderhouden, of de kerkelijke tucht der kracht oefent, of haar kerkverband rust op zuivere belijdenis, of de regeling van haar kerkelijk leven in overeenstemming is met de beginselen van Gereformeerde Kerkregeering." NGK, *Acta,* p. 22; cf. Pol, *Midden Java,* p. 62.

48. "... te leiden tot het institueeren van gemeenten naar gereformeerde ordening." Cachet, *Een Jaar,* p. 844.

49. See "Zendingcongres," p. 90; Kuyper, p. 13.

in practice. The concept of *kerkelijke zending*, which viewed missions as a direct function of the church, carried with it the "mother-daughter" relationship between the sending church and the mission church.[50] Positively, such a relationship model brought the two churches closer. Support for mission churches from the home front increased as a result. However, the contextualization of indigenous churches remained of little or no importance. In fact, the mother-daughter relationship actually served to thwart contextualization since the goal was for the "daughter church" to resemble the "mother church" as much as possible in such areas as church order and polity, creeds, order of worship, music, and theology.

In order for a mission church to be considered independent, Bakker proposed three requirements: a creed, a church order, and a liturgy.[51] Such a statement seems to imply, although Bakker did not so intend it, that there were several types of "ready-made" creeds, church orders, and liturgies to choose from, and that once they were chosen, the church would be independent. This, however, was not the case, and demonstrates that although rhetorically contextualization was a concern for some missionaries, in reality, nineteenth century Reformed mission efforts focused on developing "copy" churches of those found in the Netherlands, unaware of the importance of contextualizing the Christian message.

The failure of the missionaries to distinguish Western culture from the Christian message had the potential to develop into impatience and intolerance toward other faiths, as well as toward indigenous expressions of Christianity in different cultural contexts. Such intolerance and impatience was manifested in the attitude of the missionaries. Their approach to missions seemed to be like that of the crusaders, "fighting" against a non-Christian world. In our opinion, their world view divided the world into two factions — the Christian world, which was identified with light, and the non-Christian world, which was identified with darkness. The major task of missions was to bring the light into the world of darkness. While it is true, theoretically, that Reformed missions distinguished between "the preaching of the Gospel among the Heathens" and "the preaching of the Gospel among the Mohammedans," as stated in the constitution of the NGZV,[52] in practice this distinction did not

50. Chapter IV, Section A.
51. Bakker, *De Zending,* p. 14.
52. "de Evangelie-verkondiging onder de Heidenen" and "de Evangelie-verkondiging onder Heidenen en Mohammedanen." NGZV's Constitution, Article 1, *Heidenbode* (October, 1883), pp. 21-22, and (May, 1896), pp. 170-171; cf. also Van Den End, *Gereformeerde Zending,* pp. 71-73.

make a great deal of difference. In both instances, the above mentioned world view was implicit.

The more patient and tolerant attitude toward other faiths and cultures, which was still in the process of formation at that time, was also urgently need in the mission policy of the nineteenth century. Such an attitude is fundamental for the stimulation and facilitation of indigenous expressions of Christianity, which results in the formation of truly contextualized churches — churches of the land. We are reminded by Samartha, who viewed the missionaries as empowered by a crusading spirit, that we must listen to each other in dialogue rather than only letting others listen to us in monologue:

> The noise of old crusades, the shelter of ancient fortresses, and the spent bullets of past theological armouries must be left behind. What we need today is a theology that is not less but more true to God by being generous and open, a theology not less but more loving towards the neighbours by being friendly and willing to listen, a theology that does not separate us from our fellow human being but supports us in our common struggles and hopes. As we live together with our neighbors, what we need today is a theology that refuses to be inpregnable but which, in the spirit of Christ, is both ready and willing to be vulnerable.[53]

D. A Reconstruction of Sadrach's Christology and Soteriology

It is important to view Sadrach's teachings on the person of Jesus Christ (Christology) and Christ's redemptive work (Soteriology) in connection with the close relationship Sadrach's community had with the Javanese *Islam abangan* context. Because the missionaries perceived Sadrach's teachings as "Javanism" rather than the true Gospel, he was highly suspected by the Board of the NGZV, as was made evident in a letter sent to Wilhelm dated November 12, 1889.[54] It was the judgment of Cachet, among others, that Christ had no place in Sadrach's community, and Sadrach was accused of taking the place of God. In order to understand and evaluate this harsh judgment, three influential elements of Sadrach's background must be taken into account: Javanese elements including elements from Hinduism and Buddhism, Moslem elements, and "Christian," i.e., pietistic, elements.

It is true that Sadrach proclaimed Jesus as guru, *panutan* and *ratu adil*, who taught a "certain *ngelmu*" for human salvation.[55] Sadrach's

---

53. S.J. Samartha, *Courage for Dialogue* (New York, 1982), p. 77.
54. Wilhelm, 1889, p. 109
55. Chapter IV, Section B.

perception of Jesus and the Gospel, however, must be seen in light of his background as a Javanese. He grew up according to Javanese tradition which incorporated aspects of Hinduism and Buddhism, was educated in the *pesantren*, became a *santri*, lived in a *kauman*, and became a *guru ngelmu*. His introduction to Christianity was by orthodox missionaries and lay Christians who nurtured Sadrach in a pietistic Christianity to which he was later converted.[56] It was inevitable that Sadrach's understanding of Christ and the Gospel would be colored by these rich life experiences, some of which we will consider in more detail.

First, Sadrach's background in a *ngelmu*-seeking tradition had an impact on his way of thinking. The highest concern of the *ngelmu*-seeker was the essence and meaning of life itself, the objective being the perfection of life. In Javanese, this was described as *hanggayuh kasampurnaning hurip* (striving after the perfect life), *berbudi bawa leksana* (great noble soul), and *ngudi sajatining becik* (devotion to true goodness).[57] To achieve the final goal of perfection, one needed to obtain knowledge of *pitutur* (advice, direction) and *wewaler* (prohibition, taboo), which was handed down orally by one's ancestors and found in written form in Javanese classical literature.[58] Self-discipline ran parallel to such knowledge, for knowledge without its active expression in life was considered vain and insignificant, like a tree which does not bear fruit.[59]

Thus, to reach the goal of perfection, a mediator was required. The mediator functioned not only as the guru who taught and interpreted

56. Chapter II, Section A.
57. Soeharto, ed., "Butir-Butir Budaya Jawa" [The Elements of Javanese Culture], *TEMPO* (March 12, 1988), p. 46. This represents the basic Javanese world view from ancient times. This concurs with Mulder's statement that "although times have changed, the very basic Javanese culture and identity does not change much, and the Javanese people are very aware of and proud of the continuity of their culture," Mulder, p. 11; cf. Anderson, *Mythology*; regarding Javanese world view, see S. De Jong, *Een Javaanse Levenshouding* (Wageningen, 1973) and his *Salah satu sikap hidup orang Jawa* [A World and Life View of the Javanese People] (Yogyakarta, 1976). Emphasis on moral conduct, the good life, the perfection of life, the noble life, etc., is a prevailing characteristic of the Javanese world view. Marbangun Hardjowirogo states that "perhaps there is no people like the Javanese who are satiated with the doctrine of *kautamaning urip* (perfection of life)," Hardjowirogo, *Manusia Jawa* [Javanese Man] (Jakarta, 1984), p. 18.
58. Some examples of nineteenth century Javanese classical literature which emphasize moral ethical teachings are: *Serat Wulang Reh* by King Pakubuwana IV (1788-1820), *Serat Wedhatama* by King Mangkunagara IV (1855-1881), *Serat Jaka Lodhang* by R. Ng. Ranggawarsita (1803-1873); see Koentjaranigrat, *Javanese Culture*, p. 326; *Kebudayaan Jawa* (Jakarta, 1984), p. 320.
59. This understanding can be compared to the major theme of the Letter of James regarding faith and works.

pitutur and *wewaler*, but also as a *panutan*. A guru whose life was not blameless could not function as a *panutan*, and was therefore considered a false guru. The Javanese classical literature contained warnings in seeking a guru. One needed to seek carefully in order to find a true guru, a true *panutan* – a perfect man as demonstrated through moral conduct.[60] We can conclude, therefore, that Sadrach was concerned with achieving perfection by fulfilling the "law" (*pitutur* and *wewaler*) through the help of a guru and *panutan*.

Second, Sadrach's education in the *pesantren* system influenced his thought and spirituality. Besides benefitting from the spirit of independence which he learned through his education, the basic Moslem teaching of the merit (*amal*) of good moral conduct was also integrated into his thought. *Amal* was achieved by fulfilling the *syariat* as revealed by God to Mohammed, and following the example (*sunnah*) of Mohammed. Like the guru in Javanese tradition, Mohammed also functioned as a *panutan*.

Third, the pietistic spirit of Anthing in particular, seems to have influenced Sadrach's spirituality. During the period of his work with Anthing in Batavia, Sadrach was exposed to several missionaries and lay people from a pietistic background who emphasized individual piety through obedience to God's law.

Although each of these environments differ, the common stress on good moral conduct and obedience to the law can be seen. Moral discipline through fulfilling the law of *pitutur* and *wewaler* in Javanese thought, of *syariat* in Moslem thought, and of Christian morality in pietistic thought, was required. The function of a mediator as guru and *panutan* merges well with the Christian mediator, Jesus Christ. Discipleship meant following the path of the exemplary figure. Thus one could achieve perfection and become truly Javanese, truly *santri*, and truly Christian.

Keeping this background in mind, Sadrach's Christology and soteriology become clear. It was easy for Sadrach to understand the Gospel as the law or norm of life, similar to the *pitutur* and *wewaler* of the Javanese, and the *syariat* of the Moslems. It is understandable that moral conduct and a disciplined life became, for Sadrach, tangible evidence of the real Christian, even to the point of partial merit unto salvation. Christ, in his thinking, was comparable to the Javanese guru/*panutan* who acted as mediator, and to the prophet Mohammed, who taught the "divine" law.

This analysis of Sadrach's thought, however, is inadequate until one

60. Cf. Mulder, pp. 29-30.

understands his reasons for converting to Christianity. Unless he saw something more in the Gospel and in the person of Christ to distinguish them from the Javanese *ngelmu abangan* and *ngelmu santrian* he already possessed, his conversion does not make sense. What was the appeal of Christianity?

The answer to this question lies in the attitude of the Javanese *ngelmu*-seeker and guru. This attitude continually drove one forward in search of what was considered the highest *ngelmu*, and satisfaction was not achieved until the highest *ngelmu* was found. Therefore, it was common for *ngelmu*-seekers to move from one teacher to another more famous one, in search of the highest truth. This attitude was also prevalent among the *santris* who moved from *pesantren* to *pesantren*, always searching for a more famous *kyai*.[61] Public debate served not only to win students, but also to increase the fame and prestige of the guru. Winning in public debate also served as evidence of the superiority of the *ngelmu* which was debated.

In his experience, Sadrach found the Christian *ngelmu* to be superior to the rest. The conversion of his former guru, Pak Kurmen, in public debate with Tunggul Wulung,[62] seems to have deeply impressed Sadrach. Another factor was the acceptance of Christianity without abandoning one's "Javanese-ness." Sadrach's success in public debate served to further demonstrate the superiority of the Christian *ngelmu*. Even the most powerful and famous Javanese *guru ngelmu* of his time, Kyai Seja Wiguna, was defeated in public debate, and he, together with a number of his followers, became convinced of the triumphant Christian *ngelmu* which Sadrach possessed.[63]

It is clear that Sadrach understood the Gospel as a type of *ngelmu*, but he viewed it as a "*ngelmu* plus," the highest, noblest, and true *ngelmu* (*ngelmu sejati*), distinct from and superior to the other *ngelmus* he had learned. This was the *ngelmu* from the guru and *panutan* Jesus, who died and was risen, as Sadrach stressed in his debates. Because of his background as a *pesantren* graduate, it is not surprising that Sadrach viewed Jesus as a distinctive prophet, nabi Ngisa Rohullah, Isa the Spirit of God.

Sadrach's perception of Jesus was as a guru, *panutan*, nabi Ngisa Rohullah, and also *ratu adil*, carried with it some implications regarding his view of Christianity. Emphasis was placed on Christian ethics and the obedient fulfillment of the divine law which was taught by nabi Ngisa

61. Cf. Dhofier, pp. 24-25.
62. Chapter II, Section A.
63. Chapter IV, Section B.

Rohullah. Jesus was the exemplary figure whose entire life, as viewed by Sadrach, consistently proved the truth and triumph of his Christian *ngelmu* through obedience to the law even unto death. His resurrection proves the triumph of his *ngelmu*, a fact stressed by Sadrach in his proclamation of the Gospel. Salvation, then, stressed following the example of Jesus. Focus was upon *imitatio Christi* (the imitation of Christ) as the most perfect man, as demonstrated in his complete obedience to divine law.

Sadrach's Christology and soteriology were strengthened by the Christian literature circulating among the Javanese Christian community in the nineteenth century. Adriaanse mentioned two books in particular, written in Javanese, which were used for evangelization. The first, the title of which translates as, *Good Instruction Showing the Way of Salvation*, presented Christianity as the way of salvation. It contained a story about a Javanese who found Jesus and followed him as a *panutan*. He then told of his experience to his fellows. According to the author, because of his close relationship to God, Jesus was called God's beloved son. He became a powerful prophet whose knowledge surpassed that of all other prophets. The contents of the book can be summarized as follows.

All men have sinned and, as a result, are far from God. But God still loves sinners. He seeks them and calls them to Himself. For this reason God sent His son, Jesus Christ, to teach them the divine law. By observing this law one's life will be cleansed and sanctified. Loving Jesus means following in his footsteps as the perfect example, namely, obediently fulfilling the law of God.[64] According to Adriaanse, attention was focused on Jesus' command to love one's neighbors. He concluded, therefore, that this book served to strengthen the Javanese Moslem idea that salvation could be achieved through good works and through following the example of the prophet or guru, making the transition from Mohammed to Jesus an easier one.[65]

The second book, entitled *Instruction Concerning the Religion of the Heart Which is Pleasing to God*, presented Christianity as a religion of the heart. It began with the premise that good and evil originate in the human heart. The core prerequisite for salvation, therefore, is sanctification of the heart as the source of will and deed. Religion which emphasizes outward things is, according to the author, meaningless. True religion, on the other hand, is always focused inwardly (*batiniah*). It touches and

64. Adriaanse, *Sadrach's Kring*, pp. 225-227.
65. Ibid., p. 228.

sanctifies the human heart, and accordingly, is called religion of the heart. The true religion of the heart is the religion of Ngisa (Jesus), whom God has given for the renewal of the human heart. This is the only religion which is basically spiritual in character. Salvation is essentially understood as sanctification of the heart, which only God knows in its essence.[66] Such quotations from Scripture as "Blessed are the pure in heart, for they shall see God," "Serve God with your whole heart and soul," and "You shall find Me if you seek Me with your whole heart" were used as evidence.[67]

According to Van Den Berg, the values taught by Jesus in the Sermon on the Mount became central to Sadrach's message.[68] Adriaanse concluded that such values were very appealing to the Javanese gurus, who often lived an ascetic, hermit-like existence in search of perfection.[69] In Adriaanse's opinion, these two books, with their emphasis on individual piety, fulfillment of the law, and following the example of the guru or teacher, served to strengthen Sadrach's "Javanese-colored" view of the person and work of Jesus Christ.

In light of the above, the question of Sadrach's ability to respond to the Gospel from the Javanese context of the nineteenth century must be addressed. Did Sadrach, through his theological understanding of the person and work of Christ, proclaim Javanism or Christianity? In other words, how should Sadrach's theological standpoint be properly understood?

In considering this question, it must be kept in mind that Sadrach was not theologically trained at the seminary level. His main concern as an evangelist was how best to communicate his newly found faith (Christian *ngelmu*) to his fellow Javanese. He did not attempt to build a comprehensive, "scientific" theology to touch upon every aspect of the meaning of Jesus and His work. His goal was simply to make the Christian faith more communicable to his audience. His faith, rather than something primarily intellectual, was based on his personal encounter with the Gospel. His recognition of Jesus as guru, *panutan*, and *ratu adil* was based on his experience of what Jesus meant for him. His experience, however, in our opinion, also manifested itself in his theology. Thus, Sadrach was doing theology in the sense that "he was reflecting on the meaning of his life in relation to its ultimate values, sources and

66. Ibid., pp. 230-232.
67. Ibid., p. 231.
68. Van Den Berg, "Javaansch Christendom," p. 225.
69. Adraanse, *Sadrach's Kring*, p. 232.

destiny."[70] His theology developed from his experience and functioned in his work. It spoke to the real situation — the Javanese context of the nineteenth century in which guru, *panutan*, and *ratu adil* were living issues.

The meaning of Jesus and the Gospel is ultimately an existential question requiring a personal answer. Sadrach found his answer, similar to the disciples who expressed their personal confession when Jesus posed the question: "But who do you say that I am?"[71] The disciples could not have answered apart from their personal experience of Jesus. This was the case with the early church as well, which developed its confession based on actual experiences of Jesus, both His life and work.

Trying to understand Sadrach's theology, therefore, means understanding his personal experience resulting from his encounter with Jesus, living and working through the Spirit. We must keep in mind that the Scriptures, to a certain extent, record personal human experiences and encounters with Jesus. In them we find a variety of experiences which range from the common to the unique. The image of Jesus is not the same for everyone. Through these various personal experiences, different images of Jesus are portrayed which are of benefit to the readers. The image of a guru who teaches and gives up his life as an example, and the image of the just king who reigns with wisdom and justice are familiar images of God and Christ in Scripture. While the immediate context — Javanese culture — may be different, the basic meaning of these concepts is the same. The concepts of Jesus as guru[72] and Jesus as *ratu adil*[73] are images which are accepted by Javanese Christians even at the present time.

In the opinion of the Dutch missionaries, Sadrach's theology was one-sided and fragmentary, ignoring the principles of *sola fide* (by faith alone) and *sola gratia* (by grace alone). They accused Sadrach of ignoring rebirth by the Holy Spirit and denying the essence of Jesus as the incarnation of God. They felt that he belittled the significance of Jesus' suffering and death, concluding that Christ had no place in Sadrach's community.

70. Doing theology as meant by Tissa Balasuriya, " Towards the Liberation of Theology in Asia," *Asia's Struggle for Full Humanity*, Virginia Fabella, ed. (Maryknoll, 1980), p. 17.

71. Matt. 16:13-20; Mk. 8:27-30; Lk. 9:18-21.

72. B.J. Banawiratma, *Yesus Sang Guru* (Yogyakarta, 1977); see also a review of Baniwiratma's book in "Jesus Sang Guru," *Exchange* 13 (1984).

73. In a church song used by Javanese Christian churches, Jesus is called "Gusti Jesus ratu adil panetep panatagama" (Jesus the just king, sustainer of religion), *Kidung Pasamuwan Kristen Jawa* 139 (Yogyakarta, n.d.), p. 308.

It is true that Sadrach, in many instances, did not follow the official teaching of the mission church. He chose, rather, to find his own way — the Javanese way. From the very beginning he was "outside" the mission church. To choose this route was not without risk, and required a great deal of courage, as can be seen in his struggles with the missionaries and the *Indische Kerk*. The theological concept of *extra ecclesiam nulla sallus* (no salvation outside the church)[74] led to the view that everything outside the official church was false, a view which, to a certain extent, colored the missionaries' attitude toward all "non-Christian" elements as pseudo-religion, false faith, lying faith, idolatry, and heathenism.[75] In addition, the "denominationalism" which colored the theological thinking of the NGZV missionaries produced theological intolerance for anything outside of Reformed doctrines.[76] It is our opinion, therefore, that Sadrach's theology was viewed from a biased standpoint. The approach to missions used in the nineteenth century by the Dutch missionaries presupposed that Reformed theology was the authentic theology, and any theology which departed from Reformed principles was suspect. This approach we find to be unnecessarily intolerant. Such an approach to missions by its very nature failed to support any efforts to contextualize.

It must also be noted that Sadrach's Christology and soteriology, as developed within the Javanese context, emphasized crucial elements of the Gospel which were de-emphasized in the theology of the Dutch missionaries. Such elements include the importance of good deeds, piety, self-discipline, obedience to God's law, following Christ as an example, and the ministry of healing and exorcism. In our opinion, these are important Christian values which, while often discarded by the missionaries, ought to be included in the theology and lives of those who claim to be followers of Jesus. Was not Jesus, in fact, the truly pious guru who fulfilled God's law unto death? Was not Jesus the powerful guru whose ministry included healing and exorcism?[77] *To follow in the steps of Jesus* as guru and *panutan*, the perfect, pious, exemplary figure whom Sadrach preached, was the essence of Sadrach's Christology.[78]

---

74. A Latin saying derived from Cyprianus (200-258) which, in 1863 was developed and adopted by Pope Pius IX; see K.A. Steenbrink, *Pertumbangan Teologi dalam dunia Kristen Modern* [Theological Development in the Modern Christian World] (Yogyakarta, 1987), p. 168.

75. Cf. *Belgic Confession*, Articles XXVIII and XXIX.

76. Regarding the intolerant attitude of Western missionaries, cf. Balasuriya, p. 69.

77. See G. Vermes, *Jesus the Jew* (London, 1973), for a discussion of Jesus as an exorcist. The image of Jesus as exorcist is also used by the African Independent Church. Cf. M.L. Daneel, "Towards a Theologia Africana? The Contribution of Independent Churches to African Theology," *Missionalia* 12:2 (August, 1984).

78. Wilhelm, 1889, p. 93.

We must acknowledge the right of Sadrach, together with others from different cultures throughout Asia, Africa, and Latin America, to build their own images of Jesus — images which speak *from* and *to* their own concrete situation. Determining whether those images are authentic or a betrayal requires cautious judgment, since, as Wessels states, "the meaning of giving over (*overlevering*) and betrayal (*verraad*) is very close."[79] He goes on to point out that Jesus cannot be restricted to one context alone, neither Eastern or Western. Different contexts will naturally result in the creation of different images as a response to Christ.[80] Not only do we agree with this conclusion, but are convinced that the various images of Jesus which were developed in Central Java by Sadrach, who at the synod meeting of December, 1890, declared, "I am a servant of our Lord Jesus Christ, he is my Mediator and my Righteous King!"[81] should be sincerely regarded as equal to other images of Christ. The images developed by Sadrach and those developed by Tunggul Wulung in North Central Java, Coolen in East Java, as well as those of other Javanese evangelists must be viewed as an effort toward an authentic, obedient response to Christ and His redemptive work.

E.   A Genuine Community of Christ — Javanese culture "op een stoel" (on a chair)

J. Wilhelm once honored Sadrach by asking him to sit in a chair. While this seems an odd occurrance in our day and age, it was extremely extraordinary in the nineteenth century when the superiority of Western culture and the colonial mentality still captured the minds of the Dutch, including the missionaries.[82] It was even more striking that a Dutchman paid such honor to a common Javanese, since even the Javanese aristocrats never paid honor to commoners in this manner. It was customary for a commoner to approach the king or other aristocrats at a distance, bowing down to render homage. When seated, one sat on the floor, never in a chair. Wilhelm's attitude toward Sadrach, when seen in this context, was a revolutionary break with the feudal-colonial customs of the day.

79. A. Wessels, *Jesus zien* (Baarn, 1986), p. 20.

80. Ibid., p. 165.

81. At this meeting held in Purwareja in December, 1890, allegations against Sadrach were discussed. Sadrach recognized "ik ben een dienaar van onzen Heere Jesus Christus, die is mijn Middelaar en mijn Koning, die rechtvaardig is." Adriaanse, *Sadrach's Kring*, p. 270.

82. Graaf Van Randwijck, p. 390.

Wilhelm's attitude toward Sadrach made the headlines but created problems at the same time. A photo of Wilhelm and Sadrach seated side by side with two Javanese evangelists in traditional dress standing behind them was circulated among the missionary societies in Central Java and the Netherlands. According to Wilhelm's diary, this picture was taken on July 14, 1885, three years after he began his ministry in Sadrach's community.[83]

A hundred years after the "Sadrach-Wilhelm affair" this photo is interpreted in a variety of ways. P. Quarles Van Ufford views the affair as Sadrach's struggle for religious freedom in the early stages of the Javanese church in Central Java. In his article, "Why Don't You Sit Down?," he argues that Sadrach's religious movement must be placed in the wider context of a general religious opposition to Dutch colonial domination in Java at the end of the nineteenth century. This opposition, he claims, was not so much resistance to the overall political and economic power of the Dutch as it was a reaction against the colonial expression of Dutch Christianity as superior to Javanese Christianity.[84] From this point of view, Sadrach's movement is comparable to the other religious protest movements which flooded Java in the nineteenth century. This is made clear as well in Sartono's study.[85] Guillot, on the other hand, approaches Sadrach's community from the aspect of social emancipation, that is, the struggle of the Javanese people for social equality in a discriminating colonial system.[86] Other interpretations have been offered from different perspectives, for example, H.J. De Graaf, in a series of short articles, who views Sadrach as a misunderstood prophet and warrior.[87]

These writings are significant in that they offer a broader horizon of interpretation for a complex issue with social and political implications. While these aspects should not be ignored, the event itself, in which Wilhelm offered Sadrach a chair, demonstrated Wilhelm's distinctiveness as a Dutch missionary. Through this act he separated himself from his fellow missionaries, not only by his intellectual understanding of Javanese culture, but by his appreciation for it. He demonstrated that he

83. Wilhelm, 1886, p. 229. The picture appeared in *Heidenbode* (November, 1886).

84. P. Quarles van Ufford, "Why Don't You Sit Down?" *Man, Meaning and History*, R. Schefold, ed. (The Hague, 1980), p. 207.

85. Chapter I, Section A.

86. See Guillot, *L'Affaire Sadrach*; *Kiai Sadrach*.

87. H.J. De Graaf, "Sadrach de Profeet," *Tong-Tong* (May, 15, 1971), pp. 6-7; "Sadrach de Strijder," *Tong-Tong* (June 1, 1971), pp. 6-7; "Sadrach de Miskende," *Tong-Tong* (July 15, 1971), pp. 6-7.

knew how a respected Javanese guru ought to be treated. Wilhelm's strategy for working with Sadrach was brilliant. Rather than fighting against him, he gained Sadrach's trust, thereby opening the doors and gaining access into the community itself. Because of his approach, the authority sought in vain by Bieger and Vermeer to lead the community into the genuine church of Christ as they perceived it, was given to him.[88]

On the other hand, however, this promising start was never understood by either his colleagues or the Board of the NGZV. Suspicious of his tolerant and cooperative attitude, they accused Wilhelm of not only gaining access into the community, but also opening the door for syncretism to permeate the church of Christ. They felt that the church needed to be protected from the so-called Javanese syncretism, which they felt posed the greatest danger to their mission. They bitterly said that while Wilhelm may sit together with Balaam, Jesus may not be seated beside Baal.

Wilhelm's strongest opponent was Horstman, and their polemical conflict is evident from their letters.[89] Although they both had the goal of "purifying" the Javanese Christian community from syncretistic elements, their approach differed drastically. Horstman was convinced that the only way to achieve this goal was to dismiss Sadrach, whom he viewed as the source of error in the community. He wrote Wilhelm that the time had come to force Sadrach to sit back on the floor.[90] Wilhelm refused, claiming that Sadrach had the right to remain in the chair. Without Sadrach in the chair, the mission would fail since the community would follow Sadrach.[91] Wilhelm viewed Horstman's approach as *verhollandiseren* (to force the Javanese to become Dutch), which would only serve to alienate the Javanese Christians from their cultural and social environment, making them foreigners in their own home.[92]

In our opinion, Wilhelm's action expressed the very crucial aspect of contextualization in Christian missions, an aspect which in the past was

---

88. Chapter II, Section B; see also Van Der Linden.

89. See Horstman to Cachet, June 30, 1893.

90. " 't is tijd, 't hoogste tijd dat Sadrach weer op een matje gaat zitten, zal er iets van ons werk voor Gods Koninkrijk terecht komen." Adriaanse, *Sadrach's Kring*, p. 307. Our opinion is just the opposite, that the kingdom of God will rightly come if Sadrach remained seated "op een stoel" not "weer op een matje." Recognition of Sadrach as he really was includes the recognition of Javanese culture, which is significant for the coming of God's kingdom.

91. Chapter II, Section B. When the relationship with Sadrach was broken, almost all the members of the community sided with Sadrach (1893).

92. The term *verhollandiseren* was used in Wilhelm's letter of September 25, 1891, and in Horstman's letter of October, 1891.

largely overlooked. It is clear from Wilhelm's diary and letters to the Board of the NGZV that he, to a certain extent at least, devoted attention to the issue of contexualization. He felt that the proclamation of the Gospel in Java needed to be directed to the nature and needs of the Javanese people, which included taking into account the social, cultural, religious, and educational aspects of the local situation. In contemporary language, the context needed to be addressed.[93]

Recognition of indigenous people as partners in missions includes a recognition of their culture. The relationship between missions and the indigenous culture must be one in which the indigenous culture is "op een stoel" if contextualization is going to occur successfully. While culture is not and should not be the primary concern of missions, neither can it be ignored. The main concern of missions is to cultivate faith and obedience to Christ, but this cannot be done apart from culture. It is impossible to "bring Christ to the nations and the nations to Christ" in a cultural vacuum. Conversion, new life in Christ, and Christian obedience must all find expression in the cultural identity. The tension between missions and culture lies most often in the dilemma between obedience to Christ or cultural identity. When similarity is stressed over difference, a solution can be reached through compromise, as has been the case with the Javanese Christians.

The tension between missions and indigenous culture can be resolved in at least three different ways. The first is to break down the indigenous culture without providing a substitute. This method results in cultural emptiness and an identity crisis for the people involved. A second method is to break down the indigenous culture and replace it with a new (considered Christian) culture. This method has been used throughout the history of missions. The result is cultural chauvinism, similar to the Jewish Christians in the New Testament who demanded circumcision for gentile converts. According to Kraft, this type of "conversion" is not conversion to Christ, but rather conversion to a new cultural allegiance. The result is often nominal Christianity with little understanding of essential Christian doctrine on the part of the converts.[94]

A third choice lies in the method of breaking down the unchristian aspects of the indigenous culture and facilitating or stimulating a process of cultural transformation. The result is a genuine indigenous Christian community — a group of believers who can live out their Christianity according to the patterns of the local society. The church is itself a kind of

---

93. This was the reason why Van Der Linden entitled his articles with full appreciation, "Den Javanen een Javaan."
94. Kraft, p. 340.

society, and as such it needs patterns of interaction. According to William A. Smalley, those patterns of a truly indigenous church will be based upon the patterns already existing in the local society. This is only natural, he argues, since patterns of interaction are learned through the process of enculturation. These learned, normal habits are then simply carried over into the structure of the church.[95] It becomes obvious, then, that the indigenous people themselves should play a significant role in the process of "self-contextualization" by finding ways to become more communicative with their neighbors while at the same time living out their Christian faith. It is our opinion that Sadrach successfully made such an effort in his work in Central Java.

Today the relationship between missionaries and indigenous Christians is characterized by partnership in obedience rather than the paternalism and superiority which characterized missions in the nineteenth century. The question today, then, becomes one of the role of missionaries in the indigenous context. In Sadrach's era the important question was: Is there *any* opportunity for the indigenous people and culture to play a role in missions? Today the question has become: Is there *still* opportunity for the missionary to play a role in missions? Emphasis has shifted from the missionary's responsibility to the responsibility of the indigenous Christian. In today's mission strategies it is felt that indigenous Christians should be the primary bearers of the Gospel to their land. Thus the decisive role is in the hand of the indigenous Christian rather than of the missionary. The missionary now functions as a sort of catalyst — a source of new ideas and information based on his or her greater knowledge of history, other cultures, and the way in which God deals with mankind as recorded in Scripture. Through their broader knowledge and awareness of the ecumenical horizon, missionaries are in a position to suggest alternatives and aid in the decision-making process, thereby helping the indigenous workers to avoid the pitfall of short-sightedness. Missionaries can also offer constructive criticism on the work of the indigenous Christians, although this must be done with great care to avoid alienation and resentment. To ensure success, it is essential that missionaries fully understand the indigenous culture in which they find themselves, and always approach their work in a spirit of partnership with the indigenous Christians. To ignore these cautions is to invite the accusation of paternalism and interference.[96]

95. William A. Smalley, "Cultural Implications of an Indigenous Church," *Reading in Missionary Anthropology*, Vol. II, William A. Smalley, ed. (Pasadena, 1978), p. 366.
96. It is our opinion that Wilhelm's success in his approach to Sadrach lay in the fact that his attitude was not paternalistic; regarding the "new roles" of indigenous

Cultivating this type of working climate between missionaries and indigenous Christians will allow the process of cultural transformation to take place naturally. The goal "to increase the suitability of the culture to serve as a vehicle for divine-human interaction"[97] and, to use Bavinck's phrase, to lay the basis for forming a new culture,[98] can thus be achieved. The "new" culture can be described as a Christian culture which is totally renewed — reborn, as it were, through the process of conversion by the work of the Holy Spirit. Javanese Christians are then able to speak of a Christian Javanese culture or *adat*.[99]

It is hoped that in the present age the old patterns of missions have been renewed and replaced with patterns more conducive to cooperation and understanding. Everyone has a right to be "op een stoel" in one's own culture, from where one's faith can be freely expressed without hesitation, utilizing the colorful images of Christ which hold meaning in each particular context as the expected obedient response to Christ.

It is our opinion that the cooperation experienced between Wilhelm and Sadrach was fashioned after the model just presented. It provides an example of cooperation between a missionary with broader knowledge and understanding of Christianity and an indigenous Christian with broader knowledge and understanding of the Javanese culture. It is truly a pity that at the time this cooperation was considered unacceptable, which in turn served to accentuate the misunderstanding and impatience of those involved.

F. Sadrach's Warning to the Churches: the Serious Danger of Uprootedness and Alienation

J. Mooij described the *Indische Kerk* and the indigenous churches which resulted from its mission during the period of the VOC as "a Western plant in Asian soil."[100] His conclusion is not without reason. It is evident that the organization, creeds, church order, music, etc. of these churches were patterned after the "mother" church, the Reformed churches in the Netherlands.[101] As has already been noted, contextualization had not yet

evangelists and missionaries in the new era of mission, see Crommelin, "De Inlandsche Voorganger," pp. 978-994, and "Pandita Jawa," *MNZG* 61 (1917), pp. 2-16.

97. Kraft, p. 345.
98. Bavinck, "Zending," p. 62.
99. Cf. Bakker, "Theologische Opleiding," pp. 324-325.
100. Chapter I, section B.
101. Müller Krüger, pp. 38, 48; with his own words R. Soedarmo acknowledges a

become a concern of missionaries and church leaders. In addition, most Reformed missionaries and church leaders were not in a position to do much for the indigenous people since the church was essentially government supported. The impression that the *Indische Kerk* was a "state church" was unavoidable under the circumstances.

The inability of the missionaries to contexualize their mission, however, was not entirely the fault of government control over their mission work. The root of the problem lay deeper. The missionaries suffered from what is commonly called "Western captivity"; that is, they were so thoroughly westernized that they were unable to view the world from another perspective. Everything was viewed according to their Western standard. Such "captivity" was obvious when, in the early nineteenth century, the colonial government took a neutral stance toward religion. Various missionary organization began their work in Indonesia, each of which began mission churches that resembled churches of the same denominations in Europe in almost all areas of life. Such a phenomenon can still be seen today. The experience of I. Wayan Mastra from the Balinese church serves as an example of what was occurring in churches throughout Indonesia. In his article on the problem of contextualization, he writes:

> But when Christianity was introduced in Bali the missionaries identified the European Christian culture with the Gospel and tried to impose it on the new converts. Missionaries told the newly-converted people that their culture and religion belonged to the demons and urged their destruction. They did not distinguish between Western culture and Christian culture, between European Christian culture and the Gospel. Alarmed by this kind of attitude, a strong reaction arose among non-Christian Balinese and foreigners in Bali, mostly archeologists, artists, linguists, and novelists who had come to Bali to find inspiration for their work and who had a genuine sympathy for Balinese culture. They worried that the beauty of the unique Balinese culture would collapse because of Christianity.[102]

The strong reaction of *non*-Christian Balinese and foreigners against what was happening to Balinese culture is not surprising. They understandably

---

similar fact, that "Het Christendom was vroeger, voor de Tweede Wereldoorlog, min of meer een vreemd lichaam in het volk." (Christianity was earlier, before the Second World War, more or less a Foreign body among the people.) But he quickly adds his statement, "heden ten dage is het Gode zij dank niet meer zo." (Nowadays, thank God, that is no longer true.) R. Soedarmo, "Waarom is er zo weinig inheems Christendom in Indonesia?" *Christus prediking in de wereld* (Kampen, 1965), pp. 198-209.

102. I. Wayan Mastra, "Contextualization of the Church in Bali: A Case Study from Indonesia," *Gospel and Culture*, John Stott and Robert T. Coote, eds. (Pasadena, 1979), p. 371.

saw a serious threat in the missionaries' attitude. What is striking is that some of the Balinese Christians did not realize this attitude as a threat to their culture. Wayan Mastra continues:

> The church becomes conscious of the fact that if it wants to win the people for Christ, it should take some steps in bringing the culture as much as possible to the church. This thought is especially strong among the younger generation Christians. But these efforts have not always been welcomed by all Christians, particularly the older generation, those baptized in the 1930's. They well believe these things belonged to demons. They said: 'Why should we try to use these cultural practices that we have tried to avoid and to leave behind?'

> Once I met a minister who was converted during the 1930's. He wanted to build a new church building for the congregation. I suggested building the church in Balinese style by using Balinese artistic expression and philosophy. But the minister said: 'Why do I have to build a church which does not look like a church?' Consequently, he built the church as a garage with a small window, because that was the kind of church building first built in Bali. The minister gave a magical meaning to the small window — so that the Word of God would not *run away* from the people. But in Bali there is no winter — it is summer all year round. Such a church, therefore, is very hot inside. This Western style construction is also too expensive, because many things have to be imported, and the local village carpenter cannot make them.[103]

Even today one can hear a similar voice among members of the older generation, although, of course, one must take care not to generalize. Those who view Christianity like the Balinese minister in the above story are called "generasi zending,"[104] or "mission generation." They often nostalgically remind the younger generation of the mission era in which the missionary played the decisive role and all decisions regarding church life rested in his hands. A personal experience in my own pastorate serves as an example.

I began my pastorate in a small Javanese congregation which had no ordained minister. Since I was only a candidate for ministry at the time, I did not have the full rights of an ordained minister. As a candidate, I found that it was often best to keep silent and learn by listening to what was going on in the congregation.

As is usual, Christmas was celebrated in a special way. In addition to a church service, a fragment of the Javanese version of the Fall of Adam and Eve was performed. A Javanese *gamelan* (musical instrument) was used to accompany the performance. Curiously, the *gamelan* was placed outside the church near the left entrance rather than inside. A few days

---

103. Ibid., pp. 371-372.
104. *Generasi Zending* refers to the generation belonging to the mission era before the autonomy of the Javanese Christian Church in Central Java (1931).

later I asked the oldest church elder why the *gamelan* was placed outside
when there was plenty of room inside the church. His response took me
by surprise. He said, "Kula tiyang *gereformeerd* nganggep bilih gamelan
Jawi boten prayogi kalebetaken wonten ing greja!" (As a member of the
Reformed church, I am of the opinion that the Javanese *gamelan* is not
worthy of a place in the church!). My initial reaction was one of
astonishment, but I did not respond, because it is also not appropriate to
debate with one's elders. My mind, however, was occupied with the
question. What was wrong with the Javanese *gamelan* from a Christian
point of view?

I did not understand the situation until a few years later after I had had
more experience as a pastor and learned a few things from other
ministers. Now we, that is, the younger ministers, simply say, "Oh, he is
of the *generasi zending*." In other words, people from that generation
should be treated with great understanding.

The elder in our example viewed the Javanese *gamelan* with some
disdain. He had never before seen the *gamelan* used by the church. He
had been taught that to become a Christian meant leaving his *old life*,
which, according to him, included rejecting anything which was not
specifically Christian. The tendency to impose the attitude of "Christ
against culture"[105] had characterized the missionaries' dealings with his
generation. Such an attitude among the Javanese reveals the deeper
problem of "split identity" from which they suffer. Deep in their hearts
they remain appreciative of their culture, yet they are captured by the
"Christian" understanding that Javanese culture is demonic.

Another feature of this elder's response was confusing. He said that his
opinion was based on the fact that he was *gereformeerd*. At the time I did
not know what he meant by this. It seems that at the time of his
conversion, conversion was understood as inseparable from denominational allegiance. Therefore, to become a Christian was identical with
becoming a member of a specific denomination.

Through these examples we are again reminded that the churches in
Asia, including Indonesia, are not yet rooted enough in the Asian
context. Mooij was not alone in warning of the dangers of uprootedness
as caused by the mission efforts in the early 1920's. Since that time the
alarm has been sounded by other observers as well. Half a century later,
Christianity is still viewed by some as a potted plant which has been
transported but not transplanted. Most Asians regard the Christian

---

105. Cf. H. Richard Niebuhr, *Christ and Culture* (New York, 1975), pp. 45-76,
where he deals with the attitude of "Christ against culture."

church as a foreign import.[106] The research undertaken by Frank L. Cooley in cooperation with the Research and Study Institute of the Indonesia Council of Churches reveals a similar situation. The research resulted in the following conclusions:

> It should be self-evident that basic theological ideas and formulations would have come to Indonesian churches from the missionary churches. Just as Reformed, Christian Reformed, Lutheran, Methodist, Mennonite, and Pentecostal polities were inherited from the West with little change, even more so were the catechism and patterns of theological thought. One difference is worth noting, however, while polities and catechism remained practically the same wherever they crossed over the Indonesian shores from the land of their birth, not so theological interpretation, particularly in the decades immediately preceeding autonomy when missionaries with differing theological positions preached and taught in the Indonesian churches.... In a word, Indonesian Christianity, prior to national independence and the autonomy of the churches, was very Western in forms and content, so much so that outside the church it was often referred to as *agama Belanda* or "Dutch" (meaning foreign) religion.[107]

While it is true that historically Indonesian churches have borne a Western stamp, changes are now taking place within the churches which indicate that this Western stamp will gradually disappear. At present serious efforts are being made to root the churches in the indigenous culture and to take account of the social and political circumstances. In other words, there has been a growing awareness of contextualization in the Indonesian churches,[108] an appropriate response to the warning that as been sounded since the beginning of the twentieth century, or, more accurately, since the time of Sadrach during the second half of the nineteenth century. It is interesting, from a historical perspective, that while missionaries in the nineteenth century were sounding the alarm to warn of the great danger of syncretism, Sadrach had started beating the *bedug* (drum used by the mosque to call Moslems to prayer) as a warning to Javanese Christians of the threatening danger of alienation from their Javanese context.

At present, alienation is the greatest danger for the Christian churches in Indonesia, which make up only a tiny portion of the predominately non-Christian population. The tendency is to become introverted and isolated; however, such a response prevents them from being a living

106. Gerald H. Anderson, *Asian Voices in Christian Theology* (New York, 1976), p. 5.

107. Frank L. Cooley, *The Growing Seed: The Christian Church in Indonesia* (New York, 1981), p. 309.

108. See K.A. Steenbrink, "Christian Faith in the Indonesian Environment," *Exchange* 5 (1973); A.G. Hoekema, "Indonesian Churches: Moving towards Maturity," *Exchange* 21 (1978); "Jesus Sang Guru."

witness to Christ in the midst of Indonesian society. On the other hand, Cachet's judgment that Javanese converts lacked sufficient biblical knowledge may also function as an alarm for the church. Along with its attempts to root itself in the context, such an effort must be coupled with a profound understanding of the biblical message.

Only the church which is a part of the context can speak from inside the particular concrete situation in which it is placed. The need for its voice has been realized, and it has received good preparation through Christian pioneers like Sadrach. The discovry that Christianity and "Javanese-ness" are not mutually exclusive has opened the door for conscious efforts to contextualize the church in Indonesia. As a result, attention has focused on the work of Javanese mission figures. The Mennonite missionary, A.G. Hoekema, who taught for several years at the Theological School in Pati, North Central Java, made the following observation: "There is a tremendous challenge for the churches here. The Javanese Christians are right in pointing to their Christian ancestors like Sadrach, who, back in the nineteenth century, presented the Gospel in a Javanese way: as *guru ngelmu*, mystic, and wisdom teacher."[109]

As the Javanese churches continue to search for their contextual identity, they would do well to take as their starting point the challenge presented by the figure and community of Sadrach. For in him we find an unashamedly Javanese expression of Christianity rooted in its Javanese context, nourished by the riches of Javanese tradition, and flourishing in its Javanese environment. Only in such a way will Javanese culture be transformed for Christ, and the liberating work of Christ be made manifest in all areas of life.

109. Hoekema, "Indonesian Churches," p. 11.

SAMENVATTING

Deze dissertatie behandelt de inspanningen van de javaanse evangelist kyai Sadrach Surapranata om het Evangelie aan de Javanen te verkondigen en een christelijke gemeente op te bouwen op basis van de 19e eeuwse javaanse kontekst. Zijn gemeente vormde in die tijd een fenomeen met javaanse karakteristieken. Veel Nederlandse zendelingen van gereformeerde huize wezen hem af omdat zij hem niet konden begrijpen. Kyai Sadrach werd als een valse profeet beschouwd en zijn gemeente was naar hun mening geen echte christelijke gemeente.

In deze studie wordt nagegaan in hoeverre de javaans gekleurde gemeentevorm en benaderingswijze van kyai Sadrach Surapranata, die afgewezen werden door de Nederlandse zendelingen, juist relevant waren voor de samenleving van die tijd, daar zij geworteld waren in de javaanse cultuur (javaanse kontekst).

Het eerste hoofdstuk behandelt het sociale, culturele en religieuze leven van de 19e eeuwse javaanse samenleving en de verkondiging van het Evangelie, zowel door leken als door Nederlandse zendelingen vanuit hun eigen kerkelijke achtergronden.

De Evangelieverkondiging in de 19e eeuw en in het bijzonder het autochtone christelijke leven in die tijd kan pas goed worden begrepen, als men kennis heeft genomen van de gang van zaken in de voorafgaande eeuw. Daarom wordt ook in dit hoofdstuk in grote lijnen een beschrijving gegeven van de Evangelieverkondiging door de eerste katholieke missionarissen, vervolgens ten tijde van de VOC en door de Indische Kerk.

Sociaal cultureel gezien bestond de javaanse samenleving in de 19e eeuw uit twee standen, t.w. de adelijke stand of priyayi, die vaak "wong gedhe" werd genoemd en de stand der "wong cilik", de kleine man, waartoe de meenderheid van de bevolking behoorde. In het algemeen woonde de "wong cilik" op het platteland. De priyayi's waren de heersers en velen van hen werden betrokken bij het Nederlands Indische bestuur. De relatie tussen de twee standen was een relatie tussen de heerser en de onderworpene, tussen "bendara en kawula" die gekenmerkt werd door een absolute onderworpenheid van de "kawula" aan de "bendara". Adelijke titels en waardigheidssymbolen die de verhevenheid van de adelijke stand weerspiegelden en kenmerkend waren voor de javaanse feodale samenleving, waren in die tijd nog een zeer begerenswaard levensideaal. De

Nederlandse koloniale overheid veranderde het feodale overheersings-
systeem niet, maar droeg er zelfs bij tot de bestendiging ervan. De adelijke
stand profiteerde veel meer van de mogelijkheden en voorzieningen van
het koloniale systeem, met name op onderwijsgebied, zodat de kloof tussen
beide groeperingen onoverbrugbaar bleef.

Ter wille van het eigen belang en van het behoud van de status quo was
de javaanse adel er toe geneigd de belangen van de koloniale overheerser
boven die van het volk te stellen. Op deze manier vond er geen verandering
plaats in de levensomstandigheden van het gewone volk en de kleine man
bleef onderontwikkeld. Daarnaast werden de traditionele waarden hoe
langer hoe meer bedreigd door de binnendringing van "westerse" in-
vloeden. Het is dan ook niet verwonderlijk dat er in de 19e eeuw op vele
plaatsen protestbewegingen, oorspronkelijk van religieuze aard, de kop
opstaken. Deze bewegingen ontstonden rondom religieuze leiders, die
vaak *kyai* of *guru* werden genoemd. Doordat deze informele leiders buiten
de struktuur van het koloniale bestuur stonden, konden zij zich meer
vrijheid permitteren en het gewone volk vestigde dan ook zijn hoop op hen.
De koloniale overheid voelde zich bedreigd door zulke protestbewegingen
en in naam van "rust en orde" trad zij hoe langer hoe repressiever op. Van
direkte invloed op de Evangelieverkondiging op Java was de afkondiging
van de Landsverordening Nr. 123 (later bekend als Regeringsreglement
177), waarin bepaald werd dat alle zendelingen een "werkvergunning"
moesten bezitten. De overheid wilde daarmee de bewegingsvrijheid van
zendelingen aan banden leggen, om de in de ogen van de koloniale
overheid mohammedaanse Javanen niet voor het hoofd te stoten.

Sociaal-religieus gezien waren de Javanen Islamieten. Maar de door hen
beleden Islam was een godsdienst met eigen karakteristieken, die vaak
javaanse Islam wordt genoemd en te onderscheiden viel in *santri Islam* en
abangan Islam. De *santri Islam* is meer puriteins en fanatiek van aard. De
abangan Islam daarentegen was meer vatbaar voor de javaanse spirituali-
teit en cultuur. In de geschiedenis van de Evangelieverkondiging tot op de
huidige dag blijkt de *abangan Islam* ontvankelijker te zijn dan de *santri
Islam*.

Het tweede deel van het eerste hoofdstuk bepreekt de Evangelieverkondiging, zowel door de "officiële" kerk als door het initiatief van
individuele christenen, die zich geroepen voelden om de blijde boodschap
aan de "inboorlingen" te brengen. In tegenstelling tot de gewesten in het
oostelijk deel van Indonesië, waar de verkondiging reeds plaats vond met
de komst van rooms katholieke missionarissen en onder de VOC, traden in
het bijzonder op Midden Java pas in de tweede helft van de 19e eeuw enkele
"inboorlingen" tot het christendom. Dit laatste was het resultaat van het

werk van enkele christen leken, zoals mevrouw Philips-Stevens te Purwareja, mevrouw Van Ostroom-Philips te Banyumas en mevrouw Le
Jolle-de Wildt te Salatiga. Eigenlijk was de protestantse Indische Kerk
reeds sinds de 17e eeuw werkzaam op Java, maar omdat haar activiteiten
beperkt waren tot enkele grote steden en zij geen belangstelling had voor
verkondiging onder de inboorlingen, waren er dan ook geen Javaanse
bekeerlingen in die tijd.

Bijna gelijktijdig met de vorming van christelijke groepen op Java
kwamen enkele Nederlandse zendelingen naar Midden Java. Zij werden
uitgezonden door genootschappen die gelieerd waren met bepaalde
kerkelijke gezindten. De door hun arbeid ontstane christelijke groepen op
Java kregen dan ook ieder de specifieke kerkelijke tinten van het zendende
genootschap in Nederland. Qua aantal was het resultaat van de pioniers-
arbeid van deze zendelingen erg teleurstellend. Een van de redenen
daarvoor was de "zeer hoge standaard", die geeist werd van de bekeerde
Javanen om als echte christenen aangemerkt te kunnen worden, gezuiverd
van traditionele gewoonten, die in de ogen van de zendelingen beheerst
waren door bijgeloof en magie. Van eeuw tot eeuw hoort men hetzelfde
oordeel, dat de autochtone christen nog steeds in zijn oude leefwereld
verkeert en niet leeft zoals een echt christen betaamt.

Hierbij moet worden aangetekend dat onder de Javanen in die tijd het
christendom beschouwd werd als de godsdienst van de Nederlandse
koloniale overheerser, derhalve werd iemand die deze godsdienst aanvaardde ook gezien als een tot Hollander (Blanda) geworden Javaan. Men
was van oordeel dat een christen geworden Javaan eigenlijk geen Javaan
meer kon zijn, omdat hij de tradities heeft verlaten.

Het tweede hoofdstuk behandelt de rol van kyai Sadrach in de opbouw
en ontwikkeling van zijn javaanse gemeente. De evangelist kyai Sadrach
kwam voort uit een *abangan Islam* achtergrond en kreeg een pesantren
opleiding in Oost Java. Zoals gebruikelijk was in de javaanse samenleving
van die tijd, wanneer men naar "ngelmu"/de waarheid wilde zoeken, trok
ook Sadrach van de ene guru naar de andere, todat hij op een gegeven
moment de hoogste "ngelmu" vond, namelijk het christelijk geloof. De
ontmoeting met de hoogste "ngelmu" had Sadrach te danken aan zijn
kontakten met christen leken zoals F.L. Anthing en met Nederlandse
zendelingen. Het scheen dat hij erg onder de indruk kwam van het
standpunt van Tunggul Wulung, een javaanse evangelist uit Jepara, dat
men christen kon worden zonder dat men de javaanse cultuur en traditie
hoefde te verlaten. In zijn verdere ontwikkeling bleek dat Sadrach een
sterke persoonlijkheid en leiderschapscapaciteiten bezat. Na zijn doop in
Batavia (tegenwoordig Jakarta) werd Sadrach evengelist in het gebied

Bagelen/Purwareja. Daar verwierf hij al spoedig bekendheid, vooral door zijn methode van verkondiging. Hij hanteerde de traditionele methode van debatteren tussen guru's die "ngelmu" doceerden. Een debat kon soms dagen in beslag nemen en werd bijgewoond door de leerlingen van de beide debatterende guru's. De guru die het debat verloor, moest zich inclusief zijn leerlingen onderwerpen aan zijn tegenstander en bij hem in de leer gaan. Kyai Sadrach verloor nimmer een debat en binnen relatief korte tijd verwierf hij grote bekendheid als een christen guru en een behoorlijk aantal leerlingen. Zijn nieuwe dorp Karangjasa werd een centrum voor zijn volgelingen. De invloed van kyai Sadrach was zo groot, dat hij in de ogen van het plaatselijke koloniale bestuur verdacht werd en op beschuldiging van samenspannen tot opstand of op zijn minst tot ordeverstoring, werd hij dan ook gearresteerd. Maar het rapport van de resident over de "Sadrach beweging" was niet overtuigend genoeg voor Batavia en op bevel van de Gouverneur Generaal werd Sadrach op virje voeten gesteld. Zijn vrijstelling werd niet alleen met vreugde ontvangen door zijn volgelingen, maar deed ook zijn "pamor" of prestige enorm toenemen. Kyai Sadrach Surapranata steeg hiermede in eer en werd een alom zeer gerespecteerde en charismatische leider.

Het aantal volgelingen van Sadrach nam snel toe en overal op het platteland van Midden Java werden christelijke groepen gevormd. Gedurende bijna tien jaar was er een goede samenwerking met zendeling J. Wilhelm van de NGZV. Maar het sceptisisme van andere zendelingen en vooral van de kant van het NGZV-bestuur in Nederland was zo toegenomen, dat de samenwerking op den duur verbroken werden. Dit sceptisisme was in principe gebaseerd op de volgende vooronderstellingen.
1e. de Javanse christenen waren nog niet in staat om als echte christenen te leven;
2e. de te grote persoonlijke macht van Sadrach was niet in overeenstemming met de christelijke beginselen;
3e. Sadrach verpreidde een dwaalleer.
Toen de samenwerking verbroken werd, koos het grootste deel van de javaanse christenen de kant van Sadrach en slechts een klein deel bleef trouw aan de zendelingen. Dit bewees te meer hoe groot het gezag van kyai Sadrach wel was onder de "inboorlingen".

Daar hij zich vernederd voelde door de "Zending" en inzag dat hij geen sacrament mocht bedienen, besloot Sadrach later om een door de Apostolischen "aangeboden" apostelschap te aanvaarden. Aan deze ambt bleef Sadrach trouw tot aan zijn dood in 1924. Bij zijn begravenis waren niet alleen zijn volgelingen, maar ook verschillende plaatselijke hoogwaardigheidsbekleders aanwezig, zoals de Bupati. Dit was een bewijs dat hij inderdaad een geëerd leider was, zowel in zijn eigen kring als daar buiten. Het valt te betreuren dat de Sadrach-gemeente na zijn dood verbrokkelde en achteruitging. De reden daarvan was dat Yotham Martareja, zijn pleegzoon, waaraan de leiding was overgegeven niet de charisma bezat van de overleden leider. Daarnaast vereiste de veranderde maatschappelijke situatie in de eerste helft van de 20e eeuw een ander soort leiderschap.

In hoofdstuk drie wordt het eigene, specifiek javaanse besproken, dat tot uitdrukking kwam in organisatievorm, leiderschap, lidmaatschap, mystieke levenshouding, godsdienstige plechtigheden, spiritueel leven en opvallende innerlijke vrijheid bij de Sadrach-gemeente. Zoals het geval was bij de javaanse "paguron" of relatie tussen de guru en zijn leerlingen, waarbij meer nadruk werd gelegd op innerlijke verbondenheid/broeder-schap dan op een bepaalde organisatievorm, zo bekommerde de Sadrach-gemeente zich weinig om organisatievormen. De gemeente was een gemeenschap tussen de guru en zijn leerlingen en kon worden beschouwd als een grote familie, waarin de relaties sterk van persoonlijke en informele aard zijn. Het is daarom niet verwonderlijk dat de volgelingen van Sadrach zich beschouwden (of door Sadrach werden beschouwd) als zijn kinderen en kleinkinderen.

De plaatselijke gemeente werd geleid door een imam (voorganger). De door Sadrach aangestelde imams waren merendeels gewezen kyai's en "ngelmu"-gurus, die tot het dorpselite behoorden. Sadrach zelf werd ter zijde gestaan door drie assistenten op "supra lokaal" nivo. Samen met deze drie assistenten vormde Sadrach de hoogste leiding van de Sadrach-kring als geheel. Deze primordiale javaanse organisatievorm bleef intern van kracht, ook nadat men de door zendeling Wilhem geintroduceerde kerkelijke organisatie naar gereformeerd model had aanvaard en toe-gepast. Deze laatste vorm had slechts een externe functie, namelijk om aan het gouvernement en aan andere nederlanders te laten zien, dat de Sadrach-kring werkelijk een *kerk* was met een kerkorde, classes en een soort synode. Sadrach en zendeling Wilhelm vulden elkaar aan. De aanwezigheid van Wilhelm in de Sadrach-gemeente bestendigde de autonomie van de gemeente, terwijl de steun die Sadrach aan deze zendeling gaf op den duur het gezag van de zendeling in de ogen van de gemeente bestendigde.

De imams, die verantwoordelijk waren voor de plaatselijke kring, leidden de kerkdiensten en andere godsdienstige plechtigheden. De liturgie was uiterst eenvoudig en flexibel en de regeling ervan werd overgelaten aan de Imam. De preken hielden meestal persoonlijke getuigenissen in, getuigenissen over de imam's ervaring in het zoeken naar de nieuwe "ngelmu", namelijk de boven alle andere "ngelmu" verheven "Christen ngelmu", de ngelmu van "nabi Ngisa Rohulla", die ook de *ratu adil* is (de rechtvaardige vorst, een messiaanse figuur uit de javaanse religie). De persoonlijke getuigenissen waren bedoeld om de gemeente aan te sporen tot gehoorzaamheid aan de geboden van nabi Ngisa. Het was daarom opvallend dat volgens bepaalde gouvernements waarnemers op de moraal van de Sadrach-gemeente leden over het algemeen weinig aan te merken viel en dat deze leden tot het beste deel van de bevolking behoorden. De chronische maatschappelijke ziektes van die tijd, zoals het schuiven opium en het gokken waren nagenoeg onbekend onder de Sadrach-gemeente.

De javaanse traditie, zeden en gewoonten bleven in de Sadrach-gemeente gehandhaafd met slechts hier en daar enkele aanpassingen. Er vond een soort selectie plaats ten opzichte van de javaanse zeden en gewoonten, naar wat "gechristianiseerd" kon worden en wat niet. Het standpunt van Sadrach was dat een javaanse christen in de eerste plaats Javaan moest blijven met al zijn zeden en gewoonten, zodat hij de javaanse tradities zo goed en zo veel mogelijk zou weten aan te passen in een christelijk leven. Dit was een opvallende karakteristiek van de Sadrach-gemeente.

Een ander opvallend kenmerk was de zelfstandige en vrije geest, overeenkomstig de in den beginne voor deze kring gekozen naam: Golongane Wong Kristen Kang Mardika (de groep van vrije christenen). Volgens sociologisch onderzoek was de zelfstandige en vrije geest kenmerkend voor het javaanse platteland en bestond er sinds mensen huigenis, waar de dorpen in alles zichzelf regelden. Deze onafhankelijke geest was klaarblijkelijk een specifieke karakteristiek van het plattelands leven in de 19e eeuw, daar de levensbehoeften in de dorpen niet zo veelvuldig waren als in de steden. De gebouwen waarin men de eredienst hield werden opgetrokken van plaatselijk materiaal, in *gotong royong* (onderlinge hulp en samenwerking) en gewoonlijk op het erf van de imams. De "kerkelijke functionarissen" werden niet bezoldigd, maar leefden van hun eigen handenarbeid. Men aanvaardde een "kerkelijke functie" op vrijwillige basis, misschien ook wel om prestige redenen.

In het vierde hoofdstuk worden de vele beschuldigingen aan de orde gesteld, die door Nederlandse zendelingen gericht werden aan het adres van Sadrach en zijn gemeente. De motieven van degenen die de beschuldigingen uitten waren verschillend; er waren er die uit eigen ambitie niet graag een inlander als Sadrach zagen als leider, weer anderen deden dat uit jaloezie over de successen van Sadrach en de zijnen bij de verkondiging van het Evangelie. Duidelijk was wel het betrekkelijk grote verschil dat er bestond tussen de wereld van de Nederlanders en die van de Javanen, zowel sociaal-politiek als sociaal-cultureel.

In dit hoofdstuk wordt ook de theologie van de gereformeerde zending aan de orde gesteld. Sinds de aanvang hield de gereformeerde zending vast aan haar orthodoxe visie om het Evangelie zo louter en zuiver mogelijk te verkondigen en dat de blijde boodschap over de redding van de mensheid door het bloed van Christus de kern van de verkondiging moet vormen. In de praktijk bleek echter dat dit beginsel niet zo makkelijk uit te voeren viel, te meer omdat er in de beginperiode van de gereformeerde zending geen konkrete en gedetailleerde richtlijnen bestonden voor de uitvoering van de zendingsarbeid. Pogingen werden ondernomen om te komen tot een konkrete formulering van wat eigenlijk gereformeerde zending is. In dit verband sprongen enkele namen in het oog, zoals ds. Lion Cachet die zeer nauw betrokken was bij de zendingsarbeid inMidden Java en dr. A. Kuyper. Steeds meer brak de visie baan, dat de kerk direct verant- woordelijk is voor de zending en dat deze opdracht niet kan worden overgelaten aan verenigingen. Dit begingsel dat vaak *kerkelijke zending* genoemd wordt, werd later aanvaard door de gereformeerde kerken. Een grondige en gedetailleerde formulering over wat eigenlijk gereformeerde zending is, werd gepresenteerd op het zendingscongres van 1890 te Amsterdam, waar het referaat van dr. A. Kuyper van beslissende invloed was. Op grond van de resultaten van het congres van Amsterdam werd ten slotte op de Generale Synode van de Gereformeerde Kerken in 1896 te Middelburg een officiële formulering aanvaard van de visie op de zending.

Naast de theologische fundering van de zendingsarbeid waren deze formuleringen met betrekking tot het zendingswerk in Midden Java van belang door het onderscheid dat gemaakt werd tussen verkondiging aan Islamieten en aan "heidenen". Daarbij werd ook gewezen op de gevoelig- heid voor de lokale kontekst en op het verschil tussen de situatie op het thuisfront en op het zendingsveld. Verder werd daarin sterke nadruk gelegd op het stichten van een gereformeerde kerk op het zendingsveld (Midden Java), als doel van verkondiging. Men kan zeggen dat deze formuleringen eigenlijk de *geest* vormden van de gereformeerde zending sinds de aanvang van haar arbeid op Midden Java.

Betrekkelijk uitvoerig wordt vervolgens in dit hoofdstuk de aantijgingen aan het adres van sadrach en zijn gemeente besproken. De aantijgingen begonnen reeds in 1870 toen zendeling P. Bieger pogingen deed om de Sadrach-gemeenten te "annexeren". Er waren geruchten over moei- lijkheden met het bestuur, die culmineerden in het vaccinatie-incident. Sadrach werd in hechtenis genomen en een tijdje vastgehouden op beschuldiging van overtreding van de vaccinatieverordening. Volgens de zendeling verwierp Sadrach de vaccinatie omdat hij de Bijbel onvoldoende begreep. Zulke beschuldigingen werden telkens geuit door zendelingen. Op grond van de beschikbare bronnen kan gesteld worden dat Sadrach afgetekend werd als een op macht beluste, arrogante inlander, die zich titels aanmat waarop hij geen recht had met de bedoeling zich religieuze verering te laten aanleunen, waardoor hij door zijn volgelingen als een *sakti* (onkwetsbare) kon worden beschouwd; dat hij in zijn positie als leider zich verrijkt heeft door de gemeenten af te persen, etc. In de ogen van de zendelingen was Sadrach niet meer dan een javaanse evangelist met onvoldoende opleiding, ontoereikende kennis over de Bijbel en over de ware christelijke leer, zodat hij niet het Evangelie predikte, maar Java-nisme. Zij zagen Sadrach als de bron van alle "droevige" situaties onder de christen Javanen, zoals het levenspatroon dat voortdurend beheerst werd door bijgeloof en door met de christelijke leer strijdige zeden en gewoonten. Zij konkludeerden dan ook dat Sadrach de zendingsarbeid in Midden Java heeft *vergiftigd*.

Naast de ongegronde beschuldigingen, die aangewakkerd werden door onder de christenen verspreide geruchten, waren er ook beschuldigingen uit theologisch oogpunt. Deze kunnen samengevat worden rondom vier thema's. Ten eerste, de te grote autoriteit van Sadrach over zijn gemeente werd beschouwd als strijdig te zijn met het ware christelijke leiderschap op basis van Calvijn's leer over de relatie tussen de voorganger en de gemeente. Ten tweede, dat Christus begrepen en verkondigd werd door Sadrach als de *ratu adil*, wiens voorbeeld gevolgd dient te worden. Dit was volgens de zendelingen in strijd met de aard van Christus, de mens geworden zoon van God zelf. Ten derde, dat het Evangelie begrepen en verkondigd werd door Sadrach als "ngelmu", hetgeen in de ogen van de zendelingen niet in overeenstemming was met de leer over rechtvaardiging alleen door geloof, niet door goede daden. Ten vierde, dat in de gemeente van Sadrach de oude javaanse zeden en gewoonten nog voortleefden, hetgeen in strijd was met de leer omtrent wedergeboorte en nieuw leven, waarin volgens de zendelingen de christen zijn "oude leven" moest verlaten.

Ten slotte kan konkluderend worden gesteld dat de problemen waar-voor men zich geplaatst zag op Midden Java in die tijd eigenlijk voortvloeiden uit de onmacht van de zendelingen om de javaanse geest en cultuur te begrijpen, uit de orthodoxe christelijke leer van de gerefor-meerde zendelingen en uit het ontbreken van konkrete en gedetailleeerde richtlijnen voor de uitvoering van de zendingsarbeid te velde, waardoor veel geimproviseerd moest worden. Dit zijn de voornaamste oorzaken van de door de gereformeerde zendelingen vertoonde onverdraagzaamheid tegen over de werkelijkheid van het zendingsveld op Midden Java.

In hoofdstuk vijf, het laatste hoofdstuk wordt de betekenis nagegaan van sadrach's bijdrage aan de kontekstualisering van de kerk, door het in deze studie gepresenteerde materiaal samen te vatten, ter onderbouwing van de geldigheid van onze (oorspronkelijke) hypothese, dat de inspanningen van sadrach, hoewel vaak onbegrepen, eigenlijk een vroeg voorbeeld vormden van echte gekontekstualiseerde javaanse christenheid en is daarom van uitzonderlijke betekenis voor de geschiedenis van de Javaanse kerk. Onze konklusie is dat Sadrach een uitdrukking aan het christelijk geloof verschafte, die dicht bij het hart van de mensen lag, die aansloot bij hun ontvankelijkheden en ervaringen, die effectief aansloot bij aan hun noden en verwachtingen, hun hoop en hun streven. De verder in dit hoofdstuk uitgewerkte punten ondersteunen onze konklusie.

A. De leiderschapsstijl van de vrije en onafhankelijke Sadrach was van beslissende invloed voor de ontwikkeling en de aard van zijn gemeente. Zijn leiderschap vormde een weerspiegeling van zijn sterke persoonlijkheid en van een hecht zelfvertrouwen, dat gevormd werd door zijn opvoeding en levenservaring als kyai. Zijn vrije en zelfstandige geest bleek uit het feit dat hij nooit lang heeft gewerkt onder toezicht van een ander. De relatie en samenwerking met mevrouw Philips-Stevens was van dien aard dat daardoor juist de ontwikkeling naar een vrij en zelfstandig leiderschap bevorderd werd.

B. De Sadrach-gemeente wa een gemeente die was geworteld in de kontekst van de traditionele javaanse samenleving. Het bestaan van korrelaties tussen de Sadrach-gemeente en haar javaanse kontekst, verklaart en levert tegelijkertijd het bewijs dat de gemeente geworteld was in haar omgeving, die een sleutel faktor vormde voor de ontwikkeling van de gemeente. Ten eerste moet het feit genoemd worden, dat de Sadrach-gemeente een plattelandsgemeente was. Daarom absorbeerde deze gemeente vele kenmerken van een plattelandssamenleving, zoals sober leven, gotong royong (waarbij de individuele belangen ondergeschikt worden gesteld aan die van de gemeenschap), de zeer beslissende rol van de leider, die tegelijkertijd als *primus inter pares* en als symbool fungeerde van communaal leven. Ten tweede, de Sadrach-gemeente ontstond in en had als achtergrond de *abangan Islam* samenleving, zodat zij de waarden van deze samenleving in zich opnam. Dit bleek uit haar *respect voor* en *affiniteit met* de javaanse zeden en gewoonten. Ten derde, stond de gemeente midden in een feodale en koloniale samenleving, waarin de meerderheid van de Javanen, vooral onder de plattelandsbevolking, nagenoeg geen mogelijkheid kreeg tot het ontwikkelen van persoonlijkheid, zelfvertrouwen, kennis en initiatief. Een vooraanstaande autochtoon werd in zo'n uitzichtloze situatie beschouwd als "brenger van een verlossingsboodschap" voor duizenden "wong cilik", zonder zich op te werpen als politiek leider. Het besef bij Sadrach over de noodzaak van emancipatie van de "wong cilik" heeft hem niet verleid tot een verandering van zijn kring in een politieke beweging.

C. Zonder af te doen aan onze waardering voor de eerlijke motivatie van westerse en in het bijzonder Nederlandse zendelingen, die het Evangelie in Indonesië brachten, moet gesteld worden dat deze zendelingen bewust of onbewust, direct of indirect niet alleen de autochtonen kerstenden, maar hen ook "verhollandiseerden". Dit kwam klaarblijkelijk omdat de zendelingen niet goed inzagen dat er twee konteksten bestonden die van elkaar verschilden, namelijk de kontekst van het thuisfront en die van het zendingsveld. Zij beoordeelden en pasten alles toe volgens de in het thuisfront geldende maatstaven, zodat bekering een "opname" betekende van de autochtoon in de kontekst van de zendelingen. Het valt moeilijk te ontkennen dat in de voorafgaande eeuwen, zoals dat blijkt uit de zendingsgeschiedenis, de zendelingen onverdraagzaam waren ten opzichte van de autochtone cultuur. Tot het einde van de 19e eeuw bleven de gereformeerde zendelingen sterk onverdraagzaam. Hun orthodoxe zendingstheologie bleek krachtig genoeg te zijn om de houding van onverdraagzaamheid te bestendigen. Het is duidelijk dat zulk een houding het proces van kontekstualisering niet bevordert.

D. De visie van Sadrach op de persoon van Christus en Zijn verlossingswerk werd uiteraard gekleurd door zijn javaanse achtergrond. Sadrach bouwde geen comprehensieve theologie, maar als evangelist was zijn eerste zorg de verkondiging van de blijde boodschap aan zijn volksgenoten door middel van methoden en begrippen, die vatbaar waren voor hen. Christus werd door Sadrach als een guru gezien, als een "panutan" (iemand wiens voorbeeld gevolgd dient te worden), zelfs als ratu adil, wiens leer "ngelmu plus" werd genoemd, de allerhoogste ngelmu. Het ontzagwekkende van deze "christelijke ngelmu" ligt in het feit dat Christus de *nabi Ngisa Rohullah*, opgestaan is uit de dood en wiens macht groter is dan die van alle andere nabi's. Daarom legde Sadrach sterke nadruk op de plicht de bevelen van Christus te gehoorzamen en Zijn voorbeeld te volgen, opdat in de christenen, die immers volgelingen zijn van Christus, een goede levenswandel zichtbaar mag worden, een levenswandel zoals ook benadrukt werd door de traditionele javaanse leer "pitutur dan wewaler". In elk geval moet deze "Sadrach theologie" gezien worden als een poging om een zo authentiek mogelijk antwoord te geven in gehoorzaamheid aan Christus en Zijn verlossingswerk.

E. De Kerk van Christus op Midden Java kan alleen een autochtone kerk worden, als de javaanse cultuur een plaats krijgt in het kerkelijk leven en daarmee serieus rekening wordt gehouden. De mening dat de javaanse cultuur alleen maar het Evangelie zal vertroebelen, of zelfs syncretisme en pseudo-Christendom zou doen ontstaan, moet thans worden verlaten. Bekering dient niet gezien te worden als een afwerpen van eigen cultuur bij het aanvaarden van een andere cultuur, maar als het aanvaarden van gehoorzaamheid aan Christus in eigen cultuur. De erkenning dat de autochtone cultuur een plaats dient te krijgen in de verkondiging van het Evangelie en in het kerkelijk leven, zal de oplegging van een vreemde cultuur verhinderen. Ook de erkenning dat autochtone christenen de voornaamste dragers van zending dienen te zijn en een beslissende rol moeten spelen in het kerkelijk leven, zal verhinderen dat er een hiërarchische en paternalistische relatie zal ontstaan tussen deze autochtonen en de buitenlandse zendelingen. Dit was klaarblijkelijk waarvoor Sadrach heeft "gestreden". In onze eeuw, in dit nieuwe tijdperk van zending dient de relatie tussen autochtone christenen en buitenlandse zendelingen te groeien in de richting van "partnerschap in gehoorzaamheid", want alleen zulk een partnerschap kan het kontekstualiseringsproces bevorderen.

F. Een serieus gevaar in de geschiedenis van zending sinds het prille begin vormt de ontworteling en vervreemding van autochtone christenen van hun eigen maatschappij. De kerk wordt een afdruk van de kerk in het vaderland van de zendeling en een *Fremdkörper* in eigen land. De konkrete feiten hierover op Java en in het algemeen in Indonesië vormen moeilijk te ontkennen bewijzen. Maar de situatie is nu gelukkig aan het veranderen. Er vinden hoopvolle ontwikkelingen plaats in de Indonesiche kerken, namelijk het groeiende besef om zich in te wortelen in de eigen maatschappij. De groeiende betrokkenheid van de kerken in de problemen waarmee de Indonesische samenleving en natie gekonfronteerd worden, moet gezien worden in het kader van pogingen tot kontekstualisering, tot het voorkomen van vervreemding en om niet als "westers" te worden bestempeld. Wat reeds door Sadrach is gedaan, vormt tegenwoordig een uitdaging bij de pogingen om de kerken wortel te doen schieten in de eigen samenleving.

RINGKASAN ISI DESERTASI

Desertasi ini membicarakan seorang pekabar Injil Jawa kyai Sadrach Surapranata dalam usaha mengabarkan Injil kepada orang Jawa dan membangun jemaat berdasarkan konteks sosial dan budaya Jawa abad ke-19. Jemaatnya merupakan fenomena yang bersifat Jawa. Banyak pekabar Injil Belanda dari golongan *gereformeerd* yang tidak dapat memahaminya, karena itu mereka menolaknya. Kyai Sadrach dianggap sebagai penyesat dan jemaatnya dianggap bukan sebagai jemaat Kristen yang benar. Dalam studi ini kita mempersoalkan adanya kemungkinan bahwa wujud jemaat yang bercorak Jawa itu, yang ditolak oleh para pekabar Injil Belanda, justru merupakan jemaat yang berakar dalam masyarakat Jawa pada waktu itu.

Dalam bab pertama buku ini dibicarakan tentang kehidupan sosial, kultural dan religius masyarakat Jawa abad ke 19 dan pekabaran Injil yang dilakukan baik oleh beberapa kaum awam Kristen maupun para pekabar Injil Belanda dengan latar belakang denominasinya. Pekabaran Injil pada abad ke-19, khususnya kepada penduduk pribumi, hanya akan dapat dipahami secara tepat jikalau kita memahami pekabaran Injil pada abad sebelumnya. Karena itu disini secara garis besar juga dikemukakan tentang pekabaran Injil yang telah dimulai oleh missionaris2 Roma Katolik dan berlanjut dengan pekabaran Injil pada masa VOC (Vereenigde Oost Indische Compagnie, yaitu kongsi dagang Belanda di Hindia Timur), serta gereja Protestan *Indische Kerk.*

Secara sosial budaya, masyarakat Jawa abad ke-19 terdiri dari golongan masyarakat tinggi yang sering disebut "wong gedhe" atau priyayi (bangsawan) dan golongan masyarakat kebanyakan yang disebut juga sebagai rakyat kecil atau "wong cilik". Jumlah yang kedua jauh lebih besar dari yang pertama, pada umumnya mereka hidup dipedesaan. Para bangsawan Jawa merupakan golongan yang memerintah (ruling class) dan banyak dari mereka menjadi pegawai pemerintah kolonial Belanda. Hubungan antara dua kelas masyarakat itu dapat dikatakan sebagai hubungan antara golongan yang memerintah dan diperintah, antara "bendara dan kawula" yang ditandai oleh ketaatan yang luar biasa dari pihak kedua terhadap yang pertama. Gelar2 dan simbol2 kebangsawanan yang mencerminkan keagungan bangsawan Jawa yang merupakan ciri masyarakat feudalistis masih merupakan cita2 ideal. Pemerintah kolonial

Belanda tidak mengubah sistim masyarakat semacam ini, bahkan dapat dikatakan makin memantabkan. Golongan bangsawan lebih banyak menikmati kesempatan dan kemudahan2 dari sistim kolonial, terlebih-lebih dalam bidang pendidikan, dan karenanya jarak antara kedua golongan itu tetap tidak terjembatani.

Golongan bangsawan Jawa yang memerintah pada umumnya, demi kepentingan sendiri dan memelihara *status quo*, lebih bersikap mewakili kepentingan pemerintah kolonial dari kepentingan rakyat banyak. Akibatnya kondisi kehidupan mereka tidak diperbaiki dan mereka tetap hidup dalam keterbelakangan. Disamping itu pengaruh "Barat" makin dirasakan mengancam nilai2 tradisional kehidupan Jawa. Karena itu tidak mengherankan kalau pada abad ke-19 gerakan2 protest yang pada mulanya bersifat religius muncul dimana-mana. Gerakan2 ini terpusat disekitar tokoh2 keagamaan yang sering disebut *kyai* atau *guru*. Pemimpin2 informal ini yang karena berada diluar struktur birokrasi pemerintah kolonial dapat lebih leluasa bergerak dan kelihatannya menjadi tumpuan harapan rakyat banyak. Pemerintah kolonial merasa terancam oleh gerakan2 semacam ini, dan atas nama *"rust en orde"* (ketenangan dan ketertiban) tindakan2 yang represif makin diberlakukan. Akibat langsung dari sikap pemerintah yang represif ini bagi pekabaran Injil di Jawa ialah dikeluarkannya peraturan nomor 123 (kemudian dikenal *Regeringsreglement* 177) yang berisi bahwa semua pekabar Injil harus mempunyai ijin "kerja" dari pemerintah. Dengan demikian kebebasan bergerak dari para pekabar Injil sangat dibatasi, supaya tidak membangkitkan amarah orang2 Jawa yang dimata pemerintah kolonial dianggap Islam.

Secara sosial-keagamaan orang2 Jawa memang dapat dikatakan menganut agama Islam. Tetapi ke-Islaman mereka bercorak ke-Jawaan, sehingga sering disebut Islam Jawa atau Islam abangan. Mereka ini lebih terbuka dan dekat kepada spiritualitas dan budaya Jawa, berbeda dengan Islam santri yang lebih puritan dalam ajaran dan fanatik sikapnya. Dalam hubungannya dengan pekabaran Injil, Islam abangan lebih reseptip dari pada Islam santri, dan hal ini terbukti dalam sejarah pekabaran Injil di Jawa sampai sekarang.

Bagian kedua dari bab pertama ini membicarakan pekabaran Injil baik yang dilakukan oleh gereja "resmi" maupun atas inisiatip sementara orang Kristen yang merasa terpanggil dirinya untuk menyampaikan kabar kesukaan itu kepada orang2 pribumi. Berbeda dengan daerah2 dibagian Timur Indonesia yang terlebih dahulu menerima Injil sejak missionaris Roma Katolik dan zaman VOC, di Jawa Tengah khususnya baru ada orang2 Jawa yang menjadi Kristen pada parohan kedua abad ke-19, sebagai hasil pekabaran Injil atas inisiatip berapa orang Kristen awam seperti nyonya Philips-Stevens di Purwareja dan nyonya Van Ostroom-

Philips di Banyumas, serta nyonya Le Jolle-de Wildt di Salatiga. Sebenarnya Gereja Protestan *Indische Kerk* sudah berada di Jawa sejak abad ke-17, tetapi karena terbatas hanya dibeberapa kota besar dan memang gereja ini tidak berminat dalam pekabaran Injil untuk orang2 pribumi, tidak ada orang2 Jawa yang bertobat pada waktu itu.

Hampir bersamaan dengan timbulnya kelompok2 Kristen Jawa itu datanglah beberapa pekabar Injil Belanda di Jawa Tengah. Mereka mewakili organisasi2 pekabaran Injil yang denominasional dinegerinya, karena itu kelompok2 Kristen yang timbul bersifat denominasional. Pekerjaan2 perintisan para pekabar Injil ini boleh dikatakan sangat mengecewakan hasilnya secara jumlah, salah satu sebab diantaranya ialah mereka menuntut "standard yang tinggi" bagi orang2 Jawa yang bertobat supaya menjadi orang2 yang benar2 Kristen, bersih dari kebiasaan2 lamanya yang menurut para pekabar Injil itu kehidupan mereka penuh dengan takhayul dan magi. Penilaian seperti ini yang selalu kita dengar dari abad keabad, bahwa orang2 Kristen pribumi masih hidup dalam kehidupan "lamanya" dan belum hidup sebagaimana orang2 Kristen yang benar.

Perlu dikemukakan bahwa pada waktu itu pandangan terhadap agama Kristen sebagai agama penjajah Belanda dan menjadi Kristen berarti "menjadi Belanda" masih cukup kuat dikalangan orang2 Jawa. Ada anggapan bahwa orang2 Jawa yang masuk agama Kristen sudah meninggalkan adat-istiadatnya dan dengan demikian tidak lagi sebagai orang Jawa.

Bab kedua membicarakan tentang peranan kyai Sadrach dalam memperkembangkan dan membangun jemaat Jawa kelompoknya. Ia seorang penginjil Jawa yang berlatar belakang Islam Jawa abangan, berpendidikan pesantren didaerah Jawa Timur. Sebagaimana kebiasaan yang ada dalam masyarakat Jawa untuk mencari ngelmu/kebenaran, begitulah Sadrach tidak henti2nya kesana-kemari berguru dari seorang guru yang satu ke yang lainnya, sampai pada suatu saat ia menemukan *ngelmu* yang paling tinggi yaitu keyakinan Kristen, berkat hubungannya dengan orang2 Kristen awam seperti F.L. Anthing yang aktip dalam pekabaran Injil kepada orang2 Jawa maupun para pekabar Injil Belanda. Agaknya ia sangat terkesan kepada pribadi dan sikap Tunggul Wulung, seorang pekabar Injil Jawa dari daerah Jepara yang berpendirian bahwa menjadi orang Kristen tidak perlu meninggalkan budaya dan adat istiadat Jawa. Dalam perkembangan hidup Sadrach nampak bahwa ia memang mempunyai pribadi yang kuat dan mempunyai bakat pemimpin. Setelah ia dibaptiskan di Batavia (Jakarta sekarang), ia menjadi pekabar Injil didaerah Bagelen/Purwareja. Namanya segera menjadi terkenal, karena cara ia mengabarkan Injil sama seperti guru2 Jawa yang menantang perdebatan tentang ngelmu yang dimiliki. Barang siapa yang kalah dalam perdebatan, yang kadang2 membutuhkan waktu berhari-hari dengan disaksikan oleh para murid dari guru yang berdebat, ia beserta murid2nya harus tunduk menyerah dan berguru kepada guru yang menang. Begitulah Sadrach dalam mengabarkan Injil, dan tidak pernah ia dikalahkan, sehingga dalam waktu yang relatip singkat ia sebagai seorang guru dan kyai Kristen memperoleh pengikut banyak dan menjadi terkenal. Ia menjadikan desanya yang baru, yaitu Karangjasa menjadi pusat bagi orang2 Kristen Jawa para pengikutnya. Pengaruhnya begitu besar dan meluas, sehingga pada suatu saat ia sempat dicurigai oleh pemerintah kolonial setempat dan ditahan atas tuduhan merencanakan pemberontakan atau paling sedikit keonaran. Tetapi laporan pemerintah daerah tentang gerakan Sadrah tidak meyakinkan pemerintah pusat, dalam hal ini Gubernur Jendral, sehingga atas keputusannya Sadrach dibebaskan dari segala macam tuduhan, karena memang tidak terbukti. Pembebasan Sadrach tidak hanya disambut oleh para pengikut2nya dengan kegembiraan, melainkan justru pembebasan itu menaikkan pamor (gengsi, dan wibawa) Sadrach dimata para pendukung2nya. Sadrach diakui sebagai pemimpin mereka yang kharismatis, dan karenanya sangat dihormati.

Jemaat kelompoknya begitu cepat berkembang dan meliputi sebagian besar daerah Jawa Tengah, terutama didaerah2 pedesaan. Kerjasama dengan pekabar Injil J. Wilhelm dari *NGZV* dapat berkembang selama hampir sepuluh tahun. Tetapi kecurigaan dari pekabar Injil *NGZV* lainnya dan pengurus *NGZV* dinegeri Belanda pada akhirnya membuat putus hubungan kerja sama itu. Kecurigaan itu pada pokoknya berkisar bahwa orang2 Kristen Jawa dianggap belum hidup secara Kristen yang benar dan Sadrach terlalu berkuasa dan dianggap sebagai yang bertentangan dengan prinsip2 Kristen, dan lagi ia dicap sebagai penyebar ajaran sesat. Pada saat putusnya hubungan itu, sebagian besar orang2 Kristen Jawa memihak kepada Sadrach, dan hanya sebagian kecil saja yang mengikut para pekabar Injil Belanda. Hal ini membutikan bahwa kyai Sadrach memiliki wibawa besar dan sangat berpengaruh.

Merasa sangat direndahkan oleh pihak *"Zending"* dan menyadari dirinya tidak berhak melayankan sacrament (baptis dan perjamuan kudus), ia kemudian mengambil keputusan untuk menerima "tawaran" diangkat menjadi rasul, jabatan mana dipeganginya dengan taat dan hormat sampai meninggalnya pada tahun 1924. Yang hadir pada waktu penguburannya tidak hanya para pengikutnya, melainkan juga beberapa penjabat penting setempat seperti bupati, hal ini membuktikan ia memang pemimpin yang dikenal baik didalam jemaat maupun diluar jemaatnya. Sayang, bahwa sepeninggal Sadrach, jemaat mengalami perpecahan dan kemunduran. Sebabnya ialah karena Yotham Martareja, anak angkatnya yang menjadi pengganti memimpin jemaat, tidak memiliki kharisma seperti mendiang ayahnya, disamping memang situasi baru yang dihadapi sudah berubah, yang menuntut kepemimpinan yang berbeda dalam perubahan masyarakat memasuki zaman baru dan modern pada permulaan abad kita ini.

Bab ketiga menggambarkan sifat yang unik khas Jawa yang mengexpressi dalam bentuk organisasi, kepemimpinan, keanggotaan, kebaktian dan upacara2 keagamaan serta kehidupan spiritual dan jiwa kemerdekaan yang menonjol dalam jemaat Sadrach. Seperti dalam paguron Jawa yaitu persekutuan antara guru dengan para muridnya yang lebih menekankan persekutuan / ikatan batiniah daripada suatu wujud organisasi, demikianlah sifat khas dari jemaat Sadrach, pada dasarnya tidak menekankan bentuk2 organisasi. Persekutuan itu hanya merupakan persekutuan antara guru dan para murid, atau persekutuan sebagai keluarga besar dimana hubungan2 itu sangat bersifat personal dan informal. Karena itu tidak mengherankan kalau para pengikut Sadrach menganggap diri (atau dianggap oleh Sadrach) sebagai anak2 dan cucu2nya.

Jemaat setempat dipimpin oleh seorang imam yang diangkat oleh Sadrach. Mereka ini kebanyakan adalah bekas kyai dan guru ngelmu dan secara sosial ekonomi termasuk "elite" pedesaan. Sedangkan Sadrach dengan ketiga pembantu utamanya memiliki wibawa "supra lokal" yang merupakan kepemimpinan tertinggi dalam jemaat Sadrach secara keseluruhan. Model organisasi Jawa yang "primitif" ini tetap berlaku dan berfungsi *intern*, sementara model baru yang diintrodusir oleh pekabar Injil Wilhelm, yaitu model organisasi gereja *gereformeerd* juga diterima dan diberlakukan. Tetapi yang kedua ini lebih berfungsi *extern*, yaitu untuk menunjukkan kepada pemerintah dan pejabat2 Belanda lainnya bahwa jemaat Sadrach adalah merupakan *gereja* berdasarkan tatagereja *gereformeerd*, lengkap dengan semacam klasis dan synode. Kedua pemimpin ini, Wilhelm dan Sadrach, fungsinya saling mendukung dan melengkapi. Kehadiran Wilhelm dalam jemaat Sadrach makin memantabkan autonomi jemaat, sementara dukungan Sadrach terhadap Wilhelm makin memantabkan wibawa Wilhelm dimata jemaat.

Para imam, yang pada dasarnya penanggungjawab atas kelompok persekutuan setempat, juga bertanggungjawab atas kebaktian dan upacara2 agamaniah yang dilakukan. Ia menjadi pemimpin kebaktian dan pemimpin upacara2. Liturgi kebaktian sangat sederhana dan bersifat fleksible, tergantung pengaturannya oleh imam. Khotbah para imam agaknya lebih merupakan kesaksian2 pribadi, kesaksian2 tentang pengalaman mereka memperoleh *ngelmu* yang baru, yaitu "ngelmu Kristen" yang lebih unggul dari segala ngelmu, ngelmu dari "nabi Ngisa Rohullah" yang juga adalah ratu adil. Khotbah yang merupakan kesaksian2 pribadi itu dimaksudkan untuk membangkitkan kemauan hidup dalam ketaatan kepada perintah2 nabi Ngisa, karena itu tidak mengherankan bahwa berdasarkan pengamatan pejabat2 pemerintah kehidupan ethis/moral jemaat Sadrach secara rata2 baik, dan mereka merupakan bagian yang terbaik dari penduduk. Penyakit kronis masyarakat pada waktu itu, antara lain mengisap candu dan berjudi, kelihatannya tidak terlalu menjangkiti jemaat Sadrach.

Adat dan tatacara Jawa masih dipertahankan dalam kehidupan jemaat Sadrach, hanya saja dengan penyesuaian2 seperlunya. Ada semacam penseleksian terhadap adat dan tatacara Jawa, mana yang dapat di "kristen" kan dan mana yang tidak. Prinsip Sadrach adalah bahwa orang Kristen Jawa harus tetap tinggal sebagai orang Jawa dengan segala adat kebiasaannya, sehingga berusaha mengakomodasikan adat dan tatacara Jawa sedapat dan sebanyak mungkin bagi kehidupan Kristen. Hal ini merupakan ciri yang menonjol dalam jemaat Sadrach.

Ciri yang menonjol lainnya ialah jiwa yang mandiri dan merdeka, sesuai dengan nama yang sejak semula mereka pilih untuk kelompok jemaat mereka yaitu: *Golongane Wong Kristen Kang Mardika* (Vrije Christenen). Berdasarkan penelitian sosiologis, sebenarnya jiwa yang mandiri dan merdeka merupakan jiwa yang asli dari pedesaan di Jawa sejak zaman dahulu, dimana desa2 pada dasarnya mengatur dirinya sendiri hampir dalam segala hal. Jiwa ketidak-tergantungan ini memang sangat mungkin menjadi ciri khusus dalam kehidupan pedesaan abad ke-19, dimana tuntutan kebutuhan hidup juga tidak setinggi di-daerah2 perkotaan. Rumah2 kebaktian mereka bangun atas dasar bahan2 yang ada didesa, secara gotong royong dan biasanya dibangun diatas pekarangan para imam. Juga para "pejabat gereja" jemaat Sadrach sama sekali tidak menggantungkan hidupnya dari jemaat, melainkan mereka mempunyai pekerjaan masing2. Kesediaan untuk menjadi imam atau "pejabat gereja" hanyalah karena kesukarelaan, mungkin juga semacam *prestige*.

Bab keempat membicarakan berbagai tuduhan yang dilontarkan oleh para pekabar Injil Belanda terhadap Sadrach dan jemaatnya. Motif tuduhan-tuduhan itu memang bervariasi, ada yang karena ambisi pribadi yang tidak suka melihat seorang "inlander" seperti Sadrach memegang pimpinan, atau karena rasa irihati atas keberhasilan pekabaran Injil yang dilakukan oleh Sadrach dan kawan2nya yang didukung oleh Wilhelm. Yang cukup jelas ialah adanya kenyataan perbedaan yang cukup besar antara dunia Belanda dan dunia orang Jawa, baik secara sosial politik maupun sosial budaya.

Pada bagian ini juga disinggung tentang theologia pekabaran Injil *zending gereformeerd* yang sejak dari semula mempertahankan sifatnya yang orthodox, yaitu menekankan pekabaran Injil semurni mungkin sesuai dengan Alkitab, bahwa kabar kesukaan oleh darah Kristus untuk keselamatan umat manusia tetap harus menjadi inti dalam pemberitaan Injil. Namun dalam prakteknya prinsip ini tidaklah begitu mudah dilaksanakan. Apalagi pada waktu permulaan berdirinya *zending gereformeerd*, belum ada pedoman yang konkrit dan terperinci bagi pelaksanaan pekerjaan pekabaran Injil. Usaha2 untuk merumuskan secara konkrit apa sebenarnya *zending gereformeerd* itu dilakukan oleh para pengurus dan penasehatnya, seperti Ds. Lion Cachet yang sangat terlibat langsung dalam pekerjaan pekabaran Injil di Jawa Tengah dan Dr. A. Kuyper. Makin disadari bahwa gerejalah yang mempunyai tanggung jawab langsung terhadap pekabaran Injil, bukan organisasi2 pekabaran Injil seperti yang sudah berlaku. Prinsip ini, yaitu yang sering disebut *kerkelijk zending* kemudian dapat diterima sepenuhnya dilingkungan geraja2 *gereformeerd*. Perumusan yang cukup mendasar dan terperinci tentang apakah sebenarnya *zending gereformeerd* itu nyata pada *zending-congres* yang diadakan pada tahun 1890 di Amsterdam dimana makalah Dr. A. Kuyper sangat menentukan. Akhirnya sidang sinode gereja2 *gereformeerd* di Middelburg pada tahun 1896 secara resmi dapat merumuskan pemahaman *gereformeerd* tentang pekabaran Injil berdasarkan atas apa yang telah dirumuskan dalam *zending-congres* di Amsterdam.

Disamping memberikan dasar2 theologis bagi pekerjaan pekabaran Injil, relevansi rumusan2 itu dalam hubungannya dengan pekabaran Injil di Jawa Tengah ialah dibedakannya pekabaran Injil kepada orang Islam dan kepada orang kafir. Dan juga kepekaan terhadap konteks setempat, perbedaan antara situasi *thuisfront* dan *zendingsveld* sudah disadari. Disamping itu pengertian pekabaran Injil untuk mendirikan gereja *gereformeerd* dilapangan pekabaran Injil di Jawa Tengah sangat ditekankan. Dapat dikatakan bahwa rumusan2 itu sebenarnya sudah menjadi *jiwa* pekerjaan *zending gereformeerd* sejak memulai pekerjaannya di Jawa Tengah.

Selanjutnya secara agak panjang dikemukakan tentang berbagai *issue* yang negatip terhadap/tentang Sadrach dan jemaatnya. Sebenarnya issue2 negatip itu sudah timbul sejak tahun 1870-an ketika pekabar Injil P. Bieger bermaksud mengambil alih kepemimpinan atas orang2 Kristen Jawa dari tangan Sadrach, yang memuncak kemudian dalam peristiwa "vaksinasi", yaitu ketika Sadrach ditahan beberapa waktu lamanya atas tuduhan menentang peraturan pemerintah tentang pencacaran. Menurut tuduhan itu Sadrach menentang pencacaran karena kekurang-pengertiaannya tentang Alkitab. Tuduhan2 semacam inilah yang selalu dilancarkan oleh para pekabar Injil Belanda. Dari sumber-sumber yang ada dapat dikemukakan bahwa tuduhan2 yang menyangkut diri Sadrach adalah bahwa ia seorang "inlander" yang haus kekuasaan, tinggi hati, memakai gelar2 yang sebenarnya tidak berhak ia pakai yang tujuannya hanya untuk mengagungkan diri, supaya ia dianggap oleh para pengikutnya sebagai orang sakti, dan dalam kedudukannya sebagai pemimpin ia mengumpulkan uang dengan memeras jemaat untuk memperkaya diri dll. Dimata para pekabar Injil Belanda Sadrach tidak lebih dari seorang pekabar Injil Jawa yang tidak berpendidikan cukup, kurang pengetahuannya tentang Alkitab dan ajaran Kristen yang benar, sehingga ia bukan mengajarkan Injil melainkan Javanisme. Keadaan hidup orang2 Kristen Jawa yang menurut para pekabar Injil Belanda tidak bersifat Kristen, penuh dengan takhayul dan kebiasaan-kebiasaan yang bertentangan dengan ajaran Kristen, semua keadaan yang "menyedihkan" ini sumbernya, menurut mereka, adalah pada diri Sadrach. Karena itu mereka berpendapat bahwa Sadrach telah *meracuni* pekerjaan pekabaran Injil di Jawa Tengah.

Disamping tuduhan2 yang sebenarnya tidak berdasar, karena hanya berdasarkan suara2 yang tersebar dilingkungan orang2 Kristen yang tidak dapat dibuktikan kebenarannya, ada tuduhan2 yang dilatar belakangi oleh alasan theologis. Tuduhan ini dapat diringkaskan disekitar empat macam thema. Pertama, bahwa kekuasaan dan wibawa Sadrach atas jemaatnya terlalu besar sehingga kepemimpinannya dianggap bertentangan dengan kepemimpinan Kristen yang benar berdasarkan prinsip ajaran Calvin (Calvinisme) tentang hubungan antara pelayan Firman dan jemaat. Kedua, bahwa Kristus dipahami dan diberitakan oleh Sadrach sebagai ratu adil dan panutan sehingga ini dianggap bertentangan dengan hakekat Kristus yang adalah Allah sendiri yang telah menjadi manusia (inkarnasi Allah). Ketiga, bahwa Injil dipahami dan diberitakan oleh Sadrach sebagai *ngelmu* dan ini dianggap oleh para pekabar Injil Belanda sebagai yang bertentangan dengan ajaran tentang keselamatan hanya karena imam, bukan karena oleh perbuatan baik. Keempat, bahwa dalam jemaat Sadrach masih terdapat kebiasaan-kebiasaan (adat dan tradisi) Jawa yang dipegangi dan ini dianggap sebagai yang bertentangan dengan ajaran tentang kelahiran/hidup baru dimana orang Kristen harus meninggalkan "kehidupan lamanya".

Akhirnya dapat dikatakan sebagai kesimpulan bahwa problema-problema pekabaran Injil yang muncul/dihadapi di Jawa Tengah pada waktu itu sebenarnya disebabkan oleh ketidakmampuan para pekabar Injil Belanda untuk mengenal jiwa dan budaya Jawa, dan sifat orthodox ajaran Kristen yang menjiwai mereka serta belum adanya pedoman yang konkrit dan terperinci yang membekali mereka dalam mengabarkan Injil schingga pelaksanaan pekerjaan lcbih banyak didasarkan oleh improvisasi. Hal2 ini melatarbelakangi kecenderungan para pekabar Injil *gereformeerd* untuk bersikap intoleran terhadap kenyataan2 yang mereka hadapi di Jawa Tengah.

Bab kelima, yang merupakan bagian terakhir dari desertasi mengemukakan tentang penting nya kontribusi Sadrach bagi usaha2 kontekstualisasi gereja-gereja. Kita akan mengadakan evaluasi terhadap apa yang sudah disajikan dalam bab-bab terdahulu untuk menunjukkan validitas *hypothesis* kita bahwa apa yang Sadrach telah usahakan dan capai, yang sering kali disalah mengerti oleh para pekabar Injil Belanda, sebenarnya merupakan contoh permulaan dari ke-kristenan Jawa yang kontekstuil, karenanya merupakan hal yang penting dalam sejarah Gereja Jawa.Kesimpulan kita adalah bahwa Sadrach telah mengungkapkan suatu wujud iman Kristen yang dekat dengan jiwa dan pikiran Jawa, bersesuaian dengan perasaan dan pengalaman serta memenuhi kebutuhan, harapan dan aspirasi mereka. Hal-hal yang diuraikan selanjutnya dalam bab kelima ini mendukung kesimpulan kita.

A. Sifat kepemimpinan Sadrach yang bebas dan mandiri sangat menentukan perkembangan dan corak dari jemaat yang dibangunnya. Kepemimpinannya merupakan pencerminan dari pribadinya yang begitu teguh dan percaya diri yang kuat, yang dibentuk oleh latar belakang pendidikan dan kehidupannya sebagai seorang kyai. Jiwa bebas dan kemandiriannya terbukti bahwa Sadrach tidak pernah lama dalam perkerjaan dibawah pengawasan seseorang. Hubungan dan kerjasamanya dengan nyonya Philips-Stevens sedemikian rupa justru mendukung berkembangnya kepemimpinan yang bebas dan mandiri itu.

B. Jemaat Sadrach merupakan jemaat yang berakar dalam konteks masyarakat Jawa tradisional. Adanya korelasi2 antara jemaat Sadrach dengan konteks Jawanya menjelaskan dan sekaligus membuktikan bagaimana jemaat itu berakar pada lingkungannya yang merupakan faktor kunci dibalik perkembangan jemaat itu. Pertama perlu disebut bahwa jemaat Sadrach adalah jamaat pedesaan, karenanya juga menyerap ciri2 komunitas pedesaan dengan kehidupan yang sederhana, menekankan kebersamaan (gotong royong) yang menempatkan kepentingan individu dibawah kepentingan orang banyak, peranan pemimpin sangat menentukan dan berfungsi sebagai *primus inter pares* serta sekaligus ia sebagai simbol persatuan. Kedua, jemaat Sadrach adalah jemaat yang berlatar belakang dan hidup dalam masyarakat Islam abangan, sehingga ia menyerap nilai2 masyarakat itu, sebagai contoh misalnya penghargaan dan kedekatannya dengan adat dan tradisi Jawa. Ketiga, hidup dalam masyarakat yang feudal dan kolonial, dimana mayoritas orang Jawa lebih2 penduduk pedesaan hampir tidak mempunyai kesempatan untuk memperkembangkan kepribadian, percaya diri dan akal budi serta inisiatip, tokoh pribumi seperti Sadrach dapat dipandang sebagai "pembawa berita pembebasan" bagi beribu-ribu "wong cilik", tanpa merubah gerakannya yang agamaniah itu menjadi gerakan politik. Kesadaran Sadrach terhadap emansipasi bagi "wong cilik" ternyata tidak mengubah dirinya menjadi pemimpin politik.

C. Tanpa mengurangi penghargaan kita adanya motif yang tulus dari para pekabar Injil Barat, khususnya Belanda yang mengabarkan Injil ke Indonesia, secara sadar atau tidak sadar, langsung atau tidak langsung mereka tidak sekedar mengkristenkan orang2 pribumi, tetapi juga "membelandakan" nya. Hal ini disebabkan oleh karena para pekabar Injil itu kurang menyadari adanya dua konteks yang berbeda, yaitu konteks mereka (*thuisfront*) dan konteks pribumi (*zendingsveld*). Mereka menilai dan mengetrapkan segala sesuatu berdasar konteks dinegerinya, sehingga pertobatan bagi orang2 pribumi berarti "memasukkan" mereka kedalam konteks para pekabar Injil Belanda. Sukar diingkari bahwa pada abad2 lalu, sebagaimana nyata dalam sejarah pekabaran Injil, mereka bersikap intoleran terhadap budaya pribumi. Para pekabar Injil *gereformeerdpun* sampai dengan akhir abad ke-19 masih memiliki sikap intoleransi yang cukup kuat. Dan theologia pekabaran Injilnya yang bersifat orthodox itu cukup potensial untuk melestarikan sikapnya yang intoleran. Sikap seperti ini jelas tidak mendukung proses kontekstualisasi.

D. Pemahaman Sadrach terhadap pribadi Kristus (Christology) dan perkerjaan penyelamatanNya (Soteriology) bagaimanapun juga diwarnai oleh laterbelakang ke-jawaannya. Ia tidak membangun theologia yang komprehensif, melainkan sebagai seorang pekabar Injil (praktisi) ia hanya memiliki *concern* utama untuk mengabarkan Injil kepada orang2 Jawa sebangsanya dengan cara2 dan pengertian2 yang mudah mereka terima. Ia memandang Kristus sebagai seorang guru, seorang panutan bahkan ratu adil yang mengajarkan "ngelmu plus" yang paling tinggi melebihi semua ngelmu yang ada. Kehebatan "ngelmu Kristen" ini terletak pada kenyataan bahwa Kristus adalah *nabi Ngisa Rohullah* yang bangkit dari kematian dan yang berkuasa, melebihi para nabi lainnya sebagaimana diakui oleh Sadrach. Karenanya ia juga menekankan perlunya mentaati perintah2 Kristus dan mengikuti teladanNya (imitatio Christi), sehingga orang Kristen yang pada dasarnya *pengikut*2 Kristus, dapat menampakkan kehidupan yang baik, hal yang juga sangat ditckankan dalam ajaran2 (*pitutur dan wewaler*) Jawa. Bagaimanapun juga "theologia Sadrach" pada dasarnya harus dipandang sebagai usaha ketaatan dalam menjawab Injil Kristus secara relevan sesuai dengan konteks masyarakat Jawa pada abad ke-19.

E. Gereja Kristus di Jawa Tengah hanya akan menjadi gereja pribumi jikalau budaya Jawa secara serius diperhitungkan dan mendapat tempat dalam kehidupan gereja. Anggapan bahwa budaya Jawa hanya akan menggelapkan Injil, atau bahkan mejadikan kekristenan yang syncretistis dan palsu (pseudo-Christianity) seperti pada abad yang lalu haruslah ditinggalkan. Pertobatan bukanlah berarti meninggalkan budayanya sendiri dan ketaatan kepada budaya lain yang baru, melainkan ketaatan kepada Kristus dalam budaya mereka sendiri. Pengakuan bahwa budaya pribumi harus mendapat tempat dalam pekabaran Injil dan hidup gereja akan menghindarkan penerimaan budaya asing secara paksa. Demikian juga pengakuan bahwa orang Kristen pribumi harus menjadi pengemban utama dalam pekabaran Injil dan berperanan dalam kehidupan gereja, akan menghindarkan terjadinya hubungan yang hierarkis paternalistis antara mereka dengan para pekabar Injil asing. Dan inilah yang "diperjuangkan" oleh Sadrach. Dalam abad kita sekarang, yaitu zaman baru dalam pekabaran Injil, hubungan antara orang Kristen pribumi dengan para pekabar Injil asing harus berpola pada "partnership in obedience" sebab hanya pola ini yang dapat membangkitkan dan mendorong proses kontekstualisasi.

F. Bahaya yang serius dalam sejarah pekabaran Injil sejak dahulu adalah ketidakterakaran dan keterasingan orang2 Kristen pribumi dari masyarakatnya. Gereja mcnjadi "*copy gereja zendeling*" ditanah air/negeri asalnya, tetapi sebaliknya ia merupakan *tubuh asing* pada bangsanya sendiri. Kenyataan2 konkrit di Jawa dan Indonesia pada umumnya merupakan bukti2 yang tidak dapat diingkari. Namun sekarang keadaan sudah mulai berubah. Ada perkembangan dari gereja2 di Indonesia yang menggembirakan, yaitu kesadaran dan usaha untuk mengakarkan diri dalam masyarakat makin nyata. Makin adanya keterlibatan gereja2 dalam problema2 yang dihadapi oleh masyarakat dan bangsa Indonesia harus dilihat dalam rangka usaha2 kontekstualisasi, mengatasi dan mencegah keterasingan serta meniadakan "cap Barat". Apa yang dilakukan oleh Sadrach merupakan salah satu usaha yang menantang bagi kelanjutan usaha2 pengakaran gereja2 dalam masyarakatnya.

APPENDICES

APPENDIX I

SYNOPSIS OF REFORMED CHURCHES AND
REFORMED MISSION ORGANIZATIONS

The history of the Reformed churches in the Netherlands is long and complicated, compounded not least by the confusion caused by the two terms *hervormde* and *gereformeerde*, which both translate into English as "reformed." Although a work on a certain aspect of Javanese church history is not the place to write at length on the history of Reformed churches in the Netherlands, we thought it best to include a short synopsis of that history by way of an appendix. As can be seen from the chart on the opposing page, the reformed Church in the Netherlands was relatively united until 1834 under the name *Nederlandsche Hervormde Kerk* (NHK), a name made official by Willem I in his (in)famous *Algemene Regelment* in 1816. The adjectives *hervormd* and *gereformeerd*, however, continued to coexist in public parlance, and even in official church circles, until well beyond that date.

In 1834 the first major split occurred, known as the *Afscheiding*, which resulted by 1869 in the *Christelijke Gereformeerde Kerk* (CGK). Although this led to several more splinters, they do not pertain directly to our subject and therefore will not be singled out for mention here. The next major split from the *Nederlandsche Hervormde Kerk*, also of interest for our subject, took place in 1886 and was known as the *Doleantie*. The resulting denomination called itself the *Nederduitsche Gereformeerde Kerken* (NGK). In 1892, the two dissenting denominations joined forces and adopted the name *Gereformeerde Kerken in Nederland* (GKN).

In this book, the following translations are used consistently to facilitate as much as possible an understanding of the historical situation. When accompanied by careful reading, ambiguity can be avoided.

Nederlandsche Hervormde Kerk (NHK): the Dutch Reformed Church
Christelijke Gereformeerde Kerk (CGK): the Christian Reformed Church
Nederduitsche Gereformeerde Kerken (NGK): the Netherlands Reformed Church
Gereformeerde Kerken in Nederland (GKN): the Reformed Churches in the Netherlands.

Furthermore, the various Reformed mission agencies, both denominational and independent, can add to the confusion. The most important of the agencies and their relationship to the churches are as follows:

Nederlandsch Zendeling Genootschap (NZG): the Dutch Missionary Society, founded in 1797 as an independent organization, but almost exclusively made up of NHK members.

Nederlandsche Zendings Vereeniging (NZV): the Dutch Mission Organization, founded in 1858 as an independent organization closely associated with orthodox members of the Dutch Reformed Church (NHK).

Nederlandsche Gereformeerde Zendings Vereeniging (NGZV): the Dutch Reformed Mission Organization, founded in 1859 as an independent organization, but also closely associated with orthodox members of the Dutch Reformed Church (NHK).

Zending van de Gereformeerde Kerken in Nederland (ZGKN): the Mission of the Reformed Churches in the Netherlands, founded in 1892 as the denominational mission of the Reformed Churches in the Netherlands (GKN), which in 1894 took over responsibility for the mission in Central Java from the NGZV.

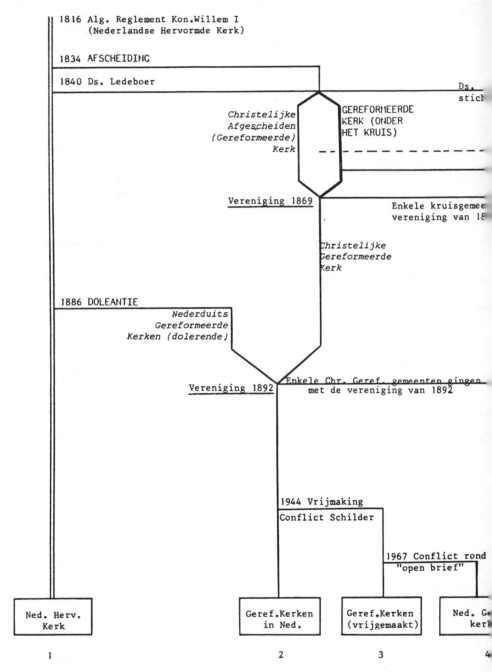

1816 Alg. Reglement Kon.Willem I
(Nederlandse Hervormde Kerk)

1834 AFSCHEIDING

1840 Ds. Ledeboer

Ds.
stich

*Christelijke
Afgescheiden
(Gereformeerde)
Kerk*

GEREFORMEERDE
KERK (ONDER
HET KRUIS)

Vereniging 1869

Enkele kruisgemee
vereniging van 18

*Christelijke
Gereformeerde
Kerk*

1886 DOLEANTIE

*Nederduits
Gereformeerde
Kerken (dolerende)*

Vereniging 1892

Enkele Chr. Geref. gemeenten gingen
met de vereniging van 1892

1944 Vrijmaking

Conflict Schilder

1967 Conflict rond
"open brief"

Ned. Herv.
Kerk

Geref.Kerken
in Ned.

Geref.Kerken
(vrijgemaakt)

Ned. G
ker

1   2   3   4

Chart taken from "DC-nieuws" (1982), an internal newsletter of the Centrum voor
Zending en Werelddiakonaat, Burgemeester de Beaufortweg 18, 3833 AG Leusden.

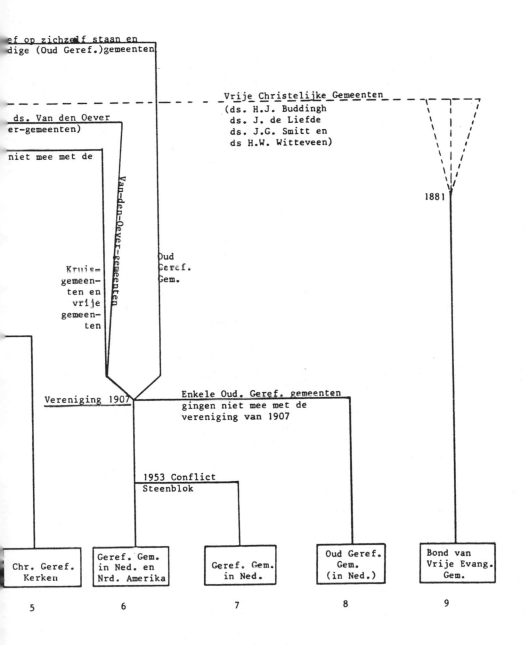

ef op zichzelf staan en
dige (Oud Geref.)gemeenten

Vrije Christelijke Gemeenten
(ds. H.J. Buddingh
  ds. J. de Liefde
  ds. J.G. Smitt en
  ds H.W. Witteveen)

ds. Van den Oever
er-gemeenten)

niet mee met de

Van den Oever-gemeenten

1881

Kruis-
gemeen-
ten en
vrije
gemeen-
ten

Oud
Geref.
Gem.

Vereniging 1907

Enkele Oud. Geref. gemeenten
gingen niet mee met de
vereniging van 1907

1953 Conflict
Steenblok

Chr. Geref.
Kerken

Geref. Gem.
in Ned. en
Nrd. Amerika

Geref. Gem.
in Ned.

Oud Geref.
Gem.
(in Ned.)

Bond van
Vrije Evang.
Gem.

5   6   7   8   9

APPENDIX II

WILHELM'S LETTER OF CALL FROM SADRACH'S COMMUNITY

Following is a list of villages where Javanese Christians live with their teachers who want to choose a minister. All the teachers do bear witnesss that the stated is true that they all unanimously choose Rev. Wilhelm, minister in Bagelen.

Karangjasa	18	Yohanes Kramawijaya
		Markus Bangsareja
		Musa Wirawijaya
		Ibrahim Dipawikrama
Hawu-hawu	34	Arun
Banjur	144	Filipus Suraleksana
Pagedangan	140	Soleman Nayaresa
Kedungdawa	91	Dawud Amatdiman
Kedungpring	274	Ismail Admawijaya
Karangpucung	230	Yonathan Asmadiwangsa
Sampang	262	Yesaya Citrawangsa
Pondokgede	160	Paulus Sadrana
Purwareja	114	Barnabas Kertamenggala
Jelok	231	Simon Wirasana
Bulu	101	Simon Wirasana
Sapuran	135	Yakub Resadiwangsa
		Zakaryas Wirasetra
Ciluluk	72	Asrom Sariyan
Bandar	81	Stefanus
Jambangan	96	Yakub Resadiwangsa
Purba	110	Aser
Derma	236	Saul Waryajaya
Kebitingan	35	Sostenus Kartadiwirya
Telagahabang	110	Aliya Casemita
Bendawuluh	47	Eliya Casemita

I have noticed there are twenty-two "mosques" with 3,039 members who want Rev. Wilhelm in Bagelen as their minister.

On behalf of,
Imam Sadrach

Karangjasa 10 April 1883

It is quite clear that each *mesjid* had its own elder with the exceptions of Jelok, Bulu, Telagahabang, and Bendawuluh who had one elder for two *mesjids*. Karangjasa, with only eighteen members had five elders. This does not mean, however, that all five elders were for *mesjid* Karangjasa alone. The first three became Sadrach's deputies, and worked for the entire community. In the Almanac of 1891 (cight years later) *guru igama* (religious teacher) is distinguished from *pangirid* (elder). The words *mesjid* and imam are used for the church and the leader of the community in general. The moslem terms were kept to symbolize a continuity with the past. The calling letter above proves that Sadrach had been widely recognized as the leader of the whole Javanese community.

Cf. Chapter III, section A.

APPENDIX III

STATISTICAL TABLES

Sadrach's Community

Residency Pekalongan:	Bandar-8, Ciluluk-3, Barang-10, Karanganyar-11, total 33
Residency Banyumas:	Banjarnegara-4, Singamarta-2, Karangkobar-7, Batur-19
Residency Bagelen:	Purwareja-12, Cangkreb-12, Loano-4, Karanganyar-4, Soka-6, Gombong-1, Petanahan-9, Karangbolong-1, Puring-13, Wanasaba-2, Kalielang-2, Sapuran-4, Kaliwiro-2, Kutaarja-6, Jenar-2, Wanarata-2, Kebumen-3, Kedungtawon-14, Ambal-7, Prembun-4.

Missionary Group

Bieger:	Purwareja-5, Cangkreb-4, Loano-1, total-10 congregations with 57 members.
Vermeer:	Purbalingga-11, Purwakerta-1, Cilacap-1, Banyumas-1, Banyumas district-6, Purwareja-1, Kalireja-3, total-24 with 277 members.

Total membership of missionary group-334 people living in 34 villages.
- from Heyting, Appendices A, B, C, D.

Residency	Number of local congregations	Number of elders	Membership adult	child	Number of villages
Bagelen	27	110	1,185	1,250	150
Banyumas	13	36	358	371	44
Yogyakarta	14	71	854	877	103
Kedu	7	26	552	511	53
Pekalongan	7	26	267	250	39
Tegal	4	13	150	169	22
Total	72	282	3,366	3,428	411

- from Almanac of 1891, p. 67.

Year	Baptisms	Year	Baptisms
1907	49*	1920	293
1908	166	1921	319
1909	227	1922	546
1910	380	1923	274
1911	115	1924†	512
1912	203	1925	210
1913	414	1926	253
1914	610	1927	89
1915	490	1928	787‡
1916	430	1929	168
1917	613		
1918	331	*smallest number of batisms	
1919	85	†year of Sadrach's death	
		‡largest number of baptisms	

- from Karangjasa Document (Karangjasa, Indonesia).

No.	Location	Leader	M	F	M	F	Total
1	Karangjasa	Sadrach Surapranata	103	97	82	180	382
2	Pituruh	Lasarus Resaleksana	13	13	8	11	45
3	Jenar	Jakobus Somawijaya	18	15	20	12	65
4	Sendang	Kornelius Joyowinangun	5	8	5	3	21
5	Bonjok	Paul Dipaleksana	16	14	5	12	47
6	Kaibon	Yohanes Rejaleksana	3	3	7	2	17
7	Pagedangan	Kalep Kertawikrama	20	13	12	11	56
8	Pamriyan	Asrabil Bangsakrama	29	31	40	29	129
9	Kedungdawa	Yakub Surawirya	15	18	17	23	73
10	Banjur Mungkadan	Senod Nayawikrama	22	21	26	26	95
11	Kedungpring	Ismael Admawijaya	28	37	26	32	123
12	Lirab	Elias Resawijaya	14	15	11	8	48
13	Kedungwaru	Tomas Atmadikrama	20	21	23	24	88
14	Pondokgede	Yotam Wangsadikrama	53	48	31	42	174
15	Sampang Oasuruhan	Lukas Wangsadikrama	100	96	92	83	371
16	Karangpucung	Elias Martadikrama	45	43	40	30	158
17	Jambeyan	Barta Kasangutama	24	24	15	24	87
18	Jelok	Simon Wirasana	20	23	18	19	80
19	Kalimade	Sustenis Wangsadrana	18	18	14	14	62
20	Sapuran	Wangsasetra	8	9	8	4	29
21	Talun amba	Yonatan Kasanklijaya	15	17	25	15	72
22	Tripis	Rajin Reksaleksana	11	14	20	17	82
23	Siwadas	Sakariyas Setrawijaya	9	8	8	4	29
24	Primasan	Andreas Singadrana	9	10	9	5	33
25	Gondokan	Prayin Karyadiwangsa	9	8	7	3	27
26	Bintaro	Eliya Sejawiguna	44	46	40	44	174
27	Gunungsari	Samuel Cakrawijaya	24	25	18	28	95
28	Pringamba	Eliasar Mangundrana	31	31	29	22	113

2,735

- From Karangjasa Document (Karangjasa, Indonesia).

Purwareja:	Kebumen:	Wanasaba:
1. Karangjasa*	1. Kedungdawa	1. Kalimade
2. Pituruh	2. Pamrian	2. Kecis
3. Jambeyan*	3. Pagedangan	3. Talunamba
4. Gowok*	4. Banjur*	4. Prumasan
5. Kranon	5. Bonjok	5. Gandokan
6. Purwasari	6. Kedungpring*	6. Tripis
	7. Tangeran/Sumpiuh	7. Sapuran

Banyumas:	Magelang:	Solo:
1. Karanggedang	1. Adigunung	1. Kartasura
2. Karangtawang		2. Slanggen
3. Grujugan		3. Pakis
4. Langgen (Priangan)		4. Kingkang
		5. Birit
		6. Tawing*

Yogyakarta	Semarang (belong to Salatigasche Zending:	Pekalongan (belong to Salatigasche Zending:
1. Wanagiri	1. Sirendeng	1. Gintung
	2. Pidadawetan	2. Jebed
		3. Sokowangi
		4. Temuireng
		5. Sidakare
		6. Panjuman
		7. Kendaldoyong
		8. Krasakgede
		9. Purba
		10. Dermakesimpar
		11. Tembelan
		12. Bawang

*partly

Van Dijk's "Sadrach's Kring," p. 90.

Purwareja:	Kebumen:	Banyumas:
1. Karangjoso*	1. Kedungwaru	1. Grujugan
2. Jelok	2. Lirap	2. Cengal
3. Gawok*	3. Banjur	3. Adireja
	4. Kedungpring*	4. Tritis
	5. Sampang	5. Sidareja
	6. Pondokgede	6. Selangegara
		7. Kalilamdak/ Pengantulan*

Magelang:	Yogyakarta:	
1. Ngawen	1. Pakualaman	11. Pare
2. Wiranayan	2. Randubanteng	12. Sodan
3. Beningan	3. Jetis	13. Tempuran
4. Pringamba	4. Dero	14. Prangkokan
5. Ngawangga	5. Kemirikebo	15. Ngabeyanmangir
	6. Ngangkrik	16. Krakitan
	7. Jaten	17. Gamol
	8. Gabukan	18. Gupit
	9. Gatak	19. Sumber
	10. Kebonagung	

Solo:
1. Purwosari
2. Mawen*
3. Kurung
4. Bulureja
5. Ngledok
6. Tawing*
7. Watusigar

*partly
Two or three local communities in Kebumen did not recognize Citrawirya as their apostle; some in Solo and Banyumas have minimal contact. Van Dijk, "Sadrach's Kring," p. 90.

APPENDIX IV

Letter of recognition of Sadrach's apostleship
Legitimatie en Erkenningsbewijs

Met deze verklaart ondergetekende: dat de heer Sadrach wettig erkend en gezonden is, door het Bestuur der Aposteleenheid van de Internationale Hersteld Apostolische Zendinggemeente, om als Apostelzendeling naar vermogen, te arbeiden in Nederlandsch-Indië, eiland Java en omgeving, en wel tot opbouw van genoemde Zendinggemeente aldaar. En verklaart hij mitsdien dat genoemde Heer Sadrach mede behoort tot deze Apostel-eenheid en zending, het recht hebbende om alle sacramenten van Doopen en Avondmaal toetedienen. Leden aantenemen en mededienaren der Zending te ordenen en uittezenden in dezen arbeid. Doch in alle zaken van bedoelden dienst, verantwoording schuldig is, overeenkomstig de gestelde orde, aan meer gemeld Bestuur der Internationale Hersteld Apostolische Zendinggemeente welks voorzitter domicilie heeft te Braunschweig Hedwigstrasse no. 13 (Duitschalnd). Van bovengenoemde Zending is eene afdeeling in Holland, erkend bij H.M. Koninklijk Besluit van 20 October 1897 no. 33 en vermeld in de Nederlandsche Staatscourant van 12 November d.a.v. no. 266 onder de benaming der vereeniging "De Apostolisch Kas" gevestigd te Enkhuizen; alwaar ook haar voorzitter en Apostel der afdeeling de Heer J. Kofman Rz. woont, onder wiens leiding de zendingsarbeid op Java meer speciaal gesteld is geworden, in ver-eeniging met de aldaar arbeidende apostelzendelingen zijnde de Heeren G.L Hanibals, J.G.R. Jacobs en Sadrach van Midden Java.

Deze zendingarbeid is natuurlijk aan alle daar gestelde Landswetten onderworpen en moet dezelve stipt eerbiedigen.

Gedaan te Enkhuizen in opdracht van vorenstaande Bestuur dezer Internationale Zendingarbeid.

Mei negentienhonderd een
J. Kofman Rz.
Voorzitter der bovengenoemde vereeniging als afdeeling gevestigt te Enkhuizen

APPENDIX V

LITURGICAL USE OF CREEDS, TEN COMMANDMENTS AND PRAYERS IN SADRACH'S COMMUNITY

Niceno-Constantinopolitan Creed, the Ten Commandments, the Apostles' Creed, the Lord's Prayer and other prayers for special occassions used in Sadrach's community according to Almanac of 1891 (transcribted from Javanese script)

The Niceno-Constantinopolitan Creed. (pp. 68-71)

Kawula pitados dumateng Allah satunggal, ingkang maha kawasa, ingkang nitahaken langit lan bumi, tuwin samukawis ingkang katingal lan ingkang boten katingal.

Kawula pitados dumateng Gusti satunggal, Jesus Kristus, putra Allah ingkang ontang-anting, anggening kayogakaken dening ingkang Rama saderenging dumadosipun jagad, inggih punika Allah ingkang mijil saking Allah, saha padang ingkang mijil saking pepadang, sejatinipun Allah ingkang mijil saking Allah sejati, anggening kayoga dening Allah dene saking pakaryanipun Allah, wujudipun sami kaliyan ingkang Rama, dumadosipun samukawis sadaya amargi saking Panjenenganipun, punapa dene anggening tumedak saking swarga awit saking kawula, karsa amilujengaken kawula, anggening dados manuswa mijil saking pakaryanipun Roh Suci, miyos saking prawan Maryam, tumunten dados tiyang, ingkang kakurbanaken dados sesulih kawula, ing nalika kabawah dumateng panjenenganipun bupati Pontius Pilatus, ingkang kasangsara saha kapetak, ing tigang dintenipun lajeng wungu, anyondongi pamecanipun para nabi, lajeng sumengka dateng swarga, pinarak wonten satengenipun ingkang Rama, tuwin ingkang benjing bade rawuh angagem kamulyan, karsa angadili tiyang ingkang gesang kaliyan ingkang pejah, *ingkang ajumeneng ratu adil, kratonipun tanpa wekasan.*

Kawula pitados dumateng Roh Suci, ingkang ginustigusti, ingkang akarya gesang, ingkang mijil saking Allah ingkang Rama, lan Allah ingkang Putra, ingkang sinebut-sebut, ingkang kasaosan pakurmatan, sami ugi kalayan Allah ingkang Rama, Allah ingkang Putra, ingkang pangandikanipun kasabdakaken dening para nabi.

Kawula angaken yen baptis punika minangka panjering pangapuntenipun dosa, tuwin kawula anggadahi pengajeng-ajeng menggah tangipun badan kawula ingkang bade pejah, miwah gesang langgeng wonten ing bumi enggal lan langit enggal. Amin.

Pepaken sadasa prekawis (the Ten Commandments). (pp. 91-95)

SEKAR KINANTI

1. Nyawa ulun kang den emut maring Hayang kang maha widhi, ingkang angagem kamulyan rikalanya karsa paring, dawuh pepakene ngarga, Horeb den ajrih kang suci.

2. Wondene dedawuhipun kadya kang kocap puniki, ingsun iki Yehuwah Hayang, myang ratunira kang uwis angluwari sira seka, ing kanistan mulya ngirid.

3. Metu sing pangwasanipun, iblis marmanya sireki, ywa nganggep Allah liyannya, kejabannya ingsun iki, sira aywa samya karya, ukir-ukiran utawi.

4. Mubarang prasemon iku, ingkang aneng langit nginggil, utawa kang neng buntala, sarta ingkang munggwing warih, ing sangisornya buntala, aywa sira samya kongsi.

5. Sujud myang ngabekti iku, deningg amung ingsun iki, Yehuwah Hyang agungira, ingkang datan anglilani, lamun kaurmataningwang, den suna mring liyaneki.

6. Kang males durakanipun, bapa marang para siwi, ngamti turun kaping tiga, myang turunnya pingpat neki, turune janma kang samya, anyengiti marang mami.

7. Nanging ingsun welas sagung, janma kang tresna mring mami, utawa ingkang sumedya, anetepi prentah mami, apan angantya tumeka, turune ping sewu neki.

8. Sireku aywa anyebut, ngala-ala asmaneki, Yehuwah Hyang agungira, awit Pangeran tan prapti, ngluwarna sing paukuman, kang nglahala mring asmeki.

9. Sira wajib ngemut-emut dina Sabat nggonireki, anetepi dedawuhan, ing sajroning anem ari, sira anggarapa karya, myang anglakonana salir.

10. Pakaryanira sadarum, nanging ing dina kang kaping, pitu iku sabbatira, Yehuwah Allahireki, aywa nganti nggarap karya, apa-apa nadyan silih.

11. Sira utawa anakmu, priya sarta pawestri, apadene baturira, kang lanang myang wadoneki, utawa wongira anyar, kang neng jro wismanire-ki.

12. Wit sajroning nem dineku, Yehuwah nitahken langit, lan bumi samodra lawan, saisenisenireki, dene dina ping pitunya, anulya kendel Hyang Widhi.

13. Pramilanipun Hayang Agung, amberkahi sabbat sari, kinarya suci sanyata, sira wajib angajeni, rama lawan ibunira, kang kadyeku supayeki.

14. Den dawakena umurmu, aneng tanahira sami, sing peparinge Yehuwah, Allahira mring sireki, sira ywa karya palastra, ywa laku bandrek sireki.

15. Sira aywa nyolong jupuk, aywa sira anekseni, goroh marang kancanira, sarta aywa sira melik, ing wismane kancanira, ywa sira nduweni melik.

16. Bojone sanak sadulur, myang bature jaluestri, apadene sapinira, miwah kebone utawi, sabarang darbek-darbeknya, mitranira sadayeki.

17. Duh ingkang mahamulyagung, mugi karsa apeparing, sihwelasan dateng kita, kang supadi dasih neki, sageda darbeni sedya, netepi dateng saliring.

18. Dedawuh Gusti puniku, myang mugi karsa aparing, kekiyatan anggen kita, anglampahi mijil saking, panrimah tuwin pracaya, mring Yesus Kristus jeng Gusti.

Pengakening Pitados (the Apostles' Creed). (pp. 95-97)

SINOM

1. Ulun pitados mring Allah, rama kang kawasa yekti, ingkang nitah aken akasa, bumi saisineki, amba pitados maring, Yesus Kristus putranipun, ontang anting sanyata, inggih niku Gusti mami, ingkang sampun kagarbini sing Rohulah.

2. Miyos saking kenya Maryam, ingkang kasangsareng nguni, rikala aneng bawahnya, Pontyus Pilatus dipati, kasalib tekeng pati, apan nulya dipun kubur, ngraosken girisannya, naraka: dupi tri ari, wungu malih anggeni pun seda.

3. Nulya mekrad mring suwarga, munggah munggweng tengeneki. Allah Ramanipun ingkang, maha kawasa: myang inggih, saking ngriku anggening, bade rawuh ngasta kukum, ngadili mring tyang gesang, tuwin kang sampun ngemasi, ulun inggih pitados dateng roh Allah.

4. Myang amba samya pracaya, dateng kawontenaneki, kratone Hyang agung ingkang, neng saenggen-nggen tur suci, lan pitepanganeki, dateng

satunggiling prakudus, pangapuntening dosa, tangining tyang saking pati, wah pitados lamun wonten gesang lana.

Pandonga Rama kawula (The Lord's prayer) (pp. 97-98)

PUCUNG

1. Duh Rama ulun, ingkang munggeng suwarga gung, mugi asma Tuwan linuhurna sagung jalmi, kraton tuwan mugi rawuh mring pra umat.

2. Ing sakayun Tuwan mugi den pituhu, kadya neng suwarga, inggih makatena ugi, aneng bumi dumateng sagung sujalma.

3. Mugi ulun ing sadinten-dintenipun Tuwan paringana, rejekinya diri mami, sarta Tuwan mugi angaksama.

4. Dateng sagung dosengong kang mring pukulun, den ulun pan samya ngapunteni dateng jalmi, ingkang samya kalepatan dateng amba.

5. Myang Hyang agung, ywa ngantya nandukken ulun, dumateng panggoda, nanging ingkang mugi-mugi, kauwalaken saking sagunging piala.

6. Wit Hyang agung, ingkang kagungan karatun, tuwin pamisesa, miwah kamulyan sajati, ingkang ngantya tumekeng neng kalanggengan.

7. Amin sestu, kabula pandonga ulun, amargi sawabnya, Yesus Kristus Gusti mami, kadya ingkang sampun dados prasetyanya.

Pandonga yen bade nampeni piwulang (Opening prayer for worship). (pp. 98-100)

DANDANGGULA

1. Duh Allah ingkang dados rama kami, ingkang ngempalaken kita, sing Gusti ulun margine, putra paduka Yesus; lamun amba pinuju sami, sumedya kakempalan, asageda ulun, nganggep mring asma paduka, myang kelamun pangandikannya Hyang Widhi, lagya kajarwakken.

2. Amba mugi den saged cumawis, anggen kita samya midangetna, margi saking dumununge, eroh kang maha kudus, myang paduka bukaa batin, tuwin tutuk ingkang, ngimami memuruk, mugi asunga katrangan mring kang muruk myang dumateng para dasih, supaya kajarwakna.

3. Ambanguna dateng santosaning, pitados ngong dumateng paduka, margi saking prasetyane, Hyang agung kang mring ulun, wah malihnya

panuwun mami, ywa amba samya ngantya, keneng sasar klimput, nging sageda gesang kita, lumaksana myang nderek prasetya widhi, ingkang dateng pra umat.

Rerepen Pandonga ing wanci enjang (Morning prayer). (pp. 100-103)

MASKEMAMBANG

1. Duh Hyang agung Allah ingkang angasihi, myang maha welasan, kang matah gadangan mami, amba sami anyaosna.

2. Sokur ageng dumateng Paduka Gusti, awit anggen Tuwan angrimat lan anjageni, temen-temen dateng amba.

3. Kala wanci dalu wau nggenngong guling, myang paring ganjaran aso dateng angga mami, supayannya badaning wang.

4. Tuk sakeca lan Gusti ugi paring, seger kasarasan malih saha mugi paring, kekiyatan anggenamba.

5. Lumaksana kesengsem samya nandangi pakaryan kawula, supaya daya netepi, men temen mring pangkat amba.

6. Tuwin dateng saliring kwajiban mami, nggih kang minangkaa kaurmatnya mring Hayang widhi, duh Gusti sihwlasan Tuwan.

7. Mugi dados berkahnya pakaryan mami, myang eroh paduka, mugi dumununga tuwin anunda dateng kawula.

8. Mugi Gusti anjangkunga mring pra dasih, mawi sih welasan supados pakaryan mami, sabenari lestantuna.

9. Duh Gusti kang kagungan sihwlasan mugi, ngaksama sakwehnya, dosanya pra abdineki, wah madangna nalar kita.

10. Ingkang peteng myang mugi ngereha salir lumaksana ing wang, supaya aywa nglampahi ingkang tan tuwan karsakna.

11. Marma mugi amerdi dateng sami, sregep nglampahana ing sakarsanipun Gusti, lan mugi amberkahana.

12. Mring sakwehning jalma kang miarsa tuding, paduka myang muga, nyirnakken kratonnya iblis, tuwin mugi angiyatna.

13. Para abdi Paduka saha sakehing, pamarentah donya supaya wignya netepi dumateng kwajibanira.

14. Miwah mugi nglipura sawarnineki, janma kang sesambat dumateng paduka yekti bab saliring prakawisnya.

15. Saha malih mugi anglilihken mami, yen pinuju manggya pakawed sahariari, duh Allah mugi anggala.

16. Anjurungi sakwehning panyuwun mami, mijil sing karsannya Yesus Kristus Gusti kami, putra Tuwan ingkang lana.

Rerepen pandonga yen bade neda (Prayer before meal). (pp. 103-104)

MIJIL

1. Duh Rama ulun ingkang peparing, ingoning tumuwoh, nggih mring ingkang gesang sadayane, tuwan mugi karsa amberkahi mring ambengan iki, myang mugi pukulun.

2. Aparinga sawarnining bukti lan mbenombeningong apan mawi sagung rejckine ingkang mijil sing mirahan Widhi tuwin mugi-mugi amulang mring ulun.

3. Aywa nganti kaduk anggen mami bukti: nagning ingong, gadahana gung duga-dugane myang paduka mugi mardi mami, samya angukih kang neng suwarga gung.

4. Miwah mugi-mugi Hayang Maha Widhi, akarya akukoh dateng driyo ulun salamine, supayeng ngong aywa ngantya gingsir mawi sabdeng Widhi yeku pamintenglun.

Rerepen pandonga sasampuning neda (Prayer after meal). (pp. 104-105

MEGATRUH

1. Aduh Gusti kawula asaos sokur, panarimah trusing galih, mring paduka maha agung, dene tuwan sampun paring rejeki malah angantos.

2. Maksih wonten sawatawis langkungipun, sarehning katah sujanmi, kang dumawah ing pakewuh, paduka nuwuki tetedan dumateng ingong.

3. Apan mawi kamirahannya Hyang agung, lan cekap sahari-ari, tuwin tuwan mugi ayun angampah tyas ulun bilih ngraketi barang kang katon.

4. Panggesangan ingkang bade sirna niku, nanging mugi-mugi mami

kasagedna amituhu, pangandikanipun Gusti, myang tresna tekeng ing batos.

5. Wah malihnya ingkang supadosing pungkur, anunggila mring Hyang Widhi, gesang neng klanggengan sestu ingkang mugi den jurungi donga ulun mring Hyang Manon.

Rerepen pamuji ing wanci sonten (Evening prayer). (pp. 105-108)

GAMBUH

1. Duh Gusti kita Yesus, Kristus padang kang langgeng satuhu, saha ingkang anupiksani sakalir, myang ingkang madangi ulun, ing pundi-pundiya enggon,

2. Anggen ulun lumaku, nadyan surya tan nyunari ulun, myang rem bulan datan amadangi mami, kang mugi-mugi pukulun, nglairken dumateng ingong.

3. Kamirahan myang tutulung, wit saking pangreksanya mring ulun, ing wancinya dalu sapunika Gusti, mugi karsa anjangkung supaya amba ywa manggoh.

4. Bebaya myang pakewuh, lan den tulus mitulungi ulun, Gusti mugi anyekecakaken mami, margi saking anggen ulun jetmiko rikala ngaso.

5. Supados amba baut, anglampahi sawarnining laku, ingkang enggal lan mugi nggen ulun guling ingkang sakeca puniku, tanginya temah dados.

6. Kluhurannya Hyang agung, Gusti mugi anyawisken ulun, myang sageda kelayan bingah-nggen mami, jeng ngajeng rawuh pukulun, ngan-tya tumekeng ing ngendon.

7. Paduka mugi ayun paring andel-andel dasihipun, ingkang saged ngayemaken diri mami, nggih niku lamun Hyang agung, yun ngaksama dosaningong.

8. Myang mugi ngreksaa ulun, neng sajroning jaman sengareku, nggih punika kelamun nyawa ngong manggih, panggoda kang karya limut lan kelamun badaningong.

9. Siniya myang pinupuh wah ywa ngantya iblis mengsah ulun, saged damel pitunannya angga mami, mugi rumeksaa sagung, umat paduka Hyang Manon.

10. Saha malih yen mangguh, kasusahan kang mugi Gustingsun, karsa

paring sembulih anulya salin kabingahan myang Hyang agung, karsa nglipur sagunging wong.

11. Saderek kang was kalbu, miwah ingkang lagya samya ambruk, kenging sakit mugi kasarasna aglis, duh Rama tresna pukulun, klaira dumateng ingong.

12. Duh putra mugi pukulun karsa anunggilken wujudipun prasemonnya sarira paduka Gusti nggih dumateng badan ulun, duh roh suci mugi manggon.

13. Kang mugi-mugi pukulun karsa maringken tentrem rahayu, dateng amba myang dateng pra dasih neki, duh Allah sarira telu dados ajuga sayektos.

14. Mung Tuwan ingkang sinung, kaluhuran langgeng laminipun, mugi-mugi Hyang Sukma karsa njurungi panuwun amba sadarum mijil sing wlasan kemawon.

Z E E

Pedada
Baluk
Kendal
Sirendeng
□ SEMARANG

S E M A R A N G

R E M B A N G

K E D O E

Pringhombo
MAGELANG □ Glagah
Boeloe
Bintaroe
oenoengsari
Prangkokkan
Ngangkrik
Djelok
Djomblang
Gaboeggan
Djaten
ibean
Dermasari
II
Semboeh
Penten
DJOKDJA
Selong
Temon
Ngabeam

S O E R A K A R T A

□ SOERAKARTA

Pagerdjoesang
Birit
Sarab
Karangasem
Nganwen

D J O K D J A K A R T A

Tjombongan

M A D I O E N

A A N

, behoorende tot den kring van VERMEER en UHLENBUSCH.
PS vóór 1869 gesticht
ring van SADRACH (1899)

GLOSSARY OF FOREIGN TERMS

abangan — red; used to designate the Moslem religious group which was characterized by its incorporation of Javanese religious elements. This group was quite tolerant

adat — ancient Javanese traditions

agama Allah — the true religion of God

agama Belanda — "Dutch" or foreign religion

agami Islam santri — Islam as observed by the *santris*

agami Jawi — Javanese religion

aja melu-melu — a warning not to follow the missionaries

akad nikah — Moslem marriage ceremony

algemeene kerkeraad — the general synod

anak angkat — foster child

angker — haunted places; the dwelling places of evil spirits

apostel zendelingen — missionary apostles of the *Apostolische Kerk*

apostolische gemeenten — congregations of the *Apostolische Kerk*

babu — female servant

bangsa — people

bapa — father

batik — Javanese printed cloth

batiniah — the inward focus of true religion

bawa swara — introductory melody

bedug — drum used at the mosque to call Moslems to prayer

belijdenis — confession of belief

bengkok — the part of communal land of a village which was cultivated by the *lurah* and his staff in lieu of a salary

berbudi bawa leksana — great noble soul

bersih desa - slametan ceremony observed to cleanse the village from evil, disaster, and misfortune

bhagawan — a distinguished person, possessing perfect *ngelmu*, whose advice was willingly accepted as good for everyone; used in our book to refer to the Dutch missionaries

bhiksu — Hindu or Buddhist monk

brahman — upper caste Hindu

bujana pirukunan — meal of reconciliation

bupati — regent

cacad — physical scar

cakra — a disc with several protruding arrows, used on the roof of the Christian church in Karangjasa; the weapon of Sri Kresna

carik — secretary; the record keeper of the village or community

cela — physical scar

Cultuurstelsel — the Dutch colonial government's policy of forced cultivation (1833-1867)

desa — village

deva — god

dhukun — traditional healer

dhukun sunat — healer who performs the rite of circumcision

dominee — minister

dubbele kwaliteit "double capacity" — the term used by Lion Cachet to describe his assignment to Central Java

dupa — clay pot in which incense was burned

dzikiran — Thursday evening gatherings

ei-pandita — "egg minister"; nickname given to the Dutch missionaries

emban — female attendant of a Javanese noble

Erucakra — Master of the *cakra*; another name for *ratu adil*

extra ecclesiam nulla salus — no salvation outside the church

gaiban — communal song used in worship

gamelan — Javanese musical instrument

gembala agung — the great shepherd

gending — Javanese instrumental and vocal combination

generasi zending — "mission generation" referring to those Javanese who became Christians under the guidance of the Dutch missionaries

gethok-tular — personal contact, which was the primary means of direct communication in nineteenth century Java

Golongane Wong Kristen Kang Mardika — The Group of Free Christians; the name chosen by Sadrach's community

gotong royong — concerted action; solidarity, harmony, and cooperation between community members

grojogan — cooperation among village members, including such activities as hoeing, planting rice seedlings, and weeding the rice fields

guru — in general, a teacher, and also used specifically for a traditional religious teacher

guru igama — religious teacher

guru Injil — a missionary helper who served to bridge the gap between the missionaries and the Javanese

guru linuwih — a distinguished Javanese guru; one who was considered invulnerable

guru ngelmu — traditional Javanese religious teacher of a specific *ngelmu* or knowledge *gusti* — master; also used as a title for God

hagama tahi asu — the religion of dog manure; name given to Christianity by some of the Javanese

hajji — a Moslem who has made the pilgrimage to Mecca

hanggayuh kasampurnaning hurip — striving after the perfect life

heilig volk — holy people; a term sometimes applied to the adherents of *Islam putihan*

high ngelmu — religious knowledge; the term was used in the past for Javanese mysticism

huis-gemeente — house church

hulpzendeling — missionary helper, usually an indigenous person

Idhul Fitri — celebration held the day after the month-long fast of Ramadan

imam — Islamic priest; used for the local community leaders in Sadrach's community

imitatio Christi — the imitation of Christ

imperium in imperio — kingdom within a kingdom

Injil — the Gospel

jamu — herbal medicine (drunk especially by young women for health and beauty)

japa — formula

japamantra — incantation, magic sentence

Javaansche ambtenaren — Javanese civil servants

jimat — talisman

jimatsrapal — amulet

jongos — male servant

kafad — the symbolic circumcision performed on girls, usually at the time of their first menstrual period

kafir — unbeliever

kangjeng — his majesty

kasepuhan — the council of elders who acted as advisors to the village administration

kasunyatan — the highest reality; also used to describe God, the Absolute

kaum — Moslem offical who performed the religious rituals and ceremonies

kauman — exclusive Moslem priestly community

kawula — servant

keberdikarian — literally, "to stand on one's own feet;" spirit of independence

kekah (aqiqah) — *slametan* held among *santri* Moslems when a child was seven days old for the naming of the child and its first haircut

kemis — Thursday

kenduren — religious meal

kentongan — hollow tube made of wood or bamboo, normally used to sound an alarm; used sometimes as a call to worship

kereta kencana — the golden cart of a Javanese sultan

keris — dagger

kerkelijke zending — ecclesiastical mission; the new mission policy of the ZGKN when it took over in Central Java from the NGZV which emphasized that mission was the responsibility of the church and not of independent organizations

kerkeraad — the church council

kesaktian — the power of invulnerability

khitan — to cut; a term used for circumcision

kiyamat — the last days

kramas — hair washing; the ritual of hair washing which accompanied the symbolic circumcision of girls who had reached the age of puberty

kraton — the King's palace

kring — circle

Kristen abangan — Javanese Christianity, developed by the indigenous evangelists, which was more closely bound to the culture

Kristen Jawa — Javanese Christianity; Christianity as developed by the indigenous evangelists

Kristen Landa — Dutch Christianity; Christianity as developed by the Dutch missionaries

Kristen putihan — Javanese Christianity, developed by the Dutch missionaries, which was suspicious of Javanese culture

kuli — landowners who were usually descendants of the original legendary settlers of a village

kumpulan — a special evening house-gathering

kumpulan gedhe — the annual great gathering in Karangjasa comparable to a synod meeting

kuwalat — to become "overburdened" or "cursed"

kyai — traditional religious leader

langgar — building used for daily prayers and the recital of the Koran

Lebaran — the festival held after the month-long fast of Ramadan

levende wet — "living law"

lindung — landless villagers who owned a house and garden but were dependent on the landowners for their livelihood

louter en zuiver — "pure and unadulterated"; term used by the Dutch to describe the "proper" proclamation of God's Word

lumbung miskin — rice barn set up for the care of the poor

lumbung padi — rice barn for storing part of the harvest in case of a poor harvest the following year *lurah* — the village leader or head who was appointed for life by the village administration

magang — apprenticeship

Mahdi — messiah; the one who will come; another name for *ratu adil* according to Islamic belief

manca negari — foreign country

mardika — free, independent

matang puluh — *slametan* observed on the fourtieth day following a funeral

mendak pindo — *slametan* held on the second anniversary of a death

mendak pisan — *slametan* held on the first anniversary of a death

menyelamken — corruption of *meng-Islam-kan*, to islamize

mesjid — literally, mosque; used by Sadrach's community to indicate church or individual community of Christians

missionaire predikant — ordained missionary

mitoni — *slametan* observed in the seventh month of pregnancy

mitung dinani — *slametan* observed on the seventh day following a funeral

modin — Moslem official who performed the religious rituals and ceremonies

momong — persuasive

momot — accomodative

murid — pupil of a *ngelmu* teacher

nabine Landa — "the prophet of the Dutch"

naik haji — pilgrimage to Mecca; an Islamic obligation

negara — the state

negari gung — the great state

nelung dinani — *slametan* observed on the third day after a funeral

ngelmu — knowledge

ngelmu dowa — knowledge of prayer

ngelmu pasek — *ngelmu* which is dominated by elements of the native religion

ngelmu santrian — *ngelmu* which is dominated by Islamic elements

ngelmu sejati — true and noble knowledge

ngemis — literally, begging; sometimes used in the sense of raising funds for religious activities and charity work

ngenger — patronage entailing some obligations

ngesur tanah — *slametan* observed in the evening of the day of a funeral

Ngisa Rohullah — Jesus, the Spirit of God

nglimani — *slametan* observed in the fifth month of pregnancy

ngudi sjatining becik — devotion to true goodness

nyewu — *slametan* held on the third anniversary of a death

nyuwita — outright patronage

opperherder — chief shepherd; a term used to describe Sadrach's position in the community

ouderling — ecclesiastical elder

oudste — elder

overlevering van Jezus Christus — interpretation of Jesus Christ in another culture

paguron — discipleship system

palanquin — a carried chair used for transporting Javanese and Dutch officials

palungguh — the part of communal land of a village cultivated by the *lurah* and his staff in lieu of a salary

panakawan — attendants thought to possess divine wisdom

pandita — minister; in this specific case refers to white ministers

pandita mardika — free minister; the minister of Sadrach's community

pangirid — the official who led a procession who was responsible for giving directions as well as encouraging and motivating the participants; used in the community for elder or leader

panutan — exemplary figure

payung — umbrella

pekarangan — mixed gardens around the village houses

pengandelan — the creed

pengulu — Moslem marriage official

pepujan — The Lord's Prayer

perkampungan Arab — Arab villages; sections of the cities where the *putihan* and Arabic descendants lived

pesantren — Moslem secondary school, also called *pondok pesantren*

pitra or *fitrah* — almsgiving

pitutur — advice, direction

pondok — landless immigrants, newcomers, and other landless who generally owned no house

pondok pesantren — housing complex of *santris*; Moslem secondary school

prabot dusun — the village administration which in the past usually consisted of families belonging to the rural elite

pranatan — law; regulation

primus inter pares — first among equals

priyayi — aristocrats composing the ruling class, many of whom were government officials

priyayi gunung — the local bureaucratic elite, appointed by the King to assure security and manage court affairs

puasa — fasting; an Islamic obligation

putihan — white; used to designate the Moslem religious group which was characterized by its orthodoxy; composed of *santris*

Raad van Indië — the Indies Council

rapal — chanted formula

rasul — apostle

ratu adil — the "just king," a messianic figure in Javanese religious thought

ronggeng — public performers

rukun iman — Islamic belief, namely, belief in God, angels, sacred books, prophets, the last days, and predestination

rukun Islam — Islamic obligation, which included confession, prayer, fasting, almsgiving, and making a pilgrimage to Mecca

Sadrach's Kring — Sadrach's Circle

sahosan — tribute

sajen — offering meals (held during a woman's first pregnancy, child birth, etc.)

sangar — haunted places; the dwelling places of evil spirits

sangkan paraning urip — the origin and destiny of life

santri — Moslem student or graduate of a *pesantren*

sapu — a brush of palm leaf ribs; the symbol chosen by Sadrach to unite the community

sarana — actions which accompanied *rapal*

sarasehan — a Javanese style of discussion which entailed sharing views and opinions as well as asking questions

sawah — wet rice fields

sawah janda — "widowed rice fields"; the name given to rice fields which were considered haunted by evil spirits

sedekah — alms or charity; common meal

sedekah-bumi — offering for land; harvest festival

selapan — a thirty-five day period, the unit of the Javanese calendar; also the name given to the *slametan* observed when a child was thirty-five days old (*selapanan*)

sembah — (ritual) bowing

semedi — meditation

sepasar — *slametan* held among the *Islam abangan* when a child was five days old

sesajen — offering meal

sesepuh — elder

sesirah — head or chairman

sholat — prayer; an Islamic obligation

sholat Ied — communal prayers offered during the celebration following the month-long fast of Ramadan usually done in an open square

Sinoman — literally, youth; a cooperative organization which provided funds at low or no interest for those who needed capital to start a small business

siratul-mustakim — term used by the *santri* for a swinging bridge constructed of one-seventh of a female hair which the soul must pass over before entering heaven

slametan — ceremonial communal meal

slametan barakah — literally, blessing or grace; *slametan* held on the 15th of Ruwah, the night in which Allah was believed to decide who would die in the coming year

slametan memule sedulur — *slametan* observed in the ninth month of pregnancy to honor the "twin brothers," the placenta and the amniotic fluid

slametan suran — *slametan* held to commemorate the death of Husein, Mohammed's grandson

sola fide — by faith alone

sola gratia — by grace alone

stam — literally "trunk"; used to describe a preeminent apostle

sunat — circumcision

sunnah — the example of Mohammed, which was to be followed

supit — to cut; a term used for circumcision

Surapranata — the name taken by Sadrach when he became an independent guru; literally translated it means "he who has the courage to administer" from *sura* — courageous, daring and *pranata/mranata* —to administer, govern

surjan — Javanese shirt

syahadat — confession of faith; an Islamic obligation

syariat — divine law

takdir — predestination

tandak — erotic dancer

tapa — asceticism

tayuban — an erotic dance feast

tedak siti — touching the ground; the name of the *slametan* held on a child's seventh "birthday" (7 x 35 days) to symbolize the first stage of learning to walk

tegalan — dry fields

telekim — prayers for the dead performed by a Moslem official

tembang — Javanese poetry; a particular musical form found only among the Javanese and Sundanese

tetak — to cut; a term used for circumcision

theologia praxeos — theology of action

tijdgeest — the spirit of age

tingkeb — *slametan* observed in the seventh month of pregnancy *tirakat* — deliberately seeking hardship

tiyang baku — the main settlers of a village who belonged to the landowning class

tiyang pasek — godless; a derogatory term sometimes used for adherents of *Islam abangan*

tledek — erotic dancer

toelating (als inlandsche hulpzendeling) — permission or license to work as an evangelist, granted by the colonial government according to Regulation 123

tukang maca — professional reader

ummat Allah — God's chosen people

verlichte piëtisten — "enlightened pietists"

verraad — betrayal

voedstervrouw — "foster mother"

voorganger — religious leader

wangsit — a divine calling

warung — simple stores where everyday goods were sold

wayang — shadow puppets

wewaler — prohibition, taboo

wong cilik — one of two social groups in nineteenth century Java called the little people

wong gede — one of two social groups in nineteenth century Java called the great people

wot ogal-agil — term used by the *abangan* for a swinging bridge, constructed of one-seventh of a female hair which the soul had to pass over before entering heaven

zakat-fitrah — almsgiving; an Islamic obligation

zamzam — holy Arab water from the sacred well of Mecca, the well of Ishmael

zelfverheffing — self-aggrandizing

zendeling leraar — missionary teacher

zendingsfeest — mission festival

zendingsreis — missionary tour

zieketrooster — lay pastor for the sick

zuivere verkondiging — pure preaching; the emphasis of many of the Dutch missionaries

zuiverheid — "purity," regarding the proclamation of the Word of God

SOURCES CONSULTED

The sources are divided into three sections for the sake of convenience. The first section includes documents which are available in the various archives. The listings can be found alphabetically according to the archives in which they are preserved. The second section includes all articles found either in books, journals, or periodicals. Included also in this section are unpublished papers and manuscripts which have been preserved in places other than the archives listed above. The third section includes all book references.

ARCHIVES

National Archives Office Jakarta, Indonesia:

Documents regarding Sadrach's movements:
  Decision of the Governor-General of the Dutch Indies No. 94. August 11, 1180.
  Decision of the Governor-General of the Dutch Indies No. 5. April 10, 1884.
  Decision of the Resident of Yogjakarta 1548/TB. November 30, 1887.
  Missive Government Secretary No. 117 to the new Resident of Bagelen, July 1, 1882.
  Missive Government Secretary No. 2405 to the new Resident of Bagelen, September 15, 1882.
Bieger, P. to the Governor-General of the Dutch Indies, July 19, 1880.
— to Rev. Heyting, minister of the *Indische Kerk* in Purwareja, June 11, 1882.
Central Board of the *Indische Kerk* in Batavia to the Governor-General of the Dutch Indies, July 31, 1882.
Central Board of the *Indische Kerk* in Batavia to the Governor-General of the Dutch Indies, February 13, 1884.
Heyting, Petrus. *Verslag van den toestand de verspreiding enz. der Inlandsche Christenen in de residentie Bagelen en aangrenzende gewesten.*
Ligtvoet, W. to the Governor-General of the Dutch Indies, June 22, 1880.
— to the Governor-General of the Dutch Indies, July 19, 1880.
— to the Governor-General of the Dutch Indies, July 27, 1880.
— to the Governor-General of the Dutch Indies, March 27, 1882.
— to the Central Board of the *Indische Kerk* in Batavia, July 31, 1883.
Wilhelm, J. to the Governor-General of the Dutch Indies, April 17, 1883.
— to the Board of the *Indische Kerk* in Batavia, May 23, 1887.

Karangjasa Documents. Preserved by Sadrach's descendents in Karangjasa, Central Java:

Baku Pengakuan Kaprecayan Cara Agama Karasulan [Creed of the *Apostolische Kerk*]. Batavia: 1907.
Extract from the Register of the Decisions of the Governor General. *Toelating* No. 1/c for Sadrach. October 4, 1886.
Toelating No. 2/c for Markus Bangsareja. March 21, 1887.
Toelating No. 2/c for Yohanes Kramawijaya. March 21, 1887.
Hersteld Apostolische Zendinggemeente in de Eenheid der Apostelen. *Apakah ada Kebenaran itu?* [Is There Truth?]. Originally issued in Enkhuizen, The Netherlands.
— *Legitimatie en Erkenningsbewijs* [Legitimation and Recognition]. May, 1901.
Martareja, Yotham. *Bab Anane Panjenengane Rasulku Jawa* [The Origin of my Javanese Apostle]. Unpublished MSS.
— *Layang gagasan kang perlu dilakoni supaya bisane lestari uripe klayan kemaremaning ati* [The Ideal to be Achieved for Continuing Life with Satisfaction]: *Saupama aku dadi rasul* [Supposing I were an Apostle]. Unpublished MSS.
— *Sejarah Adeging Greja Pasamuan Karangjasa* [History of the Establishment of the Christian Community in Karangjasa]. Unpublished MSS.
Record of annual number of baptisms in Sadrach's community (1907-1929).
Record of local communities elders, and number of members in 1907.
Serat pramandian (baptis) [certificate of baptism] for Perhimpoenan Mesehi Kerasoelan Hoeloebalang Zeboelon.

Archives of the Dutch Reformed Missionary Society, Leusden.

Almanac of 1891, "Serat penanggalan ing taun agami Kirsten 1891 kangge ing para golonganing tiyang Kristen ing tanah Jawi Tengahan."
Horstman, R.J. to F.L. Cachet, June 30, 1892.
— to J. Wilhelm, October, 1891.
Nederlandsche Gereformeerde Zendings Vereniging, Minutes, October 15, 1881.
— Minutes, June 15, 1882.
— Minutes, November 8, 1886.
— Minutes, May 27, 1889.
— Minutes, May, 1890.
— Minutes, March 9, 1891.
— Minutes, September 14, 1894.
Wilhelm, J. *Aantekeningen.*
— *Dagboek 1881-1890.* Unpublished MSS.
— to R.J. Horstman, September 25, 1891.

ARTICLES

Adriaanse, L. "Syncretisme in Britsch-Indië op Java." *De Macedoniër* 39 (1935). Pp. 293ff.
— to Deputaten voor de Zending op Midden Java ten Zuiden. *Heidenbode* (March, 1897). Pp. 268-271.
— to Deputaten voor de Zending op Midden Java ten Zuiden, July 2, 1897. *Heidenbode* (December 1897).

— to Deputaten voor de Zending op Midden Java ten Zuiden. *Heidenbode* (January, 1898).

— to Deputaten voor de Zending op Midden Java ten Zuiden. *Heidenbode* (December, 1899).

Bachtiar, Harsja W. "The Religion of Java: Sebuah Komentar [A Commentary]." Supplement in *Abangan, Santri, dan Priyayi dalam Masyarakat* by C. Geertz. Jakarta: 1981. Also in *Majalah Ilmu-Ilmu Sastra Indonesia*. Vol. 5. No. 1. Jakarta: 1973.

"Bagelen." *De Macedoniër* 8 (1890). P. 215.

Bakker, D. "Christelijke Hollandsche-Javaansche Scholen." *De Macedoniër* 15 (1911). Pp. 266-276.

— "De Gereformeerde Kerken in Nederland en Zending." *De Macedoniër* 12 (1908). Pp. 3-12.

— "De Godsdienst van de Javaan." *De Macedoniër* 12 (1908). Pp. 225ff.

— "De Mohammedaansche Eredienst." *De Macedoniër* 14 (1910). Pp. 136-145.

— "De Mohammedaansche Geloofsbelijdenis." *De Macedoniër* 14 (1910). Pp. 11-20.

— "Het Godsbegrip van de Javaan." *De Macedoniër* 15 (1911). Pp. 337-345.

— "Het Schuldbesef van de Javaan." *De Macedoniër* 15 (1911). Pp. 240ff.

— "Java: cultuur." *De Macedoniër* 12 (1908). Pp. 69ff.

— "Java: wat Zending den Inlander moet brengen." *De Macedoniër* 15 (1911). Pp. 112-117.

— "Mohammedaansch zedenwet." *De Macedoniër* 14 (1910). Pp. 33-41.

— "Nationaal Christendom." *De Macedoniër* 26 (1922). Pp. 289-301.

— "Ons Zendingsterrein op Midden Java." *De Macedoniër* 15 (1911). Pp. 353-366.

— "Organisatie van het kerkelijk leven op het Zendingsterrein." *De Macedoniër* 15 (1911). Pp. 193-197.

— "Theologische opleiding van Javanen." *De Macedoniër* (1917). Pp. 321-327.

— "Verhoudingen in de zendingsarbeid contra ds. Fernhout." *Utrechtsche Kerkbode*. Amsterdam: n.d. Appendix II.

— "Wat zending den Inlander moet brengen." *De Macedoniër* 15 (1911). Pp. 112-117.

Bakker, F.L. "De Stichting van der Kerk op het Zendingsveld." *De Macedoniër* 44 (1939). Pp. 144-152.

— "Opleiding van Voorgangers." *De Macedoniër*" (1937). Pp. 225-232.

Balasuriya, Tisa. "Towards the Liberation of Theology in Asia." *Asia's Struggle for Full Humanity*. Edited by Virginia Fabella. Maryknoll: 1980. Pp. 16-27.

"Banyumas-Bagelen." *De Macedoniër* 2 (1884). Pp. 168-174.

Bavinck, J.H. "De Mystieke Achtergrond van het Javaanse denken." *Schakels* 43 (1951). Pp. 3-8.

— "Het goed recht van het Christelijk onderwijs in Indië." *De Macedoniër* 42 (1937). Pp. 341ff.

— "Wat kan het Christelijk onderwijs aan de bevolking in Indië brengen?" *De Macedoniër* (1937). Pp. 214ff.

— "Zending en Cultuur." *Indische dag*. Heemstede: n.d. Pp. 49-64.

Berg, C.C. "Toekomstverwachtingen in het Javaanse denken." *Schakels* 43 (1951). Pp. 9-12.

Bergema, H. "Karakter en Doel van de opleiding van inheemse helpers." *De Macedoniër* 42 (1937). Pp. 214ff.

Bevans, Stephen. "Models of Contextual Theology." *Missiology: An International Review* 13 (April, 1985). Pp. 185-201.

Bieger, P. "Javaansche Volksverhalen." *Mededeelingen van wege het Nederlandsche Zendeling genootschap* 35 (1891). Pp. 213-223.

— Letters of March 28, and July 1, 1878. *Heidenbode* (October, 1878). Pp. 21-22.

— to the Board of the NGZV, May 21, 1882. *Heidenbode* (October, 1882). P. 24.

Bliek, A.J. "De Anthingsche Christen Inlandsche Gemeenten in Batavia's Ommelanden." *De Opwekker* 70 (January, 1925). Pp. 278ff.

— "Een Pionier in de Zending op west-Java herdacht." *Mededeelingen van wege het Nederlandsche Zendeling genootschap* 67 (1923). Pp. 298-308.

Bode, J. "Onze Zending op Java in harde werking beschouwd." *Mededeelingen van wege het Nederlandsch Zendeling genootschap* 25 (1881). Pp. 210-235.

Bong Rin Ro. "Contextualization: Asian Theology." *What Asian Christians are Thinking*. Edited by Douglas J. Elwood. Queen City: 1976. Pp. 47-58.

Brandes, J.L.A. "Iets over een Ouderen Dipanegara in verband met een prototijpe van voorspellingen van Jaya baya." *Tijdschrift voor Taal-, Land- en Volkenkunde* 32 (1889). Pp. 305-327.

Brumund J.F.G. "Het Landbezit op Java." *Tijdschrift voor Nederlandsch-Indië* (1859). Pp. 48ff.

Cachet, F. Lion. "Sadrach's Kring." *Heidenbode* (1889). Pp. 613-614.

Carey, P.B.R. "The Javanese Messiah." *Orientation* (December, 1972). Pp. 53-58.

Christelijke Gereformeerde Kerk. "Verslag van de Zendingsdag van de Zending der Christelijke Gereformeerde Kerk te Leiden op September, 1883." *Het Mosterdzaad* (October, 1883). Pp. 148-158.

Coe, Shaki. "Contextualizing Theology." *Mission Trends* 3. Edited by Gerald H. Anderson and Thomas F. Stransky. Grand Rapids: 1976.

Coolsma, S. "E.W. King." *De Macedoniër* 3 (1885). Pp. 177-197.

Crommelin, D. "De Inlandsche voorganger in de Oost Java-Zending." *Stemmen voor Waarheid en Vrede* 50 (1913). Pp. 978-994.

— "Pandita Djawa." *Mededeelingen van wege het Nederlandsch Zendeling genootschap* 61 (1917). Pp. 2-16.

"Culture and Identity." A Report of Section I of the Bangkok Conference. *International Review of Missions*. Vol. 52. No. 246 (1973). Pp. 185-197.

Daneel. M.L. "Towards a Theologia Africana? The Contribution of Independent Churches to African Theology." *Missionalia* 12 (August, 1984).

"De Geoctroyeerde Oost Indische Compagnie." *De Macedoniër* 8 (1890). Pp. 55-167.

"De Geschiedenis en beschrijving der Ned. bezittingen in Oost Indië." *De Macedoniër* 8 (1890). Pp. 18-55.

De Graaf, H.J. "De Oorsprong van der Javaansche moskee." *Indonesia*. Vol. I (1947-1948). Pp. 289-306.

— "Kyai Ibrahim Tunggul Wulung." *Tong-Tong* 15 (May, 1970). Pp. 8-9.

— "Sadrach de Miskende." *Tong-Tong* 16 (July 15, 1971). Pp. 6-7.

— "Sadrach de Profeet." *Tong-Tong* 15 (May 15, 1971). Pp. 6-7.

— Sadrach de Strijder." *Tong-Tong* 15 (June 1, 1971). Pp. 6-7.

"De Islam op Java." *De Macedoniër* 2 (1884). Pp. 5-15.

"De Toestand van Bagelen in 1830." *TNI* 20 (1858). Pp. 65-84.

"De Wijze van werken op Java." *De Macedoniër* 2 (1884). Pp. 260-277.

"De Zending op de Synode." *Heidenbode* (September/October, 1896). Pp. 203-223.

"De Zendingsorganen en Zendingsmethode der Oost Indië Compagnie." *De Macedoniër* (1890). Pp. 193-240.

Dijkstra, H. "Article 123 van het Indisch Regeerings-reglement." *De Macedoniër* 19 (1915). Pp. 203-210.

— "Overzicht van het zendingsveld in Nederlandsch Oost-Indië, De Zending der Gereformeerde Kerken." *Nederlandsch Zendingstijdschrift* 8 (1896). Pp. 277-321.

— "Wat kan, mag en moet de Koloniale Regeering doen in het belang van de uitbreiding van het Koningkrijk Gods." *De Macedoniër* 15 (1911). Pp. 289-302.

Donner, J.H. "Wat moet de Zending de Heidenen brengen?" *Het Mosterdzaad* (June, 1882). Pp. 81-84. (July, 1882). Pp. 97-100.

"Ds. J.H. Donner." *Heidenbode* 4 (1889). Pp. 633-634.

Elwood, Douglas J. "Asian Christian Theology in the Making." *What Asian Christians are Thinking*. Edited by Douglas J. Elwood. Queen City: 1976. Pp. 19-38.

Enklaar, I.H. "Groen van Prinsterer en het NZG." *Aspecten van het Reveil*. Edited by *Het Nederlandsch Zendeling Genootschap*. Kampen: 1980. Pp. 89-105.

Esser, I. "Apostolische Gemeenten of Irvingianen." *De Macedoniër* 2 (1844). Pp. 165-167.

— "Iets over de houding die ons gouvernment in Indië tegen over de zending aanneemt." *De Macedoniër* 3 (1885). Pp. 272-275.

— "Inlandsche Christen gemeenten in Nederlandsch-Oost Indië." *De Macedoniër* 1 (1883). Pp. 273-275.

Fernhout, K. "Sadrach." *Heidenbode* (1889). Pp. 799-801.

"Gereformeerde Kerken in Nederland, concept regeling voor de Zending, Generaale Synode te Groningen 1899." *Heidenbode* (1899). Pp. 582-590.

Gispen, W.H. "Kerkelijke Zending in de practijk." *De Macedoniër* 8 (1890). Pp. 280-297.

Graafland, N. "De oorsprong, de grondslag en de methode der Zending." *Mededeelingen van het Nederlandsch Zendeling genootschap* 8 (1864). Pp. 264-297.

— "Evangelisatie op Java." *Mededeelingen van wege het Nederlandsch Zendeling genootschap* 8 (1864). Pp. 109-164.

— "Het Oogpunt waaruit de Zending de niet-christelijke godsdiensten in Nederlandsch Indië te beschouwen heeft." *Mededeelingen van wege het Nederlandsch Zendeling genootschap*. Pp. 388-403.

— "Over het Onderwijs voor inlanders." *Mededeelingen van wege het Nederlandsch Zendeling genootschap* 24 (1880). Pp. 230-267.

Harthoorn, S.E. "De Zending op Java en meer bepaald die van Malang (Uit zijn jaarverslag van 1857)." *Mededeelingen van wege het Nederlandsch Zendeling genootschap* 4 (1860). Pp. 105ff.

— "Iets over den Javaanschen Mohammedaan en Javaanschen Christen." *Mededeelingen van wege het Nederlandsch Zendeling genootschap* 1 (1857). Pp. 183-212.

Heleblian Krikor. "The Problem of Contextualization." *Missiology* XI: 1 Pp. 95-111.

"Hermanus Willem Witteveen." *De Macedoniër* 2 (1884). Pp. 197-206.

"Het Aftreden van Minister Keuchenius." *De Macedoniër* 8 (1890). Pp. 169-177.

"Het Besluit van Generale Synode van de Gereformeerde Kerken in Nederland in zake overneming van het werk der NGZV." *De Macedoniër* 11 (1893). Pp. 275-276.

Hidding, K.A. "Religieuze waarden in den volksgodsdiensten op Java." *De Opwekker* 77 (1932). Pp. 429-445.

Hoekema, A.G. "Indonesian Churches: Moving Towards Maturity." *Exchange* 21 (1978). Pp. 1-58.

— "Kiai Ibrahim Tunggul Wulung (1800-1885)." *Peninjau* 7 (1980). Pp. 3-24.
— "Pieter Jansz (1820-1904), First Mennonite Missionary to Java." *Mennonite Quarterly Review* 52 (January, 1978). Pp. 58-76.
Hoekendijk, C.J. "Evangelie en Ngelmu." *Mededeelingen van wege het Nederlandsch Zendeling genootschap* 61 (1917). Pp. 25-26.
"Hoe men op Java het waarschuwt voor het Christendom." *De Macedoniër* 11 (1893). Pp. 207-208.
Hoezoo, W. "Achiring Zaman." *Mededeelingen van wege het Nederlandsch Zendeling genootschap* 27 (1883), Pp. 1-42.
— "Bijdrage tot de kennis van de Bijbelsche legenden der Mohammedanen." *Mededeelingen van wege het Nederlandsch Zendeling genootschap* 9 (1865). Pp. 227-240.
— "Evangelisatie op Java, onderzoek naar de tot gevolgde met de voornamelijk met betrekking tot oprigten van gemeente." *Mededeelingen van wege het Nederlandsch Zendeling genootschap* 9 (1865). Pp. 1-74.
— "Fragment van het Javaansch geschrift 'Achiring Zaman.'" *Mededeelingen van wege het Nederlandsch Zendeling genootschap* 13 (1869). Pp. 307-312.
— "Het Javaansch geschrift 'Anbio' — geschiedenis van nabi Ngisa." *Mededeelingen van wege het Nederlandsch Zendeling genootschap* 9 (1865). Pp. 227-240.
— "Majawarna en Semarang." *Mededeelingen van wege het Nederlandsch Zendeling genootschap* 9 (1865). Pp. 277-282.
— "Nog eene legende over nabi Ngisa." *Mededeelingen van wege het Nederlandsch Zendeling genootschap* 17 (1873). Pp. 266-271.
— "Uit de Inlandsche School op Java." *Mededeelingen van wege het Nederlandsch Zendeling genootschap* 17 (1873). Pp. 48-55.
— "Verslag over de gemeente te Majawarna, 1861." *Mededeelingen van wege het Nederlandsch Zendeling genootschap* 7 (1863). P. 170.
Inggris. "Volksgewoonten in Bagelen." *Djawa* 1 (1921). Pp. 89-91.
Ingwersen, H.P. "Iets over Sadrach." *De Macedoniër* 19 (1915). Pp. 225ff.
"Inlandsche Ambtenaren en Inlandsche Christenen." *De Macedoniër* 8 (1890). Pp. 305-312.
"In Memoriam Johannes Hendrikus Donner (18 October 1824-31 Augustus 1903)." *Het Mosterdzaad* 17 (1903). Pp. 165-167.
"Inspectie reis." *Heidenbode* (June, 1890). Pp. 124-125.
"Jaarlijksch Overzicht van 't Zendingswerk in onze overzeesche Bezittingen." *De Macedoniër* 1 (1883). Pp. 148-149.
Jellesma, J.E. "Hoe kan op beste en minst kostbare wijze worden voorzien in de groote behoefte van Evangelieverkondigers in Nederlandsch Oost Indië, zoo onder Mohammedanen en Heidenen, als bij verlaten Christen gemeenten?" *Mededeelingen van wege het Nederlandsch Zendeling genootschap* 1 (1857). Pp. 329-350.
"Jepara-Margareja." *De Macedoniër* 11 (1893). Pp. 89-91.
"Jepara-Puntjel." *De Macedoniër* 1 (1883). Pp. 141-151.
"Jesus Sang Guru." *Exchange* 13 (1984).
Kampert, Henk. *Christendom en Javaanse Goddienstigheid naar een lokale theologie in Indonesië.* January, 1972. Unpublished paper.
"Kan mag zal, Concept regeling voor Zending." *Heidenbode* (1889). Pp. 607-608.
Knibbe, W.A. "Onderwijs en opvoeding der Javaansche bevolking." *Tijdschrift voor Nederlandsch-Indië* 11 (1849). Pp. 275-288.
Koentjaraningrat. "Javanese Religion." *The Encyclopedia of Religion.* Edited by Mircea Eliade. New York: 1987. Pp. 559-563.

Kollmann, M.H.J. "Bagelen onder het Bestuur van Soerakarta en Djokjakarta." *Bataviaasch Genootschap van Kunsten en Wetenschappen*. Vol. 14. n.p.: 1864. Pp. 352-368.

Koopman, C.H. "Aan het Hoofd bestuur der Nederlandsche Gereformeerde Zending-vereeniging." *Heidenbode* (August, 1878). Pp. 14-15.

— to the Board of the NGZV. *Heidenbode* (September, 1878). Pp. 17-18.

Kraemer, H. "De Positie der Christen Javanen te midden hun volk." *De Opwekker* 69 (1924). Pp. 313-326.

— "Nationaal Christendom op Java." *De Opwekker* 69 (January, 1925). Pp. 103-112.

Kreemer, J. "Iets over djimat." *Mededeelingen van wege het Nederlandsch Zendeling genootschap* 32 (1888). Pp. 349-354.

— "Onze heerschappij over Java en de aloude Javaansche-profetien." *Mededeelingen van wege het Nederlandsch Zendeling genootschap* 27 (1883). Pp. 101-108.

— "Wat de Javanen zoo als van ons denken." *Mededeelingen van wege het Nederlandsch Zendeling genootschap* 32 (1888). Pp. 121-125.

Kruyt, A.C. "Hoe het evangelie door natuurvolken ontvangen wordt." *De Inlander en Zending: vier lezingen*. Edited by A.C. Kruyt. Amsterdam: 1907. Pp. 81-125.

Kuitert, H.M. "Contextueel of academisch? Op zoek naar relevante theologie." *Gereformeerd Theologisch Tijdschrift* 83 (August, 1983). Pp. 188-203.

Lindenborn, M. "Evangelie en *Ngelmu*." *Mededeelingen van wege het Nederlandsch Zondeling genootschap* 60 (1916). Pp. 249-269.

— "Nationaal Christendom op Java." *Stemmen voor Waarheid en Vrede* 59 (1922). Pp. 529ff.

Lonergan, B.J.F. "Theology in New Context." *Theology of Renewal*. Edited by L.K. Shook. New York: 1968. Pp. 34-46.

Mastra, I. Wayan. "Contextualization of the Church in Bali: A Case Study from Indonesia." *Gospel and Culture*. Edited by John Stott and Robert T. Coote. Pasadena, 1979.

Meriso, R. Soedibjo. *Paulus Tosari, pemrakarsa pembangunan gedung greja Maja-wama*. Unpublished MSS. 1975.

Merkelijn, A. "Enkele gegeven over Zendingsterreinen van de Gereformeerde Kerken over 1923." *De Opwekker* 69 (January, 1924). Pp. 155-159.

"Methodologische Gedachten." *De Macedoniër* 2 (1884). Pp. 200-202.

Millies, H.C. "Islam en Christendom, ook met betrekking tot Nederlandsch-Indië." *Mededeelingen van wege het Nederlandsch Zendeling genootschap* 14 (1870). Pp. 325-356.

Mulder, D.C. "The Christian Message to a Changing World." *IRB* 35 (October, 1968). Pp. 40-47.

"Nederlandsch Gereformeerd Zendingvereniging." *De Macedoniër* 11 (1893). Pp. 271-274.

Neurdenburg, J.C. "De Eischen van het Inlandsch Onderwijs in Nederlandsch-Indië." *Mededeelingen van wege het Nederlandsch Zendeling genootschap* 23 (1897). Pp. 79ff.

— "De Opleiding van onze Zendelingen." *Mededeelingen van wege het Nederlandsch Zendeling genootschap* 34 (1890). Pp. 416-436.

— "De wijze van werken op Java." *Mededeelingen van wege het Nederlandsch Zendeling genootschap* 29 (1885). Pp. 93ff.

— "De Zendeling in zijn karakter en werk." *Mededeelingen van wege het Nederlandsch Zendeling genootschap* 32 (1888). Pp. 187ff.

— "Zendelingen en Hulpprediker." *Mededeelingen van wege het Nederlandsch Zendeling genootschap* 24 (1880). Pp. 170ff.

Nortier, C.W. "Het Geestelijk leven van den Dessa-Javaan." *Mededeelingen van wege het Nederlandsch Zendeling genootschap* 70 (1926). Pp. 47-56.

Offerhaus, H.J. "Eenige denkbeelden omtrent de verhouding van de staat tot de Inlandsche Christenen en omtrent den toestand, waarin de Christen Inlanders zich nu bevinden, inzonderheid op Java." *Mededeelingen van wege het Nederlandsch Zendeling genootschap* 38 (1894). Pp. 86-95.

"Oost Java-Majawarna." *De Macedoniër* 11 (1893). Pp. 116-119.

Pieris, A. "Toward an Asian Theology of Liberation: Some Religio-Cultural Guidelines." *Asia's Struggle for Full Humanity.* Edited by Virginia Fabella. Maryknoll: 1980. Pp. 75-95.

Poensen, C. "Bijdrage tot de kennis van Godsdienstigen en zedelijke toestand." *Mededeelingen van wege het Nederlandsch Zendeling genootschap* 9 (1865). Pp. 333-357. Also in *Mededeelingen van wege het Nederlandsch Zendeling genootschap* 13 (1869). Pp. 153ff. And in *Mededeelingen van wege het Nederlandsch Zendeling genootschap* 14 (1870). Pp. 161-202.

— "De Javanen en het Evangelie." *Mededeelingen van wege het Nederlandsch Zendeling genootschap* 14 (1870). Pp. 123-216.

— "Djimat." *Mededeelingen van wege het Nederlandsch Zendeling genootschap* 23 (1879). Pp. 229ff.

— "Een beschouwing van den inhoud van eenige voorname geschriften der Javaansche literatuur 'Serat Pataq'." *Mededeelingen van wege het Nederlandsch Zendeling genootschap* 13 (1869). Pp. 345-356.

— "Een en ander over de Godsdienstigen toestand van den Javaan." *Mededeelingen van wege het Nederlandsch Zendeling genootschap* 8(1864). Pp. 214-263. Also in *Mededeelingen van wege het Nederlandsch Zendeling genootschap* 9 (1865). Pp. 161-202.

— "Gatolotjo." *Mededeelingen van wege het Nederlandsch Zendeling genootschap* 17 (1873). Pp. 227-265.

— "Het Evangelie op Java." *Mededeelingen van wege het Nederlandsch Zendeling genootschap* 34 (1890). Pp. 391-415.

— "Het geschrift Djatikusuma." *Mededeelingen van wege het Nederlandsch Zendeling genootschap* 24 (1880). Pp. 97ff.

— "Iets over den Javaan als mensch." *Mededeelingen van wege het Nederlandsch Zendeling genootschap* 29 (1885). Pp. 26ff.

— "Iets over de Javaansche Desa." *Mededeelingen van wege het Nederlandsch Zendeling genootschap* 38 (1894). Pp. 24ff.

— "Iets over Javaansche naamgeving en eigennamen." *Mededeelingen van wege het Nederlandsch Zendeling genootschap* 14 (1870). Pp. 304-317.

— "Johanes Pak Dasimah." *Mededeelingen van wege het Nederlandsch Zendeling genootschap* 27 (1883). Pp. 161-171.

— "Karakterschetsen uit het desa leven op Java." *Mededeelingen van wege het Nederlandsch Zendeling genootschap* 23 (1879). Pp. 157-176.

— "Mattheus Aniep." *Mededeelingen van wege het Nederlandsch Zendeling genootschap* 24 (1880). Pp. 338-391.

— "Paulus Tosari." *Mededeelingen van wege het Nederlandsch Zendeling genootschap* 27 (1883). Pp. 283ff.

— "Sembur-suwug, japa-mantra." *Mededeelingen van wege het Nederlandsch Zendeling genootschap* 34 (1890). Pp. 333-365.

Pol, D. "Article 177." *De Macedoniër* 38 (1934). Pp. 344-345.

— "Sadrach Christenen." *De Macedoniër* 38 (1934). Pp. 155ff.

Quarles Van Ufford, P. "Cycles of Concern: Dutch Reformed Mission in Central Java, 1896-1970." *Religion and Development*. Edited by P. Quarles Van Ufford and Matthew Schoffeleers. Amsterdam, 1988. Pp. 73-94.

— "Mengapa Anda tidak duduk?" [Why Don't You Sit Down?]. *Peninjau* Vol. 9/10 (1982/1983). Pp. 3-23.

— "Why Don't You Sit Down?" *Man, Meaning and History*. Edited by R. Schefold. The Hague: 1980. Pp. 204-229.

"Rapport in zake de Zending." *Heidenbode* (September/October, 1896). Pp. 203-218.

Rullman, J.A.C. Sr. "De Sadrach Christenen, hun betekenis voor vandaag." *Allerwegen*. Vol. 2. No. 3.

Rutting, H.C.G. "Evangelie en Elmoe." *De Opwekker* 62 (1917). Pp. 303-308.

Schilstra, S.A. "De band des huwelijk op Java." *De Macedoniër* 11 (1893). Pp. 357-366.

— "Langgar en Pesantren." *De Macedoniër* 11 (1893). Pp. 325-336.

Schot, C.C. "Iets over de vragen aan Indische Regeering om Sadrach in zijn arbeid te bemoeilijken en over Sadrach." *De Macedoeniër* 11 (1893). Pp 13-22.

Schuurmans, N.D. "Nog eens, wat de Javanen zoo als van ons denken." *Mededeelingen van wege het Nederlandsch Zendeling genootschap* 32 (1888). Pp. 355-358.

— "Staat der Zending in Nederlandsch Oost Indië anno 1895." *Nederlandsch Zendingstijdschrift* 8 (1896). Pp. 129-163.

"Semarang." *De Macedoniër* 11 (1893). Pp. 50-54.

Soedarmo, Raden. "Waarom is er zo weinig inheems Christendom in Indië?" *Christus prediking in de wereld*. Kampen: 1965. Pp. 199-209.

"Butir-Butir Budaya Jawa." [The Elements of Javanese Culture]. TEMPO (March 12, 1988). Pp. 46-47.

Steenbrink, K.A. "Christian Faith in the Indonesian Environment." *Exchange* 5 (1973).

Supono Martasaputra, interviewed in Karangjasa. February, 1896.

Suprapto Martasaputra, interviewed in Karangjasa. February, 1986.

Sutapa, C. *Sejarah hidup Sadrach dan kegiatannya* [Sadrach's Biography and his Activities]. Duta Wacana Theological Seminary. Unpublished MSS. 1971.

Ten Zeldam Ganswijk, D.J. "Iets over de Javanen in betrekking tot Evangelieprediking in Oostelijk Java." *Mededeelingen van wege het Nederlandsch Zendeling genootschap* 1 (1857). Pp. 89-121.

"Uit Indië." *Heidenbode* (August, 1889). Pp. 1-7.

Van Andel, H.A. "De Godsdiensten en cultuur der Heidenen." *De Opwekker* 77 (1932). Pp. 355-385.

Van Den Berg, L.W.C. "Article 123 RR Nederlandsch-Indië." *De Opwekker* 69 (1924). Pp. 413-418.

— "Javaansch Christendom." *De Gids* 25 (1907). Pp. 235-269.

Van Den End, T. "Dutch Protestant Mission Activity: A Survey." *Itinerario* 7 (1983). Pp. 86-106.

Van Der Chijs, J.A. "Bijdragen tot de Geschiedenis van het Inlandsch Onderwijs in Nederlandsch-Indië." *Tijdscrift voor Indische Taal-, Land- en Volkenkunde* 14 (1864). Pp. 121-323.

Van Der Kroef, J.M. "Javanese Messianic Expectations: Their Origin and Cultural Context." *Comparative Studies in Society and History*. Supplement I. New York: 1959. Pp. 299-323.

— "Messianic Movements in Celebes, Sumatra, and Borneo." *Comparative Studies in Society and History*. Supplement II. New York: 1962. Pp. 80-121.

Van Der Linden, J. "Den Javanen een Javaan, zendeling J. Wilhelm van Purwareja 1883-1892." *Licht stralen op den akker der wereld* 48 (1947).

— "Enkele grepen uit het leven en werken van zendeling J. Wilhelm (Naar zijn dagboek en brieven)." *De Macedoniër* 41 (1937). Pp. 73ff.

Van Dijk, K. "Article 177 van de wet op Staatsinrichting van Nederlandsch-Indië." *De Macedoniër* 38 (1934). Pp. 55ff.

— "In Memoriam J.P. Zuidema." *De Opwekker* 77 (1932). Pp. 561-569.

— "Sadrach." *De Macedoniër* 39 (1935). Pp. 242ff.

— "Sadrach's Kring na 1922." *De Macedoniër* 42 (1938). Pp. 266ff. Also in *De Macedoniër* 43 (1939). Pp. 19ff.

Van Dijk, W. "Article 177 van de wet op de Staatsinrichting van Nederlandsch-Indië en zoogenaamde dubbele Zending." *De Macedoniër* 43 (1939). Pp. 1-9.

— "De Organisatie van de Kerk op het Zendingsterrein." *De Macedoniër* 39 (1935). Pp. 321ff.

— "Het monogame huwelijk in de Inlandsche Kringen en Gemeenten." *De Macedoniër* 43 (1939). Pp. 193-206.

Van Eijk, P.H. "De Sadrach Gemeenten." *De Macedoniër* 38 (1934). Pp. 33-44.

"Van ons arbeidsveld in Indië." *Heidenbode* (February, 1890). Pp. 74-77.

"Van ons Zendingsveld in Indië." *Heidenbode* (March, 1891). Pp. 229-230.

Van Troostenburg De Bruijn, C.A.L. "De Zendingspost Majawarna." *Mededeelingen van wege het Nederlandsch Zendeling genootschap* 24 (1880). Pp. 1-32.

Van Wijk, P. "Mr. F.L. Anthing en zijn werk te Batavia." De Macedoniër 3 (1885). Pp. 28-33.

Wagenaar, L. "In Memoriam Ds. Frans Lion Cachet." *Heidenbode* (December, 1899). Pp. 651-656.

Weitjens, J. "Pastor van Lith mengenai kyai Sadrach." [Pastor Van Lith's Opinion on Kyai Sadrach]. *Orientasi* 6 (1974). Pp. 183-202.

Wessels, A. "Op weg naar een contextuele missiologie." *Religies in Nieuw Perspectief.* Edited by R. Bakker et al. Kampen: 1985. Pp. 109-136.

Wiselius, J.A.B. "Jayabaya, zijn leven en profetiën." *Bijdragen tot de Taal-, Land- en Volkenkunde* 19 (1872). Pp. 172-207.

Wolterbeek, J.D. "Sadrach." *Christelijke Encyclopedie.* Edited by G.F.W. Grosheide. Kampen: 1965. Pp. 17-18.

"Zending congres." *Heidenbode* (March, 1890). Pp. 89-92.

Zuidema, J.P. to the Board of the NGZV. *Heidenbode* (July, 1897). P. 323.

BOOKS

Adriaanse, L. *De Zendingsarbeid onzer Gereformeerde Kerken onder de Javanen en Chinesen op midden Java.* Zeist: 1940.

— *Sadrach's Kring.* Leiden: 1899.

Anderson, Benedict R.O.G. *Mythology and the Tolerance of Java.* New York: 1965.

Anderson, Gerald H. *Asian Voices in Christian Theology.* New York: 1976.

Anggaran Dasar Rumahtangga dan Syahadat Kerasulan Baru untuk para anggota dari Gereja Kerasulan Baru [Constitution and Creed of the New Apostolic Church]. Bandung: 1966.

Arnold, T.W. *The Preaching of Islam.* London: 1913.

Bakker, D. *De Zending van de Gereformeerde Kerken.* Groningen: n.d.

Banawiratma, B.J. *Yesus Sang Guru.* Yogyakarta: 1977.

Bavinck, J.H. *Christus en de mystiek van het Oosten.* Kampen: 1934.

— *De Absoluutheid van het Christendom.* Javaansche Boekhandel en Drukkerij: n.d.

— *Religious besef en Christelijk geloof.* Kampen: 1949.

— *The Church Between Temple and Mosque: A Study of the Relationship Between the Christian Faith and Other Religions.* Grand Rapids: 1981.

Benson, Purnell Handy. *Religion in Contemporary Culture: A Study of Religion Through Social Science.* New York: 1960.

Berkhof, H. *Sejarah Gereja* [Church History]. Translated and edited by I.H. Enklaar. Jakarta: 1967.

Bliek, A.J. *Mr. F.L. Anthing.* 1938.

Blom Van Geel, J.F. *Overzicht van het ontstaan en de ontwikkeling der Salatiga-Zending.* Utrecht: 1911.

Board of Publications of the Christian Reformed Church. *Belgic Confession* in *Ecumenical Creeds and Reformed Confessions.* Grand Rapids: 1979.

Boersma, J.A. *Sadrach's Kring: Beschreven in zijn historisch verloop.* Mildam: 1980.

Boerwinkel, F. *Kerk en Secte.* 's-Gravenhage: 1959.

Boissevain, H.D.J. *De Zending in Oost en West.* Vol. I. 's-Gravenhage: 1934.

— *De Zending in Oost en West.* Vol. II. Hoenderloo: 1943.

Boneschansker, J. *Het Nederlandsch Zendeling Genootschap in zijn eerste periode.* Leeuwarden: 1987.

Boston Theological Institute. *One Faith, Many Cultures.* Edited by Ruy O. Costa. New York: 1988.

Broijer, H.B. *De opium en de Zending.* Arnhem: 1887.

Brouwer, A.M. *De Eerste Schreden.* Rotterdam: 1916.

— *De Moderne richting, eene historische-dogmatische studie.* Nijmegen: n.d.

Brumund, J.F.G. *Berigten omtrent de evangelisatie van Java.* Amsterdam: 1854.

— *Het Volksonderwijs onder Javanen.* Batavia: 1857.

Burger, D.H. *Perubahan-perubahan Struktur dalam Masyarakat Jawa* [Structural Changes in Javanese Society]. Jakarta: 1983.

Cachet, F. Lion. *Een Jaar op reis in dienst der Zending.* Amsterdam: 1896.

Caldarolla, Carlo. *Christianity: The Japanese Way.* Leiden: 1979.

Camps, A. *Christendom en godsdiensten der wereld.* Baarn: 1976.

Carpenter, Edward. *Heidendom en Christendom.* Arnhem: 1925.

Chadwick, Henry. *The Early Church.* New York: 1967.

Chopp, Rebecca S. *The Praxis of Suffering: An Interpretation of Liberation and Political Theologies.* New York: 1986.

Cooley, Frank L. *The Growing Seed: The Christian Church in Indonesia.* New York: 1981.

Coolsma, S. *De Zendingseeuw voor Nederlandsch Oost-Indië.* Utrecht: 1901.

Coward, Harold. *Pluralism Challenge to World Religion.* New York: 1985.

Craandijk, J. *Het Nederlandsch Zendeling Genootschap in zijn willen en werken.* Rotterdam: 1869.

Daubanton, F.E. *Prolegomena van Protestantsche Zendingswetenschap.* Utrecht: 1911.

De Jong, S. *Een Javaanse Levenshouding.* Wageningen: 1973.

— *Salah satu sikap hidup orang Jawa* [A World and Life View of the Javanese People]. Yogyakarta: 1976.

Dhofier, Zamaksyari. *Tradisi Pesantren: suatu study tentang pandangan hidup Kyai* [*Pesantren* Tradition: A Study of *Kyai's* Life-View]. Jakarta: 1985.

Drewes, G.W.J. *Drie Javaansche Goeroe's: hun leven, onderricht en messiasprediking.* Leiden: 1925.

Eliade, Mircea, editor. *The Encyclopedia of Religion.* New York: 1987.

308

Enklaar, I.H. *De levensgeschiedenis van Johannes Theodorus van der Kemp Stichter van het NZG, Pioneer van de LMS onder Kaffers en Hottentotten in Zuid-Afrika 1747-1811 tot zijn aankomst aan Kaap in 1799*. Wageningen: 1972. English edition: *Life and Work of Dr. J.T. van der Kemp 1747-1811, Missionary Pioneer and Protagonist of Racial Equality in South Africa*. Translated by A.A. Balkema. Rotterdam: 1988.

— *De Scheiding der Sacramenten op het Zendingsveld*. Amsterdam: 1947.

— *Joseph Kam: Apostel der Molukken*. 's-Gravenhage: 1963.

Epton, N. *Magic and Mystics of Java*. London: 1974.

Esser, B.J. *De Goddelijke Leiding in de Zending, beantwoording der vraag of de Gereformeerde Kerken in Nederland een nieuw Zendingsveld in de "buiten-bezittingen" zullen zoeken*. Rotterdam: 1914.

Fabella, Virginia, editor. *Asia's Struggle for Full Humanity*. Maryknoll: 1980.

Feringa, J.H. *De Plaats der Zending onder Heidenen en Mohammedanen*. Middelburg: 1896.

Fischer, H.T. *De Verhouding tusschen het binnenlandsch bestuur en Zending in Nederlandsch-Indië*. 's-Gravenhage: 1931.

— *Inleiding tot de culturele anthropologie van Indonesië*. Haarlem: 1952.

Fleming, Bruce C.E. *Contextualization of Theology: An Evangelical Assessment*. Pasadena: 1980.

Frankforter, A. Daniel. *A History of the Christian Movement: The Development of Christian Institutions*. Chicago: 1978.

Geertz, Clifford. *Abangan, Santri, Priyayi: Dalam Masyarakat Jawa*. Translated by Aswab Mahasin. Edited by Bur Rasuanto. Jakarta: 1981.

— *Religion of Java*. Illinois: 1960.

Gereja Kristen Jawa Purwareja. *Risalah Gereja Kristen Jawa Purwareja* [Treatise of the Javanese Christian Church in Purwareja]. Purwareja: 1976.

Gilhuis, J.C. *Ecclesiocentrische Aspecten van het Zendingswerk, met name bij de ontwikkeling daarvoor in Indonesië, bijzonder op Midden Java*. Kampen: 1955.

Gore, Charles. *The Reconstruction of Belief*. London: 1926.

Graaf Van Randwijck. *Handelen en Denken in dienst der Zending*. 's-Gravenhage: 1981.

Guillot, C. *L'Affair Sadrach: Essai de Christianisation à Java ou XIXe siècle*. Paris: 1981. Indonesian edition — *Kiai Sadrach, Riwayat Kristenisasi di Jawa*. Jakarta: 1985.

Hadiwijono, Harun. *Man in the Present Javanese Mysticism*. Baarn: 1967.

Hardjamardjaja, Andre Corsini Harjaka. *Javanese Popular Belief in the Coming of Ratu Adil, a Righteous King*. Rome: 1965.

Hardjowirogo, Marbangun. *Manusia Jawa* [Javanese Man]. Jakarta: 1984.

Harthoorn, S.E. *Het Inlandsche karakter en de Nederlandsche invloed*. Batavia: 1875.

Hoekstra, E.G. and M.H. Ipenburg. *Wegwijs in gelovig Nederland: Een alfabetische beschrijving van Nederlandse kerken en religieuze groeperingen*. Kampen: n.d.

Hoult, Thomas Ford. *The Sociology of Religion*. New York: 1958.

Hyma, Albert. *The Dutch Far East*. Ann Arbor: 1942.

Jansz, Pieter. *Landontginning en Evangelisatie op Java*. [Land Reclamation and Evangelism in Java]. Amsterdam: 1874.

Jensma, Theodoor Erik. *Doopsgezinde Zending in Indonesië*. 's-Gravenhage: 1968.

Jones, Howard P. *Indonesia, Possible Dream*. California: 1971.

Kerr, Martin Jarret. *Patterns of Christian Acceptance*. London: 1972.

Kidung Pasamuwan Kristen Jawa 139. Yogyakarta: n.d.

Kluin, H. *Het Geestesleven der Natuurvolken*. 's-Gravenhage: 1924.

Knitter, Paul F. *No Other Name?* London: 1985.

309

Koentjaraningrat. *Javanese Culture*. Oxford: 1985. Indonesian edition: *Kebudayaan Jawa*. Jakarta: 1984.

Köhler, J.M. *Het Irvingisme: Eene historisch-critisch proeve*. 's-Gravenhage: 1876.

Koopmans, J. *Nederlandsche Geloofsbelijdenis*. Amsterdam: 1940.

Kraemer, H. *De strijd over Bali en de Zending*. Amsterdam: 1933.

— *De wortelen van het syncretisme*. 's-Gravenhage: 1937.

— *Een Javaansche Primbon uit de zestiende eeuw*. Leiden: 1921.

— *From Mission Field to Independent Church*. The Hague: 1958.

— *The Christian Message in the Non-Christian World*. London: 1938.

— *World Cultures and World Religions*. London: 1960.

Kraft, Charles H. *Christianity in Culture: A Study in Dynamic Biblical Theologizing in Cross-Cultural Perspective*. New York: 1981.

Kruijf, E.F. *Geschiedenis van het Nederlandsch Zendelinggenootschap en zijne zendingsposten*. Groningen: 1894.

Kuyper, A. *Historisch Document*. Edited by J. Bootsma. Utrecht: 1940.

Lindenborn, M. *West Java*. Bussum: n.d.

Locher, G.P.H. *De Kerkorde der Protestantsche Kerk in Indonesië: bijdragen tot de kennis van haar historie en beginselen*. n.p.: n.d.

Lonergan, B.J.F. *Method in Theology*. New York: 1972.

Maijer, L.T.R. *Een Blik in het Javaansche volksleven* II. Leiden: 1897.

Malinowski, Bronislaw. *Magic, Science and Religion*. New York: 1954.

McGavran, Donald A. *Understanding Church Growth*. Grand Rapids: 1970.

Moertono, Soemarsaid. *Negara dan Usaha Bina Negara di Jawa masa lampau* [State and Statecraft in Old Java]. Jakarta: 1985.

Mooij, J. *Atlas der Protestantsche Kerk in Nederlandsch Oost-Indië*. Weltevreden: 1925.

— *Geschiedenis der Protestantsche Kerk in Nederlandsch-Indië*. Weltevreden: 1923.

Mulder, Niels. *Mysticism and Everyday life in Contemporary Java*. Singapore: 1978. Indonesian edition: *Kebatinan dan hidup sehari-hari orang Jawa*. Jakarta: 1983.

Müller Krüger, T. *De Protestantismus in Indonesia*. Stuttgart: 1968.

—*Sejarah Gereja di Indonesia* [Church History of Indonesia]. Jakarta: 1966.

Muskens, M.P.M. and Fr. Cornelissen, editors. *Sejarah Gereja Katolik Indonesia* I [History of the Roman Catholic Church in Indonesia]. Ende: 1974.

Nederduitsche Gereformeerde Kerken. *Acta van het Zending congres*. Amsterdam: 1890.

— *Acta Voorloopige Synode van Amsterdam, 1892*. Amsterdam:1892.

Nederlandsch Zending Vereniging. *Toelichting der Bepalingen van de Zendingsvereniging te Rotterdam*. Rotterdam: 1861.

Neill, Stephen. *A History of Christian Mission*. Middlesex: 1980.

Neurdenburg, J.C. *De Christelijke Zending der Nederlander in de 17e en 18e eeuw*. Rotterdam: 1891.

— *Geschiedenis tegen over kritiek*. Rotterdam: 1864.

Nida, Eugene A. *Customs and Cultures: Anthropology for Christian Missions*. New York: 1954.

Niebuhr, H. Richard. *Christ and Culture*. New York: 1975.

Nortier, C.W. *Ngulati Toya Wening* [Seeking Clear Water]. Bandung: 1928.

— *Tumbuh Dewasa Bertanggungjawab* [Growing Towards Responsible Maturity]. Edited by T. Van Den End and P. Siahaan. Jakarta: 1981.

— *Van Zendingsarbeid tot zelfstandige Kerk in Oost Java*. Hoenderloo: 1939.

Overzicht van de zesde zendingsconferentie van Nederlandsch-Indisch Zendingsbond gehouden te Batavia en te Depok van 26 Augustus-8 September, 1889. Rotterdam: 1889.

310

Pol, D. *Midden Java ten Zuiden.* 's-Gravenhage: 1939.
Pos, A. *Vijf en twentig jaar zendings arbeid te Jogya.* Amsterdam 1925.
Quarles Van Ufford, P. *Grenzen van internationale hulpverlening.* Assen: 1980.
Rasker, A.J. *De Nederlandse Hervormde Kerk vanaf 1795.* Kampen: 1986.
Rikin, W. Mintardja. *Ngabersihan als knoop in de Tali Paranti.* Meppel: 1973.
Risalah Gereja Kristen Jawa di Purwareja [Treatise of Javanese Christian Church in Purwareja]. Purwareja: 1976.
Rutgers, Jacqueline C. *Islam en Christendom.* The Hague: 1912.
Samartha, S.J. *Courage for Dialogue.* New York: 1982.
Sartono Kartodirdjo. *Protest Movements in Rural Java: A Study of Agrarian Unrests in the Nineteenth and Early Twentieth Centuries.* Singapore: 1973.
— *Ratu Adil* [Righteous King]. Jakarta: 1984.
— *The Peasants' Revolt of Banten in 1888.* 's-Gravenhage: 1966.
Schreiter, Robert J. *Constructing Local Theologies.* New York: 1985.
Schuurman, B.M. *Mystik und Glaube, im zusammenhang mit der Mission auf Java.* The Hague: 1933.
— *Pambiyake Kekeraning Ngaurip* [Uncovering the Mystery of Life]. Bandung: 1934.
Selosoemardjan. *Social Changes in Yogyakarta.* Ithaca, NJ: 1962.
Senior, Donald and Carrol Stuhlmueller. *The Biblical Foundations for Mission.* London: 1983.
Sir, Mardja. *Kyai Paulus Tosari.* Jakarta: 1967.
Smalley, William A. editor. *Readings in Missionary Anthropology.* Vol. II. South Pasadena: 1978.
Smit, G. *Mohammedaansche Propaganda en Christelijk Zending in onze Oost.* Amsterdam: 1912.
Soemodidjojo, R., editor. *Kitab Primbon Betaljemur Adammakna* [Book of Primbon Betaljemur Adammaknal]. Yogyakarta: 1978.
Sri Mulyono. *Wayang: asal usul filsafat, masa depannya* I [Wayang: its origin, philosophy and its future]. Jakarta: 1975.
Steenbrink, K.A. *Beberapa aspek tentang Islam di Indonesia abad ke-19* [Some Aspects of Islam in Indonesia in the Nineteenth Century]. Jakarta: 1984.
— *Perkembangan Teologi dalam dunia Kristen Modern.* [Development of Theology in the Modern Christian World]. Yogyakarta: 1987.
— *Pesantren, Madrasah, Sekolah: recente ontwikkeling in Indonesisch islamonderricht.* Meppel: 1974.
Stellingwerff, J. *Dr. Abraham Kuyper en de Vrije Universiteit.* Kampen: 1987.
Stott, John and Robert T. Coote, editors. *Gospel and Culture.* Pasadena: 1979.
Subagya, Rachmat. *Agama Asli Indonesia* [Native Religion in Indonesia]. Jakarta: 1981.
Suharto, editor. *Butir-butir Budaya Jawa* [Elements of Javanese Culture]. Jakarta: 1987.
Sumanto, I. *Kyai Sadrach pencari kebenaran* [Kyai Sadrach, the Truth Seeker]. Jakarta: 1974.
Sutherland, Heather. *The Making of a Bureaucratic Elite, the Colonial Transformation of Javanese Priyayi.* Singapore: 1979. Indonesian edition: *Terbentuknya sebuah Elite birokrasi.* Translated by Sunarto. Jakarta: 1983.
Tang, M.J. *Het Apostolische Werk in Nederland.* 's-Gravenhage: 1982.
Theological Education Fund. *Learning in Context: The Search for Innovative Patterns in Theological Education.* Bromiley: 1973.
— *Ministry in Context: The Third Mandate Program of the Theological Education Fund (1970-1977).* Bromiley: 1978.
Tosari, Paulus. *Rasa Sedjati.* Jakarta: 1953.

311

To Thi Anh. *Nilai Budaya Timur dan Barat, konflik atau harmony* [Eastern and Western Cultural Values]. Translated by John Yap Pareira. Jakarta: 1985.

Turner, J.E. *Essentials in the Development of Religion: A Philosophical and Psychological Study.* London: 1933.

Uhlenbeck, G.W. *Bijdrage tot de geschiedenis van verhoudingen tussen den staat en Christelijke Kerk genootschappen in Nederlandsch Oost Indië.* Leiden: 1887.

Van Akkeren, P. *Sri and Christ: A Study of the Indigenous Church in East Java.* London: 1970.

Van Andel, H.A. *Cultuur en Christendom onder Javanen.* Kampen: 1921.

— *De Betekenis van den Godsdienst voor zedelijke opvoeding.* Weltevreden: n.d.

Van Boetzelaer. *De Gereformeerde Kerken in Nederland en de Zending in Oost-Indië.* Utrecht: 1906.

— *De Protestantsche Kerk in Nederlandsch-Indië.* 's-Gravenhage: 1947.

Van Den Berg, L.W.C. *Nota over de Inlandsche rangen en titels op Java en Madura.* n.p.: n.d.

Van Den End, T. *Gereformeerde Zending op Sumba: 1859-1972.* Alphen aan de Rijn: 1987.

Van Der Linden, J. *Die Entstehungsgeschichte der Mission der niederländischen reformierten Kirchen, Sin Beitrag zur Geschichte der kirchlichen Mission in Holland.* Tübingen: 1934.

Van Hien, Hendrik A. *De Javaansche Geestenwereld en de betrekking, die Toeschen de Geesten en de zinnelijke wereld bestaat. Verduidelijkt door Petangan's of tellingen bij de Javanen in gebruik.* Semarang: 1896.

Van Rhijn, L.J. *Reis door een Indischen Archipel van het belang der evangelische zending.* Rotterdam: 1851.

Van Til, Cornelius. *The New Synthesis Theology of the Netherlands.* New York: 1975.

Van Troostenburg De Bruijn, C.A.L. *Biographisch Woordenboek van Oost Indische Predikanten.* Nijmegen: 1893.

Verkuyl, J. *Contemporary Missiology.* Translated by Dale Cooper. Grand Rapids: 1978.

— *Java, geographisch-ethnologisch, historisch.* Haarlem: 1896.

Vermes, G. *Jesus the Jew.* London: 1973.

Veth, P.J. *Aardrijkskundig-Statistisch Woordenboek van Nederlandsch-Indië.* Amsterdam: 1869.

— *Java, geographisch-ethnologisch, historisch.* Haarlem: 1896.

Visscher, H. *Religie en Gemeenschap bij de Natuurvolken.* Vol. I. Utrecht: 1907.

Wessels, A. *Jezus zien.* Baarn: 1986.

Winckel, A. *Animisme en Christendom.* The Hague: 1913.

— *Christianity Among World Religions.* Edited by Hans Küng and Jürgen Moltmann. Edinburg: 1986.

— *Toward a Universal Theology of Religion.* Edited by Leonard Swidler. New York: 1988.

Wolterbeek, J.D. *Babad Zending in Tanah Jawi.* [The History of Missions in Java]. Purwakerta: 1939.

World Council of Churches. *Apostolic Faith Today.* Edited by Hans-Georg Link. Geneva: 1985.

— *Sharing Jesus in the Two Thirds World.* Papers of the first Conference of Evangelical Mission Theologians from the Two Thirds World. Bangkok. March 22-25, 1982. Edited by Vinay Samuel and Chris Sugden. Bangelore: 1983.

— *The Roots of Our Common Faith: Faith in the Scriptures and in the Early Church.* Edited by Hans-Georg Link. Geneva: 1984.

INDEX OF SUBJECTS[1]

INDEX OF AUTHORS
AND NAMES